China – Politics and Economics

edited by

Prof. Dr. Doris Fischer

Prof. Dr. Jörn-Carsten Gottwald

Associate Prof. Dr. Katja Levy

Volume 6

Theresa Krause

Corporate Compliance and the Social Credit System in China

A Firm-Centered Perspective on the Regulatory State

Nomos

Funded by the Friedrich-Ebert-Foundation.

The Deutsche Nationalbibliothek lists this publication in the Deutsche Nationalbibliografie; detailed bibliographic data are available on the Internet at http://dnb.d-nb.de

a.t.: Würzburg, Univ., Diss., 2024

ISBN 978-3-7560-2436-0 (Print)
978-3-7489-4999-2 (ePDF)

Online Version
Nomos eLibrary

1st Edition 2024

"Integrity has no need of rules."

(The Myth of Sisyphus, Albert Camus)

Acknowledgments

This research would not have been possible without the support of many people.

I would like to thank everyone who helped me to improve the content of my dissertation: Prof. Dr. Doris Fischer, for her trust in my abilities, her guidance during the entire research process and her detailed feedback on my writing; Prof. Dr. Björn Alpermann and Prof. Dr. Lenz, for their input on topics of their expertise; the team at the chair of China Business and Economics for the exchanges on my dissertation; and the team involved in the research project "Learning from the "frontrunner"? A multidisciplinary analysis of the Chinese Social Credit System and its impact on Germany" for the interdisciplinary exchange on the Social Credit System, regulation and research approaches.

Many thanks to all the people and organizations, without whom this dissertation would not have been possible: All interviewees and friends in China who introduced me to new interviewees, for their selfless support and making my field trip to China unforgettable; the Friedrich Ebert foundation, for providing me with financial and non-financial support via a scholarship; BayChina, for the funding for my field trip to China in 2019; the bidt, for the financial support for publishing papers and accessing databases necessary for my research; my employer, for giving me the opportunity of an educational leave.

Last, but definitely not least, I would like to express sincere gratitude to my family, friends and teachers, who have made me the person I am today.

Table of Contents

List of Figures

List of Tables

Abbreviations

BRICS	Brazil, Russia, India, China and South Africa
CAAM	China Association of Automobile Manufacturers
CCDI	Central Commission for Discipline Inspection
CCO	Chief Compliance Officer
CCP	Chinese Communist Party
CEO	Chief Executive Officer
CICLA	China Institute of Corporate Legal Affairs
CSR	Corporate Social Responsibility
CSRC	China Securities and Regulatory Commission
EU	European Union
FDI	Foreign Direct Investment
GAC	General Administration of Customs
GDP	Gross Domestic Product
HR	Human Resources
IOSCO	International Organization of Securities Commission
IPO	Initial Public Offer
IT	Information Technology
JV	Joint Venture
LEI	Legal Entity Identifier
MEE	Ministry of Ecology and Environment
MIIT	Ministry of Industry and Information Technology
MNE	Multinational Enterprise
MOFCOM	Ministry of Commerce
MoU	Memorandum of Understanding
NCISP	National Credit Information Sharing Platform
NDRC	National Development and Reform Commission
NECIPS	National Enterprise Credit Information Publicity System
NGO	Non-Governmental Organization
NSC	National Supervision Commission

OECD	Organization for Economic Co-operation and Development
OEM	Original Equipment Manufacturer
PBoC	People's Bank of China
POE	Privately-Owned Enterprise
SAC	Securities Association of China
SAMR	State Administration for Market Regulation
SASAC	State-owned Asset Supervision and Administrative Commission of the State Council
SCS	Social Credit System
SEC	Securities and Exchange Commission
SME	Small and Medium-Sized Enterprise
SOE	State-Owned Enterprise
US	United States
WTO	World Trade Organization

1 Introduction

1.1 Background

Decades of rapid economic development in the People's Republic of China (中华人民共和国, 'China' in the following) after the reform and opening in 1978 have not only lifted more than 850 million Chinese people out of poverty (The World Bank, 2018, p. 19), but also modernized the country and helped China regain status in the international arena. This transformation has, however, at the same time, caused various problems, such as inequality and environmental degradation. In 1997, the World Bank already estimated that China's annual economic costs of air and water pollution during the mid-1990s was as high as 3.5 to 7.7 percent of the country's gross domestic product (GDP) (The World Bank, 1997, p. 2f).

Furthermore, many traditional societal structures and institutions have eroded in this modernization process leading to low levels of trust in society. For instance, the transition from a face-to-face society to a modern internationalized society has rendered 'interpersonal relationships' (or guanxi, 关系 [1]), from being the main to constituting one among other trust-building mechanisms. Since interactions in all aspects of modern life frequently extend beyond personal contacts, establishing trust towards strangers becomes a key ingredient for a healthy society and business environment. However, in a survey of Chinese villagers from 2011, only 5.8 percent of respondents indicated that outsiders could be trusted (Xia, 2011, p. 145f). More recent studies corroborate these results: The World Value Survey 2014 found that only 11 percent of the Chinese population agree that people they meet for the first time can be completely or somewhat trusted[2] (World Value Survey Association, 2014). In addition, Kostka's (2018, p. 20)

1 In China, these relationships are built on the basis of reciprocity and social norms. They exert a significant influence on individuals' behavior, both in the private and professional realms. For further information, refer to Lee et al. (2001, p. 51ff).

2 In comparison, in all Western countries included in the survey, at least double the share of the population trust people they meet for the first time (e.g. Netherlands 22 percent, Germany 31 percent, the US 35 percent, Sweden 57 percent) (World Value Survey Association, 2014).

survey in 2018 showed that 76 percent of the Chinese respondents felt mistrust between citizens was a problem in China.

The dissolution of these traditional trust and social control mechanisms has created a vacuum that has readily been exploited for personal gain, especially in the corporate sector. This void becomes apparent, on the one hand, in the high levels of corruption that have taken hold of China. Based on data released by Chinese media outlets, Pei (1999, p. 96) estimated in 1999 that corruption cost the country about 4 percent of the country's annual GDP[3]. On the other hand, a seemingly unbroken chain of corporate scandals, such as the melamine-tainted milk scandal of 2008 (Dong et al., 2018, p. 543), has further dissipated consumer trust in corporations. All these elements of trust erosion in Chinese society have led to a loss in credibility that increases companies' transaction costs[4] and thereby deteriorates the efficiency of Chinese markets. This, in turn, carries the risk that "the game becomes so unreliable that no one [in the business community] will want to play" (Handy, 2002).

The Chinese leadership has attempted to counteract these developments with various measures to establish a more rules-based society[5]: After the turbulences of the Mao-era, such as the Cultural Revolution, Deng Xiaoping (1978-1989) focused on establishing a more stable order and strengthened the legal system, e.g. by increasing legal personnel and enacting a large number of laws. Nevertheless, no rule of law was established, since Deng also asserted that laws were bound by the 'Four Cardinal Principles' (四项基本原则)[6] (Lubman, 1999, p. 128). His successor, Jiang Zemin

---

3 The real number is presumably much higher, since media outlets are unlikely to uncover all prevailing corruption incidents, especially in a country where media is state-controlled and certain corruption practices may intentionally be kept under wraps.

4 Transaction costs are friction costs that appear in economic relationships. Economic actors should reduce them to a minimum, while still defending themselves against opportunism on the part of competitors and business partners (den Butter and Mosch, 2003, p. 3f). For further information, refer to Section 2.3.

5 When the term 'rules-based' in the Chinese context is used in this book, it does not refer to institutionalized rules made in a setting where the rule of law is in place. Instead, it describes to the development that authoritarian rulers use rules (e.g. a legal system) as a means to legitimize their political system and control society rather than to constrain their own power (Fewsmith 2021, p. 3f; Whiting 2017, p. 1934f).

6 The 'Four Cardinal Principles' were stated by Deng in the context of the reform and opening and entail 1) adhering to the socialist path (坚持社会主义道路), 2) upholding people's democratic dictatorship (坚持人民民主专政), 3) upholding Chinese Communist Party leadership (坚持中国共产党的领导) and 4) embracing Marx-

(1989-2003), followed Deng's path and strengthened order and control, for example via stricter market regulations. He reinforced that the country should be governed according to the law, one of the features of 'Socialism with Chinese Characteristics' (中国特色社会主义) (Lubman, 1999, p. 128). During Hu Jintao's rule (2003-2013), the social and environmental costs of rapid economic development had become problems that could no longer be neglected. With the push for a 'Harmonious Society' (和谐社会), his administration made a first step to mitigate the negative side-effects of economic development (Webnews of the CCP, 2005). At the same time, Hu strove for greater accountability within the Chinese Communist Party (CCP) and the population, for example by propagating the moral code 'Eight Honors and Eight Shames' (八荣八耻), which, among other considerations, promotes trustworthiness, law abidance and service to the people (Webnews of the CCP, 2006). Nevertheless, great social inequalities, omnipresent environmental destruction, rampant corruption as well as enforcement problems regarding the increasingly exhaustive body of law, remained critical problems when Xi Jinping took office in 2013. Three of Xi Jinping's most prominent endeavors to counter the negative developments have so far been the 'Anti-Corruption Campaign' (反腐败工作), the campaign to 'Comprehensively Govern the Country According to the Law' (全面依法治国) and the set-up of the 'Social Credit System' (SCS, 社会信用体系), a socio-technical system that adopts a variety of mechanisms to enhance rule enforcement[7]. While the former two have gained a lot of attention from researchers and the press early on in Xi's presidency (e.g. Brown, 2018, Hongdao et al., 2018, Lu and Lorentzen, 2018, Trevaskes, 2018, Xu and Yano, 2017, DeLisle, 2015, Minzner, 2015), the SCS is still comparatively under-researched and has only recently started to gain attention in the academic community.

This Chinese turn towards a more rules-based society is, in fact, part of a larger global development. Since the 1970s, there has been a massive increase in regulations and government-imposed formalities in most member countries of the Organization for Economic Co-operation and Development (OECD); conditions that have led researchers to characterize the era as 'regulatory capitalism'. Regulatory capitalism, with the regulatory state

ism-Leninism, as well as Mao-Zedong-Thought (坚持马克思列宁主义、毛泽东思想) (Webnews of the CCP, 2008).

7 Besides strengthening a rules-based approach, these actions also centralize power and increase Xi's legitimacy as a personalistic ruler (see Footnote 5).

as one of its key players, has two distinguishing characteristics (Levi-Faur, 2005, p. 27f): First, regulation is devolved, i.e. moves away from only the state to a larger set of actors engaging as regulators. Second, businesses are 'responsibilisized', i.e. are handed the responsibility to self-regulate in order to achieve policy goals and, in some cases, certain values that exceed mere profit generation.

These two characteristics reflect the two main perspectives from which this new trend can be examined: The regulatory regime and corporate compliance. Regulatory regimes have not only received a lot of attention from political scientists and experts in law (e.g. Oded, 2013, Braithwaite, 2000, Braithwaite and Drahos, 2002, Ayres and Braithwaite, 1992), but also from economists in the context of New Institutional Economics, which focuses on social and legal norms, as well as other rules that underlie economic activity (e.g. Williamson, 1993, North, 1990). Corporate compliance, i.e. the response of the firm to increasing regulatory complexities, initially emerged as a field for practitioners. Compliance professionals, for instance, discussed compliance best practices, when a rising number of corporations started to establish a corporate function solely dedicated to compliance management. Hence, corporate compliance has been receiving high levels of attention by practitioners (e.g. Ernst & Young, 2020, PwC, 2019, Bay and Hastenrath, 2016, Bühr et al., 2016, Schneider, 2003), but has constituted a niche topic in academic circles[8] (e.g. Edelman and Talesh, 2011, Parker and Lehmann Nielsen, 2011c, Tyler, 2011, Parker and Lehmann Nielsen, 2006). Only recently, there have been calls for research to look beyond the regulatory subjects and enforcement practices and to put the regulated actor at the center of research projects, e.g. by focusing on corporate compliance (Li, 2016).

A similar pattern is discernible in research focused on China. The Chinese regulatory regime has been under scrutiny in the context of the country's transition to a market-based economy for several decades, for instance in the discourses on the Chinese regulatory state (e.g. Hsueh, 2011,

8 At the same time, the extension of the firm's responsibility beyond purely financial goals and legal compliance is broadly discussed. This topic is captured in 'Corporate Social Responsibility' (CSR) (e.g. Jamali and Karam, 2018, Shamir, 2008), 'Sustainability' (e.g. Epstein, 2018, Ameer and Othman, 2012), 'Beyond Compliance' (e.g. Borck and Coglianese, 2011, Norman, 2011, Lam, 2009), 'Corporate Ethics' (e.g. Weber and Wasieleski, 2013, Schwartz, 2004), 'Corporate Integrity' (e.g. Maak, 2008, Brown, 2005, Brenkert, 2004, Paine, 1994) and 'Corporate Citizenship' (e.g. Mirvis and Googins, 2006) discourses.

Pearson, 2005) and the Chinese political economy (e.g. Peck and Zhang, 2013, Witt, 2010, McNally, 2007). But the firm's perspective, i.e. corporate compliance research, is barely existent (e.g. Li, 2016, Wu and Liang, 2015). The scarcity of investigations that place the firm at the center of inquiries is deplorable, as such research endeavors promise valuable contributions to our understanding of the Chinese political economy, including its regulatory system. The introduction of the SCS by the Chinese government as an enforcement instrument that attempts to spur firms' (and other actors) self-regulatory capacities, has only increased the relevance of this type of research.

1.2 Objectives

The previous section has illustrated that corporate compliance as a subject-area is academically under-researched. Typically, researchers look at compliance from the perspective of regulation and enforcement (e.g. Hodges, 2015, Levi-Faur, 2010, Braithwaite, 2002), but rarely investigate businesses' perceptions and responses to these regulations in detail (e.g. Parker and Lehmann Nielsen, 2006). In China, in particular, the corporate compliance status quo and management practices are almost exclusively addressed by reports from think tanks (e.g. CICLA et al., 2019, 2018). They lay out the state of corporate compliance in China in an objectivist fashion[9], but fail to generate a deeper understanding of the meaning and social practices of corporate compliance in the Chinese context. However, such insights are especially promising because corporate compliance, positioned at the interface between the economic and regulatory spheres, is not only affected by the endemic political economy, but also exerts influence back on it, i.e. corporate compliance possesses a systemic nature. For this reason, examinations on corporate compliance can not only further our understanding of businesses' responses to regulation, but also deepen our knowledge about the respective political economy, including its regulatory regime.

With China's increasing influence on the global stage, examining the constructed meaning and manifestation of corporate compliance in China is especially worthwhile, as it can contribute to two purposes: First, such

9 I.e. with a pre-defined understanding of the concept of compliance adopted from Western compliance management literature. For more details on the difference between objectivist and social constructionist research, refer to Section 1.3.1.

an investigation can deepen our understanding of the countries' corporate compliance management practices, regulatory regime and overall political economy. This is of recent relevance, since the set-up of the SCS as a technology-based enforcement approach since 2014 is affecting all three topics, an influence that has not been taken into account in related discussions yet. Thus, the findings can contribute to academic discourses such as the nature of the Chinese political economy and regulatory regime, which has so far remained inconclusive in adequately characterizing China (e.g. Hsueh, 2011, Witt, 2010, McNally, 2007, Pearson, 2005). Moreover, practitioners in the regulatory and business fields in China can benefit from the research results: Companies can better understand the contextual factors that affect their compliance management and adjust their practices accordingly, whereas regulators can adapt regulations and enforcement practices to the reactions of businesses. Second, the Chinese case can generate valuable insights for scholars and practitioners across the world, be it for lesson drawing in countries with similar institutional endowments, especially in the Global South, or for understanding how China shapes global governance.

To contribute to these objectives, this study addresses the following overarching research question:

> *How is corporate compliance constructed in China to deal with the increasing regulatory complexity corporate actors face?*

This inquiry is subsequently broken down into four sub-questions:

1. What are the constructed connotations of, influences on and social practices of corporate compliance in China? How do the Chinese manifestations deviate from international best practices?
2. How does the SCS affect corporate compliance construction?
3. How does the construction of corporate compliance differ between industries?
4. How does the identified construction of corporate compliance affect the nature of the Chinese political economy and regulatory regime?

The first sub-question aims to explore the meaning, influences and practices of compliance and to identify whether China-specific characteristics exist. As a concept that originated in Western industrialized nations (Baer, 2009, p. 961f), corporate compliance can either be adopted in China exactly as practiced in these countries (mimicry) or adapted to the Chinese context. Since corporate compliance is affected by the regulatory, political, economic and social environments it is embedded in (Parker and Lehmann Nielsen, 2011c, p. 5), which, in the Chinese context, differ from those in Western industrialized nations, the second option seems more likely. Therefore, answering this research questions can not only contribute to corporate compliance-related theory building, but also provide insights for business and regulatory practitioners working in and with China.

Consequently, the second and third sub-questions focus on two specific aspects of corporate compliance that are of particular interest related to China. Sub-question two addresses the Chinese trend of increasingly adopting information technologies to address regulatory problems in all realms of society (NDRC, 2020, State Council China, 2015). Via this question, the impact of the SCS on corporate compliance, as the epitome of technology adoption in regulatory enforcement in China, is examined. While academics mostly discuss the SCS branch that targets individuals (e.g. Kostka and Antoine, 2020, Knight, 2018, Liang et al., 2018), they overlook the full breadth of the system: The SCS is also intended to function as a trust-building and enforcement tool in the corporate sector. In fact, the SCS branch targeting the corporate sector had been much further developed and already been implemented nationwide back in 2018, whereas the branch targeting individuals, even to this date, remains in the pilot phase to a certain extent[10]. Therefore, by focusing on the effects the SCS has on Chinese firms' corporate compliance construction, this sub-question enhances our understanding of idiosyncrasies of corporate compliance and the regulatory regime in China.

Sub-question three, then, addresses the fact that corporate compliance has been transferred to China from Western industrialized nations. Research has found that cross-country influences within sectors are strong, leading to pronounced variations between sectors within one country (Levi-Faur, 2006, p. 368). Hence, it is likely that compliance was introduced to industries with diverging characteristics in China differently, resulting in variations in the constructed meaning and social practices of corporate compliance across industries in China. By answering sub-question three, this research captures this diversity and shows how corporate compliance can be transferred to new contexts in different manners.

10 Certain elements targeting individuals, such as the Supreme Court's Defaulter List have been rolled out nationally, whereas other aspects, such as comprehensive citizen scoring remains subject to implementation in selected pilots on the local level.

Based on the findings from the previous questions, the last sub-question then relates corporate compliance back to the Chinese political economy and regulatory regime. This is possible thanks to the systemic nature of corporate compliance at the interface between the corporate and the regulatory fields. With the help of a better understanding of corporate compliance in China, this study can contribute findings on the characterization of the Chinese regulatory regime and political economy. Furthermore, the insights can serve researchers and practitioners in countries with similar institutional endowments as China, as well as those working on global governance, since China's international influence is increasing.

In order to answer these questions, the book proceeds as follows: The next and final section of the introduction provides an overview of the methodology applied in this study. Part I then lays the theoretical groundwork by elaborating on corporate compliance. In this part, Chapter 2 defines terms, then explains institutional characteristics of compliance and introduces the corporate compliance framework adopted in the empirical part of the research. Finally, the chapter discusses best practices in corporate compliance management systems and attends to international manifestations of corporate compliance. In Chapter 3, the systemic nature of corporate compliance is explored. Here, regulatory capitalism, the regulatory state and policy transfer serve as the main theoretical pillars. They are not only discussed in general, but also specifically in the context of the Global South[11]. Part II with Chapters 4 to 6, describes the empirical research findings. It elaborates on corporate compliance in China in general (Chapter 4) and via three sub-cases: the SCS (Chapter 5) for a deeper understanding of the impacts of this new enforcement instrument on corporate compliance construction, as well as securities and automotive sectors (Chapter 6) to identify differences between industries. The discussion in Chapter 7 highlights the key findings from the empirical research on China

11 The terms 'Global South' and 'Global North' are used to distinguish between groups of countries that share similar historical backgrounds in a non-hierarchical fashion. Countries of the Global North are characterized by advanced levels of industrialization and low levels of poverty (e.g. Japan, European and North American countries). In contrast, countries of the Global South have typically experienced colonialism and are predominantly concerned with development, due to high levels of poverty (e.g. Latin American, African and Asian countries) (Pagel et al., 2014, Dubash and Morgan, 2013b, p. 3f). In this classification, China is typically categorized as a country of the Global South and therefore, a reflection on regulatory capitalism, the regulatory state and policy transfer in contexts of the Global South contributes to the understanding of the Chinese case.

in light of the systemic nature of corporate compliance and the theoretical context. Finally, this work concludes in Chapter 8 by summarizing the insights from this study, explaining their relevance as well as providing an outlook for future research.

1.3 Methodology

1.3.1 Epistemology

The epistemological basis of this research is social constructivism. This epistemological school asserts that knowledge and our reality do not possess an absolute or objective truth and even if there were one, humans would not be able to obtain it (e.g. Murphy, 1997, Berger and Luckmann, 1966, Foucault, 1966). The key cause of this inability to gain objective knowledge lies in the human approach to knowledge generation: Knowledge-seekers interpret phenomena and construct their reality based on their own personal experiences, social conditioning and exchanges with their environment (Von Glaserfeld, 1995, p. 7). Thus,

> "things we typically take for granted (e.g. the objectivity of scientific facts) are actually products of contingent social processes" (Khalifa, 2010, p. 46).

This means that terms and concepts, or epistemes as Foucault (1966, p. XXIII) calls them, that allow us to comprehend and communicate about the world, also constitute social artifacts. As such, knowledge itself is constructed and finding *the* truth becomes impossible. Therefore, truth as a concept in research is replaced by viability, i.e. the object of a study's adequacy in the context it is located in (Von Glaserfeld, 1995, p. 7). This perspective stands in contrast to objectivism, which claims that the essence of properties can be identified and remains relatively unchanged (Jonassen, 1991). While objectivism as an epistemology can be criticized for its simplification of reality and its often positivist features, relativism poses significant limits to social constructivist investigations. Therefore, research based on the two approaches should complement each other.

To date, objectivist research still dominates the field of management and organization studies (Samra-Fredericks, 2008). This is the case even though the social constructionist movement[12] has been criticizing the underlying epistemological assumptions of objectivist research and provided new empirical perspectives starting from the 1960s. Specifically, social constructionist research investigates the social construction processes in different fields of management and organization research, thereby unearthing "both the dynamic contours of social reality and the processes by which social reality is put together and assigned meaning" (Holstein and Gubrium, 2008, p. 3). Still, social constructionism is not a streamlined research program. Instead, various social constructionist approaches have been developing simultaneously (Flick, 2009, p. 69).

In line with management and organization studies, empirical corporate compliance research predominantly employs the objectivist approach, while social constructionist research remains comparably underrepresented. Objectivist corporate compliance research aims to determine factors that influence corporate compliance both positively and negatively. By setting (non-) compliance as the dependent variable and drawing a direct connection between corporate compliance behavior and its influencing factors, this type of research assumes that an ideal corporate compliance behavior, which can be clearly defined and measured quantitatively, exists. Hence, results from this type of research is deemed adequate to provide practical policy advice on how to design regulations and enforcement strategies (Parker and Lehmann Nielsen, 2011c, p. 5). However, this approach is criticized for neglecting the complex relationship between different factors and actors affecting corporate compliance, which ultimately defy the definition of one ideal state of corporate compliance. Specifically, researchers adopting an objectivist approach regard corporate compliance only as a means to reach regulatory objectives. By adopting such an understanding of corporate compliance without critically reflecting its normative assumptions, this type of research easily falls prey to cultural and ethical biases (Parker and Lehmann Nielsen, 2011c, p. 7). Furthermore, critics raise concerns about data collection and the measurement methods of corporate compliance levels: Related company data is highly sensitive and often not accessible to external researchers. Solutions to circumvent this problem, however, also have their limits: Self-reported data on corporate compliance levels,

12 The terms social constructivism and social constructionism are used interchangeably in the academic discourse. In this project, social constructivism is used to highlight the philosophical school of thought, whereas social constructionism refers to the scientific research approach.

on the one hand, runs a high risk of producing biases due to research subjects' proclivity to provide socially accepted instead of truthful answers (Parker and Nielsen, 2009, p. 58ff). On the other hand, the implementation of compliance management systems can also not serve as a proxy for measuring corporate compliance levels, because compliance behavior cannot necessarily be directly attributed to formal structures (e.g. in the case of creative compliance[13]) (Parker and Gilad, 2011, p. 185).

Social constructionist compliance research, in contrast, regards corporate compliance as social practices that emerge from complex interactions among actors within networks, instead of a state that is brought about by direct one-way relationships of influence. This approach, therefore, focuses on uncovering the influences that generate the meaning of corporate compliance, motivations for corporate compliance and corporate compliance practices in different contexts and among different actors. It does not regard corporate compliance as binary states (either in or out of compliance), but rather acknowledges that the meaning of corporate compliance itself differs depending on the context and the actors involved. One understanding of corporate compliance even interprets the transition between compliance and non-compliance as a gradual continuum (Bird and Kim Park, 2017). Doing so, this perspective can contribute to social science theory-building by bridging the gap between the corporate, the state/political and social spheres and thereby reveal the inner-workings of corporate capitalism (Parker and Lehmann Nielsen, 2011c, p. 8). By nature, such research is interactive, dynamic and consequently conducive to qualitative methods (e.g. qualitative interviews, participatory observations, text analysis). But this approach's attention to the complexity of social interactions also bears the risk of generating findings that are too context-specific to be generalized and constraint to the ivory tower of research.

With the advantages and disadvantages of both approaches at hand, corporate compliance research should ideally combine the two epistemologies: Social constructionist corporate compliance research should enrich factors and trends detected in objectivist research by identifying normative biases and interpreting the findings from quantitative data via qualitative approaches (Parker and Lehmann Nielsen, 2009, p. 61). 'China's Annual Corporate Compliance Blue Book' (中国年度企业合规蓝皮书) (e.g. CICLA

13 'Creative compliance' is defined as "finding ways to accomplish compliance with the letter of the law while totally undermining the policy behind the words" (McBarnet, 2017, p. 229).

et al., 2019, 2018) provides the results of a comprehensive objectivist corporate compliance survey in China annually. Therefore, this study adopts a social constructionist perspective on corporate compliance. This approach not only allows the researcher to contextualize the findings of these reports, but also provides an opportunity to critically scrutinize and potentially challenge the Western normative underpinnings of corporate compliance, an endeavor that the majority of previous corporate compliance research on China has not taken on (e.g. Yee et al., 2016, Wu and Liang, 2015, Ma and Ortolando, 2000).

1.3.2 Research method

The above elaborations have shown that qualitative approaches are most suitable for investigations of corporate compliance from a social constructionist perspective. Thus, this project applies the qualitative case study method. This method serves two main objectives: Case studies can, first, validate findings and theories that were derived from quantitative research; and second, develop an initial understanding for a research field which stimulates hypotheses- and theory-building that can later be refined and advanced by more research (Odell, 2001). These objectives are in line with this project's goals: On the one hand, this research adds to the already existing findings from corporate compliance research in general and the objectivist corporate compliance reports for China in particular. On the other hand, the examination of corporate compliance from a social constructionist angle is the first of its kind in the Chinese context and therefore helps to develop a foundation for further research in this field. Furthermore, case study research lends itself to the analysis of contemporary events and evolutionary paths (Yin, 2009), both of which are central elements of this project; the establishment of the SCS as a contemporary event and the evolution of the concept of corporate compliance in the Chinese context.

With a multitude of definitions of the term 'case study' circulating among academics, this project adopts Yin's (2009) understanding, which sees a case study as

> "an empirical inquiry that investigates a contemporary phenomenon (the "case") in depth and within its real-life context, especially when the boundaries between phenomenon and context may not be clearly evident" (Yin, 2009, p. 16).

Within this method, different ways to set up a case study exist. First and foremost, the researcher has to decide on the level of depth, in which a single case is to be studied: The focus can either be on illustrating one particular phenomenon in depth or on drawing general conclusions from larger n-case studies (Gerring, 2017, p. 37ff). In an extensive case study design, several cases are studied and compared. This enables breadth and generalization, while compromising on depth to a certain extent. In contrast, the intensive case study design focuses on one case and studies it in great detail. With a high degree of depth, this set-up draws a more comprehensive picture of the examined unit, but limits the researcher's ability to generalize from one case to many (Gerring, 2017, p. 41). Since the intensive case design is most useful for topics that are investigated for the first time or in a novel way (Gerring, 2017, p. 40), this project focuses on a single case, namely 'Corporate Compliance in China'.

Figure 1: Illustration of this project's case study set-up

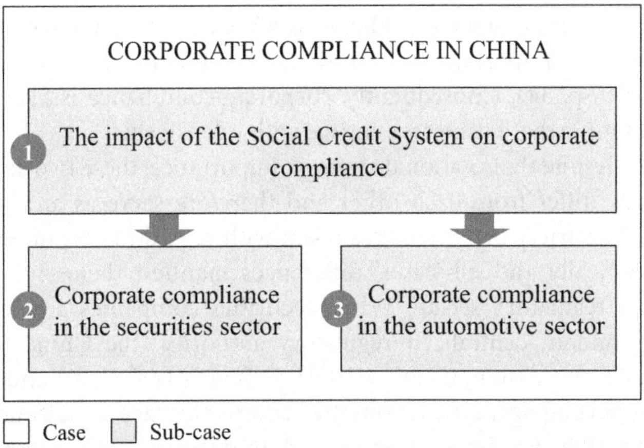

The single case 'corporate compliance in China' contains three embedded units of analysis, i.e. three sub-cases (Figure 1). Sub-case one, 'the impact of the Social Credit System on corporate compliance' provides insights into research sub-questions one and two. In this research, the SCS is regarded as a unique enforcement instrument and key component of the Chinese government's larger 'Internet Plus' strategy (互联网+). This strategy attempts to solve a broad range of regulatory problems, promote economic growth, do propaganda and foster social inclusion with the help of information technologies (NDRC, 2020, State Council China, 2015). Therefore, as one of the most comprehensive instruments developed for the corporate sector in the 'Internet Plus' context, sub-case one (Section 5) not only exemplifies the impact such tools have on the meaning and social practices of corporate compliance (sub-question two), but also contributes to the examination of potential deviations in the Chinese corporate compliance practices from international best practices (sub-question one).

Embedded in the context of compliance in general, including the SCS's influence, sub-case two, 'corporate compliance in the securities sector' (Section 6.1) and sub-case three 'corporate compliance in the automotive sector' (Section 6.2) answer research sub-questions one and three: They each analyze the evolution and status quo of corporate compliance in one industry, since differences in industries have proven to be an important cause for variations in regulatory regimes (Levi-Faur, 2006).

The choice fell on the securities and automotive sectors for three reasons. First, both of these sectors are of high national strategic importance, since they significantly contribute to national security and the creation of a national technology base. The government tends to regulate and control strategically important industries, such as the above, more rigorously (Hsueh, 2011, p. 34). Consequently, corporate compliance is likely to be a prominent topic that businesses engage with intensively.

Second, despite their national strategic importance, these two sectors still significantly differ from each other and therefore serve as an illustration to depict the variety of approaches taken with regard to corporate compliance. Specifically, the sub-cases' differences manifest themselves in their contrariant regulatory set-up. While securities companies are supervised by one dominant centralized regulatory authority (the China Securities Regulatory Commission, CSRC, 中国证券监督管理委员会) and only few minor supporting agencies, automotive companies face a multitude of different authorities for different topics and on different levels of government (central and local). In addition, the natures of these two types of industries differ because one is located in the secondary (automotive) and one in the tertiary (securities) sector. Moreover, the two industries lie at the two ends of the spectrum on international exposure, which has a strong influence on how the state intervenes within an industry (Hsueh, 2011, p. 43). Automotive companies in China are an integral part of international supply chains and produce for the domestic market at the same time as exporting their goods internationally. In contrast, securities companies are part of the highly protected Chinese financial market, which has been shielded from international influences to a large extent and is only recently slowly opening up. Therefore, the juxtaposition of these two sub-cases also allows researchers to understand how international influences affect the construction of corporate compliance in China.

Third, the researcher had access to sufficient data in these two sectors. On the one hand, pertinent publicly available official documents exist to trace the emergence and construction of corporate compliance. Since the concept of compliance originated and spread from the financial sector in China[14], this sector needs to be part of the examination. The securities sector was chosen instead of the banking or insurance sectors, because only in the securities sector the regulatory structure has not changed since the first appearance of the word 'compliance' in official documents[15]. The consistency in terms of the regulatory set-up allowed the researcher to delineate the evolution of corporate compliance as found in official documents better. On the other hand, data access also pertains to the field research. The researcher's network[16] allowed her to identify a sufficient amount of suitable interview partners in both sectors. The interviewees were often part of networks of compliance professionals, which then opened up further interview opportunities.

Overall, the insights from the three sub-cases do not only paint an in-depth picture of corporate compliance in China, but also provide a new perspective on the Chinese political economy and regulatory regime from the regulatees' viewpoint (sub-question four).

Findings from the case study with its three sub-cases are generated by applying two techniques that Yin (2009, p. 141ff) describes for analyzing case study evidence: Explanation building and cross-case synthesis. First, the researcher adopts 'explanation building' in an iterative process to understand how compliance is constructed in each of the sub-cases. Based on the collected material, explanatory propositions are made, which are then revised on a continuous basis in light of the empirical data. Once the sub-cases are analyzed in this manner, further explanations are gener-

---

14 For further details, see Section 4.3.

15 Specifically, the CSRC has remained the main regulatory body in this sector, whereas the China Banking Regulatory Commission and the China Insurance Regulatory Commission merged into the China Banking and Insurance Regulatory Commission (中国银行保险监督管理委员会) in 2018 (State Council China, 2018a).

16 This network consists of long-term contacts from previous visits to China, her supervisor's network in China as well as several contacts to German organizations with a China focus and their respective contacts.

ated on the level of the main case ('Corporate compliance in China') by comprehensively examining the collected evidence from an overarching perspective. During this process, 'cross-case synthesis' is also used, since it allows to identify differences and similarities between the comparative sub-cases two and three.

1.3.3 Data collection and analysis

When developing case studies, it is essential to rely on different sources of evidence (triangulation) in order to ensure validity (Yin, 2009, 114ff). Hence, this project builds the case study on four main data sources: Semi-structured interviews, non-participant observations, official documents and secondary sources.

In one seven-week field trip to China (November to December 2019) and additional virtual field work between February and June 2021, a total of 68 semi-structured interviews[17] with business representatives and corporate compliance experts (incl. government officials) were conducted (for further details, see Figure 2 and Appendix A[18]). Purposive sampling was adopted, meaning that the sample structure was developed from the material inductively (Flick, 2009, p. 122f). Therefore, in order to identify key topics and trends, initially, all types of companies, including international multinational enterprises (MNEs), domestic state-owned enterprises (SOEs) and domestic privately-owned enterprises (POEs) in a large variety of industrial sectors and of different sizes were interviewed. In a second step, the focus was narrowed to companies from the securities and the automotive sector, as well as actors that were of particular relevance for the third sub-case (e.g. businesses involved in the SCS's set-up). Chief executive officers (CEOs), managers or professionals responsible for corporate compliance were interviewed as representatives for their companies with respect to corporate compliance. In addition, expert interviews (e.g. lawyers, government officials, researchers, consultants) were conducted to complement the insights, understand the broader context and connect the

17 Thereof three interviewees were interviewed twice.

18 The interview lists contain the citation code for the interviews based on the interview classification ('BUS' for business representatives, 'EXP' for expert interviews and 'GOV' for interviews with government officials) and year. The Appendix is available digitally on www.nomos-shop.de.

dots between the information obtained from the company interviews. The interviews ranged from 30 minutes to around two hours in length and were conducted in Chinese with Chinese counterparts and English with counterparts from other countries[19].

Figure 2: Overview of interviews by type

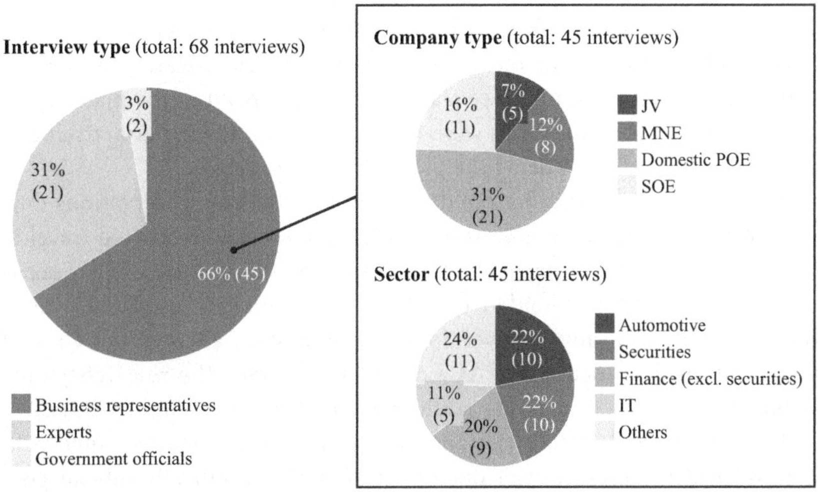

The interviews' aim was to understand the different elements influencing corporate compliance according to the compliance framework (introduced in Section 2.4), interviewees' understanding of the concept of compliance, their companies' compliance management practices as well as the impact of the SCS on their businesses (for details on the interview guidelines, contact the author). Due to the sensitivity of the subject, the researcher kept minutes during the conversations (simultaneous minutes) and immediately after each conversation (memory minutes) instead of recording the interviews. An insistence on recordings could have caused informants to withhold information or decline to be interviewed all together (Vogel and Funck, 2018). The data was anonymized for the protection of individuals and entities.

19 In rare occasions, interviewees were non-Chinese, for example experts from international consultancies or law firms. The language in which the interview was conducted is indicated in Appendix A (available digitally on www.nomos-shop.de).

With a theoretically unlimited number of further potential interviewees, the researcher adopted the logic of theoretical saturation to the sampling process: The selection of the interviewees and the amount of persons interviewed was guided by their relevance to the case study rather than a predetermined fixed target and interviewing was stopped when no additional data could be identified that would contribute to theory-building (Flick, 2009, p. 138). Interview data was analyzed with the help of the software MAXQDA in accordance with structuring qualitative content analysis (Flick, 2009, p. 327). This means that first, coding categories were derived from the theoretical compliance framework and applied to the material. In a second step, these categories were refined based on the material itself and continuously modified during the data collection process.

In addition, the researcher conducted non-participant observations during the trip and virtually, after the COVID-19 pandemic restricted travel to China (for a list of non-participant observations, see Appendix B[20]). Specifically, the researcher attended four SCS- and compliance-related events, but refrained from any interventions that may have affected the content produced on these occasions. As a complete observer, the researcher only wrote minutes, which served as additional data for analysis in MAXQDA.

The data from the interviews and observations were complemented with data from desk research and document analysis, specifically official government publications and secondary sources, such as company websites, SCS-related websites (incl. publicly available corporate data) and media reports. Documents were selected and analyzed either unsystematically on an on-demand basis to add to the original data where necessary or systematically in the context of the process tracing.

According to Beach and Pedersen (2013, p. 2),

> "[p]rocess-tracing methods are tools to study causal mechanisms in a single-case research design".

The causal mechanisms under investigation are processes that produce a certain outcome and can be studied in theory-testing, theory-building or explaining-outcome process tracing. Theory-testing and theory-building process tracing are theory-centric: Theory-testing process tracing seeks to prove the existence of certain causal mechanisms that have previously been deduced from theory. Theory-building process tracing, on the other

20 The Appendix is available digitally on www.nomos-shop.de.

hand, focuses on identifying generalizable causal mechanisms from cases in order to build theory. In contrast, explaining-outcome process tracing is case-centric and aims to find a minimally sufficient explanation of an outcome[21] (Beach and Pedersen, 2013, p. 3).

This study adopts explaining-outcome process tracing, as it pursues explanations for the construction of corporate compliance in China. Specifically, the goal is to reproduce the development path that the concept of corporate compliance has taken in official government documents since the first appearance of the word compliance (合规) in 1994. As the construction of corporate compliance in China is a little studied field, the mechanisms were initially identified in inductive process tracing and then compared in an iterative process and finally re-conceptualized based on existing theoretical concepts.

For the collection of documents for the process tracing, the main regulatory authorities' websites, both in general and for the three sub-cases, were identified and compliance-related documents retrieved by entering '合规'[22] in the search bar. A pre-selection regarding their relevancy to the topic was made[23]. Finally, a total of 547 documents on Party-state websites from the earliest release in 1994 to June 2021 were included in the process tracing (see Figure 3; for a list of all cited documents, refer to Appendix C[24]; for a list of all documents used in the process tracing and details on the document selection, contact the author)[25]. With 335 documents (61 per-

21 For more details on the differences between the different types of process tracing, see Beach and Pedersen (2013).

22 The search only focused on this term, which is the direct translation of 'compliance', and did not include related terms or terms with the opposite meaning. The main goal of the research is to understand how exactly this concept has been constructed in the official discourse and non-compliance was not referenced a lot in this context. Hence, considering research aim and workload required, this narrowing of focus was applied.

23 For example, certain Chinese authorities regulate various industries, such as the National Development and Reform Commission (NDRC, 国家发展和改革委员会). Therefore, the search for '合规' on such authorities' websites not only provides results on compliance in general and specific to the automotive and securities sectors, but also specific to other industries. The former two types of documents are included, whereas the latter type of documents was excluded from the analysis.

24 The Appendix is available digitally on www.nomos-shop.de.

25 The document lists in the Appendix (available on www.nomos-shop.de) contain further information on the cited documents from the process tracing. To each document, a citation code was allocated based on the sub-section of the process tracing the document belongs to ('GEN' for the general overarching, 'SCS' for the

cent), the securities sector contributes the greatest amount of documents, i.e. compliance has gained most dedicated attention in this industry (e.g. via industry regulations). With the help of MAXQDA, the sections of the texts relevant to corporate compliance were coded and analyzed. The insights from this analysis on the evolution of the concept of compliance in each sector could then be compared in order to synthesize findings across the two sub-cases.

Figure 3: Number of documents (incl. percentage share) collected for the process tracing split by topic area

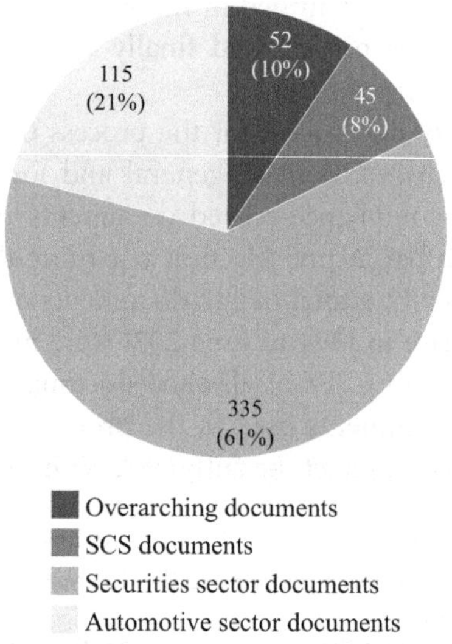

1.3.4 Limitations

The main limitations of this research lie in four areas: Corporate compliance as a research field, the applied methodology, data collection and data analysis.

Corporate compliance research in its very nature bears a rather high risk of biases due to its sensitivity and social expectations (Parker and Nielsen, 2009, p. 61). Validity and reliability of self-reported data by businesses has

SCS-specific, 'SEC' for the securities sector's and 'AUT' for the automotive sector's process tracing) and its publication date.

to be questioned, since businesses are clearly aware of socially desirable behavior and therefore fall prey to expectation bias. Moreover, government information (e.g. the government documents analyzed during process tracing) are likely to deviate from reality to a certain extent: First, the government may postulate actions and publish rules on paper that are not implemented in practice. Second, government information regarding corporate compliance levels is never complete, since not all non-compliance cases are detected. In addition, a certain level of discretion in corporate compliance supervision and high levels of corruption in China potentially distort results (Transparency International, 2017). At the same time, the direct observation of corporate compliance and related management practices by researchers, which could mitigate these problems, is nearly impossible in practice. However, these limitations carry a much heavier weight in objectivist, compared to social constructionist corporate compliance research. While a risk of biased and intentionally false answers in interviews still exists, the focus on understanding the meaning and influencing factors for corporate compliance practices is to a much lesser extent normatively charged as compared to objectivist surveys on businesses' ostensibly 'correct' or 'incorrect' corporate compliance behavior. Moreover, even though the government's perspective may not depict the complete reality of corporate compliance-related efforts, their viewpoint does, nevertheless, provide the research with insights into the active construction of the concept of corporate compliance from the authorities' side.

In addition, the applied methodology limits the generalizability of the findings in two regards. First, the perspective of compliance on an organizational, instead of an individual, level limits generalizations. In this project, the CEO or (compliance) managers' perspective on corporate compliance is used as a proxy for companies' construction and social practice of compliance. While these managers are exposed to employees' understanding and practices of compliance and therefore likely incorporate these practices in their own view on corporate compliance, their perspective is nevertheless biased to a certain extent and can never fully represent the organization as a whole. Therefore, the statements on companies' corporate compliance need to always be read as generalizations from those individuals to their organizations. Second, the social constructionist perspective itself draws the generalization of findings into question. This epistemology considers research as a second degree construction process (i.e. research constructs knowledge based on phenomena that are socially constructed themselves) (Flick, 2009, p. 77). The high level of subjectivity caused by the multiple levels of social construction during the research process raises question on general conclusions per se. Moreover, as mentioned above, the qualitative single-case method only depicts and re-constructs a narrow window of reality, which further constrains the generalizability of insights. Thus, this project's findings and its manifestations in theory have to be regarded as preliminary and further research is encouraged to challenge and/or validate the study's findings.

Moreover, data collection is subject to limitations, both in general and due to the COVID-19 pandemic. In general, qualitative research via semi-structured interviews is subject to several biases. First, the interview situation itself is prone to distortions, due to the personal interactions between the interviewer and interviewee. Even for well-versed researchers it is impossible to stay entirely neutral: Every inquiry, even if no leading questions are posed, carries certain expectations to which the interviewee responds. To the extent possible, such biases were reduced by asking open questions that invite the interviewee to narrate.

Second, the documentation of the interviews via minutes is more prone to biases compared to the use of transcripts from recordings, since the researcher unavoidably filters the content in the note-taking process and could not always document all details the interviewees mentioned. Nevertheless, in the context of this research topic, the benefits of this approach still outweigh the disadvantages, as explained in Section 1.3.3. The combination of simultaneous and memory minutes allowed the researcher to recreate the content discussed rather comprehensively. In case gaps in the documentation were identified after the interview, the researcher followed up with the interviewees for further clarification (e.g. via social media).

Third, language is a source of potential distortions. The interviews were mostly conducted in Chinese in order to ensure that the interviewees were able to fully, concisely and comfortably express their thoughts in their mother tongue. That way, the quality and quantity of the content generated could be maximized. However, this approach also necessitates translation of the content into English, a process that is interpretative in its nature. In cases where the researcher was unclear about the gist of meaning of what was being said, she followed up with the interviewee, either immediately during the conversation or afterwards in writing.

Fourth, in some cases the interview environment also made a mutual understanding harder. Even though in-person interviews were held in offices or quiet cafés mostly, background noises could not be fully avoided. During virtual interviews, internet connection problems were a disturbing factor.

However, in most cases the instability of the connection could be mitigated by turning off the video. In cases where information got lost due to the environmental factors, the researcher repeated the question or asked for clarification of the specific points that got lost.

The COVID-19 pandemic further inhibited data collection. Following the first exploratory field work in China at the end of 2019, a second research trip was planned for March to July 2020. Due to the COVID-19 outbreak in China in early 2020 and its subsequent global spread, the second research stay was not possible. Instead, the researcher had to rely on online research to compensate for the impossibility of conducting face-to-face interviews. Both online interviews (conducted via WeChat) and online event attendance were possible, but virtual encounters could not fully replace in-person meetings, since trust-building in the online context is more difficult and a lower level of anonymity can be granted (especially given China's digital surveillance practices and low levels of data privacy). For these reasons, the virtual setting did likely not only limit the willingness to provide certain information during the interviews, it also reduced the circle of potential interviewees. For instance, it was not possible to interview business representatives from less developed areas in western China[26] or government officials online due to the Chinese state's strict rules regarding civil servants' interactions with foreign researchers. In addition, it was impossible to conduct interviews with black-listed[27] firms in the context of the SCS, since this would have required physical presence and extensive trust-building. Consequently, information on the impacts of blacklist entries could only be deduced from second-hand accounts and official documents. Nevertheless, the online interviews provided additional valuable insights. Moreover, additional analyses besides the interviews and observations that were originally not included in the scope of the study (such as the process tracing) were added to secure a comprehensive picture of the topic under investigation.

26 The data collection during the first field trip focused on eastern regions. The following online research had to rely on the contacts established during the field trip for the recommendation of additional interview partners as well as WeChat groups. These methods were effective, but did not help to achieve a broad regional spread of interviewees. While the phenomena identified in the interviews therefore not necessarily apply to the entirety of China, they nevertheless provide helpful insights into the status quo in the further developed regions of China and thereby the potential development direction related to corporate compliance in the rest of the country.

27 For further information on this SCS mechanism, see 5.2.4.

Lastly, qualitative data analysis is subjective by its nature. Even experienced researchers cannot fully avoid interpretation biases in coding and analyzing qualitative data. To mitigate the risks of distortions, the researcher adopted cross-referencing of content with academic literature and official documents, where applicable. In addition, the researcher manually coded, interpreted and reflected upon all data in MAXQDA. The software's functions for automatic visualization and quantitative evaluation were only used to complement the researcher's own reflections after the content analysis. This way, the influence of (nontransparent) algorithms on the results could be reduced.

Part I Theoretical foundations

2 Corporate compliance

As the first part of this study lays the theoretical basis for the empirical case study on China, which will follow in Part II, this chapter introduces corporate compliance from a theoretical perspective comprehensively. After a literature review (Section 2.1) and the definition of corporate compliance-related terms (Section 2.2), corporate compliance is positioned as an institution (Section 2.3), which is influenced by a variety of different factors. The factors are summarized in a corporate compliance framework, which is discussed in Section 2.4. The corporate compliance practices resulting from these influences manifest themselves in the form of compliance management systems and are described in Section 2.5. Based on these elaborations, this chapter concludes by discussing the difference in the manifestations of corporate compliance internationally (Section 2.6).

2.1 Literature review

The concept of compliance originates from medicine, where it describes patients' abidance to doctors' therapeutic prescriptions (Behringer, 2013, p. 34). Research tracing the roots of compliance in the corporate sector and delineating its historical development mostly focuses on the United States (US) (e.g. Haugh, 2018, Ford and Hess, 2009, Baer, 2009). In the business context, the term was first predominantly used in the finance sector, for example related to companies' obedience to stock market laws and banks' adherence to regulations in high risk business areas (Behringer, 2013, p. 35; Mengel, 2009, p. 5f). However, over time, the concept expanded to all other business sectors and contexts and is now generally associated with rule abidance in the corporate sector. In light of the increasing number of regulations passed globally to regulate capitalism starting from the 1970s, and the ensuing legal complexity, the concept of corporate compliance increasingly gained traction. Corporate compliance turned into a standard corporate function in businesses (similar to Human Resources (HR) or Information Technology (IT)) (Soltes, 2018, p. 968f). Over the course of corporate compliance's gradual emergence, legal changes acted as catalysts for the establishment of corporate compliance as a corporate function (Head, 1998, p. 537f). Especially the acknowledgment of companies' compliance programs for the mitigation of sentences played an important role, for example in the US Sentencing Guidelines or the World Bank's Integrity Compliance Guidelines (Griffith, 2016, p. 2085; The World Bank, 2010). The publication of ISO19600[28] (compliance management systems) in 2014 (ISO, 2014) as the first international compliance management standard, marked another milestone in the institutionalization of corporate compliance. In April 2021, this institutionalization was further reinforced by replacing ISO19600, which only served as a guideline, with the first certifiable compliance management standard, ISO37301 (ISO, 2021b).

Corporate compliance, as a concept and as a business function, is located at the intersection of many academic disciplines, since it not only focuses on the interpretation of legal texts and other rules, but also covers ensuing business and management practices. These, in turn, are affected by the individuals working in an enterprise. Therefore, over time, several academic disciplines have picked up the topic from different perspectives. Legal and political science scholars have looked into the interpretation of laws, the meaning of corporate compliance, but also the way rules should be drafted and enforced to improve corporate compliance levels (e.g. Hodges, 2015, Oded, 2013, Parker, 2006, Braithwaite and Drahos, 2002). Economic and organizational scholars have aimed to comprehend the financial implications of regulations and cost-benefit calculations related to rule abidance in businesses (e.g. Pearce and Tombs, 1990, Becker, 1968). In addition, researchers in this field have aimed to understand the organizational requirements and set-ups that are conducive to compliance (e.g. Habisch, 2012, Weaver and Klebe Trevino, 2001, Klebe Trevino et al., 1999). Sociologists and psychologists, in contrast, have focused on understanding the social norms and interactions (e.g. Edelman, 1990, O'Neill, 1986, Meyer and Rowan, 1977), as well as individual decision-making processes related to rule conformity (e.g. Tyler, 2011, Jenkins, 1994). Within these different disciplines, certain compliance topics have received particular attention, for example corporate compliance with environmental (e.g. Stretesky and

28 ISO is an independent, non-governmental international organization. Because the name 'International Organization for Standardization' would have been abbreviated differently in different languages, ISO is not an acronym, but rather derived from the Greek word 'isos' (equal) (ISO, 2021a).

Lynch, 2011, Gunningham, Thornton and Kagan, 2004, Winter and May, 2001, Dasgupta et al., 2000, Heyes, 2000) and tax regulations (e.g. Hasan et al., 2017, McBarnet, 2017, Picciotto, 2007, Street and Gray, 2002). Often, such topic-specific research focuses on certain technical details of corporate compliance in an objectivist fashion, but at times, findings are also generalized to the overall topic of corporate compliance.

Overall, as mentioned in Section 1.3.1, two types of research approaches can be identified in the corporate compliance literature across disciplines: Objectivist and social constructionist research. The objectivist compliance research is not only shaped by academic research findings (e.g. Kaspereit et al., 2015, Craig Smith et al., 2007, Dalton and Kesner, 1988), but also by reports from practitioners such as legal consultancies and think tanks (e.g. Ernst & Young, 2020, PwC, 2019, 2018). However, comparability between the individual studies is often limited, as the research set-ups vary. The definition of compliance, its operationalization and the sample (e.g. country, industry) of these studies differ. For example, Kaspereit et al. (2015) examined German companies' compliance levels with corporate governance regulations using self-reported corporate data, whereas Dalton and Kesner (1988) analyzed data from US courts about Fortune 500-companies' violations of anti-trust laws and the Federal Trade Commission Act to understand the relationship between corporate illegal activity and company size. Similarly, social constructionist research was characterized by high fragmentation addressing issues, such as compliance motivations, compliance management practices and external influences on corporate compliance, separately, until Parker and Nielsen (eds) summarized the state of social constructionist corporate compliance research in their book 'Explaining Compliance' in 2011 (Parker and Lehmann Nielsen, 2011b). Since 2011, further studies in that area have been published (e.g. Hodges, 2015, Habisch, 2012), however, the general direction of research lined out in Parker and Nielsen's book has remained.

One of the major gaps in the current corporate compliance research landscape are studies of non-Western, non-democratic countries, e.g. countries in the Global South. Most of the work regarding corporate compliance so far has been conducted in Western industrialized democracies, such as the US, Canada, the Netherlands and Australia (e.g. Van Erp, 2010, Parker and Lehmann Nielsen, 2006, Gunningham, Kagan and Thornton, 2004). Only comparatively few scholars have focused on nations exhibiting other characteristics (e.g. Nguyen et al., 2020, Liu et al., 2018, Van Rooij, 2006). The latter accounts focus on examining how the contextual differences in countries, such as China, Vietnam and Mexico, affect corporate compliance.

2.2 Terms

2.2.1 Governance, regulation and enforcement

The brief historical outline of the emergence of the concept of corporate compliance highlighted the regulatory environment as a key trigger for the concept's gain in importance. Thus, before defining corporate compliance, three important terms related to the regulatory environment need to be defined: Governance, regulation and enforcement. In this study, governance is understood as an umbrella term, which incorporates the elements of regulation and enforcement.

Namely, *governance* refers to

> "all processes of governing, whether undertaken by a government, market, or network; whether over a family, tribe, corporation, or territory; and whether by laws, norms, power, or language. Governance is a broader term than government because it focuses not only on the state and its institutions but also on the creation of rule and order in social practices" (Bevir, 2013, p. 1).

Within this context of governance, some scholars refer to *regulation* as a power or control that is exercised by the power-holder over the subject. Thereby, scholars incorporate both the rules and their implementation (enforcement) into this one concept (e.g. Levi-Faur, 2010, Morgan and Yeung, 2007, Baldwin et al., 1998, Selznick, 1985). While such an understanding holds certain benefits[29], it does not create a clear linguistic distinction between the rules and their implementation. Since a differentiation between these two aspects is important when investigating corporate compliance, this project adopts a definition of regulation that focuses on the rules and refers to enforcement as the modes to ensure implementation of these rules. Another distinction is often made between regulation and legislation. But as with regulation, no clear consensus among academics exists as to the relationship and differentiation between the two terms. While some scholars regard laws as rules passed by the legislature and regulation as a

29 For more information, refer to Levi-Faur (2010), for instance.

sub-set of laws, i.e. guidelines created by the administration, the regulatory governance perspective understands legislation as a subset of regulation (Kosti et al., 2019, p. 172). Since corporate compliance is affected by any type of rule, this project adopts the regulatory governance perspective on regulation. In this line, the OECD defines regulation as

> "the diverse set of instruments by which governments establish requirements for enterprises and citizens. Regulations include laws, formal and informal orders, subordinate rules issued by all levels of government, and rules issued by non-governmental or self-regulatory bodies to whom governments have delegated regulatory powers" (OECD, 2000, p. 9).

Importantly, in contrast to other definitions of regulation (e.g. Yeung, 2004, Laffont, 1994), this definition does not exclusively focus on formal rules provided by the government. Instead, it takes a broader perspective by also including informal orders by the government as well as rules issued by other entities that the government has delegated responsibility to. Hence, this definition still regards the government as the central regulator who possesses the ultimate responsibility to regulate, but at the same time provides space for other entities to also engage in the process of regulating. Therefore, the term regulator in this study cannot be equated with the government or the state, but refers to any entity involved in issuing regulations.

Three categories of rules are subsumed under the term regulation (OECD, 2000, p. 9):

- *Economic:* Regulations that directly intervene in the market, e.g. in competition and pricing
- *Social:* Regulations that serve the protection of public interest, such as the environment and health
- *Administrative:* Regulations that are related to formal procedures, for instance related to information collection and transparency

Regulations in all three categories affect corporate actors and therefore their corporate compliance practices to varying degrees, depending, for example, on the company's field of business and size.

In line with this definition of regulation, this research also adopts a broad understanding of (regulatory) *enforcement.* According to the OECD (2014, p. 11), this term encompasses

> "all activities of state structures (or structures delegated by the state) aimed at promoting compliance and reaching regulations' outcomes –

e.g. lowering risks to safety, health and the environment, ensuring the achievement of some public goods including state revenue collection, safeguarding certain legally recognised rights, ensuring transparent functioning of markets etc. These activities may include: information, guidance and prevention; data collection and analysis; inspections; enforcement actions in the narrower sense, i.e. warnings, improvement notices, fines, prosecutions etc.".

2.2.2 Corporate compliance

In the review of the academic corporate compliance literature, terminological inconsistency in the way 'corporate compliance' is used was detected, regarding both the concept's scope and the process stage. The scope of corporate compliance can be defined broadly and narrowly depending on the type of regulation addressed: Corporate compliance either purely focuses on alignment with government-issued rules (e.g. Grützner and Bärenbrinker, 2015, Ramezani et al., 2012, Wieland, 2009) or encompasses a broad range of rules. In the latter case, the concept sometimes even exceeds the scope of external regulations by also including internal rules set by the business itself (e.g. ISO, 2014, Sadiq and Governatori, 2010, Rohde-Liebenau, 2007, Schneider, 2003). This means that in a narrow definition of compliance, theories of business ethics, such as 'Beyond Compliance', 'Corporate Social Responsibility' (CSR), 'Sustainability', 'Corporate Integrity' or 'Corporate Citizenship'[30] fall outside the scope of corporate compliance. In fact, these aspects can be considered a step up from corporate compliance. In contrast, when a broad definition of corporate compliance is applied, theories regarding business ethics are no longer completely separate from compliance, but partially overlapping. Hence topics related to business ethics are incorporated into corporate compliance to the extent that the internal rules a business sets itself often surpass requirements defined by the regulatory system. With regard to the process stage, some definitions refer to corporate compliance as a condition, i.e. the end-result of activities that ensure the obedience of rules (e.g. Mengel, 2009, Biegelman, 2008, OECD, 2000). Others encapsulate these activities themselves when they discuss corporate compliance (e.g. Behringer, 2013, Sadiq and Governatori, 2010).

30 These are research fields in their own right. An elaboration on these concepts therefore goes beyond the scope of this study.

In this study, corporate compliance is defined as a company's

> "state of being in accordance with established guidelines, specifications, or legislation" (Biegelman, 2008, p. 8),

i.e. in a broad way and as a status. Such an understanding is, on the one hand, in line with the broad definition of regulation and enforcement introduced in the previous section. Therefore, it allows for a more comprehensive investigation of firms' reaction to and implementation of regulations and internally set rules, based on where businesses themselves draw the line between compliance and business ethics. On the other hand, by considering corporate compliance as a status, it is possible to examine which qualities different actors attribute to this condition, how they construct its meaning and attempt to achieve it. Such an understanding is in line with the social constructionist approach to corporate compliance, since it does not regard corporate compliance as an ideal-type that can be objectively reached as in objectivist thinking. Instead it regards compliance as a constructed state, whose achievement is contested. In the following, for purposes of simplification, this study only uses 'compliance' when referring to 'corporate compliance'.

With compliance defined as a condition, activities undertaken by firms to achieve this condition, i.e. the social practices of compliance, are subsumed under 'compliance management'. Therefore, compliance management comprises

> "all activities and methods to ensure that a company follows all guidance and implements all measures required by an external or internal regulation" (El Kharbili and Pulvermüller, 2009, p. 61).

In case a company sets up a management system[31] related to compliance, i.e. takes comprehensive and strategic action, this research refers to it as a 'compliance management system'[32].

While closely related to corporate governance, internal control and risk management, compliance management nevertheless constitutes a distinct function in companies. Corporate governance refers to the management structures within a firm that enable the organization to efficiently and effectively reach its goals. Of course, these structures need to be in line with

31 A "set of interrelated and interacting elements of an organization [...] to establish policies [...,] objectives [...] and processes [...] to achieve those objectives" (ISO, 2014).

32 Some scholars also use the term compliance (management) program (e.g. Bay and Hastenrath, 2016, Angelucci and Han, 2011).

regulations and are therefore to a certain extent shaped by compliance and compliance management (Rohde-Liebenau, 2007, p. 276). Internal control, in contrast, focuses on ensuring that control mechanisms within a company work effectively and efficiently. This means that the internal control department also monitors the compliance work of a company. The monitoring happens on a meta-level and is process-related (e.g. checking whether the compliance function is independent and whistleblowing structures exist), but does not include content-related compliance decisions. Risk management, again, serves the objective of identifying, analyzing and evaluating risks in order to implement adequate corporate responses. Because the violation of regulations or any other compliance requirement internally constitutes a risk that needs to be mitigated (via compliance management), these two corporate functions need to work together closely (Ramezani et al., 2012, p. 459). However, compliance management is not necessarily exclusively motivated by risk considerations and therefore demands its own separate considerations. To the extent that sustainability or CSR functions in companies exist and ensure the accordance of the company with certain (internally or externally set) rules, the activities of these functions are considered a part of compliance management as well. If they are, however, only operatively executing corporate ethics programs (volunteering, etc.), they fall outside the scope of compliance management.

2.3 Corporate compliance as an institution

With the above definition of compliance as well as the social constructionist perspective in mind, this study regards compliance as an institution. The following paragraphs first introduce the concept of institutions and institutionalism in general and then draw parallels to the context of compliance research.

This project adopts Jepperson's (1991, p. 145) definition of institutions as

> "those social patterns that, when chronically reproduced, owe their survival to relatively self-activating social processes. [...] [R]outine reproductive procedures support and sustain the[se] pattern[s], furthering [their] reproduction – unless collective action blocks, or environmental shock disrupts the reproductive process".

These social patterns, alias institutions, facilitate human interaction by providing constraints that reduce complexity. Consequently, they fundamentally shape how society as a whole and any of its spheres (economy, politics...) manifests itself. However, this facilitative capacity does not imply that institutions necessarily are efficient themselves or lead to higher efficiency, but rather stresses the predictability and consistency stemming from the reproduction of patterns. With this definition at hand, a variegated spectrum of institutions emerges, ranging from highly formal institutions (such as laws) to highly informal institutions (for instance social conventions) (North, 1990, p. 4). No matter which type of institution, each emerges from a process of self-perpetuation, namely institutionalization.

As a consequence, the term 'institutionalism' describes the study of these types of institutions. This field of study invokes institutions as causes for empirical phenomena. In contrast to other research areas, this field is characterized by a high level of social construction taking place at a high order of organization (i.e. not the individual level, but in some form of organized activity, such as businesses or government departments) (Jepperson, 1991, p. 50). Institutionalism has undergone significant developments, which have led to a differentiation between 'old' and 'new' institutionalism. While old institutionalism emphasizes the inward-look at institutions within an organization (e.g. Selznick, 1949), new institutionalism, starting from the 1970s, has extended this perspective to include institutions from the organizational environment. New institutionalists (such as John Meyer, Brian Rowan Paul DiMaggio and Walter Powell) regard organizations as deeply embedded in their environments (e.g. DiMaggio and Powell, 1983, Meyer and Rowan, 1977). Therefore, they consider organizational actions and structures as reflections and responses to institutions in their environment (Powell and Colyvas, 2008, p. 977). Essentially, organizations both accommodate institutions affecting them and create their own institutions.

This new institutionalism has been incorporated into the field of economics by New Institutional Economics. In this academic discipline, institutions impact the performance of economies, while not necessarily being efficient themselves[33] (North, 1990, p. 6). They shape business interactions and have the capacity to reduce uncertainty in economic exchange. This is especially important in complex exchanges with unknown counterparts in modern economies, where uncertainty is high. North (1990, p. 34f) describes how different formal and informal institutions have structured

33 They are rather created to serve the interests of those who hold the power over rule-making (North, 1990, p. 6).

economic exchange over time: Personal exchange in local communities is characterized by cultural homogeneity and frequent exchanges with the same known counterparts. Therefore, uncertainty in exchanges is minimal thanks to the informal institutions emerging from a shared culture. But along with economic development comes the need to exchange with strangers, i.e. a high level of uncertainty. For these impersonal exchanges, business partners rely on institutions, such as merchant codes of conduct or kinship ties. However, for an economy to successfully transition into a modern economy one more step is essential, namely the establishment of third-party enforcement in impersonal exchanges. Otherwise economic actors can significantly gain from cheating, opportunism and other untrustworthy behavior in complex modern societies. But this does not mean that in modern economies only third-party enforcement exists. Instead, all types of institutions described complement each other to different degrees in different situations and, thus, lower the costs of business transactions to varying extents. These so-called 'transaction costs'[34] play an important role in the overall costs of production (North, 1990, p. 27ff). They are, to a large degree, caused by uncertainties, due to information asymmetries, and can be minimized by building formal and informal institutions. However, these rules of the game must be well balanced to positively affect transaction costs. If they are exaggerated or too complex, they are very costly to abide by and enforce and ultimately increase transaction costs.

In this context of various formal and informal institutions conditioning companies' behavior and transaction costs, compliance plays a central role: First, the concept of compliance and compliance management are considerably shaped by institutions, which organizations are exposed to (Edelman and Talesh, 2011). Therefore, the social, economic, political and legal (regulation and enforcement) environments are key influencing factors in the negotiation and construction processes surrounding compliance (Hutter, 2011, p. 305). Second, with such a broad set of external influencing institutions, an equally wide variety of external actors need to be considered as regulators for businesses, including the media, business partners and local residents, just to name a few (Parker and Lehmann Nielsen, 2011c,

34 The emergence of the concept of transaction costs is largely attributed to Coase (1937) and his 'Theory of the Firm'. It refers to the costs endured when conducting market operations. Later scholars have specified the concept as the opposite of frictions (Williamson, 1981, p. 552), and by listing cost that this term entails, such as "search and information costs, bargaining and decision costs, policing and enforcement costs" (Dahlman, 1979, p. 148).

p. 1). And third, since new institutionalism also suggests that organizations create their own institutions, compliance can be regarded as one of the institutions created by businesses. Companies construct what compliance entails and develop structures (e.g. compliance departments), as well as behavioral rules (e.g. codes of conduct) to achieve the status of compliance in order to reduce their transaction costs and as a response to regulations. These structures and behaviors are social patterns reproduced within and across organizations. Often it is professionals moving between organizations (such as consultants, standard setters) who transport and reproduce these compliance-related patterns (for further details on the transmission of compliance patterns between organizations, refer to Section 2.5) (Sahlin-Andersson and Engwall, 2002, DiMaggio and Powell, 1983).

The degree to which compliance is formalized as an institution largely depends on the context it is placed in. Sometimes compliance practices are formally prescribed in regulations (e.g. industry associations' compliance guidelines or businesses' code of conduct). In other cases, companies invoke informal rules (e.g. ethical norms) to ensure compliance. Sometimes businesses and regulators resort to both. Essentially, all these patterns constitute symbols for the condition of compliance and therefore collectively construct its meaning (Edelman, 1992). This collective construction of compliance as an institution points to the high order of organization that characterizes institutionalist examinations. In line with institutionalism, by examining the accumulated effects on the organizational level, this study conducts research at a high order of organization. Specifically, the study regards business leaders and decision-makers related to compliance as representatives for their organization and interprets the organization's compliance (management) as the collectively constructed connotations and social practices of compliance by members of the organization. With this approach, individuals' understanding and practices of compliance are also accounted for to a certain extent, but on an aggregated level. At the same time, the analysis at this higher level allows the researcher to compare different organizations and draw conclusions on an industry- and even the national level.

2.4 Corporate compliance framework

In line with old and new institutionalism, academic compliance literature has identified a variety of factors that affect compliance, both company-internal influences and impacts from institutions in companies' social, economic, political and legal (regulation and enforcement) environments[35] (Edelman and Talesh, 2011, Hutter, 2011, p. 305). However, efforts to determine the specific degrees and interrelations between these influences in an objectivist manner have remained fragmented. This is the case, because compliance-related studies tend to use highly diverging research set-ups, making comparability difficult. Nevertheless, Parker and Nielsen have undertaken a seminal consolidation effort of the related academic discourse, where they incorporated existing academic findings on compliance into their 'holistic and plural model of business compliance' (Parker and Lehmann Nielsen, 2011c, p. 5). Only when taking a social constructionist perspective on compliance, is this consolidation effort of the existing, often divergent research valid. This is the case, because the focus lies on understanding how the different factors that are mentioned affect the construction process of the concept and the social practices of compliance, instead of the exact degree to which these factors affect companies' compliance levels. In addition, from this viewpoint, the framework provided is not understood as an answer to compliance-related research questions, but rather as a starting point, from which the researcher can depart and investigate. This project adopts this comprehensive framework exactly in such a manner, but makes slight adaptions to the framework itself.

Parker and Nielsen (2011c, p. 5) identify four sets of factors that affect compliance behavior:

- *Social, economic and political environments:* The social, economic and political institutions and actors in the business environment
- *Regulation and enforcement:* The regulatory institutions that businesses are in contact with
- *Organizational capacities and characteristics:* Personal and organizational decision-making attributes, decision-implementation attributes and decision-implementation resources attributes, including organizational

35 For further details, see Section 2.4.1 and 2.4.2.

decision-making structures, managerial capacities, economic resources, technical know-how and legal knowledge[36]
- *Motives:* Motivation of individuals and businesses to comply (economic, social and normative)[37]

They provide a graphic reflection of these influences (Parker and Lehmann Nielsen, 2011c, p. 5), which indicates that these factors do not only impact compliance behavior in the short term, but also exert influence on each other in the long term. In this manner, they then affect compliance behavior. Such long-term mutual effects are attributed to the relationship between all factors, except the one between motives and organizational capacities and characteristics. In addition, compliance is presented as the endpoint, not a determinant that influences any of the four factors.

This model faces several limitations and needs to be updated (see Figure 4). First, in the visualization of the influences on compliance behavior, the political environment is not reflected, even though it is mentioned by Parker and Nielsen (2011c) as a determining factor outside the graphic representation. Since the authors do not provide any explanation for this omission and later research underlined the importance of the political environment's influence on compliance (e.g. Hodges 2015, Haines 2011, Hutter 2011, Tyler 2011), this factor needs to be captured in any visual representation of compliance in the same way as the social and economic spheres. Second, Parker and Nielsen (2011c) do not provide any reason for listing four categories of influences in their elaborations, but in their visualization then merging two into one category under formal and informal institutions. To do justice to all factors equally, the four factors should be depicted separately, but clustered into two categories: Company internal and external factors of influence. Third, for improved clarity, the subsets for the factors 'motives' and 'organizational capacities and characteristics' are removed in the visualization. Fourth, the two internal factors, 'motives' and 'organizational capacities and characteristics', have been shown to mutually influence one another, similar to the other long-term influences depicted in the original framework (e.g. Feldman and Lobel, 2011, Kagan et al., 2011, McKendall and Wagner, 1997). All these long-term mutual influences

36 For further information on the decision-making attributes, decision-implementation attributes and decision-implementation resources mentioned, refer to Lehmann and Nielsen (2012).

37 For more details on the economic, social and normative motives, refer to Section 2.4.2.2.

between the four factors are indicated by dotted arrows in the updated Figure 4. Fifth, based on the definitions adopted in this paper and the social constructionist perspective on compliance, 'compliance behavior' is renamed 'compliance' with three elements: The meaning of the concept of compliance, the compliance status based on that meaning and compliance management activities. Sixth, compliance is no longer considered the result, but also a mutually influencing determinant in the relationship with the other factors (e.g. Talesh, 2009, Edelman, 2007, Picciotto, 2007). To indicate this new understanding, compliance is placed at the center of the model, overlapping with all the influencing factors.

Figure 4: Updated compliance framework (author's design)

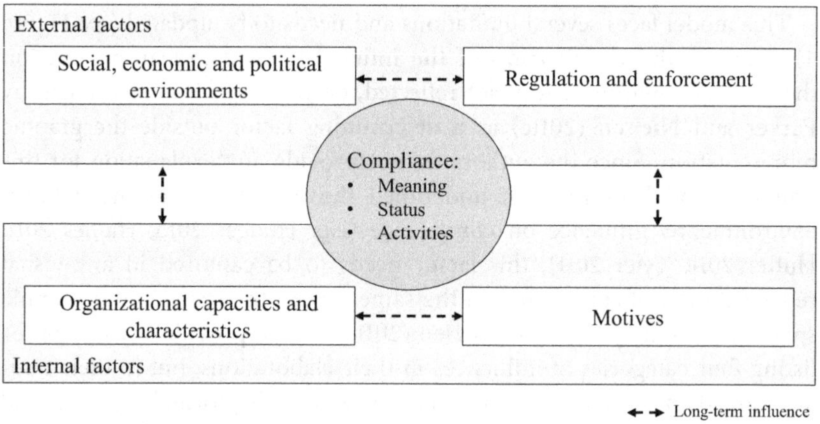

This updated comprehensive compliance framework serves as a basis for the empirical research conducted and discussed in Part II. Therefore, the remainder of this section discusses existing compliance research along the dimensions of this framework, starting with the external followed by the internal factors.

2.4.1 External factors

External factors that influence compliance are social, economic and political environments as well as regulation and enforcement. The status quo of the academic discourse on these dimensions is discussed hereafter.

2.4.1.1 Social, economic and political environments

Social environment

The social environment subsumes all societal influences outside the scope of government, state bureaucracy, judiciary and market actors. These influencing forces are often rooted in and evoked by cultural and normative institutions (e.g. norms and values), which have emerged in a particular place over the long term and are subject to constant change and contestation. According to Haines (2011, p. 289), cultural norms can provide a sense of order and rightness ('how things are done'). This then leads to a societal understanding of what is considered legitimate behavior and therefore rewarded, and what is illegitimate conduct and thus sanctioned. By affecting every individual's value compass, these cultural and normative institutions also automatically influence companies, which are essentially organized groups of people, in their understandings of and approaches to compliance. Research suggests that the key in the design of regulation is to be in line with these cultural and normative institutions in order to ensure that companies adopt related compliance management practices smoothly (e.g. Feldman and Lobel, 2011, OECD, 2000, Gilboy, 1998).

But the social environment also exerts influence on businesses' compliance in more proactive and organized ways. Three main means of influence are discussed in the literature on compliance. First, the broad population has a direct way of affecting businesses as consumers, e.g. by sanctioning behavior via boycotts. Therefore, companies tend to consider consumers as stakeholders in their compliance-related decisions (risk mitigation) (Hutter and Jones 2007, p. 317; Hutter and Jones 2007, p. 36f). Second, the public discourse, often molded by the media, also changes how corporate actors go about their compliance management. On the one hand, this discourse, by highlighting certain topics, helps companies prioritize different areas of concern related to compliance. On the other hand, the media provide platforms for individuals to speak out against companies. Such whistle-blowing actions seem to become more likely when individuals are aware of and uncover previous famous whistle-blowing incidents (Feldman and Lobel, 2011, p. 273). Third, the population organizes itself directly to exert influence on companies and their compliance management, e.g. via non-governmental organizations (NGOs). NGOs increasingly take on the role of regulators and demand compliance with laws and even stricter ethical standards. In this way, they sometimes fill gaps in regulation or push authorities to pass farther-reaching laws (Parker and Nielsen, 2009, p. 49). Nevertheless, Hutter (2011, p. 318) also found that businesses' vulnerability to such organized influence from civil society varies depending on the type of regulation[38], the size of the company addressed, the firm's sensitivity to public attacks and the amount of support a civil society actor holds within society. Oded (2013, p. 206f) classified these third-party enforcers into two prototypes, bouncers and chaperons. Bouncers act as gatekeepers by refusing to support misconduct, e.g. lawyers who reject collaboration on an issue they consider unethical. Chaperons, on the other hand, are reputational intermediaries, who control information that could potentially harm non-compliant firms, for instance standardization organizations that regularly monitor businesses and in doing so detect misconduct (Oded, 2013, p. 206f). Ultimately, both prototypes' success in influencing firms' compliance depends, to a large part, on the previously described cultural and normative institutions and which issues these actors attach importance to.

Economic environment

In the economic environment, previous research has identified several aspects that affect compliance. On the macro-level, the general economic climate in a country and its regional variations influence compliance. This is the case, because a stable and growing economy allows firms to cope with the costs related to compliance more easily. Consequently, external compliance inspectors, with this knowledge in mind, tend to enforce rules more strictly (Hutter, 2011, p. 309). In contrast, the slowdown of the economy can exert high economic pressures on companies. In such a situation, firms tend to squeeze their profitability, which has been proven to impact compliance negatively, e.g. safety standards and working conditions (Haines, 2011, p. 289). Haines (2011, p. 299) therefore calls for a deeper understanding of the economic pressures companies face in the context of compliance related to the dynamics of capitalism.

On a meso-level, industry concentration and the relationship between different market actors play a role for compliance. McKendall et al. (2002,

38 For example, NGOs tend to make a bigger change when they address environmental issues as compared to food safety and hygiene (Hutter, 2011, p. 318).

p. 368) argued that a low industry concentration potentially makes compliance monitoring and the detection of non-compliance harder, simply due to the high number of firms. Consequently, firms in these sectors can more easily take the risk of managing compliance less stringently. In addition, research on business-to-business relationships in the context of compliance shows that stakeholders closer to a firm can influence its compliance to a larger extent than those with more distant relationships (Lehmann Nielsen and Parker, 2008, p. 340). In this context, investors and the stock market are mentioned as important stakeholders that potentially influence compliance (Heyes, 2000). But competitors also play a role: A study on compliance of Mexican gas stations shows that gas stations with high ratings on compliance exert peer pressure over their competitors and thereby affect compliance in the whole industry (Liu et al., 2018).

On the micro-level, Feldman and Lobel (2011, p. 273) identified the job market in remote locations as an influencing factor for compliance: If employees have easy access to other jobs, they are more willing and likely to report peers and supervisors (whistle-blowing) as compared to when they do not have many alternative career opportunities. With a higher risk of whistle-blowing, companies, in turn, are more likely to invest more money and effort in compliance management.

Political environment

In the political environment, the key factor shaping the meaning of compliance and compliance management, as discussed in the existing literature, is political legitimacy. Political legitimacy here refers to both the legitimacy of the government and political system as well as the legitimacy of the regulations passed by the political actors in charge. In case firms do not regard the political system, its actors and outputs as fair and legitimate, they also tend to compromise on compliance and interpret the requirements they face differently (Hodges 2015, p. 28; Haines 2011, p. 292).

Parker discussed this problem in the context of what she calls the 'compliance trap':

> "Where fulsome political and moral support for the enforcement regime is lacking, then the compliance trap is set. Responsive regulators find themselves in a dilemma: overcome the deterrence trap by making morally tough demands that may not only undermine business commitment to compliance in the longer term (because they lack political legitimacy),

> but also undermine their own political support (because business will respond by lobbying government to emasculate the regulatory enforcement agency). Or avoid conflict with businesses by not making any difference at all. [...] The compliance trap can only be resolved politically, external to any particular regulatory enforcement encounter" (Parker, 2006, p. 593).

Essentially, the compliance trap refers to the nature of state-business relationships, which directly affects the way a business manages compliance. Even though the compliance literature to date does not explicitly mention factors related to the state-business relationship, such as the prevalence of corruption in the political system, norms in the interaction (e.g. lobbying) and level of intimacy between the state and businesses[39], these factors seem to be worth further considerations with regard to their impact on how compliance is constructed and practiced.

2.4.1.2 Regulation and enforcement

Regulation

The above elaborations on the social constructionist perspective on compliance highlight that compliance is too complex to be attributed directly to one causal factor and should therefore be considered a social practice and construction process. As such, contrary to popular beliefs, this defies a binary perspective on compliance, where a firm can either be in compliance or not. In the same vein, regulations are also regarded as pluralistic social practices in one strand of legal research (sociology of law) (e.g. Talesh, 2009, Picciotto, 2007, Lange, 1999). Suchman and Edelman's (1996, p. 930) assertion that

> "law is often uncertain, not determinate; [...] contested, not authoritative; and [...] constitutive, not coercive",

can also be applied to regulations, which co-opt laws in the definition adopted in this research (see Section 2.2.1).

The first characteristic mentioned by Suchman and Edelman (1996, p. 930ff), uncertainty, applies to regulation on three levels: First, regulations

39 A high level of intimacy would, for instance, be given in cases of state-ownership or other forms of public-private partnerships.

are indeterminate, due to the nature of language itself. The meaning of words (including connotations) is socially constructed. Second, regulations themselves often exhibit a certain level of fuzziness and ambiguity that leaves leeway for interpretation. Third, the norms that underpin regulations are based on shared values and purposes. Therefore, their implementation is also based on value judgments and interpretations (Picciotto, 2007, p. 12). This indeterminacy of regulations essentially means that there is leeway to construct meaning. Black (2002) described this interpretation process, i.e. the interactions between regulatees and regulator, as 'regulatory conversations'. In regulatory conversations, the sovereignty over the meaning of the rules is contested, the second characteristic mentioned in the quote by Suchman and Edelman (1996, p. 930). Different stakeholders, e.g. lawyers, companies and judges, negotiate and try to achieve a consensus regarding the content and practical implications of rules (Suchman and Edelman, 1996, p. 932). Therefore a regulation is "a site for inherent conflicts and dilemmas between different interests" (Hutter, 2011, p. 307) and, consequently, has to balance the interests and needs of different interest groups. As a result, a firm's compliance management is not confined to persuading employees to act according to regulations, but also entails two more fields of activity: The company's participation in the firm-external regulatory negotiation process with other stakeholders as well as the management of the firm-internal regulatory negotiation process. In these negotiation processes, a shared perspective on the understanding of the rules and the company's reaction to these rules is constructed. The broader the acceptance of the rules, the more stable and effective a regulatory and compliance management system becomes (Picciotto, 2007, p. 18). With regulations as social practices, formal rules are constantly changed by their stakeholders (both regulators and regulatees) during the implementation process. The third characteristic mentioned by Suchman and Edelman (1996, p. 930), the constitutive nature of law, highlights the law's ability to frame how the world is perceived. Instead of emanating power via coercion, law unfolds its impact mainly by integrating its legal categories and norms into people's cognitive maps and providing commonly accepted rituals as social practices (Suchman and Edelman, 1996, p. 936).

Figure 5: Competition regime development processes according to Buß (1973, p. 69) (author's design and translation)

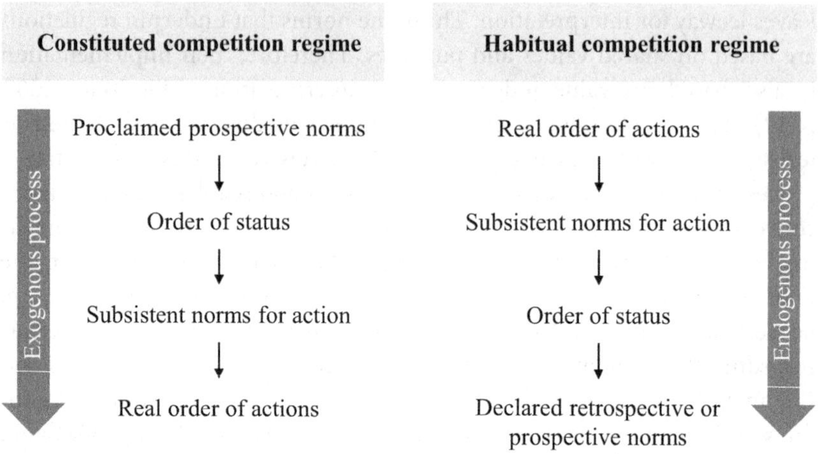

Such an understanding of regulations as pluralistic social practices has two main effects for the way regulations are conceptualized. First, regulations and related institutions emerge and evolve in a negotiation process between various actors. Using the example of competition regimes[40], Buß (1973, p. 69) delineates two ways how these regimes develop, namely an exogenous and an endogenous process (see Figure 5). The exogenous process is initiated by the government's proclamation of prospective norms, which lead to a certain 'order of the status quo' (Zustandsordnung), often laid down by certain institutions, based on the proclaimed norms. From this context, subsistent norms for action for businesses emerge, which establish a real 'order of actions' (Handlungsordnung). Ultimately, this process leads to a 'constituted competition regime' (statuierte Wettbewerbsordnung), since the norms were initially exogenously imposed. In contrast, the endogenous process starts from a real order of actions in the business community, which provides subsistent norms for action. Based on these, an order of the status quo, including norms are defined and declared, which can be both retrospective (i.e. based on existing norms) or prospective (i.e. newly defined norms). Buß (1973, p. 69) calls the set of regulations emerging

40 Competition regimes are economic institutions that are shaped by different types of regulations, such as antitrust law.

from this endogenous process a 'habitual competition regime' (habituelle Wettbewerbsordnung). In a nutshell, these two processes describe two ways in which regulations are established: They are either triggered by exogenous factors which prescribe certain norms that influence future actions (targeted top-down measure) or consolidated from existing behavioral norms and actions into an officially prescribed order (bottom-up emergence).

Second, regulations are at least partly endogenous to businesses. While most accounts of regulation and organization premise that regulations are positioned externally to and above the organization, the theory of the endogeneity of law posits that the legal and managerial/organizational fields mutually influence each other and in this process internalize one another's dominating logic: The legal logic of rights and justice becomes part of the company's management logic, which is originally based on the principle of efficiency and rationality (and vice versa) (Edelman, 2007, p. 58).

Based on research on the legal construction processes, Edelman (2007, p. 67f) defines six stages of the endogeneity of law (see Figure 6). The first step, the professional construction of the legal environment, describes the phase when law is interpreted in companies. Even though firms employ lawyers, who advise managers in understanding, interpreting and working with the law, managers ultimately dominate decision-making in companies. Since managers often do not possess a legal background and are embedded into managerial structures, regulations' interpretation tends to happen within a managerial frame of thinking. This means managers tend to consider the legal environment as a limiting factor in their business operations, similar to, for instance, resource constraints (Edelman et al., 2001, p. 69). Thus, company leaderships react to laws in a managerial fashion, e.g. by creating compliance departments, drafting governance policies, prescribing procedures or developing entirely new compliance management devices (Talesh, 2009, p. 533f). These are all symbolic forms of compliance constructed by organizations. Over time, these forms may turn into commonly accepted and adequate ways for companies' compliance management and become equated with compliance itself (step 2). With these structures in place, the members of the organization (both employers and employees) fill the structures with life via actions and decisions in their daily working environment. These behaviors are based on their own understanding of the company's rules and processes and therefore, as social practices of compliance, construct the meaning of the law within the organization (step 3) (Edelman, 2007,p. 73).

Figure 6: Process of the endogeneity of law according to Edelman (2007, p. 67f) (author's design)

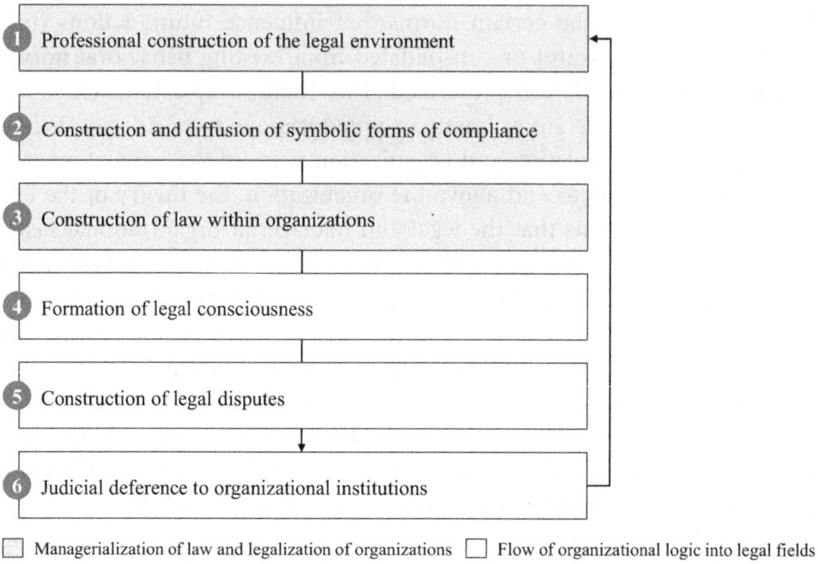

These first three process steps lead to a 'managerialization of law' as well as a 'legalization of organizations'. 'Managerialization of law' refers to the introduction of "managerial ways of thinking into the construction of law and legal ideas" (Edelman et al., 2001, p. 1597). 'Legalization of organizations', on the other hand, means that organizations "come to embody the underlying logic of the regulatory legal environment even as they try to evade its most burdensome provisions" (Edelman and Suchman, 1997, p. 495). This can be observed in organizations mimicking legislation and statutory language when determining internal rules or creating company-internal dispute processing mechanisms.

The institutionalization of managerialized legal practices in organizations, in step 4, then fosters the emergence of a legal consciousness among employers and employees, since they interact with these institutions on a regular basis (Edelman, 2007, p. 79). Consequently, these managerialized ideas of the law also affect a company's decisions on whether and how to engage in legal disputes (step 5). Via disputes or other interactions with authorities (for example when enforcement authorities assess companies' compliance), the managerialized concepts of the law are fed back into the legal sphere. This interaction then leads to the infusion of managerial approaches to law and ultimately managerial values to the legal realm. But the managerialization does not stop there. The spillovers from the managerial realm also bear the potential to create entirely new legal or bureaucratic devices for regulating and enforcing businesses' compliance (step 6). Via steps 4 to 6, organizational logic flows into the legal sphere leading to reciprocal influences between the two spheres (Edelman and Suchman, 1997, p. 79ff).

In the course of this six step process, the law has become endogenous to the organizational field and management, to a certain extent, also becomes endogenous to the legal field[41] , a point which Edelman (2007) did not explicitly state. Since these steps likely lead to legislative changes, businesses, again, have to react and the process starts anew.

Talesh (2009), for example, traced these processes of mutual influence in a study on the development of California's consumer protection laws and found that manufacturing companies construct compliance in a way that serves their own interests, rather than simply following or avoiding ambiguous regulations. Therefore, the author regards businesses as a driving force in institutional changes in public institutions. Edelman (2007, p. 89) even claimed that

> "because it operates under the political radar, the endogenous construction of social logics is likely to be an especially powerful source of field structuration and social change".

The existing research on the managerialization of law has developed hypotheses concerning factors that facilitate these processes. First, the managerialization of law is dependent on the amount of time that has passed (Edelman et al., 2001, p. 1599). The longer a law exists and is applied in the corporate context, the more interactions and social construction processes have occurred and therefore, the managerialization of older laws is likely to be more significant (Edelman et al., 2001, p. 1599). Second, the

41 Since all types of regulations are considered rules constructed in the interaction process among different social actors from a social constructionist angle, similar processes as the endogeneity of the law likely also occur in the construction process of other types of government regulations (e.g. via regulatory agencies) as well as non-governmental regulations, such as standards. Considering that businesses are often more involved in the drafting processes of other forms of regulations (e.g. standards, guidelines from self-regulatory agencies), these regulatory fields are likely to exhibit a higher degree of managerialization from the outset.

more professionals (e.g. management consultants, industry associations) promulgate a management-based interpretation of a law, the higher the chances a managerial notion is incorporated into this law. Their communication shapes the way their counterparts think about the law, for example when professionals frame legal issues in managerial terms or communicate solutions to legal problems in a pragmatic rather than punitive fashion. The role of professionals is expected to be central to managerialization, since they transmit concepts between businesses in the context of their service provision, but also in their other activities, such as publications, conferences and events (Edelman et al., 2001, p. 1596f., 1601). Sectors in which professional networks and institutions exist are predicted to experience regulations as significantly more binding and concise, as compared to industries without professional actors (Suchman and Edelman, 1996, p. 940). Lastly, highlighting the profit rational in relation to the interpretation of a law is expected to foster the managerialization process. At the same time, however, it is important that the newly managerialized concepts are still in line with the existing legal and political environment (Edelman et al., 2001, p. 1600). While these hypotheses focus on the impact that the factors have on regulations mentioned above, if proven influential, they clearly also affect the process directed at the firm. This is the case, because both the 'legalization of the organization' and the 'managerialization of the law' are part of the same interaction between the managerial and legal realm. An investigation into compliance management at the center of this interaction has the potential to provide further insights into construction processes, mutual influences and the underlying logic of compliance management itself.

Beyond its impact with regard to the processes described in the previous paragraphs, the nature of the regulation itself has also been found to directly influence compliance and compliance management. First, the amount and complexity of regulation overall affect the costs of compliance, since more complex rules and structures increase the difficulty for companies to understand and comply with guidelines (OECD, 2000, p. 14). They may need to hire dedicated legal experts or external consultancies to ensure compliant behavior, which is costly. But the complexity of regulations only affects the costs for those companies that are willing to comply. For other firms, high regulatory complexity offers more opportunities to find loopholes and avoid compliance (creative compliance) (OECD, 2000, p. 14). Second, the perceived fairness of regulations by companies has an impact on compliance. The fairer a company considers the rules, the more motivated and likely it is to comply with them. Governments try to increase perceived fairness and willingness to comply by involving firms in the drafting and implementation process of rules. This way, the rule-makers try to acknowledge the needs and concerns of the regulatory subjects by creating a cooperative and participatory relationship (Tyler, 2011, p. 90). Hence, compliance management for process-based regulations extends beyond the firm itself to also include participation in regulatory policy formulation.

Third, the type of regulation applied by the government influences the way companies conduct compliance management. Regulations can be classified on a spectrum between highly prescriptive and principles-based (Hutter, 2011, p. 307). Prescriptive regulations are characterized by detailed rules with a high degree of specificity related to their implementation. Therefore, they provide little leeway for companies to modify their compliance management regarding the regulated issue. In contrast, principles-based regulations allow for more flexible compliance management, since only the required compliance outcome and the principles that need to be adhered to are described. The measures taken to achieve the required compliance levels, however, are left to the companies to decide on (Hutter, 2011, p. 307). Such principles-based regulations are often also more ambiguous, leaving more latitude for companies to construct the notion of compliance to their benefit.

Fourth, different corporate liability regimes lead to different compliance management efforts. Depending on the level of firms' liability for their employees and the extent to which companies' executives are held responsible for their businesses' compliance violations individually, firms' compliance management systems assess compliance risks differently and thus their compliance management systems (focus topics, measures...) vary (Oded, 2013, p. 105ff).

Enforcement

Besides regulation itself, enforcement is the second key constituent in a regulatory system: The success of regulations is to a large extent contingent upon adequate enforcement. Different enforcement theories have emerged over time, which are clustered into enforcement instruments and enforcement approaches. Enforcement instruments represent the concrete methods of enforcement, such as deterrence or transparency. In contrast, enforcement approaches are understood as the logic according to which enforcement instruments are adopted, e.g. responsive, smart or meta regulation (explained later in this section). Consequently, enforcement approaches are the strategic perspectives on enforcement on a meta-level, whereas enforcement instruments describe the concrete implementation of enforcement measures.

An increasing number of enforcement instruments have emerged over time. Deterrence-based enforcement was initially predominant in academic discussions (e.g. Becker, 1968), before later other practices, namely cooperation, incentives and transparency, were recognized as enforcement instruments (e.g. Mol, 2014, Oded, 2013, Van Erp, 2011). While enforcement instruments have received varying names in different contexts and academic disciplines, scholars essentially refer to the same four styles, for which Meijer and Homburg (2009, p. 264) provide a typology: Legal, communicative, economic and network instruments (see Table 1 with examples for different terms). This typology is laid out and adopted in the following.

Table 1: Examples of different names adopted in the academic literature for the four enforcement instruments; categories based on Meijer and Homburg's (2009, p. 264) typology

Legal instruments	**Communicative instruments**	**Economic instruments**	**Network instruments**
Deterrence-based enforcement (e.g. Oded, 2013)	Cooperative enforcement (e.g. Oded, 2013)	Financial incentives (e.g. Lemos and Minzner, 2014)	Targeted transparency (e.g. Fung et al., 2007)
Coercive styles (e.g. Tang et al., 2003)	Compliance (e.g. Gunningham, 2011)	Rewards (e.g. Ben-Shahar and Bradford, 2012)	Regulatory transparency (e.g. Weil et al., 2006)
Sanctioning strategy (e.g. May and Winter, 2000)	Accommodative strategy (e.g. May and Winter, 2000)	Subsidies (e.g. Leeuw, 1997)	Regulation by revelation (e.g. Florini, 1998)
Legalistic style (e.g. Hawkins and Thomas, 1984)	Conciliatory style (e.g. Hawkins and Thomas, 1984)	Economic incentives (e.g. Mukul et al., 2014)	Naming and shaming (e.g. Braithwaite and Drahos, 2002)

Legal instruments use rules and punitive incentives to achieve a desired outcome (Meijer and Homburg, 2009, p. 264). This essentially refers to what is often called 'deterrence-based' enforcement. These instruments are based on the assumption that actors are self-interested utility maximizers (homo oeconomicus) that make decisions in a completely rational manner (rational choice theory) (Parker and Lehmann Nielsen, 2011c, p. 10). Consequently, businesses conduct cost-benefit analyses to make compliance decisions. They only comply with regulations, when, taking all factors into account (including the likelihood of detection, costs of sanctions, costs for complying, etc.), non-compliance is more costly than compliance. This implies, on the one hand, that deterrence-based enforcement is based on a one-way decision-making process from the regulator to the regulatee (Parker and Lehmann Nielsen, 2011c, p. 10). On the other hand, it portends that the only leeway that exists when designing legal enforcement instruments pertains to decisions on the type of sanctions, their severity and control mechanism (detection probability) (Oded, 2013, p. 21). In sum, this logic dictates that compliance can be achieved by coercing actors in a confrontational manner with sanctions (Oded, 2013, p. 27).

However, legal instruments have been subject to heavy criticism. First, the underlying assumptions on the homo oeconomicus and rational choice are questioned (e.g. Oded 2013, p. 43) and have in many cases been replaced by bounded rationality[42], which recognizes the ambiguity and complexity of human decision-making, i.e. individuals do not act as pure profit-maximizers (e.g. Oded, 2013, Klaes and Sent, 2005, Braithwaite and Makkai, 1991, Simon, 1972). Instead of concrete sanctions affecting companies' compliance-related cost-benefit calculations, legal enforcement instruments have rather proven to serve as a general deterrent. This means that hearing about sanctions that other non-compliant firms have to face serves as guidance for the right behavior to many companies (Thornton et al., 2005, p. 282). Moreover, even if businesses attempt to only maximize profit, they are not able to conduct correct cost-benefit-analyses regarding compliance. This inability is caused by a lack of information, as well as difficulties in identifying and calculating costs in a complete and exhaustive fashion (e.g. costs of certain injuries in case of safety incidents) (Hodges, 2015, p. 107f). Second, legal enforcement instruments are criticized for their potential negative economic side-effects. Specifically, it is extremely difficult for regulators to achieve the right level of deterrence and both over-deterrence as well as under-deterrence can cause problems (Oded, 2013, p. 22). Over-deterrence means that sanctions overwhelm firms and in the worst case can lead to insolvencies. Bankruptcies not only hurt the management of a particular firm, but also innocent employees and creditors (Hodges, 2015, p. 110). Under-deterrence, in contrast, refers to insuffi-

42 Bounded rationality acknowledges that actors do not make entirely rational decisions, e.g. due to incomplete information and cognitive limitations (Simon, 1972).

cient monitoring and weak sanctioning, which does not have a deterrent effect and thus allows firms to avoid compliance at minimal cost (Parker, 2006, p. 592). On top of risks concerning the wrong level of deterrence, Oded (2013, p. 36f) argued that even if the optimal level of sanctioning and detection measures can be identified, it often comes at too high a cost and its implementation is therefore impracticable. Third, the negative effect of legal enforcement instruments on a personal and inter-personal level are subject to criticism. Hodges (2015, p. 109) asserted that enforcement instruments with both continuous surveillance and punishments, tend "to be accusatory, confrontational, punitive and coercive and produces a culture of mistrust and resentment".

Therefore, they foster a coercive culture of mistrust and resentment in society. In addition, such instruments may lead to demotivating and antagonistic feelings among regulatees, since deterring measures tend to limit individual autonomy. This effect had been confirmed by research (e.g. Oded, 2013, Gunningham, 2011), even though it is, of course, never possible for a business to control every employee's actions or a regulatory authority to check the compliance levels of all companies at all times.

Communicative instruments can be regarded as the opposite of legal instruments. They intend to convince actors to adopt certain behaviors by providing arguments, rather than coercive measures (Meijer and Homburg, 2009, p. 264). Such an educational and advisory approach on the part of the regulator aims to persuade and incorporate the regulated actors; hence a two-way interaction, as compared to the one-way legal instruments. From this point of view, only in case all communicative efforts fail should legal instruments be adopted (Gunningham, 2011, p. 201). The difference between the two types of instruments hints at a more fundamental divergence in the respective instruments' underlying conception of human beings. Instead of regarding human beings as law-avoiding actors that need to be controlled (legal instruments), communicative instruments are based on the theory that humans generally wish to and do abide by the law, because it is the right ethical behavior. Thanks to their personal morality and the perceived legitimacy of regulators/authorities, humans are normatively committed to rules-based behavior (Oded, 2013, p. 50). Non-compliance, from this perspective, is caused by a lack of knowledge, capabilities and capacities to follow the rules. Therefore, capacity building, e.g. via education, consultation and assistance, is key to successful enforcement. One specific communicative concept, restorative justice, focuses on building compliance competences in firms, by supporting them in improving their compliance behavior, following a violation of the rules (OECD, 2000, p. 42). External audits and inspections constitute a valuable platform for capacity building, because as auditors and inspectors control company staff, these regulators can also interact with the regulatees in an educative manner (e.g. improving regulatees' knowledge on regulation) (Parker, 2003, p. 227, 234).

Communicative instruments, however, are a double-edged sword. On the one hand, they provide several evident advantages. With their focus on objectives, they leave regulatees leeway to adopt compliance approaches in the most feasible way. Thereby, regulatees are encouraged to implement objectives, the essence of regulation, instead of simply adopting a formal creative compliance approach to management (Oded, 2013, p. 54). Additionally, two-way communication facilitates the sharing of information between the regulators and regulatees, which may provide benefits for both sides beyond regulatory supervision and compliance (e.g. smoother process with other administrative procedures for firms, thanks to additional information provided to the regulatory authority) (Oded, 2013, p. 57). Lastly, since communicative instruments foster trust between the two parties, regulatory authorities can reduce their reliance on monitoring and detecting firms' non-compliance, which results in lower enforcement costs (Oded, 2013, p. 54). Nevertheless, communicative instruments also bear risks. First, during frequent interactions and cooperation, regulators and regulatees are likely to form special relationships. This may cause regulatory capture, i.e. regulators act too leniently or in a too accommodating manner towards companies they have developed bonds with (Oded, 2013, p. 66). Furthermore, the risk of corruption also increases since there is more leeway for regulated agents to react to regulations (Oded, 2013, p. 68). Lastly, even if correct for a large part of firms, the assumption that companies willingly comply may not hold true for all firms. In an approach purely based on communicative instruments, less controls take place, as compared to an approach based on legal instruments. This bears the risk of authorities being deceived by firms that can easily circumvent the rules (Oded, 2013, p. 65, 68).

Economic instruments, in contrast, actively create positive incentives for businesses to display certain behaviors, e.g. via financial rewards, grants or subsidies (Meijer and Homburg, 2009, p. 264). By providing such incentives only under certain conditions, the government influences businesses' cost-benefit-calculations (higher benefits in case of compliance) and thereby increases the likelihood of compliance (Meijer and Homburg, 2009, Leeuw, 1997). In the case of financial incentives, Wolfson (1990) identified two main beneficial effects for businesses, the income and the substitution effect. The income effect describes how firms react to increases in their income (and therefore the managers' budgets) thanks to incentives. The substitution effect subsumes companies' behavior, when they are confronted with relative prices changes (of products, materials...), because of economic instruments applied by the government.

However, similar to legal instruments, economic tools can be criticized for their assumption that businesses act as pure profit-maximizers. Since this has proven not to be the case (see discussion above), economic instruments' reach is limited. They can only motivate businesses regarding aspects where profit-maximization is the key driver of behavior, but not on topics or behaviors, where other motivators (such as norms or social pressure; for more details see Section 2.4.2.2) dominate. Furthermore, economic instruments have been criticized for their costs (e.g. Leeuw, 1997). Not only the government's beneficial treatment, be it via financial means or in administrative/decision-making processes, tends to bear high costs, but monitoring costs also remain high, because this mechanism does not eliminate controls. For example, Malik (1992) adopted economic modeling to show that, on economic grounds, such incentives can be more costly to enforce: Similar to legal and communicative instruments, the government still needs to monitor businesses' behavior to ensure they actually deserve the rewards promised by the incentives. All in all, this means that the government is charged with two sources of costs for this single enforcement instrument. Critics wonder whether the outcome is worth the burden, but profound quantitative evidence for either position has not been generated yet[43]. Another point of criticism is the vague objectives that often tend to be connected to economic incentives (Haider, 1989). This means that the behavioral conditions that need to be achieved to gain rewards offered by incentives are often not stated precisely or in a way that is easily measurable. This may render the whole instrument ineffective, since the motivating effect could be lost without clear objectives. The question arises how businesses should respond to incentives that aim to change their operations, when indications regarding what they should change their behavior to are missing. In addition, unclearly stated goals make decision on who receives rewards difficult. Consequently, this may reduce a government's credibility in case of seemingly random decisions. Some people may even

43 For further information on the difficulties of assessing economic instruments' costs and benefits, refer to Leuuw (1997).

accuse the government of only using economic incentives to pacify the population or gain more voters (Wiseman, 1977).

Lastly, network instruments use disclosure (especially via the internet) to achieve compliance (Meijer and Homburg, 2009, p. 264). The origins of these instruments can be traced back to the right-to-know movements in the 1960s and 1970s (Mol, 2014, p. 51). Due to two major developments in the more recent past, disclosure has again gained importance as an enforcement instrument. First, new technologies, such as the internet, big data and artificial intelligence, have significantly reduced the costs of disclosure and extended the reach of information, while at the same time more data points can be collected and analyzed. Second, the shift from government to governance meant an inclusion of more actors into the regulatory system besides the government (for further details see Section 3.3) (Meijer and Homburg, 2009, p. 265ff). An increase in the plurality of actors involved in enforcement is essential for disclosure, since this mechanism relies on including other information users (e.g. consumers, business partners, investors), besides the government and the targeted firm, into the enforcement process (Bunea, 2018, p. 382). The key mechanism of disclosure is the mandatory publication of "structured factual information by private or public institutions in order to advance a clear regulatory goal" (Weil et al., 2006, p. 155).

Depending on the set-up, the regulatee is obliged to disclose the information directly; otherwise the regulator acts as an intermediary and provides the information to the public. The disclosed pieces of information reduce information asymmetries and thereby potentially affect a company's reputation. Since reputation is often regarded as a proxy for the reliability and trustworthiness of an enterprise, this indicator constitutes an important form of capital in the business sector (Van Erp, 2011, p. 324f). Van Erp (2011, p. 325f) outlines two objectives of disclosure, which are addressed in network instrument to varying degrees depending on the set-up: On the one hand, disclosure empowers the recipient of the information by providing this actor with information on the regulatee (Van Erp, 2011, p. 325). Thus, it is consumer-oriented[44]. Disclosure increases market transparency and thereby allows consumers of the information to include more factors into their decision-making processes. The expectation, however, that consumers always sanction non-compliant actors based on the available

44 A consumer can be both the consumer of goods in a traditional sense, but also, beyond that, the consumer of information (e.g. a business partner or investor).

information, cannot be met by this instrument: The information users themselves only make rational decisions to a limited extent (bounded rationality), just like the businesses. On the other hand, disclosure targets the firms directly by altering the costs of potential offenses. Information transparency can lead to reputational sanctions, the fear of which serves as a deterrent in this enforcement instrument (Van Erp, 2011, p. 325). Thus, this second objective of disclosure constitutes an overlap with legal enforcement instruments. Nevertheless, network instruments are categorized as segregated enforcement instruments, since the consumer-oriented objective is clearly distinct from all other instruments. This argument is strengthened by the fact that network instruments always aim to fulfill both of the objectives explained above to a certain degree, rather than pursuing a single one of the two individually.

The effect of network instruments is, however, not guaranteed by the installation of this enforcement instrument. Research has shown that in most cases consumers do not exhibit a strong reaction to disclosure (e.g. Van Erp, 2011, Meijer and Homburg, 2009). The causes lie in the information overload for information recipients, low relevance of the information for consumers and the diverging (often not expected) interpretations of the disclosure by the information recipients (based on their existing commitments, conflicts with core values, etc.)[45]. In addition, larger firms with a solid reputation, as well as non-consumer-facing companies, show less vulnerability when confronted with the disclosure of compliance violations (Van Erp, 2011, p. 331f). Besides these firm-related hindrances, there are also potential systemic barriers to the effectiveness of disclosure instruments, especially in relation to the prevailing political and administrative culture (e.g. bribery, distrust in the bureaucracy, lacking political legitimacy) (Lee, 2010, p. 320f). Moreover, disclosure instruments bear the risk of failure due to potentially high costs for both the targeted firms and the authorities, which need to enforce the disclosure (Dalley, 2007, p. 1127). Therefore, Meijer and Homburg (2009, p. 277) recommend to use disclosure only as an enforcement instrument for small offenses, rather than for major societal risks.

45 For example, Van Erp (2011, p. 331f) highlighted that shareholders display pragmatic, instead of a morality-based, behavior related to the disclosure of offenses on the part of the invested company. Therefore, the impact of such disclosures on the firms themselves tends to be rather low.

Nevertheless, academia has also identified certain design features that increase the likelihood of success in adopting disclosure mechanisms. First, disclosure mechanisms should be doubly embedded, both in the information users' and the disclosers' decision-making processes. Only when the adoption of disclosure tools is practical, i.e. does not require significant additional efforts[46], are both parties likely to actively use the tools (e.g. Lee, 2010, Dalley, 2007, Fung et al., 2007, Weil et al., 2006). Second, to be impactful, it is important that the disclosed information addresses a specific target group and a relevant issue[47]. If the audience and the purpose of disclosure is defined too broadly or there is a great amount of information disclosed, the transparency gained loses its power and relevance (Van Erp, 2011, p. 328). Third, if intermediaries that work on an issue (e.g. environmental NGOs for the disclosure of environmental data or the media) become involved and promote the released information, disclosure mechanisms are more likely to succeed. Therefore, potential user groups and the relevance of the topic should be kept in mind when designing enforcement instruments (e.g. Fung et al., 2007, p. 55). Fourth, information that is portrayed in a clear manner increases the chances of success, e.g. via scores and color-coding. A clear message and a high level of comparability of the disclosed information simplifies the decision-making for the recipient and, hence, is more likely to be utilized (Van Erp, 2011, Fung et al., 2007). Fifth, disclosure instruments are more likely to deliver a sustainable impact if they are designed to continuously develop. Fung et al. (2007, p. 110) list three dimensions that should constantly be improved: The quality and accuracy of information, the frequency of information use by recipients and the adequacy of the scope of the information provided relative to the issue that is being addressed. Ideally, this continuous re-calibration should be based on feedback from the different stakeholders in the disclosure system. Lastly, information disclosure needs to be enforced stringently, ideally by leveraging the existing regulatory system (Fung et al., 2007, p. 177ff). Only that way, can the completeness and correctness of data be ensured and information asymmetries truly mitigated. Overall, these insights from research provide evident guidance on how the network instruments should be implemented. At the same time, however, academics also point out that

46 Fung et al. (2007, p. 50ff) used the example of restaurant hygiene ratings that are disclosed directly at the restaurant door/window. They are conveniently accessible and, thus, embedded into consumers' decision-making processes.

47 Dalley (2007, p. 1117) went as far as to state that information does not only need to be relevant, but also emotionally interesting.

research on this enforcement instrument is still in the early stages. Therefore, further research, especially on companies' reaction to disclosure and disclosure's impact on trust in public and private institutions is needed to (in)validate the existing insights from this field (e.g. Meijer et al., 2014, Lee, 2010, Fung et al., 2007). Contributing insights from the firm-perspective can be generated via compliance research.

The above elaborations on the different instruments have shown that none of them is a panacea for enforcement. Successful enforcement combines these different instruments based on the context they are embedded in[48] (Gunningham, 2011, Parker, 2006). Therefore, three main enforcement approaches have emerged in the academic discourse: Responsive regulation, smart regulation and meta regulation. Responsive regulation is an enforcement approach where the regulator takes regulated agents' existing compliance performance and capacities into consideration and responds accordingly (Gunningham, 2011, p. 206). It is an approach that was triggered by a dissatisfaction with the instruments mentioned above, which are all limited in their effectiveness. Thus, with responsive regulation, regulatory agencies can adopt different enforcement strategies for different actors based on the context, e.g. taking a cooperative approach based on communicative instruments for companies that are generally complying with regulations, but punishing the worst offenders (Gunningham, 2011, p. 202). Ayres and Braithwaite (1992) develop the concept of enforcement pyramids for responsive regulation, which highlights the escalation stages of this enforcement approach (see Figure 7). The model suggests regulators start with more lenient enforcement instruments at the bottom of the pyramid and only escalate upwards in case adopted tools do not ensure compliance. These authors' research has shown that authorities apply a range of enforcement instruments, with the softer measures at the bottom of the pyramid (often communicative instruments) being used more frequently than legal instruments higher up in the pyramid (Ayres and Braithwaite, 1992). Even though various versions of the original pyramid with variations in the enforcement instruments chosen for the different stages have been developed for different contexts (e.g. Gunningham, 2011, Lobel, 2009, Braithwaite, 2008, Healy and Braithwaite, 2006), one of the model's

48 Variables, such as the political system, social norms and values, the state of the bureaucracy, existing institutions and the type of matter and actor that are regulated, affect the choice of enforcement instruments. For further details on these variables, refer to van Rooij (2006, p. 233ff), for example.

shortcoming is that they rarely include economic or network instruments. A responsive enforcement approach should always take the utilization of all instruments into consideration. Another criticism of responsive regulation and the enforcement pyramid lies in the regulatory authority's decision to adopt enforcement instruments. As discussed previously, the perception of fairness is highly important for actors' willingness to comply. The diverging treatment of different companies could easily be regarded as arbitrary and lower the overall motivation to manage compliance (Oded, 2013, p. 92). To avoid such a response, it is essential for regulatory authorities to maintain an effective information flow and continuous dialogue with the targeted companies (Gunningham, 2011, p. 204). Parker (2006, p. 592) accentuates this point, by stating that for this enforcement approach to work, the enforced regulation needs to be considered fair in the first place. Otherwise, even high levels of communication between regulators and regulatees may not mitigate the latter's drop in compliance motivation. Furthermore, Ayres and Braithwaite (1992) only look at enforcement from a government perspective, but do not provide ideas or insights into how companies should react to such an enforcement approach.

Figure 7: Example of an enforcement pyramid according to Ayres and Braithwaite (1992, p. 35)

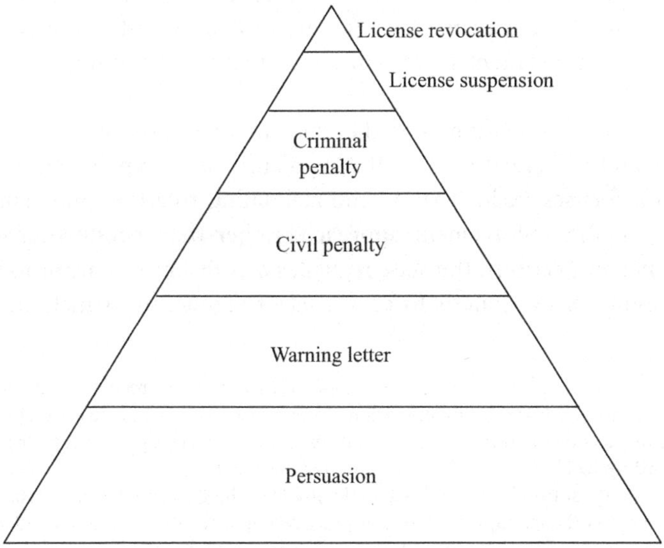

To compensate for responsive regulations shortcomings, smart regulation takes the former's advantages one step further. It is

> "a form of regulatory pluralism that embraces flexible, imaginative and innovative forms of social control. In doing so, it harnesses governments as well as business and third parties" (Gunningham and Sinclair, 2017, p. 133).

Hence, it includes more stakeholders as quasi-regulators (e.g. trading partners, financial markets, international standards organizations, industry associations) in the enforcement process to complement the role of the state. With this smaller role in direct enforcement, the state acts more as a facilitator creating the preconditions for other regulators to become involved in enforcement. But smart regulation is not just based on the pluralism of regulators, it also refers back to the use of numerous enforcement instruments, as in responsive regulation. This means that the one-dimensional enforcement pyramid of responsive regulation is expanded to three dimensions: The state enforces regulations via upwards-escalation on one side of the pyramid, while businesses (self-regulation[49]) and third parties (co-regulation[50]) each take up a similar role on the other two sides of the pyramid. How many and which regulators are responsible for which areas of enforcement depends on the context. In any case, the combination of various instruments with a broad set of regulators generates more options to tailor enforcement to the specific circumstances and is therefore considered an improvement to responsive regulation (Gunningham, 2011, p. 208).

While smart regulation sees the state in two roles, both as a direct enforcer and a facilitator for other regulators' enforcement efforts, meta regulation focuses exclusively on the facilitating role (Gunningham, 2011, p. 212f). In this enforcement approach, rather than conducting its own compliance inspections, the state regulates at a distance. Therefore the key responsibility of the state is to pass a set of regulations, which encourage

49 Self-regulation refers to a regulatory approach where those regulated take initiatives themselves to ensure compliant behavior. For instance, an industry developing and adopting a code of ethical conduct on its own initiative (Hodges, 2015, p. 466).

50 According to Hodges (2015, p. 466), co-regulation works similarly to self-regulation, but in contrast to self-regulation actually involves the government to a certain extent. He provides the example of codes of practice (e.g. accreditation and standards) that are jointly developed by an industry and a government, but then enforced by the industry on its own (e.g. via industry associations).

companies to develop their own internal control and compliance management systems for self-regulation. In addition, the state also needs to build firms' capabilities of self-reflection, self-regulation and self-reporting (Gunningham, 2011, p. 212f). The 'comply-or-explain' method can be adopted as part of this enforcement approach. In this method, companies report their compliance levels and, in case of non-compliance, provide explanations for deviations in desired behavior. This increased transparency allows stakeholders (e.g. consumers, business partners, investors) to react accordingly (Seidl et al., 2013, p. 792). The state only facilitates the process. The advantages of meta regulation are a reduction in public costs for enforcement, higher levels of flexibility to react to circumstances and adopt the most fitting compliance management approach as well as positive impacts on state-business relationships (higher degree of cooperation and consent) (OECD, 2000, p. 28). However, the disadvantages of such an approach are also evident: The risk of creative compliance is high, since only the self-reported information is checked. Thus, the enforcement process may also be considered to be unfair by actors that genuinely comply and in the process decrease their motivation to follow rules (Hodges, 2015, p. 469g). With such significant variation, the choice of enforcement approach clearly affects compliance, both in its constructed meaning[51], as well as the derived compliance management systems[52].

Irrespective of the enforcement approach and instruments adopted, inspectors play a vital role in enforcement in almost any scenario: They build the direct link between the regulators and the regulatees. However, despite the proven benefits of a high inspection frequency, the reliance on intermediaries and the setting of clear inspection priorities (May and Winter, 2011), little consensus has been reached on the most successful strategies for inspectors. On the one hand, research has shown that fewer interactions between inspectors and firms avoid regulatory capture and should therefore be preferred. The more frequent the interactions are, the smaller the relational distance becomes and the less likely inspectors apply formal sanctioning mechanisms (Hutter, 2011, p. 310). The adoption of regulatory policies to rotate inspectors regularly between different regulatees addresses this problem. On the other hand, however, research that

51 E.g. whether compliance means only accountability towards the state or also towards other actors.

52 E.g. compliance management for a company that largely self-regulates bears different compliance risks than compliance management in a company which reacts to direct enforcement actions by the state.

supports direct and frequent interaction between inspectors and regulatees also exists. Makkai and Braithwaite (1994), for example, assert that only on the basis of a good relationship will the inspector be able to make disapproval of non-compliance be heard among the senior executives of a business. Similarly, the OECD (2000, p. 72) claims that trust improves the likelihood of compliance and this trust is built through dialogue between the regulators and regulatees. Overall, the key for inspectors seems to be to establish a balance between discretion and formalism, dialogue and sanctions, relationship building and relational distance. The way inspectors decide to supervise companies influences how companies construct the meaning of compliance and which compliance management instruments they adopt. At the same time, firms' compliance management practices also affect inspectors' behavior. Therefore, it is necessary to understand the prevailing enforcement approach and instruments as part of the external factors influencing compliance when conducting related research.

2.4.2 Internal factors

In addition to external factors, organization-internal factors also affect compliance. Specifically, research has identified the dimensions of organizational capacities and characteristics as well as motives in this context, which are outlined in the following.

2.4.2.1 Organizational capacities and characteristics

From a review of the existing compliance literature, five broadly discussed sub-factors which can alter compliance (management) can be gleaned[53]: Managerial capacity, knowledge related to compliance, organizational complexity, economic pressure as well as company size. Therefore, these five factors are discussed successively in the following.

53 Parker and Nielsen (2011c, p. 5) structure compliance-related organizational capacities and characteristics along three sub-categories (decision-making attributes, decision-implementation attributes and decision-implementation resources), but they do not adopt these categories in later elaborations of their framework. Parker and Nielsen (2011c) only mention the three sub-categories and refer to Lehmann Nielsen and Parker (2012), who provide further explanations on the meaning of these categories.

High managerial capacity, i.e. management competences of those individuals in charge, has been found to benefit compliance (e.g. Gunningham, 2011, Lehmann Nielsen and Parker, 2008, Parker and Lehmann Nielsen, 2006). High levels of management oversight, commitment to a compliance culture and values conducive to compliance in managers seem to improve the social practices of compliance within a company (Lehmann Nielsen and Parker, 2008, p. 322). Parker and Lehmann Nielsen (2009, p. 28) found that good management is as important as formal compliance management systems when it comes to influencing the compliance practices of firm members. However, the results from this study should be taken with a grain of salt, since the measurement of 'good management' in their survey is focused rather narrowly by adopting only two questions regarding the level of management oversight and planning[54]. Furthermore, they rely on self-reported data from businesses (both for this question as well as the evaluation of compliance levels), which may be skewed, due to social desirability biases.

When considering the impact of knowledge related to compliance, on the other hand, a more granular investigation is necessary. In a study on Danish farmers' compliance behavior, Winter and May (2001, p. 679f) found that awareness and knowledge of the rules is linked to higher compliance levels. In addition, in a survey which includes 999 large Australian businesses, Parker and Lehmann Nielsen (2009, p. 28) identified legal, economic and technical knowledge related to compliance as significant factors that influence companies' compliance practices. However, Gunningham et al. (2004, p. 41ff) identified that the pure abstract knowledge on legal sanctions (general deterrence) only plays a small role in deterrence from legal violations. Instead, knowledge from experience (i.e. on previous sanctions against a company) has a more significant impact on compliance management. In addition, knowledge of effective enforcement by authorities (e.g. via learning about enforcement actions against other companies) can serve as a reassurance function for firms, ensuring them that compliance management is necessary and worth the investment.

Beyond these individual characteristics, structural aspects also affect compliance. This is best portrayed by three more organizational characteristics that affect compliance, namely organizational complexity, economic

54 "Our senior managers know very well what is going on in every part of our organization." and "Our managers give a lot of priority to long-term strategic planning." (Parker and Lehmann Nielsen, 2009, p. 22).

pressure and company size. High organizational complexity is considered to impact compliance negatively. Organizational complexity refers to

> "the degree of spread and segmentation in an organization's structure, reflecting the combined effects of horizontal, vertical, and spatial differentiation" (McKendall and Wagner, 1997, p. 627).

Typically, complexity increases with more operation locations, levels of hierarchy and decentralization. According to several researchers (e.g. McKendall et al., 2002, McKendall and Wagner, 1997), high complexity causes coordination, management and communication problems within companies, which then lead to violations of laws being concealed more easily from superiors. In particular, organizational decentralization, which is often praised for providing more freedom in decision-making (agility, adaption to local conditions...), potentially has negative consequences for compliance. The main reasons for this negative effect on compliance is that decentralization can cause a diffusion of responsibility, thereby reducing accountability (McKendall et al., 2002, p. 369).

Similarly, economic pressure has been found to harm compliance. Financial strains, in particular, are considered a motivator for illegal behavior (e.g. Simpson and Rorie, 2011, McKendall et al., 2002). For example, Simpson et al.'s (2007) research shows a smaller amount of reported legal environmental violations prevailing in years of high stockholder equity. Consequently, corporate actors seem to adapt their compliance levels based on external contingencies, such as the economic climate. In addition, research on legal violations in relation to industry profitability consistently provides evidence that illegality occurs more often in low-profit industries (e.g. McKendall et al., 2002, Asch and Seneca, 1976).

Lastly, researchers almost unanimously attribute a key role to company size as an influencing factor of compliance practices and levels (e.g. Parker and Lehmann Nielsen, 2011a, Lehmann Nielsen and Parker, 2008, Gunningham, Thornton and Kagan, 2004). However, due to a lack of consistency in the set-up of research designs, there are varying opinions on the way company size affects compliance (Simpson and Rorie, 2011, p. 69). On the one hand, academics hypothesize that compliance management improves with increasing company size based on the following arguments and findings. First, smaller firms tend to perform worse with regard to compliance, because the burden of compliance seems to increase with smaller business size: The costs of compliance faced by smaller firms are proportionally higher and for small firms to keep up with the increasing volume and changes in regulations is more difficult (e.g. Hutter, 2011, OECD, 2000). Second, larger firms face higher reputational and regulatory pressures, since they are subject to more publicity, as well as monitoring by authorities[55] (e.g. Kagan et al., 2011, Gunningham, Thornton and Kagan, 2004). This argument is supported by the fact that larger firms generally possess better access to resources and are thus able to spend more money on their compliance management, as well as activities that go beyond legal compliance (e.g. voluntary programs) (Lehmann Nielsen and Parker, 2008, p. 332). On the other hand, however, some research also indicates an opposite tendency in compliance levels. Dalton and Kesner (1988) and McKendall et al. (1999), for instance, found that organization size correlates with legal violations: The larger the firm, the higher the number of non-compliance incidents. The explanation for this trend is the greater capacity (resources) to absorb punitive measures, be it fines or even short-time losses due to reputational harms. Simpson and Rorie (2011) reiterated this correlation between increasing firm size and greater instances of non-compliance. However, they see its causes not in an active decision to violate, but in the fact that larger organizations are simply exposed to more regulations, and are consequently at a higher risk of (voluntarily or involuntarily) infringing upon regulations. Croall and Roos (2002) further suggested that small businesses are more likely to be responsive to advice, education and rehabilitative approaches, i.e. willing to improve, if the regulator uses communicative enforcement instruments. Despite company size's unclear direction of influence on compliance, the above shows the importance of taking this factor into account in compliance research.

The literature agrees that the mentioned intra-organizational factors are key to compliance and its social practices. This list, however, is not complete, since some factors are regularly ignored or receive little attention yet. For instance, additional factors, such as a company's location (Hutter, 2011, p. 309) or employees' background and attitudes (Lehmann Nielsen and Parker, 2008, p. 337), are only mentioned sporadically in the literature.

55 The main reason for this increased monitoring is the fact that larger companies are considered to bear greater (economic, environmental, social...) risks as compared to smaller firms.

2.4.2.2 Motives

Originally, compliance was considered from an instrumental perspective, which suggested that firms manage compliance primarily based on its immediate contribution to economic profit. From this perspective, firms' compliance motivation stems from their profit-maximization goal, and decisions for or against compliance are exclusively based on an amoral calculation and rational choice (e.g. Bird and Kim Park, 2017, Becker, 1968, Pearce and Tombs, 1997, 1990). In this logic, firms comply as long as the economic gain from bypassing a regulation is smaller than the expected losses from sanctions (including considerations on the likelihood of detection) (Nielsen, 2003, p. 425). Compliance is, thus, reduced to an economic cost-benefit calculation and firms can simply be motivated to comply by financial incentives (both positive stimuli in the form of rewards and negative impulses in the form of sanctions).

This purely economic approach to compliance motives has, however, been widely criticized (e.g. Sunstein and Ullmann-Margalit, 1998, Tversky and Kahneman, 1987). The perspective of the homo oeconomicus has long been challenged, especially since Simon (1972) introduced the concept of bounded rationality[56]. Evidence underscores that humans cannot be adequately described as rational agents and that calculative thinking regarding business compliance is limited[57]. In addition, the binary relationship between principal and agent in economic models does not adequately depict reality: Both principals and agents are always subject to multiple sources of influence that may trigger seemingly irrational behavior (Hodges, 2015, p. 669). Several studies have gathered evidence that proves this criticism of the instrumental perspective on compliance. Fisse and Braithwaite (1983), for example, highlighted that managers do not just calculate the costs of non-compliance, but also include other factors in their decision-making, such as the indeterminate costs of a bad reputation or morale. Moreover, Lehmann Nielsen and Parker (2008, p. 329) found that worries about economic losses are only weakly associated with firms' measures regarding management accountability and whistle-blowing, both elements of compliance management systems. In a similar vein, Simpson

56 For further explanations of this concept, refer to Footnote 40, Simon (1972) or Klaes and Sent (2005).

57 For example, in a study of Australian firms, Parker and Lehmann Nielsen (2011a) provide evidence that the deterrence effect, and thus the compliance level, does not increase proportionally to sanction severity.

and Rorie (2011, p. 64) asserted that management behavior often defies rational, amoral economic calculation: Managers that regard non-compliance as unethical proactively exclude certain realms of the law from economic profit-loss considerations, just for the sake of compliance.

Based on this criticism, the academic discourse has extended the purely economic motives for compliance towards a combination of multiple motivations. The various frameworks clustering compliance motives in different categories can be found in Table 2. Overall, the most commonly adopted framework that comprehensively covers the elements identified in the literature originates from Gunningham et al. (2004, p. 3). These authors investigated compliance motives in relation to environmental protection issues. Their typology introduces three categories of motives (or pressures) for compliance, which are also referred to as 'licenses to operate':

- *Economic:* Based on calculative thinking and rational choice, such as cost-benefit calculations
- *Social:* Driven by the goal to gain the respect of important people and organizations in a person's social circle, e.g. shame or reputational concerns
- *Normative:* Rooted in a person's values, norms and morality, including the trust in just authorities or a sense of moral duty

In general, companies are usually motivated to comply because of a mix of different motives. However, Etienne (2011) suggested that of the numerous motives that drive firms to comply, one usually dominates, depending on the case in point. Nevertheless, with multiple motives at play, these different motivations are not always reinforcing each other. Sometimes motivations can be contradictory, cause decision-making dilemmas and thereby hamper compliance (Lehmann Nielsen and Parker, 2012, p. 431ff). For instance, Feldman and Lobel's study from 2010 asserted that when firms are driven to comply by strong normative motivations, monetary rewards, which aim to trigger economic motives, can be counterproductive (Feldman and Lobel, 2010, p. 265).

Table 2: Summary of frameworks on compliance motives

Motive categories			**Sources**
Economic	Social	Normative	Lehmann Nielsen and Parker (2012), Parker and Lehmann Nielsen (2011c), Gunningham, Thornton and Kagan (2004)
Economic	Managerial[58]	Moral	Borck and Coglianese (2011)
Fear of detection and legal punishment	Concern about the consequences of acquiring a bad reputation	Sense of duty	Kagan et al. (2011)
Perceived certainty/severity of formal legal sanctions	Perceived certainty/ severity of informal sanctions	Perceived certainty/ severity of loss of self-respect	Paternoster and Simpson (1993)
Perceived cost of rule compliance	Characteristics of the criminal event	Perceived sense of legitimacy/fairness	
Perceived benefits of non-compliance		Moral inhibitions	
Prior offenses on the part of the person concerned			

Having already discussed the economic motive, the following sections introduce the social and normative motives in more depth. Social motives, on the one hand, include all factors in social relations that induce or disincentivize compliance. This motivation stems not only from managers' interest in protecting their businesses' reputation, but especially from them caring about their own personal reputation (Kagan et al., 2011). According to Simpson (2002), managers pay more attention to informal sanctions, such as stigma by family members after a non-compliance incident is discovered, than they worry about financial sanctions. This powerful mechanism can be leveraged especially well, when comparative information on compliance levels (e.g. environmental indicators) is available (Gunningham, Thornton and Kagan, 2004, p. 338). The social motive's drive to conform to social standards can foster institutional isomorphism, i.e. organizations embrace structures and behaviors from their social environments (for example other organizations) that are not prescribed by technical, legal or financial requirements (Edelman and Suchman, 1997). Eventually,

58 Advancement of own personal and professional relationships, not necessarily in the interest of the firm.

these informal institutions lead to the assimilation of organizations and, in the context of compliance, to the convergence of firms' compliance management[59] (DiMaggio and Powell, 1983).

The normative motive, on the other hand, comprises all intrinsic motivators for pursuing compliance. These motivators stem from norms and values that are molded in a society over the long-term. They provide the basis for what individuals consider legitimate, good and bad. Thus, they indicate which kind of behavior should be sanctioned and rewarded (Haines, 2011, p. 289). If a regulation is in line with the normative foundations upon which the population acts, the normative motive will spur compliance. Regulations then serve as guideposts and reminders of which behavior is considered 'good' (Gunningham, Thornton and Kagan, 2004, p. 53). Contrarily, when rules and their enforcement are considered unfair and illegitimate, normative motives can hamper compliance (McKendall et al., 2002, p. 368). Therefore, the congruence of rules with an individual's personal values is key to triggering self-regulation: A sense of personal responsibility for compliance held by individuals ensures their compliance. This not only holds true in state-business relationships, but also in the relationship between a company and its employees (Tyler, 2011, p. 80). Manifold research projects support the existence of a normative compliance motive. Braithwaite and Makkai (1994), as well as Wenzel (2002), for example, found that subjects to regulation exhibit higher levels of compliance when they experience respect and trust by the authorities (procedural justice). Similarly, Tyler and Degoey (1996) and Braithwaite (2002) showed how compliance is dependent on the regulatees' sense of legitimacy regarding state regulations and authorities. In addition, research by Weber and Wasieleski (2013) illustrated that US compliance programs display strong normative motivations.

Overall, these different types of motives address compliance decisions as influencing factors among individuals, but do not describe how a company is affected as a whole. Research has found that compliance within an organization depends on the motivation of its employees regarding compliance (e.g. Haugh, 2017b, Gray and Silbey, 2011). For instance, Gray's (2002) research provided evidence that individuals within companies react to regulatory regimes differently. This is especially evident in the case of corporate liability regimes. The way a company is made responsible (e.g.

59 For further details on institutional isomorphism in the context of compliance, refer to Section 2.5.

duty-based liability...) affects how managers and employees handle compliance. Overall, this means that compliance (management) is not uniform within one company and across businesses, but varies between people and contexts.

2.5 Corporate compliance management systems

In light of the many factors that influence compliance and compliance management illustrated in the previous section, readers could expect a huge variety of compliance management systems. However, this is not the case. The similarities in compliance-related practices across businesses reflect a dominant stream of new institutional literature, which highlights the processes of institutional homogenization across organizations. In their seminal work, DiMaggio and Powell (1983) called this convergence 'institutional isomorphism'. Specifically, institutional isomorphism is a

> "process by which organizations facing the same cultural rules and understandings become both increasingly similar to one another and increasingly congruent with the myths of their shared environment" (Edelman and Suchman, 1997, p. 496).

Besides competition[60] DiMaggio and Powell (1983, p. 150ff) identified three mechanisms that trigger such a homogenization process: Coercive, mimetic and normative isomorphism. In coercive isomorphism, organizations follow the requirements of actors that hold significant power over them, e.g. regulatory agencies. In contrast, in mimetic isomorphism, organizations, including businesses, emulate successful behavior from other comparable organizations that they consider best in class, or at least more successful. Normative isomorphism describes how organizations adopt practices, values and behaviors that experts, professionals and other organizations promote as best practices, potentially in an evangelizing manner. These two latter types of institutional isomorphism hint at the fact that political power does not only derive from coercive interventions, but also from controlling the standard setting process and definition of norms (DiMaggio and Powell, 1983, p. 157). Overall, this means that organizations do not exclusively pay attention to their profit motives and economic demands,

60 They deliberately excluded competition from their analysis, since their goal is to provide alternative explanations to Max Weber's (1952) concept of bureaucratization as a result of market-driven rationalization.

but actually also reflect on the norms and requirements of the institutional environment. The balance of these two aspects represents a constant challenge for businesses (Meyer and Rowan, 1977, p. 359f).

Certain circumstances are considered to be conducive to institutional isomorphism. First, a business being strongly bound on another, e.g. in strategic alliances, fosters a convergence in practices towards the dominant partner. Moreover, institutional isomorphism also benefits from a high level of professionalization and structuration in an industry, as well as few alternative organizational practices or models. In addition, trade and other professional organizations promote institutional isomorphism, since they define and promulgate certain behavioral standards and foster exchange between practitioners of different organizations. Lastly, institutional isomorphism thrives in an environment characterized by a high number of interactions among powerful actors (e.g. state agencies) (e.g. Oliver, 1997, DiMaggio and Powell, 1983).

However, some scholars criticize the one-sided focus on the process of institutional homogenization, for example by highlighting the fact that institutional heterogenization does prevail (e.g. Hall and Soskice, 2001, Whitley, 1999, 1992). Beckert (2010) bridged the divide between the two camps by arguing that institutional change actually happens in both processes of convergence and divergence. He provided examples of institutional homogenization and heterogenization for the three mechanisms laid out by DiMaggio and Powell (1983) (coercive, normative and mimetic processes), as well as competition (brought forward by Weber, 1952). Furthermore, Beckert (2010, p. 163) introduced conditions that trigger both homogenization and heterogenization processes:

> "Strong exogenous powers, perceived functional or normative attraction of institutional models, cognitive and normative congruencies among institutional entrepreneurs across national boundaries, the legitimation of institutional models among stakeholders, and direct competitive pressures in undifferentiated markets are conditions favorable to institutional homogenization. On the other side, the prevalence of powerful defenders of indigenous institutional rules, incongruent cognitive and normative frames of actors in different national settings, institutional complementarities, the interest of power holders in institutional differences, the lack of legitimacy for specific institutional models and sector-specific demands, as well as differentiated products and the structural autonomy of firms are conditions favorable to divergence".

Despite this acknowledgment of both institutional convergence and divergence, the compliance literature has so far focused to a greater extent on the convergence processes in the construction of compliance, instead of diverging approaches related to compliance. Compliance is described as a case of institutional isomorphism. Edelman (1990) traced the process of institutional isomorphism in the field of compliance in her research on the expansion of due process in organizational governance. In addition, Haugh (2018) stressed that companies that benchmark their compliance practices against their competitors, as well as compliance officers' interactions across firms, further foster isomorphism in the field of compliance management. Moreover, a significant body of literature portends that businesses copy compliance practices quicker (mimetic isomorphism), the more businesses have previously adopted them (e.g. Dobbin et al., 1993, Edelman, 1992, 1990, Mezias, 1990).

But not just mimetic isomorphism can be related to compliance. In fact, all three types of isomorphism seem to play a role in the construction of the meaning and social practices of compliance. Taking the indeterminacy and complexity of the law into consideration, businesses face a lot of uncertainties when addressing compliance issues. This impels them to seek support in their environment. They do so not only indirectly by observing other businesses' compliance management (mimetic), but also directly via experts in the field (normative) or regulators' concrete guidance (coercive) (Suchman and Edelman, 1996, p. 922). However, the emerging homogeneity between businesses is more likely caused by the previously discussed complexity, rather than by ubiquitously adopted compliance management practices that claim to improve efficiency or effectiveness. Hence, the elaborations below on compliance management systems and best practices should not be viewed as *the* answer to compliance questions, but rather as an answer that has emerged in isomorphic processes over time.

2.5.1 The compliance management process

The compliance management process consists of two main building blocks: First, the establishment and maintenance of a compliance management system and, second, the operation of this system by adopting concrete measures and activities. There are various frameworks that lay out the elements of both building blocks. Figure 8 and 9 depict two examples of compliance management models that address the first aspect. These frameworks aim to continuously improve the way compliance management is conducted in firms. Therefore, they are to be applied at regular intervals. However, since these frameworks evaluate compliance management systems from a meta-level, they do not provide concrete details on the activities undertaken to run compliance management systems. This second building block of the compliance management process is the focus of another set of frameworks, two of which are illustrated in Figure 10 and Figure 11. While these models provide more concrete guidance on the measures to be taken in compliance management operations, they do not offer advice on the establishment of compliance management systems, as in the previous two models. In addition, neither of the models emphasize the influence of the organizational context and the external environment, or other key principles that are important for compliance management.

Figure 8: Wieland's (2009, p. 22f) four levels of compliance management systems (author's translation)

1) Codification of the company's guiding values
2) Implementation of an organizational and operational structure, e.g. via codes of conduct
3) Systematization through compliance instruments, compliance communication and reviews, such as audits
4) Definition of responsibilities

Figure 9: Ramezani et al.'s (2012, p. 2ff) compliance management life cycle

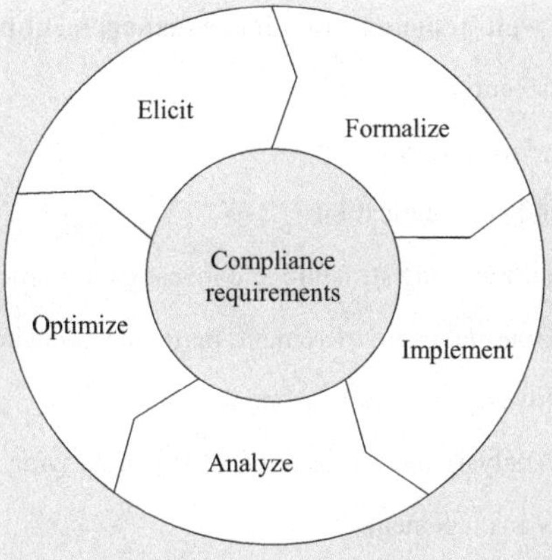

•*Elicitation:* Identification of compliance requirements relevant to an organization
•*Formalization:* Translation of abstract legal requirements into concrete compliance rules
•*Implementation:* Implementation of formalized compliance rules (incl. detection of violations)
•*Analysis:* Compliance checks (ideally supported by IT-system)
•*Optimization:* Improvement of compliance (management)

Figure 10: Elements of compliance management programs according to Bay and Hastenrath (2016, p. 123) (author's translation)

Figure 11: Description of compliance management programs by the US Department of Justice (2020)

Elements of well-designed compliance management programs:

- Risk assessment
- Policies and procedures
- Training and communication
- Confidential reporting structure and investigation process
    - Continuous improvement, periodic testing and review
    - Investigation of misconduct
    - Analysis and remediation of any underlying misconduct
- Third-party management
- Mergers and acquisitions

Figure 12: ISO37301 compliance management system (ISO, 2021b)

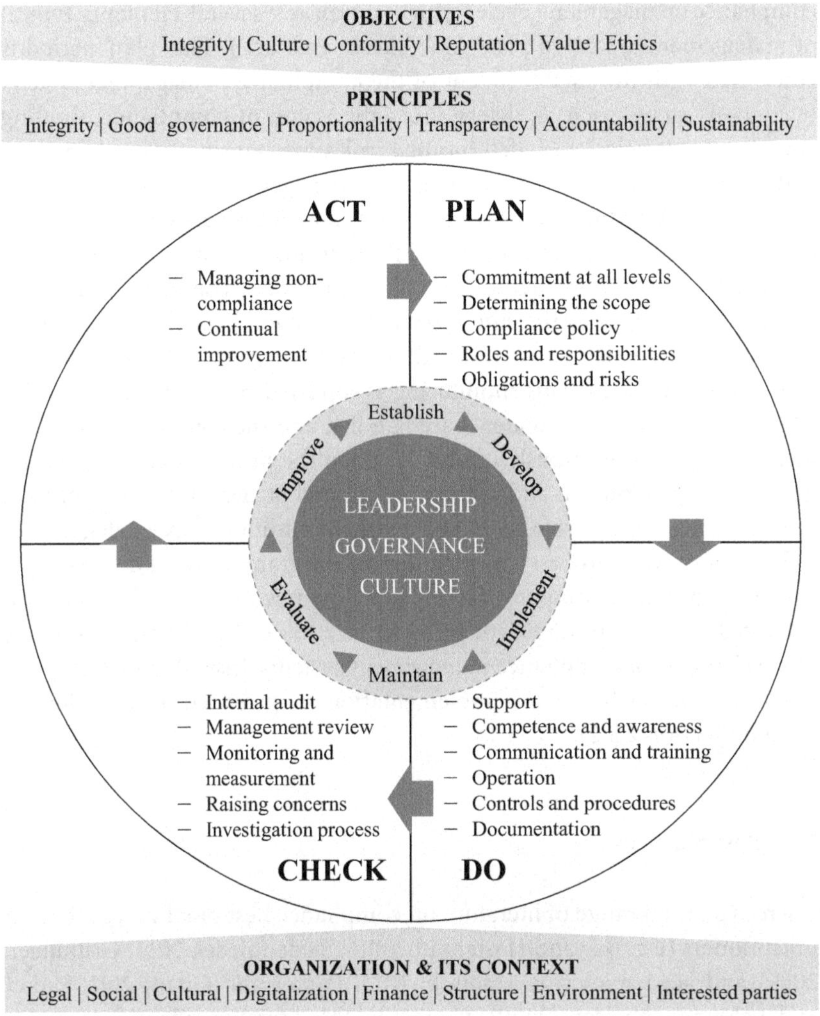

The ISO37301[61] standard for compliance management systems addresses these shortcomings by combining both building blocks in one framework

61 This internationally recognized standards was co-developed by an international expert team based on compliance best-practices and published by ISO in April 2021 (ISO, 2021b). It builds on and replaces ISO19600, a previous standard for compliance

and considering organizational contexts, the external environment and principles (see Figure 12). At the center of the ISO37301 framework is the compliance management cycle, which comprises several elements typical of management systems ('plan', 'do', 'check' and 'act'). The 'plan' period is concerned with the establishment of the compliance management system. It contains steps, such as determining the scope of compliance, drafting compliance policies and determining roles, responsibilities, obligations and risks. In the 'do' phase, compliance management is operationalized. This includes building related competences and awareness via communication and training, but also controls. Furthermore, setting up compliance procedures and documentation is important. Next, compliance management is 'checked', meaning the organization's compliance level and practices are controlled, e.g. via internal audits, management reviews and investigation processes. This monitoring is followed by a period of 'action', where non-compliance incidents are handled and the compliance management system is continuously improved. Then the process starts over again. Leadership, governance and culture are located at the core of this process to stress their central role in all segments. In addition, three categories of influences on this process are included in the framework: The objectives and principles of a company as well as its organization and the context it is located in. Overall, ISO37301 provides a rather comprehensive overview of the elements of compliance management systems. Insights into best practices regarding such systems' implementation are provided in the following section (Section 2.5.2).

2.5.2 Best practices

There is a broad range of literature on compliance best practices, both from practitioners (e.g. Bay and Hastenrath, 2016, Siedenbiedel, 2014, Grüninger, 2009) and academics (e.g. Habisch, 2012, Parker and Gilad, 2011, Parker and Lehmann Nielsen, 2009). Generally, this literature identifies success factors for compliance management, where 'success' in compliance management is defined as the prevention of non-compliance incidents in a company. While this understanding evidently reflects an objectivist per-

management systems released in 2014. While most of the content of the two standards is identical, the difference lies in ISO37301 being certifiable, whereas ISO19600 only used to function as a guideline (Deloitte Australia, 2021).

spective on compliance, where a certain predetermined, undisputed condition of compliance exists, there are still two reasons why it is worthwhile to pay attention to this strand of literature. First, an understanding of which factors are considered essential by actors involved in compliance management grants deeper insights into and allows to draw conclusions on the construction processes that determine the meaning of compliance. Second, and as explained in the methodology section, social constructionist and objectivist compliance research ideally build on each other. In order to enrich the existing objectivist compliance research as well as compliance research as a whole, it is thus necessary to gain a profound understanding of the theories and findings from objectivist compliance research.

In general, compliance-related activities should cover all three different types of compliance measures: Preventative, detective and corrective measures. Preventative activities are forward-looking and attempt to forestall non-compliance incidents from happening, e.g. via codes of conduct, training and compliance risk assessments. The detective approach complements preventative measures by evaluating present and past actions: Detective compliance practices uncover past or present compliance violations through measures, such as compliance audits and whistle-blowing hotlines. Lastly, corrective measures react to what has been found by detective compliance activities, i.e. they include any measures that rectify compliance offenses, for instance sanctions for offenders and guidelines for managing non-compliance incidents (e.g. Bay and Hastenrath, 2016, Taghiabadi, 2016). In companies that adopt a comprehensive compliance management approach, measures from all three interrelated perspectives are included in compliance management systems.

While further insights regarding compliance management best practices can be gleaned from the academic literature, most of the compliance-related studies are not dedicated to identifying detailed compliance best practices as a sole research goal. Therefore, Parker and Lehmann Nielsen's (2009) research, which is explicitly focused on determining elements of compliance management that are vital for success in ensuring compliance, is unique. They unveiled six aspects conducive to compliance: a written compliance policy, a dedicated compliance function, a clearly defined complaint handling system, standardized processes for handing compliance failures, compliance-related information (including training) for new employees and external reviews of the compliance system (Parker and Lehmann Nielsen, 2009).

In addition, the fragmented insights regarding compliance management best practices from other compliance-related literature is also valuable. The findings can be consolidated into six key characteristics that foster smooth compliance management:

- *Solid formal compliance management structures,* including codes of conduct, audits and controls, training, disciplinary mechanisms and a formal link to risk management (e.g. Hodges, 2015, Wieland, 2009, McKendall et al., 2002).
- *Embeddedness of compliance management into business practices and IT-systems,* e.g. by aligning compliance objectives with business objectives, including compliance as a criterion in performance reviews, rewards and decision-making processes as well as integrating automated compliance controls into the information systems (e.g. Ramezani et al., 2012, Parker and Gilad, 2011, Sadiq and Governatori, 2010, Grüninger, 2009).
- *Good management practices,* including sufficient management oversight, planning and organizational resources, adequate communication and dialogue with employees on compliance topics, stringency and fairness in compliance procedures and sufficient general managerial competence of the leadership (e.g. Habisch, 2012, Parker and Gilad, 2011, Tyler, 2011, Lehmann Nielsen and Parker, 2008).
- *Top-level commitment,* including direct reporting channels of the compliance management organization to the top management (e.g. Bay and Hastenrath, 2016, Habisch, 2012, Borck and Coglianese, 2011).
- *A compliance culture,* i.e. a corporate culture that supports compliance via the promotion of related values, norms and ethics (e.g. Habisch, 2012, Sokol, 2012, Parker and Lehmann Nielsen, 2006).
- *Values-based compliance management* rather than pure prescriptions, in order to cultivate ethical decision-making and behavior as well as whistle-blowing (e.g. Hodges, 2015, Siedenbiedel, 2014, Parker and Gilad, 2011, Tyler, 2011, Wieland, 2009).

In addition, 'nudging' has recently emerged as a popular and effective approach to steer individuals' actions (e.g. Sunstein, 2014, Kahneman, 2003). From a theoretical perspective, however, this approach's effect is questioned and empirical research into the impact of nudging in the compliance context is limited (Haugh, 2017a). Similarly, digitization has also taken hold of compliance, both in the context of ensuring compliance in digital initiatives and adopting digital tools for compliance management itself (PwC, 2019).

While digital tools certainly decrease costs, their actual feasibility in reaching companies' compliance goals has yet to be proven by research.

2.5.3 Criticism

Since their introduction in companies, compliance management and compliance management systems have been targets for criticism. There are two central reasons for discontent: The supposedly limited effectiveness and the lack of sincerity in firms that make an effort to implement compliance management systems. With regard to effectiveness, critics argue that the success of compliance management essentially boils down to the integrity of the executives at the top of the company. This means that each compliance management system is only as strong as the company leadership wants it to be (Barnes, 2007, p. 112). Moreover, the effectiveness of compliance programs is reduced exactly because of this top-down notion of compliance: On the one hand, passing decisions on moral problems up to higher levels can lead to employee atrophy in terms of their competence to solve such dilemmas (Habisch, 2012, p. 915). On the other hand, the indoctrination of and constraints to employee behavior from the top may "trigger reactance of employees" (Habisch, 2012, p. 913), i.e. opposition to the rules, because employees are not involved in the decision-making process and want to resist such highly hierarchical processes. Risks to the effectiveness of compliance management systems can be mitigated by including bottom-up design elements in compliance management programs to ensure employee buy-in. Additionally, Haugh (2018, p. 133) lamented that compliance programs assume a normal distribution in the likelihood of employees' non-compliance and therefore set up mechanisms to ensure compliance uniformly across the organization. Consequently, true effectiveness in compliance management can only be reached by spending more on offense-prevention efforts for the small circle of organizational members that is most likely to commit more egregious offenses (Haugh, 2018, p. 188f). However, this has not yet become a common compliance practice. Lastly, some critics claim that compliance programs have only endured for such a long time because they aid two stakeholders who foster their proliferation: The compliance industry (e.g. consultancies and law firms, who earn from providing advice and commissioning research on this topic) and the government, who benefits from corporate compliance programs that increase company-internal transparency and thus make company supervision cheaper (Baer, 2009, p. 990ff).

Related to lacking sincerity, research has shown that compliance management systems have a tendency to be realized only symbolically and perfunctorily (i.e. creative compliance instead of substantive compliance) (e.g. McBarnet, 2017, Yeung, 2004). In case of creative compliance, critics assert that too much money is poured into window dressing and covering up deliberate illegal actions, which could be better invested otherwise (Parker and Lehmann Nielsen, 2009, p. 9f). In relation to the social construction processes of compliance, it is therefore important to identify to what extent compliance is constructed 'creatively' and (if so) why companies consider it a worthwhile investment.

2.6 International manifestations

As elucidated in Section 2.4.1, the external environment is of great importance to the construction of the meaning and social practices of compliance. With that in mind, and as the majority of the literature discussed thus far has been based on compliance literature from Western, democratic and industrialized nations (e.g. Weber and Wasieleski, 2013, Van Erp, 2010, Parker and Lehmann Nielsen, 2006), which presume a rule of law and trust in the legal system, limitations with respect to the generalizability of the findings arise. Non-Western, non-democratic nations and countries from the Global South often exhibit significantly different characteristics in their external environment, such as high levels of corruption in the bureaucratic apparatus, missing government legitimacy and capacities, different cultural and social norms, missing private property right protection and the lack of or a weakly developed rule of law (Yee et al., 2016, p. 95). Furthermore, the way rules are negotiated and established also differs. Fischer (2000), for instance, highlights this point by adjusting Buß's (1973) framework for the development of competition regimes to the Chinese context. These environmental factors could not only significantly alter the understanding and management of compliance in other countries directly, but also change its meaning indirectly via internal influencing factors, namely organizational capacities and characteristics (e.g. loss of key staff, budgetary restrictions) and motives (e.g. no sense of compliance duty without trust in the legal and administrative system).

Existing literature regarding countries from the Global South, however, focuses on CSR of MNEs from industrialized nations, based on the implicit assumption that the local regulatory standards are lower or government enforcement capacities insufficient (e.g. Jamali and Karam, 2018, Jamali, 2007, Graham and Woods, 2005, Ite, 2004). Only a small number of studies have tried to close this research gap by identifying compliance issues in nations not considered countries of the Global North[62]. Dasgupta et al. (2000) investigated Mexican manufacturers' reaction to environmental regulation. They found that Mexican companies in the metal, mineral and food sector that are ISO14001-certified[63] exhibit higher compliance levels with environmental regulations, as compared to companies without certification. This result can be considered an indicator of the difficulties the Mexican government faces in enforcing regulations, which provide space for other, non-governmental regulatory institutions to step in and mitigate these problems. Moreover, there have been several studies that examined factors that impact compliance levels in the Global South. De Koker and Symington (2014), for instance, studied the compliance responses of South African banks and develop a framework of factors that influence compliance. They touch upon five main elements: Supervisory conduct, the hard law rule, applicable soft law, a company's own framework and reality as well as relevant business management considerations. While framed and named differently, these factors are congruent with the factors introduced by Parker and Nielsen's (2011c, p. 5) compliance framework (see Section 2.4). In contrast, Nguyen et al. (2020) and Ali et al. (2004) both identified influencing factors that have not been a focus topic of mainstream compliance literature. Nguyen et al. (2020) found a positive impact of business ownership on voluntary tax compliance among Vietnamese companies, whereas Ali et al. (2004) stressed the difference between multinational versus domestic companies regarding compliance in South Asia (India, Pakistan and Bangladesh). The status of a foreign MNE, here, is associated positively with compliance. The few existing studies on compliance in China are discussed in the context of the China case study (Section 4).

The research results from manifestations of compliance beyond Western industrialized democracies prompt the following summary and conclusion: Existing literature in the context of Western industrialized democracies has only pointed at compliance as a phenomenon of institutional isomor-

62 For a definition of this term, see Footnote 11.

63 A standard for environmental management systems.

phism. However, in countries of the Global South both similarities and differences in compliance practices compared to their Western industrialized democratic counterparts have been identified. At the same time, the state of research regarding compliance in a broader international context is characterized by an insufficient level of variation in international case studies, especially in countries of the Global South. Therefore, it is unclear whether, to what extent and why institutional convergence or divergence processes regarding compliance practices are in progress internationally. With its focus on the construction of compliance in China, a non-Western, non-democratic nation of the Global South (see definition in Footnote 11), this study contributes to understanding to what extent and why the construction of compliance in China converges with or diverges from the international practices identified above.

3 The systemic nature of corporate compliance

As discussed in the compliance framework in the previous chapter, compliance is influenced by external factors, especially the regulatory environment, including the enforcement approaches adopted. Essentially, compliance as a concept links the world of economics with that of regulation. Hence, those involved in constructing the meaning of and practicing compliance act as intermediaries between these two worlds. Precisely because of this role, compliance has a systemic nature: It is not only affected by the set-up of the endemic political economy, but also directly shapes how economic actors are governed and steered[64]. Therefore, the study of compliance is directly linked to research on the nature of political economies.

This research focuses on discourses on regulatory capitalism and the regulatory state to analyze political economies because these concepts' regulatory angle of examining political economies is most closely connected to compliance research. Specifically, this chapter builds the theoretical foundation for the discussion of the systemic nature of corporate compliance in the Chinese context by first providing an overview of the research landscape related to regulatory capitalism and the regulatory state (Section 3.1) and then describing the two concepts in detail (Section 3.2 and 3.3). Based

64 Governance generally refers to a non-hierarchical, networked mode of controlling and supervising in which cooperation between a multitude of actors, including non-state actors, is promoted, whereas steering indicates a more direct top-down manner (Schubert and Alpermann, 2019).

on these elaborations, Section 3.4 explains how scholars have adopted and adapted these concepts in contexts of the Global South.

3.1 Literature review

Both the discourses on regulatory capitalism and the regulatory state have a strong bias towards the Global North, especially Western industrialized nations. The literature on the regulatory state predates discourses on regulatory capitalism (Anderson, 1962), but it nevertheless took until the 1980/90s for comprehensive analyses to emerge (e.g. Majone, 1997, Seidman and Gilmour, 1986). In the following, authors such as Moran (2000) and McGowan and Wallace (1996) based their analyses of the European experience on Majone's (1997) work. Over time, the conceptualization of the regulatory state shifted from what Braithwaite called the 'old regulatory state' to the 'new regulatory state' (for details, see Section 3.3) (Braithwaite, 2000). In addition, the idea of a 'regulatory society' emerged. These developments reflect a movement of scholars away from the idea of a dominant role for the state in regulation to a more collaborative regulatory mode involving a broad number of non-state actors. On the basis of the regulatory state debates, Levi-Faur introduced the concept of regulatory capitalism in his seminal work in 2005 (Levi-Faur, 2005), which further broadened the view on the political economy and allowed researchers to delineate the relationship between capitalism and the state more effectively.

But research on regulatory capitalism and the regulatory state in the context of the Global South has been underrepresented. This research gap is only gradually being closed. Early on, researchers focused on distinguishing the regulatory state from the developmental state[65] in a similar manner as the regulatory state was compared with the welfare state in the Global North (e.g. Jayasuriya, 2005, Pearson, 2005, Braithwaite, 2000). Only later did researchers invest into identifying the idiosyncrasies of the political economies in countries of the Global South, drawing on the concept of the regulatory state, but not being limited by it. A key milestone in this context was Dubash and Morgans (2013c) edited volume 'The Rise of the Regulatory State of the South'.

65 A state form characterized by proactive state-led macroeconomic planning for the purpose of economic growth via measures, such as industrial policies (Jayasuriya, 2005).

In addition, researchers are interested in understanding the spread of the regulatory state and regulatory capitalism from their origins in the Global North to the Global South. A thread of literature focusing on the diffusion of regulatory capitalism has attempted to identify the concept's spreading patterns, mostly with a focus on Latin America (e.g. Phillips, 2013, Jordana, 2005, Jordana and Levi-Faur, 2005). Furthermore, the transfer process has been scrutinized by scholars of policy transfer. Similarly to regulatory capitalism and the regulatory state, policy transfer originated from and mainly describes transfer processes in the Global North, especially the European Union (EU) (e.g. Benson and Jordan, 2011, Prince, 2010, Bulmer et al., 2007, Dolowitz and Marsh, 1996). Dolowitz and Marsh (1996, 2000) laid the groundwork for future research in this field in 1996 with their policy transfer framework, which was updated in 2000. However, in a comprehensive treatise of this concept, Evans (2004b) collected research of transfer processes from all four corners of the world, including the Global South[66]. Nevertheless, literature on the impact of transfers on nations of the Global South, especially beyond the policy success/failure dichotomy, has been scarce.

3.2 Regulatory capitalism

Since the 1960s, there has been a massive increase in regulations and government-imposed formalities in most OECD-countries (OECD, 2000, p. 9). From 1976 to 1990, for instance, the amount of new laws in France increased by 35 percent and the number of regulatory agencies in Latin America rose from 43 to 138 between 1979 and 2002 (Jordana and Levi-Faur 2005, p. 103; OECD 2000, p. 14). Regulation and enforcement thus have become central governance tools for the state to maintain control over the economy. However, this trend also pertains to non-state regulation (Braithwaite, 2008, p. 64ff). For example, the market now plays an important role in the governance of firms, e.g. via standard setting or negative reactions on the stock market to undesired corporate behavior and ensuing firm losses. This growth in regulations also goes beyond the traditional relationship between the state and businesses to entail other contexts, for

66 Specifically, the volume edited by Evans contains work on policy transfer between nations of the Global North, from the Global South to the Global North and vice versa as well as between countries of the Global South.

instance emerging regulatory regimes within enterprises or in the social realm (Levi-Faur, 2007, p. 14). The increase even goes so far as to incorporating the state into becoming a regulated actor, e.g. by being monitored by non-state actors, such as rating agencies (Drahos, 2014).

On an overarching level, this growth in regulations can be regarded as a fundamental change in societal trust patterns. O'Neill (2002) observed a shift of trust away from elected politicians towards regulators (e.g. bureaucrats, private actors...). He highlighted the paradox of people demanding more accountability and transparency in order to trust, while actually trusting less, the more they know about actors in power. Power (1997), in contrast, focused on trust-levels and maintained that the trend to increased regulation and enforcement is caused by a lack of trust.

Moran (2000, p. 10) underscored this argument with his often cited expression:

> "We audit, and we regulate, when we cease to trust".

Hence, by providing legitimacy to markets and reducing risks in transactions, regulation and enforcement answer the demands for more trust in today's modern economies.

The fact that this surge in regulations coincided with the neoliberal era, may, at first, seem counter-intuitive. However, Levi-Faur (2005, p. 14) explained this phenomenon in his seminal work:

> "While at the ideological level neoliberalism promotes deregulation, at the practical level it promotes, or at least is accompanied by, regulation. The results are often contradictory and unintended, and the new global order may well be most aptly characterized as "regulatory capitalism." [...] Regulation is both a constitutive element of capitalism (as the framework that enables markets) and the tool that moderates and socializes it (the regulation of risk). From this point of view, the history of economic development is the history of regulation".

In essence, this means that capitalism is a regulatory institution that has, historically, both been shaped by other regulatory institutions and is shaping other institutions. At the same time, regulatory capitalism intimates the dual function of regulation as both a force controlling capitalism (by constraining or steering capitalism in certain directions) as well as a necessary demand for capitalism's survival (i.e. regulation reinforcing existing institutional patterns of capitalism) (Levi-Faur, 2017, p. 290f). Therefore, the perspective of regulatory capitalism offers a deeper understanding of the relationship between the state and the capitalist order.

Two basic capitalist institutions elucidate the nature of the relationship between regulation and capitalism aptly: The corporation and the market. Like capitalism itself, the emergence of corporations has, on the one hand, been caused by regulations and is, on the other hand, fostering regulatory growth. Braithwaite (2005, p. 20ff) tracked down the development of the corporation to the time when the concept of securities was developed: Only securities made it possible to replace family ownership of firms with more diverse ownership forms and increasingly professional management practices in firms. These new ownership forms created a demand for more state-led regulations, which smaller firms could not easily meet. Therefore, over time, mega-corporations emerged. This again triggered a new wave of state-driven regulations, especially to counter the risk of emerging monopolies (such as anti-trust regulation). This development shows how deeply intertwined corporations and the state are. The connection of businesses and the state goes as far as corporations mimicking state regulations by increasingly developing regulatory regimes within the company (e.g. codes of conduct, CSR guidelines, worker safety rules) (Levi-Faur, 2007, p. 19). And as pointed out in the previous chapter (Section 2.4.1.2), following the institutionalization of corporate management, one can observe a managerialization of the law, as companies' managerial practices (compliance management), designed to cope with internal and external regulatory demands, influence the practice of law. As a consequence, not only do regulations and the corporation (as institutions) mediate capitalism, but the same also applies to the institution of compliance.

A similar relationship can be found between capitalist markets and the state: The state constitutes markets, but in turn, markets also constitute the state (Levi-Faur, 2017, p. 290f). As discussed above, this stands in stark contrast to neoliberal views that describe an antagonistic relationship between the state and the market (Braithwaite, 2005, p. 34ff). Instead, regulatory capitalism poses that the state and the market are complementary to each other. Specifically, by providing regulations for competition, the state nurtures capital accumulation and commodification. The market is even mobilized as a regulatory institution itself (Levi-Faur, 2017, p. 290). But this support of the market is not a selfless act. The state depends on this process of capital accumulation in the market for its own wealth and legitimization. Only by commodifying more and more areas of life is it possible to continue capital accumulation (e.g. Crain, 2018, Drahos, 2017). Commodification refers to the

> "process whereby an object (in the widest sense of the term, meaning a thing, an idea, a creature, etc.) comes to be provided through, and/or represented in terms of, a market transaction" (Carvalho and Rodrigues, 2008, p. 268).

Hence, the status of being a commodity is not an intrinsic characteristic of an object, but rather assigned to it ex-post. For example, personal information has been commodified in the context of emerging internet-based business models. Commodification processes, such as of personal information, are dynamic and contested. Hence, commodification is not an organic predestined development, as portrayed by supporters of the commodification thesis[67]. Instead, it is constructed by choice, meaning it involves a certain degree of agency on the part of the actors involved (Williams, 2005). Consequently, commodification presupposed a variety of actors, such as individuals, businesses and the state (Crain, 2018). Therefore, it is important to understand which actors control and influence commodification processes to what extent. In this context, regulatory capitalism ascribes a key role to the state: The state actively promotes the commodification of an increasing number of areas of life (Levi-Faur, 2017, p. 291f).

Overall, the promotion of commodification by the state and its relationship to the capitalist market in the context of regulatory capitalism hints at two key functions the state takes on according to Levi-Faur (2017, p. 296): The regulation *of* capitalism and the regulation *for* capitalism. By regulation *of* capitalism, Levi-Faur (2017, p. 297) means the function commonly attributed to the state, namely its control over capitalism by passing regulations and setting up related institutions. In contrast, regulation *for* capitalism refers to the state facilitating the spread of capitalism to new realms via regulations and capitalist institutions, for example regulatory agencies (Levi-Faur, 2017, p. 297f).

Such stimuli for capitalism can hold both positive and negative consequences. Braithwaite (2008, p. 206) calls them 'markets in vice' and 'markets in virtue' and claims they coexist, since control via regulation, i.e. at a distance, can provide additional leeway for capitalist actors and thereby not only trigger innovation for the benefit of society, but potentially also

67 The commodification thesis purports a predetermined linear path towards increasing commodification, concomitant with economic development (Williams, 2005).

for unethical means (e.g. aggressive tax planning and transferring profits abroad to avoid tax payments). Therefore, it is key to not only regulate *for* capitalism, but always also to ensure the regulation *of* capitalism. According to Braithwaite (2008), only by regulating in both ways is it possible to harness the benefits of regulatory capitalism.

Based on this reinforcing relationship between regulation and capitalism, the division of labor between the state, businesses and society changes in regulatory capitalism (Levi-Faur, 2005, p. 15). In concrete terms, this means that compared to times predating regulatory capitalism, the state focuses more on steering via delegation as well as the creation and formalization of regulatory institutions, i.e. devolving regulatory processes towards networks of multiple regulators (Parker and Nielsen, 2009, p. 50). On the one hand, this leads to highly complex administrative structures in modern capitalist states. To cope with this complexity, a constant search for better regulatory instruments takes place. This quest leads to innovation in regulatory technologies and practices (e.g. nudging, transparency). Therefore, regulatory capitalism can also be described as a technological order (Levi-Faur, 2005, p. 22). On the other hand, businesses increasingly assume responsibility for service provision and technological innovation that the state used to hold. Parker and Nielsen (2009) called this the 'responsibilization of business'. 'Responsibilization of business' entails not only the implementation of measures for self-regulation, such as internal compliance control mechanisms, but also describes a shift of focus away from pure financial profit goals towards achieving policy goals and values (Parker and Nielsen, 2009, p. 48). With this supposedly more active role and increased responsibilities on the part of the corporate sector, scholars wonder about ensuing consequences. Some consider regulatory capitalism as a chance to provide social goods more effectively and efficiently by leveraging market mechanisms (e.g. Braithwaite, 2008, Gunningham et al., 2003), while others see the risks associated with the expansion of the market to social fields, i.e. economization of the social (e.g. Shamir, 2008, Garsten and Jacobsson, 2007). In any case, due to regulatory complexity, both realms, the state and businesses, are in need of and dependent on regulatory experts to pass, interpret and react to regulations.

Levi-Faur (2005, p. 27) summarized the characteristics of regulatory capitalism explained above in five elements:

1. A changed division of labor between the state and society (e.g. societal actors taking on the role of regulators);

2. Increased delegation by the state (e.g. to regulatory agencies) and more self-regulatory practices;
3. The proliferation of new technologies of regulation;
4. Formalized relations between regulatory actors (within and between institutions);
5. Growing influence of experts, especially international networks of experts.

These characteristics show that regulatory capitalism is not a monolithic concept to describe Western industrialized democratic political economies. Instead, it becomes manifest in a variety of shapes and sizes, depending on the location and environment it is placed in (e.g. Levi-Faur, 2007, Jordana, 2005). Specifically, Levi-Faur (2007, p. 16ff) developed a typology of four varieties that differ in the allocation of regulatory strength towards state and civil actors (civil regulation[68]): Étatist, corporatist, laizzez–faire and pluralist regulatory capitalism (see Figure 13). In étatist regulatory capitalism, the state possesses high capacities to impose sanctions and almost exclusively focuses on command and control with prescriptive rules. Since civil regulation only plays a small role in this form of regulatory capitalism, it often goes hand in hand with strict authoritarianism, unpredictable enforcement practices and comparably high compliance costs. This tends to cause adversarial relationships between the state and those regulated. Contrarily, regulatory corporatism (or corporatist regulatory capitalism) is characterized by both strong state and civil regulation and is especially prevalent in the context of states that are seeking further economic development (e.g. developmental states). In such cases, capitalism is strongly coordinated and a myriad of regulatory forms exist, such as enforced self-regulation, meta regulation and co-regulation between different entities. The complete opposite of regulatory corporatism is laissez-faire regulatory capitalism, which exhibits an expansion of market mechanism and a retreat of the political sphere as a means of control. In this context, rules in the form of vague and unspecified principles prevail. Lastly, pluralist regulatory capitalism is characterized by weak state and strong civil regulation. As in étaist regulatory capitalism, in this variety of regulatory capitalism, a critical attitude towards the state prevails, mainly stemming from the state's

68 Civil regulation here refers to voluntary global and national regulatory forms developed by non-state agents to govern the market. Civil regulation includes self-regulation and third-party regulation by actors such as private firms (e.g. consultancies), international organizations and NGOs (Levi-Faur, 2007, p. 9).

weakness, frequent changes within the regulatory regime and high rates of regime demise. By adopting process-based and performance-based regulations instead of prescriptive rules, as well as civil regulation, conflicts are avoided and enforcement costs reduced (Levi-Faur, 2007, p. 16ff).

Figure 13: Varieties of regulatory capitalism according to Levi-Faur (2007, p. 16) (author's design)

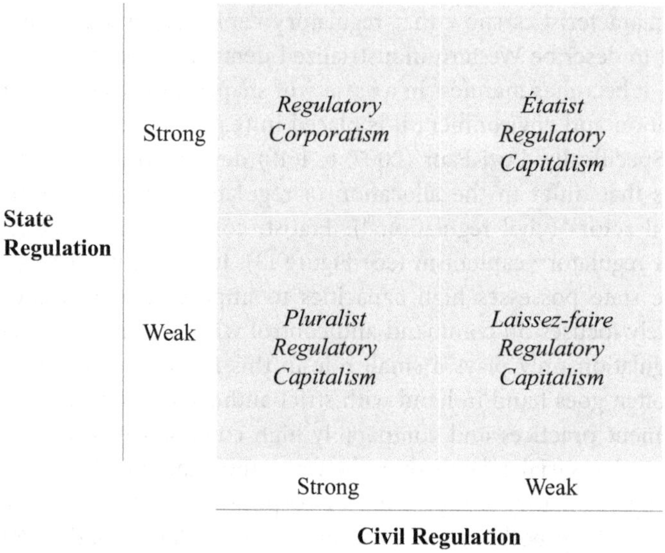

While academics tend look to the nation-state for manifestations of regulatory capitalism, Levi-Faur (2005) and Jordana (2005) highlighted that the construction of regulatory capitalism actually often goes hand in hand with the process of globalization. This means that it may spread within one sector across nation states, rather than from one country to another. Hence, the type of regulatory capitalism may look more similar in the same sector in different countries as compared to different sectors within the same nation. Overall, capitalism emerges stronger in contexts where it is facilitated by more powerful formal and informal institutions (Jordana, 2005, p. 184).

A challenge arising from either form of regulatory capitalism is ritualism. Braithwaite (2008, p. 141) defines ritualism as the

> "acceptance of institutionalised means for securing regulatory goals while losing focus on achieving the goals or outcomes themselves".

The growth in the number of regulations is conducive to stoking ritualism on the part of regulators, since the means adopted by regulations to achieve certain behaviors are less and less questioned. While ritualism can be transcended (for instance by harnessing the power of the market for innovation), when not overcome, it does bear the risk of fostering creative compliance: If regulators lose track of the overarching goals of their regulations, they are less likely to detect, whether companies comply with the rules in substance or just mechanically. Therefore, regulatory capitalism as a concept can not only contribute to explaining the institution of compliance and its manifestation in a country or sector. But compliance research, as the node between the state, business and society, can also contribute to better understanding the characteristics, workings and effects of regulatory capitalism.

Concomitantly, as the concept of regulatory capitalism has gained traction, another thread of academic literature is discussing the re-emergence of state capitalism. State capitalism can be defined as

> "the widespread influence of the government in the economy, either by owning majority or minority equity positions in companies or by providing subsidized credit and/or other privileges to private companies" (Musachio and Lazzarini, 2014, p. 2).

In a similar vein as in regulatory capitalism, different variations of state capitalism are described (e.g. Musacchio et al., 2015). But in contrast to regulatory capitalism, which lays a strong focus on the Global North, scholars of state capitalism draw on examples from Brazil, Russia, India, China and South Africa (BRICS) or other countries in the Global South to provide evidence of its existence (e.g. Bremmer, 2008). Nevertheless, there is evidence that elements of both types of capitalism can exist simultaneously (e.g. Hsueh, 2011) and therefore, instead of a dichotomous evaluation, the question is rather a matter of degree. More research is needed, especially in the context of the Global South, to understand the role regulatory capitalism plays in comparison to state capitalism and whether their amalgamation creates entirely new manifestations of capitalism. The compliance perspective can provide valuable insights in this regard, especially since the concept of compliance and its social practice, which emerged to a large extent because of regulatory capitalism, have also spread to SOEs.

3.3 The regulatory state

Along with the increase in regulations and the emergence of political economies that are now described as regulatory capitalism came a shift in the role of the state. This change is extensively discussed in the academic discourse on the regulatory state. The concept of the regulatory state emerged in the 1960s and its meaning has evolved over time. Anderson (1962) introduced what is today termed the 'old regulatory state' in 1962. This understanding is largely based on the US administrative state and dominated academic discussions until the 1980s. It focuses on the trend to establish regulatory agencies to control the economic system in order to prevent abuses of the capitalist market order (Levi-Faur, 2007, p. 6). In 1986, Seidman and Gilmour's study 'Politics, Position and Power: From the Positive to the Regulatory State' shifted the notion of the regulatory state from service delivery to a focus on monitoring compliance with rules and regulations, again with a focus on the experience in the United States (Seidman and Gilmour, 1986).

Later, Braithwaite (2000) coined the term 'new regulatory state' to highlight the new role of the state. Specifically, the new regulatory state differs from the old regulatory state in its indirect governance approach. Braithwaite (2000) characterized the new regulatory state[69] as a state that focuses less on rowing (i.e. active direct control), but more on steering (i.e. indirect control via rules). Therefore the regulatory state is a

> "polymorphic institution where source of its authority is not simply its legitimate monopoly of the means of violence, but its claim to a legitimate monopoly over rule making, rule monitoring and rule enforcement"(Levi-Faur, 2013a, p. 30). "Rules can be made, monitored, and enforced directly via bureaucratic organs of the state or indirectly via the supervision of other organizational, regulatory systems" (Levi-Faur, 2013a, p. 39).

With this approach, characterized by rule at a distance, the new regulatory state is polycentric, delegates responsibilities (upward and downward) to different specialized agencies and transfers the various state functions (policy-making, service provision, regulation) to separate actors (Levi-Faur, 2013a). To implement polymorphic power networks reliably, the

69 In the following, the term 'regulatory state' is used to refer to exactly this concept of the 'new regulatory state' for purposes of simplification.

commitment to and faith in formal rules is crucial, as compared to the previously dominant informal norms that were agreed on in private, personal interactions between people in power (Picciotto, 2007, p. 14). In this context, demands for more transparency and accountability in the regulatory context reflect changes in trust patterns (as explained in Section 3.2) and an increased risk aversion (Levi-Faur, 2007, p. 11). Therefore, Jordana and Levi-Faur (2004) called for a trust-centered interpretation of the regulatory state. From such a perspective, the nature of trust in a society and regulations as a governance instrument interact with and influence each other. Specifically, the regulatory state is regarded as an effort to address problems of trust in post-modern societies, for instance by better defining the role of politicians and authorities as well as reducing administrative discretion.

For these purposes, the actors involved in governance rely on a wide variety of soft regulatory instruments to complement the traditional use of command and control, such as self-regulation, ranking, shaming and compliance management systems (e.g. Phillips, 2006, Braithwaite, 2000). In 2004 already, these instruments were found to often be supported and promoted by new digital technologies (Jordana and Levi-Faur, 2004); a trend that has gained speed since then, since regulatory states need to be capable of overseeing the emerging information economy (Cohen, 2016). This goes hand in hand with the regulatory state's continuous search for and invention of better enforcement approaches (e.g. smart regulation) and instruments (e.g. eco-labeling, compliance awards) (Levi-Faur, 2011). Therefore, gaining a deeper understanding of these approaches and instruments, in particular the social practices of compliance, provides a new angle to examine and characterize the regulatory state.

All approaches and instruments applied in the context of the regulatory state share one common characteristic. They work through more indirect means, i.e. focus more on the process rather than outcomes (Jayasuriya, 2001, p. 103). This so-called 'proceduralism' aims to foster regulatees' capacities for self-regulation, whereas the state focuses on shaping the institutional context (e.g. via establishing regulatory agencies) and constituting new areas of governance. Hence, the state becomes a regulator of the regulatory institutions, a meta-regulator (Jayasuriya, 2005, p. 384). In this context, rule-making becomes one of the core activities undertaken by the state. This is reflected in a stage dedicated to regulation- and rule-making in the overall policy-making process in regulatory states (Levi-Faur, 2011, p. 666).

Another core feature of the regulatory state, claimed by scholars such as Majore (1997), is its autonomy. These scholars assert that the regulatory state is shaped by autonomous institutions, such as regulatory agencies, which govern with the public interest in mind. But such a conceptualization does not only seem problematic due to the shift of substantial power to non-democratically legitimized actors (technocrats in regulatory agencies, managerial elites) (Majone, 1997, p. 159). This idea of autonomy can also be challenged, due to the constant risk of regulatory capture triggered by regulators' relations to certain interest groups. In addition, the fact that regulators are often part of international networks of experts with particular agendas questions this autonomy. These networks exchange ideas and together attempt to shape global and local rules in a certain fashion. Thus, the national regulatory state becomes a multi-level player embedded in the global community (Levi-Faur, 2011). Finally, the autonomy-claim can be refuted by examining the regulatory state's relationship to the economy. Similar to the relationship between regulation and the capitalist economy in regulatory capitalism, the regulatory state, in fact, plays the role of protector and nurturer of the economy (Levi-Faur, 2017, Jayasuriya, 2013). The regulatory state

> "is likely to intervene to underpin the market rather than replace markets; it is concerned to make markets work better and thus to compensate or substitute where markets fail" (McGowan and Wallace, 1996, p. 563).

By stepping in with regulations to prevent market failures, the regulatory state can actually increase market efficiency, spur economic growth and protect markets in which information disclosure is extremely important, such as the financial service industry. At the same time, however, the regulatory state shifts the main financial burden of enforcement to companies, who need to comply with an ever-increasing amount of regulations (Majone, 1997, p. 149). Whether the benefits from these rules (i.e. reduction in transaction costs) are higher than the investment in compliance management is hard to measure. Nevertheless, it is a necessary concern when drafting new regulations that aim to improve market efficiency. Consequently, the regulatory state is actually not an entirely autonomous entity.

Overall, Levi-Faur (2013a, p. 38) summarized the regulatory state's nature in four key attributes:

- The separation of the bureaucratic functions of regulating from the functions of service delivery;
- The norm of formal rule-based relations[70];
- The separation of regulatory functions from policy-making functions;
- A policy-making process with a distinct stage of regulating and rule-making.

The concept of the regulatory state is at times criticized for the centrality of the state as a regulator. Critics, for instance, highlight the shift from a unitary state to networked governance in line with a trend in regulatory scholarship that extends the role of the regulator beyond the confines of the state (Braithwaite, 2005, p. 32). They also describe the importance of economic and social actors in the regulatory realm and thus acknowledge that political power is based on structures beyond the state (Scott, 2017, p. 280). Examples, such as the growing amount of civil regulations, self-regulation and the increasing importance of gatekeepers (e.g. debt-rating agencies, large auditing firms, external lawyers) in the context of economic regulation illustrate this point (Levi-Faur, 2007). Therefore, several scholars argue, a regulatory society is emerging, where multiple non-state actors are involved in regulatory governance[71] (e.g. Clarke, 2000, Braithwaite, 2006, Levi-Faur, 2007).

Another criticism revolves around the contrasting of the regulatory state with other conceptualizations of the state. On the one hand, scholars draw contrasts between the regulatory state and the developmental state, i.e. a state form characterized by proactive state-led macroeconomic planning for the purpose of economic growth via measures such as industrial policies (e.g. Jayasuriya, 2005). On the other hand, the regulatory state is compared with the positive state, i.e. a state that is directly involved in producing goods and services and directly providing welfare to its citizens (Majone, 1997). In this context, some scholars describe a historical timeline of different state forms replacing each other, in which the regulatory state is the positive state's successor (e.g. Braithwaite, 2000, Majone, 1997). These descriptions, however, are misguided, since they imply the complete demise

70 Replacing intimate and informal relations that characterized previous decision-making.

71 Scott (2004) uses the term post-regulatory state to describe the same trend.

of the positive state and consequently cannot explain continuing social welfare provision by the state (e.g. in central European countries).

Instead of adopting a dichotomous way of thinking on these different state forms, a differentiated approach is necessary. Levi-Faur (2011, 2013b), for example, argued that the positive state and the regulatory state should be regarded as two different modes of governance that can co-exist to a certain extent. Moreover, Krizic (2019) found evidence that the emergence of the regulatory state in the Global South is not necessarily linked to a departure from developmentalism. Consequently, the regulatory state cannot be regarded as a uniform state, but one that comes in different shapes and sizes. However, several researchers directly point out that research on these variegated forms of the regulatory state is lacking (e.g. Jayasuriya, 2005, Jordana and Levi-Faur, 2004). This is largely caused by academic discourses' concentration on the regulatory state in the context of Western liberal democracies. However, Levi-Faur (2013a) aptly pointed out that the regulatory state as a concept itself is not directly connected to any type of political or economic system:

> "The regulatory state claims a legitimate monopoly on the deployment and distribution of power through rule making, rule monitoring, and rule enforcement" (Levi-Faur, 2013a, p. 39). "It does not require agencies or democratic or economic liberalism, nor does it have any particular affinity to Anglo-Saxon or Western cultures" (Levi-Faur, 2013a, p. 45).

Consequently, research dedicated to the regulatory state in other contexts, such as the Global South, can provide further insights into the variegated forms of the regulatory state. The following section lays out related existing academic insights.

3.4 Regulatory capitalism and the regulatory state in the Global South

As the sections above have shown, both the concept of regulatory capitalism and the regulatory state emerged from developed Western democracies. Only later, research started to address the question of whether and how the same or similar phenomena surface in countries of differing development statuses, with diverging political systems and other cultural and institutional backgrounds, especially in the Global South. In the context of the Global South, the examination of two aspects is especially worthwhile, namely the proliferation processes and the context-specific manifestations of regulatory capitalism, the regulatory state as well as related ideas and practices.

3.4.1 Proliferation processes of regulatory capitalism and the regulatory state to the Global South

A number of different academic concepts are adopted to describe the spread of institutions, regulations and enforcement mechanisms and therefore fit the study of the proliferation of regulatory capitalism, the regulatory state and related institutions, such as compliance, to the Global South: Policy convergence, policy diffusion and policy transfer (e.g. Knill, 2005, Dolowitz and Marsh, 2000). Policy convergence focuses on the results, i.e. the question of whether or not regulation converges globally. In contrast, policy diffusion identifies the spreading patterns of policies and other types of regulations, institutions and enforcement mechanisms and their spatial, structural and socioeconomic reasons (Knill, 2005, p. 766). Hence, policy diffusion differs from policy convergence in that it does not predetermine the spread to be categorized in the convergence vs. non-convergence dichotomy. In addition, it identifies factors that account for the spreading processes observed. However, similar to policy convergence, it does not examine the intricacies of how institutions, regulations and enforcement mechanisms spread. Policy transfer focuses on this aspect. It is defined as the

> "process in which knowledge about policies, administrative arrangements, institutions and ideas in one political setting (past or present) is used in the development of policies, administrative arrangements, institutions and ideas in another political setting" (Dolowitz and Marsh, 2000, p. 5).

Consequently, policy transfer studies are, on the one hand, not restricted to transfers of policies, but also cover transfers of ideas and institutions, such as compliance. On the other hand, these types of investigation are not limited to cases of imitation, but can also examine cases where profound changes were made in the transfer process. Furthermore, this perspective's focus on process generates a deeper understanding of the causes and contents of individual transfer processes, as compared to policy diffusion, which provides insights on a higher level (Knill, 2005, p. 768). Therefore, policy transfer studies tend to adopt qualitative methods, especially process tracing, whereas research on policy diffusion tends towards quantitative research (Marsh and Sharman, 2009, p. 275). While there are overlaps between policy transfer and institutional isomorphism (for more details on this concept, refer to Section 2.5), the former focuses to a larger degree on the transfer of contents (e.g. of regulations and enforcement mechanisms), while the latter pertains more to organizational changes (e.g. organizational structures and processes). Hence, institutional isomorphism can be regarded as one aspect of a policy transfer, as it provides explanations for the outcomes of transfers on the organizational level (Radaelli, 2000, p. 38f). Since compliance manifests itself within the organization, but is also strongly influenced by related regulatory prescriptions and enforcement mechanisms, both aspects are important for an investigation of the spread of the concept of compliance. Therefore, a policy transfer analysis of compliance-related regulations and enforcement mechanisms contributes to the understanding of compliance construction in countries where compliance management did not originate. The insights from the transfer processes of the case of compliance, again, provide vital insights into the political economy in those countries that compliance is transferred to, explicitly the nature of their regulatory capitalism and their manifestation of the regulatory state.

In their seminal work, Dolowitz and Marsh (1996, 2000) defined a conceptual framework for policy transfer with categories that provide a deeper understanding of the transfer process (see Table 3). The framework sheds light on eight key aspects of policy transfer and permits a classification of the investigated case in each of these categories.

First, it provides different answers to questions of why a transfer happens. Policy transfer incorporates policy learning, i.e. voluntary transfers based on the principle of rationality, as one end on a continuum of causes for transfer (Dolowitz and Marsh, 2000, p. 9). Coercive transfer, i.e. transfers forced by actors, such as international organizations, constitutes the other end of the spectrum. Between these two extremes, there is a broad range of causes for transfers, such as obligations stemming from loans or norm cascades that disseminate ideas and institutions across the globe (Lutz and Sikkink, 2001).

Table 3: Policy transfer framework according to Dolowitz and Marsh (2000, p. 9)

Dimension	Subcategories	Manifestations
Reason for transfer	Voluntary	Lesson drawing (perfect rationality)
	Mixtures	Lesson drawing (bounded rationality); international pressures; externalities (image, consensus, perceptions); conditionality; obligations (loans, conditions attached to business activity)
	Coercive	Direct imposition
Transfer agents		Elected officials; bureaucrats/civil servants; pressure groups; political parties; policy entrepreneurs/experts; consultants; think tanks; transnational corporations; supranational institutions
Transfer object		Policies (goals, content, instruments); programs; negative lessons; attitudes/cultural values; institutions; ideologies
Transfer path	Past	Internal; global
	Within a nation	State governments; city governments; local authorities
	Cross-national	International organizations; regional/state/local governments; past relations
Degree of transfer		Copying; emulation; mixtures; inspiration
Constraints on transfer		Policy complexity (newspaper, magazine, TV, radio); past policies; structural institutional feasibility; ideology; cultural proximity; (technology/economic/ bureaucratic) language
Demonstration of transfer		Media; reports (commissioned/uncommissioned); conferences; meetings/visits; statements (written/verbal)
Reasons for failure		Uninformed transfer; incomplete transfer; inappropriate transfer

Second, the framework spells out nine actor groups that are potentially involved in transfers. In line with the trend of involving a broader range of actors in the regulatory process as part of regulatory capitalism, Dolowitz and Marsh (2000, p. 10) recognize the importance of non-state actors, for instance policy consultants, NGOs and think tanks, for disseminating best practices[72]. In addition, Stone (2004, 2010) elaborated on the role of

72 This extension of potential actors in policy transfers was one of the major improvements on their updated framework published 2000, as compared to the original 1996 framework.

non-state actors in policy transfer, especially in the context of soft forms of global policy transfer (e.g. norms). She claims that

> "transfer can also be facilitated by organizations outside and between the state. In other words, policy transfer is just as likely to be achieved by mechanisms embedded in markets and networks as in the hierarchies of the state" (Stone, 2004, p. 546).

Nevertheless, neither of the authors provide deeper insights into the role that transnational enterprises or business consultants play in the transfer process. Another element that is missing in Dolowitz and Marsh's discussion of actors, but is discussed in more detail by Evans and McComb (2004), is policy transfer networks, i.e. the context in which actors interact. Policy transfer networks are defined as "ad hoc action-oriented networks set up with the specific intention of engineering policy change" (Evans and McComb, 2004, p. 49).

Therefore, these policy transfer networks are ad hoc phenomena that are set up only for the purpose of the transfer, compared to epistemic communities or policy communities[73], which are also discussed in the context of policy transfer. Hence, they dissolve after the policy has been transferred. Their analysis is worthwhile, because they connect different levels of analysis in policy transfers: Micro-decision-making in organizations, macro-systems and global, transnational and international systems (Evans and McComb, 2004).

Third, the object of the transfer is specified. Both, this framework and the definition for policy transfer stated above, emphasize that the object of the policy transfer must not exclusively be policies. Instead, programs resulting from certain policies, negative lessons, attitudes/cultural values, institutions and ideologies are also subject to policy transfers. The content of policy transfers is often informed by best practices from think tanks, international organizations or other knowledge networks. Generally, what is being transferred tends to intimate areas where the recipient lacks knowledge (Evans, 2004a). Therefore, this policy transfer framework can not only be applied to compliance-related policies, but also to the institution of compliance itself.

Fourth, the framework analyzes the sources from which the content of the policy transfer is drawn. Three sub-categories are outlined: Transfers

73 Both are permanently existing networks of expert with regard to a certain topic or policy field. For a more detailed comparison, refer to Evans and McComb (2004).

from the past, from actors within the same nation (both transfers between equal levels, such as two city governments, and between differing levels, for instance from local to central authorities or the other way round) and from actors outside of the nation (e.g. international organizations, other national governments).

Fifth, the framework considers different degrees of transfer ranging from a direct and complete transfer in the form of copying to pure inspiration, where an idea from elsewhere triggers a change, but the final outcome is not designed according to the original idea. Emulation (transfer of the key ideas) and combination (merging of different ideas etc.) constitute options between these two poles. The evaluation of these transfer degrees varies. When scrutinizing literature referring to emulation, for example, Evans (2004a, p. 222) highlighted this degree's potential for locally sensitive policy transfer. However, Meseguer (2005, p. 73) pointed out that emulation, in fact, does not always refer to learning motivated by the need to solve a problem, but actually often simply becomes manifest as purely symbolic mimicry driven by a need to achieve credibility, status or conformity with certain trends.

Sixth, the policy transfer framework provides potential constraints that may hinder or limit the transfer, such as structural, ideological or linguistic challenges.

Seventh, options for promulgating the implemented transfer are listed. According to Dolowitz and Marsh (2000, p. 9), traditional information sources related to policies provide insights into these transfers, such as official statements, reports, traditional media outlets and conferences. However, more informal means, where the transfer agents have less control over the process, such as social media (blogs, podcasts, etc.), are not mentioned.

Eighth, the framework specifies three potential reasons for the failure of policy transfers: Uninformed, incomplete and inappropriate transfers. Based on the various case studies in his collective volume, Evans (2004a, p. 215) points out that the success or failure of a policy transfer depends on the compatibility of the policy with the recipient's value system and historical legacies and builds on preexisting organizational strengths and structures of the new context.

While well-established in the academic discourse, this framework has also been subject to criticism and suggestions for improvement. James and Lodge (2003), for instance, favor institutional analysis, as Dolowitz and Marsh's policy transfer framework does not allow an in-depth understanding of the power relations within states that affect the manifestations and level of success of transfers. Other scholars, such as Prince (2010), extended the scope of policy transfers by pointing out new, less scrutinized forms of transfer, such as non-transfer and policy assemblages. In addition, Benson and Jordan (2011, p. 374) portended that just like regulatory capitalism and the regulatory state, policy transfer also tends to focus on a small set of countries in the industrialized world. This omission causes a misunderstanding of the role of deeper underlying structural factors (e.g. institutional and cultural context) in transfer processes. In this context, they also point to the lack of social constructionist perspectives on policy transfer processes, which hold the potential to better account for the dynamics, interactions and construction of social practices in the transfer process.

Indeed, only few exceptions provide insights into policy transfers in other environments outside the Global North, even though the nature of a political economy, including levels of stability, are likely to affect the occurrence, process and outcome of transfers significantly (Evans, 2004a). One exception is Kwon (2009), who identified policy transfer as an effective tool for development in East Asian states (Taiwan, Korea, Japan). In addition, Jordana and Levi-Faur (2005) investigated the growth in the number of regulatory authorities in Latin America. They reveal that the likelihood to establish a new regulatory institution in one sector increases both, if similar decisions have been made in other sectors in the same country and if such authorities have been created in the same sector in other countries. However, they attest higher importance to the influence of decisions in the same sectors across countries. Post (2005) corroborated these findings with her study of the spread of food safety standards in countries of the Global South. Overall, the literature therefore attributes the global spread of regulatory capitalism rather to transfer processes than to similar, yet independent developments in different countries.

Another element that is not covered by Dolowitz and Marsh's framework is the procedural sequence of policy transfer steps. Other researchers have, however, searched for generalizable patterns in policy transfer processes. While Bulmer et al. (2007) focused exclusively on transfer patterns in the EU, Evans and McComb (2004) were one of the few that provided a process sequence for policy transfer that can supposedly be generalized across nations and contexts. They break the voluntary policy transfer process via policy transfer networks down into twelve stages (see Figure 14). The first three stages revolve around identifying the policy problem and ideas for potential solutions. Stages four to nine describe the steps of concrete policy learning via policy transfer networks. The last three steps pave the way for the implementation of the transferred content. While this process is helpful to analyze policy transfer steps that lead towards the implementation of the transferred content, it does not provide further insights into developments that are set off by the initial transfer.

Figure 14: Evans and McComb's (2004, p. 50) twelve stages of the policy transfer process (author's design)

1) Problem recognition (economic crisis, globalization, modernization, policy failure, electoral change, conflict, legitimation)
2) The search for ideas (regime, international, transnational, national, regional, local, cross-sectoral)
3) Contact with potential agents of transfer
4) The emergence of an information feeder network
5) Cognition and reception (identification of agents of transfer)
6) The emergence of a policy transfer network
7) Elite and cognitive mobilization (agenda-setting)
8) Interaction
9) Evaluation of options
10) Decision enters formal policy stream
11) Formal policy processes
12) Implementation to outcome

Yet, it is crucial to examine the occurrences that happen after the initial transfer to determine the outcome of the transfer. This importance is illustrated by discussions that classify the transferred content either as 'irritants' or 'transplants'. Teubner (2001, p. 418) aptly contributed to this discussion:

> "I think 'legal irritant' expresses things better than 'legal transplant.' To be sure, transplant makes sense in so far as it describes legal import/export in organismic, not in machinistic, terms. [...] [Legal institutions] need careful implementation and cultivation in the new environment. But 'transplant' creates the wrong impression that after a difficult surgical operation the transferred material will remain identical with itself, playing its old role in the new organism. Accordingly, it comes down to the narrow alternative: repulsion or integration. However, when a foreign rule is imposed on a domestic culture, I submit, something else is happening. It is not transplanted into another organism, rather it

> works as fundamental irritation which triggers a whole series of new and unexpected events".

Consequently, it is not only necessary to understand the initial transfer process, but attention also needs to be paid to developments that are set off by so-called irritants. This is especially important in the context policy transfers from the Global North to the Global South, since the differences in political, economic and social environments are significant. Manifestations of the transferred objects in the Global South may at times vary significantly from the original conceptualization in the Global North, which the following section will discuss.

3.4.2 Manifestations of regulatory capitalism and the regulatory state in the Global South

While countries in the Global South certainly show a high level of diversity in their political economies, they are also characterized by important commonalities. Therefore, in the same vein as Dubash and Morgan (2012, p. 262), this section intends

> "to draw out common themes that characterize a 'regulatory state of the South', while remaining sensitive to the variations in level of economic development and political institutional contexts within 'the South'".

Due to a set of shared histories[74], most countries in the Global South share several characteristics that affect the manifestation of the regulatory state and regulatory capitalism. First, countries in the Global South face powerful external pressures, e.g. from international organizations, such as the World Bank and the International Monetary Fund. Often these organizations push countries from the Global South to implement certain institutional arrangements that have been identified as best practices for development. This has also been the case for independent regulatory agencies in the past. However, these best practices from the Global North have often not proven successful in other contexts. Second, in the Global South, redistributive politics (e.g. for infrastructure and poverty alleviation) are of higher importance as compared to the Global North, because of their different development stage. Therefore, a broad set of actors outside

74 Such as colonialism, widespread poverty and a predominant concern with development as a political objective.

of the state, including international actors are involved in the politics of regulation and redistribution. Third, most countries in the Global South face limits in state capacity, both related to financial means of running state administrations and in terms of managing a diverse set of interest groups as well as balancing a range of objectives, such as economic growth and redistribution (Dubash and Morgan, 2012, p. 272ff). For instance, Pistor and Xu (2005, p. 186) highlighted that regulatory failures in transition economies are often ascribed to limited state capacity and especially to underdeveloped legal systems with high probabilities of deterrence failures. Furthermore, some authors point to the failures of policy transfer (e.g. Lavenex et al., 2021, Ozel, 2012, Pistor, 2002). They raise concerns about problems related to importing regulatory institutions in countries of the Global South, such as producing empty shells or even undermining the functioning of other important existing institutions.

As a consequence of such depictions and in the face of overt developmental aspirations in the Global South, a controversial debate about the feasibility of transition towards a regulatory state and regulatory capitalism in countries of the Global South has emerged (e.g. Lavenex et al., 2021, Pearson, 2005). However, by regarding the manifestation of the regulatory state and regulatory capitalism as a matter of degree, as pointed out in Sections 3.2 and 3.3, scholars have been able to generate an understanding of the idiosyncrasies of regulatory capitalism and the regulatory state in the Global South (Phillips, 2006, p. 35ff). Specifically, research has identified three core themes that shape the manifestation of the regulatory state and regulatory capitalism in the Global South and therefore lend themselves to further examination. In the broadest sense, all three are based on the notion that differences in institutional endowments produce various forms of regulatory risks, options, outcomes and efficiency levels (Jarvis, 2010, p. 177). Therefore it is necessary to calibrate regulatory reform based on the context.

The first theme revolves around the dichotomy of rules versus deals. Based on case studies on the regulatory state in the Global South, Dubash and Morgan (2013a) conclude that in countries of the Global South, negotiation as a form of decision-making is persistent within the arenas of the regulatory state. This finding calls into question earlier claims of exclusively neutral technocratic decision-making based on expertise in the regulatory context. Hence, the authors call for a conceptualization of the regulatory state on a spectrum between rules and deals, where problems are solved by consistently applying rules at the rules end of the spectrum and negotiation as a mode of resolving conflicts at the deals end of the spectrum. From such a perspective, different manifestations of regulatory states characterized by varying levels of negotiation and governance by rule are possible. In a regulatory state manifestation leaning strongly towards the deals end of the spectrum, regulatory agencies still exist. However, their function shifts from content-based to a stronger focus on procedural rule-making, i.e. shaping and controlling the predominant spaces for negotiation. According to Dubash and Morgan (2013a), the manifestation of regulatory agencies on the rules-deals spectrum depends on six contextual factors: The specificities of the industry, the agency's interaction with other institutions and actors, predominating bureaucratic practices, the nature of the political system, the prevalence of redistributive politics and the susceptibility to and preponderance of crises.

The second theme draws on the concept of a regulatory society discussed in Section 3.3. Scholars ponder the feasibility and benefits of this mode of governance in the context of the Global South. Braithwaite (2006), for example, raises the idea that the limitations in state capacity and the institutional environments in the Global South can be circumvented, by jumping over the regulatory state stage and instead directly adopting a 'regulatory society' approach of governance. In an era of internationally networked governance, Braithwaite (2006, p. 890) claims states in the Global South can exploit non-state regulators in their network to compensate for their own lack of enforcement capacity. Examples for such an approach could be leveraging international standardization organizations, international NGOs and industry associations to enforce certain standards or adopting qui tam statutes[75] in order to encourage whistle-blowing. Being aware of the risks of such a strategy (e.g. fostering the already rampant corruption in such states), Braithwaite (2006) nevertheless sees high potential in the transition to a regulatory society, in which the regulatory resources of the private sector are mobilized. Other scholars' research corroborates the importance of involving a wider network of actors in the regulatory process in countries of the Global South, especially since these actors can help amend imported regulatory concepts in ways relevant to the local context (e.g. Dubash and Morgan, 2013a, Ozel, 2012). Against this backdrop, the concept of state capacity needs to be re-conceptualized to fit the context of a regulatory society, since in this governance mode, the state faces new and different tasks

75 A writ of qui tam determines that a private person can receive a financial reward if they assist a prosecution (e.g. via whistle-blowing).

(e.g. engaging non-state actors in regulatory processes). Hence, Dubash and Morgan (2012, p. 273ff) call for further research to better understand this new form of state capacity.

The third theme is embeddedness. The independence of regulatory agencies has been contested in discussions on the regulatory state in the Global North, and this discussion is further amplified in the context of the Global South. Research has provided evidence that regulatory agencies in economies with a strong developmental agenda are not independent and succumb to political and bureaucratic pressures (Jordana, 2013, p. 203). It has also been shown that regulatory agencies that were transferred to states of the Global South develop a life of their own: They may not work in the way they were expected to, but instead, ex-post, become populated by prevalent norms of institutional practice, cultures, etc. (Dubash and Morgan, 2013a, p. 283f). Thereby these agencies develop new functionalities that still meaningfully contribute to the regulatory process. This underpins claims that a certain level of embeddedness of the regulatory function may be productive, despite the common assumption in discourses on the regulatory state that any substantial influence on the regulatory agency from outside is harmful (Dubash and Morgan, 2013a, p. 290). Lavenex et al. (2021, p. 456) see especially high potential in economic embeddedness, specifically in the indigenous support for certain regulatory tools by firms in internationally competitive industries based on their international experience (e.g. intellectual property protection). That way, the companies foster an ongoing process of bottom-up regulatory state building. The investigation into corporate compliance construction can provide valuable insights into this process.

Therefore, it is worthwhile to consider a variation of the regulatory state that is characterized by so-called 'embedded autonomy' (Evans, 1995). An oxymoron at first glance, this concept originated from the developmental state literature and delineates a condition in which a state exhibits both features of autonomy and embeddedness at the same time. Specifically, autonomy hints at bureaucratic autonomy and coherence in procedures, while embeddedness refers to connections of the state apparatus to societal actors, who are allowed to become involved in negotiating policies and other contents. Translated to the regulatory context, a regulatory state characterized by embedded autonomy, or an 'embedded regulatory state', consists of regulatory institutions that are deeply integrated in their societal and economic contexts. But at the same time, these institutions retain the steering function of regulatory states via rule making, monitoring and enforcement of sectors and topics within a context conducive to this kind of governance (Dubash and Morgan, 2013a). Hence, the embedded regulatory state essentially links the first two themes, by exhibiting both the notions of rules and deals at the same time and involving a broader set of actors in the regulatory process. The corporate sector plays a significant role here, since it is involved in setting regulations and at the same time constitutes an important target of regulations. This underpins the systemic nature of corporate compliance as a link between the corporate and the regulatory world.

Thus, the following case study on corporate compliance not only provides deeper insights into the construction and social practices of corporate compliance in China, a country of the Global South, which has managed to quickly transform into a major economic power. This case study also contributes to understanding China's political economy, in particular its distinct manifestations of the regulatory state and regulatory capitalism.

Part II Empirical findings from China

4 Corporate compliance in China

As the first chapter to discuss the Chinese case study and therefore the empirical findings from this research, this chapter starts with a literature review on compliance in China (Section 4.1) before providing an overview of the Chinese political economy (Section 4.2). This is followed by a discussion of the emerging trends, influencing factors and practices related to compliance in China (Sections 4.3, 4.4 and 4.5). Section 4.6 summarizes the findings by highlighting their consequences for the construction of compliance in China.

4.1 Literature review

The academic literature addresses the topic of compliance in China mostly from a regulatory perspective. On the one hand, there is a strand of literature that explores the nature of the Chinese regulatory regime in general and thereby provides insights into the state-business relationship in China. For example, Hsueh (2011) and Pearson (2005, 2007) both made significant contributions to this discussion by describing the transformation of the Chinese regulatory regime after the reform and opening against the backdrop of the regulatory state literature. Related Chinese-speaking sources also point out the gradual transformation of the Chinese Party-state[76] into a regulatory state (e.g. Liu, 2011a) and discuss shortcomings of the Chinese regulatory system as well as improvement suggestions (e.g. Xu, 2016, Hu, 2011, Liu, 2011b). However, most of these reviews of the Chinese regulatory regime date back at least ten years and therefore do not reflect the changes that have happened under Xi Jinping. More recent Chinese- and English-speaking literature delineates international policy transfer processes (incl. factors for success and failure) in the context of the development of the Chinese regulatory model (e.g. Chen and Man, 2020, Balme, 2019, Song Lei and Li Jing, 2019, Zheng and Wei, 2019, Dabrowski et al., 2018).

---

76 This study uses the term 'Party-state', because the state and the CCP are highly entangled in the Chinese authoritarian one-party system.

On the other hand, regulation scholars study contextual influences on regulatory practices and their effects: Van Rooij (2006) undertook an extensive analysis of the regulation of land and pollution in Chinese local communities. He found that, consistent with international studies, the economic, social and political contexts are important influences on compliance. Yet, the way these influences manifest themselves differs in China. For instance, the economic context plays a significantly stronger role than the regulatory context and enforcement (Van Rooij, 2006, p. 221). In addition, the political limits the influence of the social context, e.g. by the government prohibiting nationwide collective organization (Van Rooij, 2006, p. 222). Both Qi et al.'s (2014) results regarding the importance of the media as a regulator and Fu and Geng's (2019) evidence on the role of the public to improve compliance in China support Van Rooij's findings. However, Yee et al. (2016) drew contrasting conclusions to van Rooij regarding the regulatory context. Their investigation of Hong Kong-owned small and medium-sized enterprises' (SMEs) compliance in the Pearl River Delta finds that abidance by regulations is strongly driven by the regulator, i.e. potential punishments as well as local officials' priorities and actions influence firms' compliance behavior.

While these academic works study compliance from a regulatory perspective, only few researchers have explored firms' compliance management in China in itself so far. Most of these studies compare Chinese companies' compliance management with international best practices and identify shortcomings. For instance, Wu and Liang (2015, 2016) identified missing compliance management skills and compliance staff, lagging standardization of compliance management practices, unsystematic compliance management systems, unsound reporting and investigation mechanisms as well as the mentality of taking shortcuts as deficiencies in Chinese firms' compliance management. Yang et al. (2011) additionally found that corporate governance instruments fail due to firms' state ownership and a missing independent judiciary. Moreover, several researchers pointed out that weak enforcement, low discovery rates of legal violations, conflicting political agendas and lacking ethical standards for legal compliance are among the main causes for insufficient compliance management in China (e.g. Li, 2016, Jia et al., 2009, Van Rooij, 2006). Chinese-speaking compliance literature, which mostly only approaches compliance conceptually, echoes these points (e.g. Deng, 2020, Hao, 2019, Fan, 2018, Yao, 2017, Wu, 2017). Further problems this strand of literature mentions are, for instance, a shortage of financial resources for investment in compliance management and the low levels of power possessed by compliance departments within Chinese companies (e.g. Fan, 2018, Song, 2015).

The key target group discussed in this context is internationally operating central SOEs (e.g. Yao, 2017, Song, 2015). Chen (2020) explained that an increasingly strict regulatory environment domestically and internationally motivates Chinese SOEs to manage compliance. In the same vein, several authors, such as Wu (2017), Wang (2012) as well as Liu and Cao (2018), mentioned Chinese companies' blacklistings and sanctioning by the World Bank and stressed the importance of compliance management in the context of successful internationalization.

To improve compliance management in China, the Chinese-speaking literature does not only mention the implementation of international best practices by modeling international examples (e.g. Chen, 2020, Hao, 2019, Qu, 2018, Wu, 2017, Li and Lei, 2014), but also emphasizes the important role of government support for compliance management success; for instance, in the form of role modeling, advancing the regulatory environment, compliance education and propaganda as well as improving the compliance certification market (Fan, 2018). Moreover, leveraging Party structures within companies and Party ideology as well as influences from international investors is proposed (e.g. Hao, 2019, Wu, 2017, Yang, 2017c).

Besides these academic sources, think tanks publish material about compliance in China. Some provide reports about China's compliance management status quo (e.g. CICLA et al., 2019, 2018), while others release compliance management guides for international companies on the Chinese market which postulate preventative compliance management approaches (e.g. Von Busekist, 2016, Stucken, 2015).

However, most of this literature takes an objectivist[77] perspective on compliance. Thus, evidence of social constructionist compliance research from a business perspective in China is still missing. The remaining sections of Chapter 4 contribute to closing this research gap by describing compliance phenomena in China from a social constructionist perspective after providing an overview of the Chinese political economy.

77 For details on the difference between objectivist and social constructionist compliance research, refer to Section 1.3.1.

4.2 Overview of the Chinese political economy

4.2.1 Historical development

Today's Chinese political economy is to a large extent a result of the developments after 1978, when the Chinese government gradually reformed and opened up its economy after almost 30 years of running a planned economy (Naughton, 2007). From the start of the economic transformation until the mid-1990s, the reform focused on the advancement of economic development via gradually introducing economic incentives (Naughton, 2007, p. 89ff). One of the mechanisms in this context was the dual track system, which allowed the continuation of economic planning as a first track and the emergence of market mechanisms (e.g. price building) as a second track. These changes were initially made in the countryside and allowed farmers to sell their overproduction at market prices. At the same time, many farmers also chose to work in township and village enterprises, since they did not need all their work capacity to grow the produce required by the plans. Hence, local enterprises were able to grow, increase their production and also manufacture for both tracks. They became the engine of China's economic development until the mid-1990s (Naughton, 2007, p. 274f).

However, starting from the mid-1990s, achieving economic growth became more complicated. Both internal and external factors increased complexity and regulatory pressures. Internally, Chinese society had become more heterogeneous in terms of social strata and severe environmental degradation as well as a row of business scandals that highlighted the negative side effects of fast economic growth (Yang, 2017a). Externally, the entry to the World Trade Organization (WTO) in 2001 exerted pressure on the Chinese government to elevate the Chinese regulatory and economic systems to international standards and adopt international practices (e.g. regarding transparency in the administration and impartiality of regulators) (Xue and Liou, 2012, p. 116).

These developments triggered several actions by the Chinese government to improve the political economy. First, the government restructured the bureaucracy to improve its efficiency and effectiveness. For example, during the 1998 administrative reform, many of the ministries dealing with economic affairs were relinquished and the management of SOEs, previously within the responsibility of these ministries, was allocated to the State

Economic and Trade Commission[78] (Lan, 2000, p. 440). In this context, the government also made significant efforts to separate government and industry (政企分开) by abolishing SOE's market monopolies both via SOE privatization and closure (Pearson, 2005, p. 303).

Second, a wave of privatizations hit previously successful township and village enterprises, which were facing an increasing competitive market environment (Naughton, 2007, p. 285ff). This development resulted in both winners and losers, since local enterprises often had to lay off workers to stay competitive or shut down completely, a factor that, in combination with the eroded traditional social security system organized via work units, widened the poverty gap in China (Naughton, 2007, p. 288).

Third, the government made increasing efforts to institutionalize rules in order to ensure the healthy functioning of the market economy. For example, China passed its first Company Law in 1994, which regulated company structures and procedures, e.g. by requiring listed companies in China to set up governance structures similar to those in Western countries (Lau et al., 2016, p. 76; Naughton, 2007, p. 301). In addition, the CCP and the government started to propagate the idea of governing the country according to the law (依法治国) in 1997 (National Congress of the CCP, 1997, State Council China, 1997) and integrated this principle into the constitution in 1999 (Van Rooij, 2006, p. 48). For this purpose, China developed an administrative law system and adopted the Legalization Law as a key measure towards a rules-based society in 2003 (Wu, 2007, p. 766). Further international regulatory standards (e.g. related to product safety and labor) were adopted after joining the WTO (Marquis et al., 2011, p. 42).

Due to the increasing environmental destruction and social inequalities that were produced by economic development, the Chinese government started to place more emphasis on environmental and social policies in the 2000s (Hu and Wen administration) (Howell and Duckett, 2019, p. 3). However, these policies, as well as additional guidelines to stimulate domestic consumption in the context of the global financial crisis in 2007/08, were complements to previous developments rather than a redirection of the course of economic and regulatory reforms (Howell and Duckett, 2019, p. 3). An important element contributing to the developments described

78 This commission merged with the Ministry of Foreign Trade and Economic Cooperation and the State Development Planning Commission into today's Ministry of Commerce (MOFCOM, 商务部) in 2003. In the same year, the State-owned Asset Supervision and Administrative Commission of the State Council (SASAC, 国务院国有资产监督管理委员会), which oversees central SOEs, was installed.

above has been policy transfer from abroad (Zhang, 2016). While China mainly relied on policy transfers from the Soviet Union to industrialize the country during the Mao-era, the main examples from which to learn and transfer policies, systems as well as institutions after 1978 were industrialized Western and Asian countries (e.g. Miao, 2018, Feng and Cheng, 2009).

Scholars have identified two distinct features of Chinese policy transfers. First, transfers were characterized by a high level of pragmatism (Zhang and Marsh, 2016, p. 37). One element of this pragmatism was learning by doing, i.e. implementation-oriented transfers (e.g. Zhang and Yu, 2021, Zhang, 2016). Using the example of the Chinese adoption of the eco-city phenomenon, de Jong (2013) described how pragmatism featured in many transfer processes and characterized Chinese policy transfers as 'institutional bricolage': Transfer objects were not only disassembled, partially adopted or reassembled in a manner that fit the Chinese context, but they were also introduced and implemented gradually. Second, Chinese political and bureaucratic elites were the key transfer agents and therefore transfers were driven top-down (e.g. Zhang and Yu, 2021, Zhang and Marsh, 2016). While international organizations (e.g. the United Nations Development Program) also act as agents for policy transfers, they generally tend to work with local actors. In the Chinese context, these actors were mostly (related to) the political and bureaucratic elites (e.g. Zhang and Yu, 2021, p. 13). Hence international organizations only played an expert and financier role (e.g. Zhang and Yu, 2021, Zhu and Wang, 2012).

Overall, scholars see mixed results with regard to policy transfers to China: A lack of knowledge and skills locally, cultural differences and deficient localization of transfer objects were identified as key reasons for transfer failures (e.g. Zhang and Yu, 2021, Zheng and Wei, 2019, Feng and Cheng, 2009). Zhang (2016, p. 2018ff) even regarded these policy processes and the ensuing structural renewal as tools which are part of the CCP's project of ensuring legitimacy and retaining control over the economy as well as society.

Despite all the transition efforts, two idiosyncrasies of the Chinese political economy related to its regulatory framework have endured. First, the role of the Party-state in the Chinese political economy has remained very strong (Pearson, 2005, p. 297f). This is not only reflected in the high levels of state-ownership and the adoption of industrial policies to steer the economy, but also in the strict confines in which the Party-state has set complementary regulators and their enforcement mechanisms (e.g. NGOs, the media) (e.g. Fischer et al., 2021, Lin et al., 2020, Van Rooij et al., 2013). Second, the Party-state's enforcement capacities have stayed rather weak (Marquis et al., 2011). While China's set of regulations became increasingly comprehensive, strict and specific, for a long time, many of these rules only existed on paper and were regarded as a motivating aspirational standards rather than a behavioral bottom-line (Lin, 2011b, Kolk et al., 2010). This so-called 'decoupling' has been observed in many countries of the Global South and leads to minimal changes of the status quo (Marquis et al., 2011, p. 40). While efforts to implement the existing regulations and strengthen enforcement has been observed in China (Marquis et al., 2011, p. 46ff), the lack of an independent judiciary, missing checks and balances for the government[79] and insufficient resources (money, expertise, etc.) are hampering this process (e.g. Li, 2016, Yee et al., 2016, Lin, 2011b). In addition, local governments have often been protective of local economic interests, i.e. stymied the enforcement of regulations which are disadvantageous to economic development, while the comparatively weak civil society has not been able to hold local bureaucrats to account (e.g. Tan, 2014, Van Rooij et al., 2013, Ma and Ortolando, 2000). Hence, these factors have perpetuated the existing weak enforcement regime.

The current administration under Xi Jinping is reinforcing the first and attempting to counteract the second idiosyncrasy. With respect to further strengthening the Party-state, the Xi administration has centralized its power in the past decade and left less leeway for local experimentation and divergence (Ling, 2016). In addition, top-down industrial policies, such as 'Made in China 2025' (中国制造 2025)[80], and strategies, e.g. 'Internet Plus', are supposed to contribute to China's transformation from the workbench of the world to a technology-intensive economic powerhouse (Li, 2018). Since the Chinese Party-state is strongly involved in this development, its role in the Chinese political economy is being reinforced.

To counteract the second idiosyncrasy, the Xi administration makes efforts to improve the currently weak enforcement regime. Xi has not only implemented an unprecedented anti-corruption campaign, but also heightened the attention to rule-based mechanisms via the set-up of the SCS and the campaign to govern the country with the rule by law (e.g.

79 The Party stands above the law, which is why the Chinese legal system can be described as a rule *by* law rather than a rule *of* law (Ng, 2019).

80 This policy has the goal of improving manufacturing capabilities in China to transition from the production of low-tech to high-tech as well as high quality products (Li, 2018).

Brown, 2018, Hongdao et al., 2018, Meissner, 2017). These developments have produced the Chinese political economy of today with its key building blocks, the Chinese economy, the Party-state and the regulatory model, which are described in the following.

4.2.2 The Chinese economy

Thanks to the reform processes since 1978 described in the previous section, the Chinese economy has grown rapidly over the course of the past 40 years (The World Bank, 2021a). Annual GDP-growth rates between four and 15 percent have been the norm (The World Bank, 2021a). But even since 2010, when economic development started to slow down, the growth rates remained on a comparably high level (see Figure 15 for a comparison to the US) (The World Bank, 2021a). This development has catapulted China to the rank of the world's second largest economy after the US in 2020 with a GDP of 14.7 trillion US dollars[81] (The World Bank, 2021b).

Figure 15: GDP growth rates (1980-2020) in China and the US in comparison (The World Bank, 2021a)

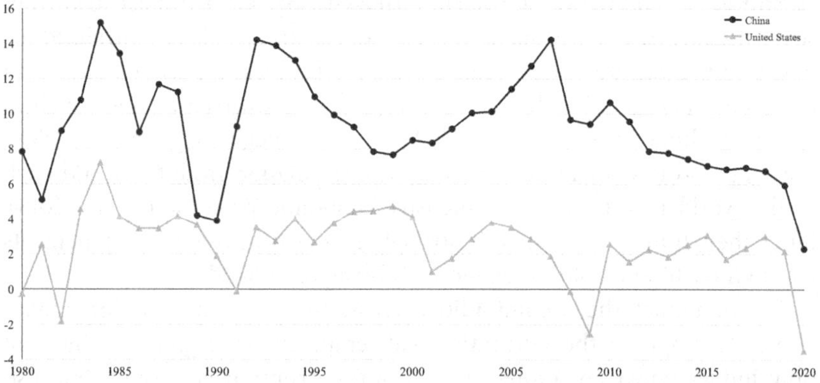

81 There are debates over the accuracy of Chinese official GDP data (Williamson et al., 2018). However, the official numbers, which can provide a rough estimate of the real GDP development trend, suffice for illustrating the general direction of economic development.

Against the background of unprecedented Chinese economic development, two basic questions regarding the characterization of the Chinese economy have been discussed in academic circles.

The first is the Chinese economy's development status. China itself claims to belong to the developing nations in the WTO[82] and according to the OECD's definition, which focuses on the per capital Gross National Income in its measurement, China is classified as upper middle income country that is eligible to receive official development assistance (OECD, 2020). However, the facts that China is now the second largest economy of the world, presents itself as a major global power and possesses highly innovative industries have raised questions about this status (Giehler, 2020, p. 63). Therefore, from 2008 onward, the amount of aid China received has continuously shrunken and the US has attempted to prevent China from being classified as a developing nation in the WTO by proposing criteria for developing nations which would exclude China[83] (Giehler, 2020, p. 64).

Independent from the label that is adopted for the Chinese economy, economists today discuss the risk of and the strategies to avoid the so-called 'middle income trap'[84] for China (e.g. Glawe and Wagner, 2017, Liu et al., 2017, Yao, 2015). Innovation plays an especially important role in this context, because it continuously fosters economic growth and helps countries to develop from a middle income country to a high income economy (e.g. Liu et al., 2017, Huang, 2016, Lewin et al., 2016). The Chinese government is aware of this risk and therefore has actively pushed a variety of different initiatives promoting innovation, for example digitization via the 'Internet Plus' strategy, transaction costs reduction in economic exchanges via the SCS (for further elaborations, see Section 5) as well as big data and artificial intelligence via the promotion of data to the rank of a production factor in 2020 (Krause and Fischer, 2021, Central Committee of the CCP and State Council China, 2020, Krause and Fischer, 2020, State Council China, 2015).

---

82 Developing nations in the WTO are eligible to special and differential treatment, e.g. the tolerance of higher market entry barriers for foreign companies (Low, 2021).

83 Previously, no clear criteria to evaluate the development status of countries in the WTO existed.

84 This term usually refers to countries that have become middle income country thanks to rapid growth in a rather short amount of time, but are stuck at this development level instead of progressing further towards becoming developed high income economies (Glawe and Wagner, 2017, p. 3). However, the definition of criteria for middle income countries is contested, i.e. scholars adopt both absolute and relative approaches (e.g. using the US as a baseline) in their research on this topic (Glawe and Wagner, 2016, p. 8ff).

The second question related to the characterization of the Chinese economy arises because of strong Party-state influence and discusses whether capitalism prevails in China. While the economic reforms saw the transition from a planned economy to a state-led market economy, high levels of state-ownership and central macro-economic planning persist: The World Bank estimates that SOEs' share of China's GDP in 2017 was between 23 and 28 percent and SOEs accounted for 39 percent of assets (Zhang, 2019). In addition, the importance of Chinese SOEs has increased in the international comparison. While in 2000, only nine Chinese SOEs were included in the Fortune Global 500 (33 percent of all SOEs included in the list), this number had risen to 75 by 2017 (74 percent of all SOEs included in the list) (Lin et al., 2020, p. 31). In 2020, three of the top ten global companies in terms of revenue were Chinese SOEs (Sinopec Group, State Grid, China National Petroleum) (Fortune, 2021). This shows that state-ownership is still a key characteristic of the Chinese political economy.

In addition, the continued authority of Party-state institutions over economic development as a legacy of central planning underpins their strong influence on economic governance: Since the 2003 administrative reform, the NDRC[85] under the State Council is responsible for macroeconomic planning (Heilmann, 2016, p. 77f). Moreover, a key feature of the CCP's economic governance are the five-year plans, the fourteenth of which was formally adopted in 2021.

Due to this communist heritage and strong Party-state influence over the Chinese economy, only in the 2000s, scholars increasingly used the term 'capitalism' in discussions on the Chinese economy (Ten Brink, 2019). While the exact labeling of the Chinese economy continues to be contested[86], a consensus appears to have emerged that China's economy is functionally capitalist (e.g. Ten Brink, 2019, Peck and Zhang, 2013, Huang, 2008), since core capitalist features, such as accumulation processes driven by profit-making and surplus values, markets as regimes for economic coordination and the existence of a capitalist class, prevail. However, under Xi Jinping, market principles have been challenged and the role of the private sector in the economy has declined. In addition, the strict lockdown policies during the COVID-19 pandemic, due to which economic activity

85 Formerly known as the State Planning Commission (1952-1998) and the State Development Planning Commission (1998-2003).

86 Terms that are used are, for instance, state capitalism (Peck and Zhang, 2013), Sino-capitalism (McNally, 2012) or capitalism with Chinese characteristics (Huang, 2008).

almost came to a standstill in large cities like Shanghai for several months in 2022, has caused a slowdown in economic growth in China. Against this backdrop, a lot of uncertainties on the future economic framework surround the 20th Party Congress in 2022 (Rudd, 2022). Exactly because of the important role of the Party-state in China, understanding the bureaucratic structures which underpin the Chinese political economy is vital. Therefore the following section elaborates on the set-up of the Party-state.

4.2.3 The Party-state

As mentioned in the previous sections, the Party-state plays an important role in market regulation and consequently in regulatory and compliance questions. Therefore, this section provides an overview of the Party-state's key institutions and structures relevant for compliance-related matters[87] (see Figure 16).

On the central level, the CCP's leading institution, the Politburo, heads two main organs (Heilmann, 2016, p. 73): The Central Committee as well as the merged Central Commission for Discipline Inspection (CCDI, 中央纪律检查委员会) and National Supervision Commission (国家监察委员会). The Central Committee oversees a range of executive Party organs, such as the Organization Department (组织部), which, as the CCP's HR department, is responsible for staffing within the CCP, the Propaganda Department (宣传部), as well as the Central Party School (中共中央党校). Furthermore, the Central Financial and Economic Affairs Commission (中央财经委员会) guides the Central Committee and the State Council in their economic work, and the Central Leading Group for Inspection Work (中央巡视工作领导小组) sends inspection teams (巡视组) on inspection tours across the country to check rule abidance by SOEs, state and Party organs (CCP, 2017).

87 This summary does not claim to be exhaustive (e.g. it does not discuss the political decision-making processes, the judiciary or the legislature), but rather combines a high-level overview of the Party-state structures that are important for the following elaborations on compliance.

Figure 16: Schematic overview of the Chinese Party-state's structures relevant from a compliance perspective (author's design)

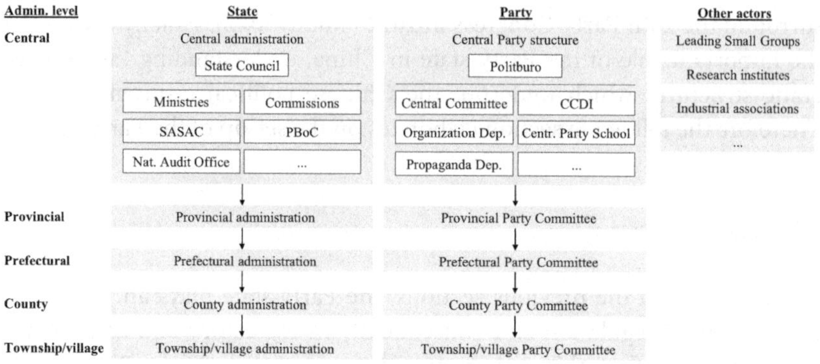

On the other hand, the CCDI, with its origins as a body dedicated to combating corruption, is the Party's internal control institution (Gang, 2017). This means that the commission collaborates closely with the Central Leading Group for Inspection Work and the Party's inspection teams. Recently, the CCDI merged its operations with the National Supervision Commission, a state body created during the 2018 administrative reforms (Liao and Tsai, 2020). In addition to the central Party structure, the CCP organization stretches across all other administrative levels. On the local level[88], Party committees represent the CCP and ensure that Party branches (党支部) exist in all important organizations (Thornton, 2012, p. 63f). One of the focus areas have been Party branches in private enterprises, since the importance of the private sector has been growing and the Party attempts to use Party cells in private companies to reinforce its power (Yan and Huang, 2017, p. 38f).

Similar to the Party structure, the Chinese state bureaucracy's highest executive organ is the State Council (国务院), headed by the premier (Heilmann, 2016, p. 76). This institution directly oversees more than twenty ministries and commissions, such as the Ministry of Industry and Information Technology (MIIT, 工业和信息化部), the NDRC, the MOFCOM and the Ministry of Ecology and Environment (MEE, 生态环境部). Further constituents of the State Council are the SASAC, which supervises central

88 I.e. all levels below the central level.

SOEs[89], the People's Bank of China (PBoC, 人民银行), China's central bank, and the National Audit Office (审计署), responsible for auditing government institutions. In addition, several ministry-level organizations are located directly under the authority of the State Council, such as the CSRC and the State Administration for Market Regulation (SAMR, 国家市场监督管理总局) (State Council China, 2018b, Heilmann, 2016, p. 80).

The state administration also stretches across all levels, i.e. complements the Party structure (Heilmann, 2016, p. 73). The administrative institutional set-up is to a large extent replicated on the provincial level (provinces, autonomous regions and municipalities). However, the central ministries can only guide the provincial ministries functionally; these two actors are not connected by direct disciplinary reporting lines. In addition to the provincial level, the local state administration includes prefecture-, county-, township- and village-level administrations. Over the course of history, there have been waves of centralization and decentralization in the Chinese bureaucracy. Under Xi's leadership, the power is palpably shifting towards the center, illustrated, for example, by the promotion of 'top-level design' (顶层设计) for the deepening of economic reforms (Lee, 2017, p. 330f).

Similarly, the relationship between the state and the Party has changed. Under Xi Jinping, the previous discussions about institutional separation (党政分开) seem to have died down and recent administrative and constitutional reforms have corroborated the CCP's overall leadership position (Grünberg and Drinhausen, 2019, p. 2). For example the CCP's leadership monopoly has been included in Article 1 of the constitution in 2018, causing Holbig to conclude:

> "If you will, the party no longer stands above the law – now it is the law" (Holbig, 2018, p. 196).

For instance, during the 2018 administrative reforms, many organizational duplicates between state and Party were removed via mergers (Grünberg and Drinhausen, 2019, p. 7). However, all these mergers resulted in the elimination of the respective state agency and thereby the strengthening of the CCP's position (Grünberg and Drinhausen, 2019, p. 7). This shows that it is impossible to separate Party from state actions in China.

Beyond and across these formal Party-state structures, other actors influence the Party-state and businesses directly or indirectly, such as Leading

89 Local SOEs are controlled by the respective local governments.

Small Groups (领导小组)[90], research institutes and industry associations (Heilmann, 2016, p. 268). Depending on the specific actor, these organizations are located on only one administrative level or spread across central and local levels. All these actors are involved in the regulatory process and together constitute the Chinese regulatory model described in the following section.

4.2.4 The Chinese regulatory model

To date, Pearson (2005, 2007) Hsueh (2011) and Yang (2017a) have provided the most comprehensive accounts of the Chinese regulatory model. They agree that neither the regulatory state nor the developmental state serves as an adequate characterization of the way the Chinese political economy is regulated. According to these authors, the concept of the regulatory state as laid out in Section 3.3 does not suit China, because the Chinese regulatory model lacks regulatory independence. For instance, Pearson (2007, p. 726) stated:

> "The process-driven establishment of a level playing field, with the regulator serving as referee without regard for who a particular player is, has not only *not* been achieved but also is unrealistic given the imperatives the party-state has demonstrated in the lifeline industries."

While she acknowledged the fundamental changes in the Chinese regulatory model towards less direct Party-state intervention via administrative reforms, Pearson (2005, p. 303ff) nevertheless identified four main characteristics of the Chinese regulatory model that constrain regulatory independence: First, the continued state-ownership of strategic economic assets provides the Chinese Party-state with direct control over economic actors (see Section 4.2.2). Second, the Party-state maintains its authority over economic governance via macro-economic planning (see Section 4.2.2, Yang, 2017a, p. 120ff). Third, the origins of the current regulatory agencies lie to a large extent in former Communist line ministries. For instance, the regulators in financial services are spin-offs from the PBoC and the MIIT is the successor of the

90 Leading Small Groups usually address and coordinate complex tasks that involve a variety of administrative state and/or Party bodies (Grünberg, 2021). They can be established for the short- or long-term depending on the topic and either cooperate with Party or state organs exclusively or involve bodies from both organizations (Grünberg, 2021).

Ministry of Information Industry, which was established through a merger of the Ministry of Post and Telecommunications and the Ministry of Electronics Industry, both former line ministries controlling the respective sectors. This means that staff and leadership from the old ministries were working in the new ministries and thereby transferring not only expertise, but also continuity in terms of culture and regulatory approaches, including the close state-business relationships that the bureaucrats had cultivated. Fourth, the fragmentation and ambiguity of authority reduces regulators' power. For instance, in the automotive sector, central (e.g. the MIIT and the MEE), provincial and local authorities are involved in the regulatory process. They often operate on the same level of hierarchy and therefore responsibilities and power are not delineated clearly. Automotive firms therefore have to answer requests from a variety of different authorities, which may have diverging interests (e.g. local authorities pursue profit as the top priority, while central authorities also focus on other aspects, such as environmental protection) (Marquis et al., 2011). This example shows that even in China's authoritarian one-party state, interests are multi-dimensional and measures therefore contested; not between political parties, but instead between central and local authorities as well as quasi-state stakeholders and powerful local actors outside of the bureaucracy's boundaries (Hsueh, 2013, p. 251). Overall, these characteristics are all not typical for a regulatory state.

However, the concept of a developmental state (as explained in Section 3.3) in also does not fully capture the Chinese regulatory framework, as illustrated by the following three examples. First, China did not restrict foreign direct investment (FDI) as developmental states, such as Japan and South Korea, used to do. Instead, China liberalized FDI on a macro-economic level to stimulate competition among market players and only set limits to the level of FDI in certain strategic industries, such as the automotive sector (Hsueh, 2011, p. 193). Second, the Chinese regulatory framework does not possess the level of centralization in its regulators as prescribed by developmental state models (Hsueh, 2011, p. 266ff). As outlined above, regulatory authority is not always delineated clearly between agencies. In addition, authority is also distributed between central and local bureaucratic levels. Hence, despite recent centralization efforts under the Xi Jinping administration, Lieberthal's (1992) characterization of the Chinese bureaucracy as 'fragmented authoritarianism'[91] still seems to be valid. For instance, five authorities are in charge of regulating

91 Fragmented authoritarianism posits that authority in the Chinese political system is disjointed and decisions are not made directly top-down, but rather emerge from a

the credit rating market (the PBoC, the NDRC, the CSRC, the China Banking and Insurance Regulatory Commission and the Ministry of Finance, 国财政部), but responsibilities are not delineated clearly (Krause et al., 2022, p. 7). Similarly, a multitude of state agencies at the central and local levels are involved in the set-up of the SCS (further details in Section 5.2.3). These ambiguities regarding responsibilities lead to negotiations between involved actors and nontransparent decision-making. Third, the Chinese Party-state's interventions in the economy often do not follow economic principles as in developmental states (Hsueh, 2011, p. 266). Developmental states, for instance, subsidize private market players and thereby foster technological development to ultimately create internationally competitive national champions. In contrast, the Chinese Party-state still strictly controls ownership structures, business activities and market entries in certain industries, etc., which are all command and control mechanisms, that limit market mechanisms from unfolding (Yang, 2017a, p. 127ff). At the same time, other industries are fully exposed to and not protected from international competition, a phenomenon untypical for a developmental state (Hsueh, 2011, p. 266ff).

Even though these lines of argument by Hsueh (2011) and Pearson (2005, 2007) at times fall prey to dichotomous thinking about state forms (either regulatory state or developmental state, for further details refer to Section 3.3), the authors nevertheless paint a differentiated picture of the Chinese regulatory approach and thereby implicitly acknowledge the possibility of a co-existence of different regulatory modes. Pearson (2005, p. 322) postulated that

> "China's government can be expected to develop a variegated set of regulatory reforms for different types of sectors; any emerging model of China's political economy must recognize this diversity."

Hsueh (2011, p. 270) specified the co-existence of different regulatory modes in the Chinese case as a "bifurcated approach toward government-business relations".

According to Hsueh (2011, p. 34), the Chinese Party-state's regulatory framework for a particular industry depends to a large extent on the sector's strategic value, which is determined by the sector's importance to national security (political and social stability, geopolitics and foreign affairs) as well as the industry's contribution to the country's technological

process of bargaining between various authorities involved in the topic (Lieberthal, 1992).

and infrastructure foundations. Specifically, a sector's strategic value affects the way the government defines the industry's development goals, who is in charge of industrial policies and what types of regulatory and enforcement measures are applied in this industry. In addition to the strategic value, a sector's institutional and structural characteristics, such as the dominating ownership types, the location in global production chains and the local industry's level of international competitiveness, play a role in the mode of governance that is employed (Hsueh, 2011, p. 39).

Based on these characteristics, Hsueh (2011, p. 58ff) specified two dominant regulatory approaches for China: Deliberate reinforcement for internationally less competitive domestic sectors of high strategic value and decentralized engagement for internationally more competitive domestic sectors of low strategic value. Deliberate reinforcement is characterized by the central government's mobilization of investments and the coordination of research and development, because the products and services from these industries often contain complex technologies and require high levels of knowledge and capital. The central government regulates other aspects in these sectors rather strictly in order to enhance state authority, such as firms' ownership structures, technical standards, product certification and market entry. This regulatory approach is dominant in sectors, such as financial services and telecommunications. In contrast, decentralized engagement means that the central government allows fierce market competition by relaxing central controls and providing the local authorities with more leeway to regulate. Therefore, sectors where decentralized engagement dominates, e.g. in the textile industry, generally face less restrictive regulations, mostly consisting of macro-economic policies, nationwide general economic rules and specific local regulations. However, such lax regulatory frameworks have caused a myriad of problems, especially environmental destruction and threats to health and safety, because the regulatory authorities' capacities do not suffice to effectively enforce the rules. Within each of the two regulatory approaches, additional, smaller regulatory variations based on sector-specific institutional and structural characteristics exist (for examples, refer to Part 2 and 3 of Hsueh's, 2011, work).

Despite updates on economic strategy and policy since 2011, such as 'Made in China 2025', McNally and Gruin's (2017) more recent analysis[92] sees Hsueh's (2011) characterization of the Chinese regulatory regime as

92 Their analysis is based on the concept of Sino-capitalism, which McNally (2012) introduced to describe the idiosyncratic nature of the Chinese political economy

bifurcated unchanged. They identify two modes of capital accumulation in the Chinese political economy: One dominated by the Party-state and dependent on the government's control over the economy for the strategically important sectors of the economy and another one, the entrepreneurial networked mode, featuring fierce market competition and a high level of global integration. Based on this dual nature of the Chinese economic governance approach, the authors regard economic liberalization and the adoption of market mechanisms in China only as an instrument to develop China's economy rather than the foundation on which the political economy is built (McNally and Gruin, 2017).

Liu (2011a) further detailed the picture of the Chinese regulatory regime and outlined four regulatory modes for China. These modes are based on the questions whether or not government and business has been separated and whether or not private capital has been introduced in a sector ('privatization'): State-owned monopolies (国有垄断), government supervision (政府监管), planned economy (计划经济) and government-business integration (政企合一) (see Figure 17).

Figure 17: Regulatory modes in China according to Liu (2011a, p. 55) (author's design and translation)

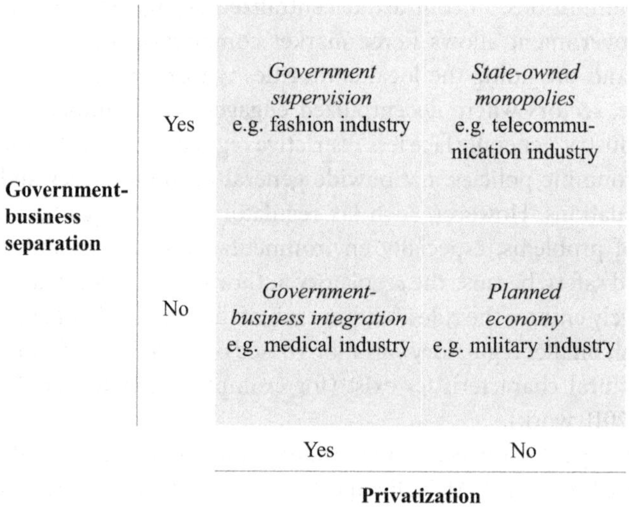

compared to political economies of the Global North (often characterized as liberal or coordinated market economies based on the Varieties of Capitalism framework).

Across these regulatory approaches, the academic literature examining regulation and enforcement has identified three main features of Chinese authorities' enforcement actions. First, the adoption of legal and communicative enforcement instruments is characterized by a high level of pragmatism. This pragmatism is visible in all aspects of enforcement. For example, Lo and Fryxell (2019) found that environmental officers tend to favor educative and collaborative means of enforcement over coercion, because their guanxi with the regulatee can be harmed by overt confrontation. Second, network enforcement instruments focusing on transparency and shaming have a long history in China (Liebman and Milhaupt, 2008, p. 979). Already during the time of China's imperial bureaucracy, the cangue, a device that was worn around the neck and restricted movement, was used for delinquents' public humiliation. But shaming mechanisms have also been adopted in modern China, for instance during the Cultural Revolution (e.g. in public struggle meetings) (Wang, 2014, p. 109). Since transparency became a subject of the public discourse in the 1990s, the Chinese Party-state has slowly implemented transparency practices and non-state actors have engaged in transparency-related initiatives, especially in the field of CSR (Mol, 2014, p. 51). For example, listed companies are required to release CSR reports and a responsibility index has been implemented at the stock exchanges (Lin, 2010, p. 76ff). Moreover, information transparency is supposed to trigger public shame, e.g. via blacklists for offenders or disclosure of other information (e.g. food quality ratings or emission levels) (Li, 2016, Mol, 2014). Originally, the government and NGOs mainly implemented this type of disclosure in the realm of environmental protection, but with the current set-up of the SCS this enforcement instrument is becoming increasingly institutionalized and important (further information on the SCS in Chapter 5).

These developments are part of a decentering of the regulatory process in China: In certain areas and situations, the Chinese Party-state has increasingly been coopting on actors outside of its own structures for business supervision, such as the media and the general public (e.g. in form of interest groups or NGOs), especially when the authorities' enforcement was weak, e.g. in the 2000s (Van Rooij et al., 2013, p. 322ff). For example, Chinese media have been covering instances of unsafe products or production processes, such as the illegal use of red dye in food by the companies Meiweiyuan and Kentucky Fried Chicken in 2005 (Xinhua, 2005). For actors outside the bureaucracy to be able to monitor corporate actors, public corporate information disclosure is essential. Hence, network enforcement instruments increasingly complement traditional legal command-and-control enforcement.

Third, apart from the two regular enforcement instruments mentioned above, campaign-style enforcement is also a common practice in China (e.g. Liu, 2015, Van Rooij, 2006). Campaign-style enforcement is defined as

> "a type of policy implementation involving extraordinary mobilization of administrative resources under political sponsorship to achieve a specific policy target within a defined period of time" (Liu et al., 2015, p. 85).

During campaigns that target the corporate sector, companies are inspected with regard to the campaign's specific topic. According to Ma and Ortolando (2000, p. 121), rules are more stringently enforced during campaigns as compared to regular day-to-day enforcement, because officials' performance is controlled more closely. Constituting a common practice in China (e.g. in environmental protection), campaigns are an important addition to regular enforcement practices that need to be considered in the context of compliance research on China. This type of ad hoc enforcement calls attention to the so-called 'shadow of the hierarchy', i.e. the state's power to intervene in the regulatory act directly at any time, especially when self-regulation or networks prove ineffective (Schubert and Alpermann, 2019).

Against the backdrop of these particularities in the Chinese regulatory model and the political economy as a whole, the following sections provide an overview of the compliance situation in China, beginning with the development of the concept of compliance over time.

4.3 The genesis of the concept of corporate compliance

Process tracing of the term 'compliance' (合规) in Chinese official documents[93] ('official discourse' in the following) has located its origins in the financial sector. The term first emerged in a document by the CSRC as early as 1994 and in a document title in 2004 (SEC-19940827, SEC-20040817). In 2006, the China Banking Regulatory Commission (中国银行业监督管理委员会) issued its first dedicated compliance management guidelines, the 'Guidelines on Commercial Banks' Compliance Risk Management' (商业银行合规风险管理指引) (GEN-20061026), followed by compliance

93 For further information on the process tracing, refer to Section 1.3.

management guidelines released by the China Insurance Regulatory Commission (保险监督管理委员会, 2007) and the CSRC (SEC-20080714).

These early compliance documents contain indicators which demonstrate that the international concept and practices of compliance were introduced to China via the global financial sector. First, the understanding of compliance adopted in these documents is the same as the one the Basel Committee on Banking Supervision laid out in 2005 (Basel Committee on Banking Supervision, 2005). Second, the documents provide detailed prescriptions on how compliance management is to be implemented by targeted companies. These rules follow international best practices, such as setting up a compliance management system with written policies, conducting compliance trainings, strengthening a compliance culture (GEN-20061026, SEC-20080714).

Later compliance-related documents from other sectors and authorities corroborate the international influences as a major driver for compliance practices being transferred to China: Foremost, the SASAC's compliance-related documents emphasize the international regulatory environment as a key motivation and learning opportunity for compliance management in the context of the 'Go Out' strategy (走出去战略)[94] (e.g. GEN-20120904, GEN-20161212). For example, the first document with a focus on compliance released by the SASAC (in 2012) provides a case study of an SOE that set up a compliance risk management system in the context of the enterprise's internationalization (GEN-20120904). The case study mentions the regulatory supervision in other countries and the increasingly strict regulations and sanctions by international organizations (e.g. the World Bank) as motivations for adopting compliance management. Moreover, it explicitly states that the SOE studied and analyzed "countries' related laws and regulations, the World Bank's compliance requirements, international compliance conventions and best practices" ("国家相关法律法规、世界银行合规要求、国际合规惯例以及国际最佳实践", GEN-20120904).

Similar references to international strategies can be found in the work of Chinese researchers (e.g. Liu and Cao, 2018, Wang, 2012) and newspaper articles. For instance, an article propagated via the Chinese government's website (GEN-20181128) claims that the urgency for companies to set up compliance systems stems from them having experienced major

94 The 'Go Out' strategy was adopted by the Chinese government in order to encourage overseas investment by Chinese enterprises.

conflicts when entering international markets (“企业合规体系建设的紧迫性，是企业走向国际市场所受到巨大冲力的体现”). Hence, according to the same article, a compliance system is a must-have for every Chinese company entering the international environment (“是中国企业走向国际市场的必由之路”). In addition, Chinese authorities conducted corporate compliance trainings in the context of the ‘Belt and Road’ Initiative (一带一路)[95] to equip Chinese companies with internationalization strategies for success (GEN-20170714, GEN-20190719). During such trainings, companies learn lessons from international actors; there is, for instance, documented evidence that the World Bank joined the CCDI in a compliance training (GEN-20190719). The fact, that Xi Jinping himself delivered a speech at this event, illustrates the importance and recognition of such collaborations and trainings for the internationalization of Chinese companies (GEN-20190719).

Moreover, Chinese authorities adopt and explicitly refer to international rules and compliance practices in their policy documents and standards (GEN-20140609, GEN-20151010). For instance, the State Council released a document to highlight that it is strengthening trade policy compliance across the country, i.e. the alignment of local authorities’ trade policies with national and WTO standards (GEN-20140609). Similar efforts were made by the central tax authorities, which require local tax policies to be in line with WTO guidelines (GEN-20151010). With regard to standards, China directly translated the compliance management guideline ISO19600 into the Chinese (recommended, but optional) standard GB/T35770-2017 in 2017 (SAMR, 2017). The transfer of the new, certifiable compliance management standard ISO37301 into a Chinese standard is already being discussed (Sohu, 2021). These examples show the influence of international rules and compliance systems on Chinese regulatory and compliance practices.

Based on international best practices, the first dedicated compliance management guidelines from the financial sector prescribe a certain way of managing compliance for their target organizations, i.e. strongly shape the construction of compliance in China. The concept of compliance propagated in these documents is closely linked to the idea of risk. Specifically, compliance is introduced as a means to mitigate business risks and

95 The Belt and Road Initiative is an infrastructure development strategy initiated by the Chinese government in 2013, which invests in infrastructure projects, especially along the routes of the ancient silk road.

thereby ensure safe and stable operations, healthy market development and improve market supervision (e.g. GEN-20061026, SEC-20080714). At the same time, these documents adopt a broad understanding of compliance, which does not only entail external regulations, but also additional business-internal rules, such as ethical standards (SEC-20080714). Moreover, the compliance management guidelines delineate compliance management as a top-down endeavor: Compliance is clearly depicted as a management and leadership task within companies (employees' role is not mentioned) (GEN-20061026, SEC-20080714). In addition, the documents explicitly mention the Party-state's top-down influence on the targeted companies in the compliance context; for example via the installment of chief compliance officers (CCOs) in securities firms, which have to be approved by the CSRC and report non-compliance incidents not only to the company management but also directly to the CSRC (SEC-20080714). Since this notion of compliance is prescribed in mandatory rules, these guidelines contribute to coercive institutional isomorphism[96] with regard to compliance if they are consistently enforced.

The conception of compliance evolved in the following years, when the idea of compliance spread to other contexts. On the one hand, compliance appeared as an increasingly prominent topic in other industries, such as the food and drug as well as the logistics sectors (GEN-20120811, GEN-20131107, GEN-20170315, GEN-20180511, GEN-20180515). On the other hand, the idea of compliance trickled down from the central to the local level. Local authorities encouraged corporate compliance and deterred non-compliance; documented, for instance, in Liaoning and Jiangsu provinces (GEN-20100728, GEN-20101209), the cities of Shanghai and Tianjin (GEN-20110906, GEN-20120712), as well as the autonomous region of Ningxia (GEN-20111130).

Across these sectors and target groups, the concept of compliance evolved in scope amid the adoption of a variety of other enforcement instruments besides legal instruments. The scope of compliance extended from a focus on financial risk mitigation towards rules-based management in various business fields and topics. For example, personal information protection has become an important compliance concern in addition to traditional compliance topics, such as anti-corruption and anti-money laundering efforts (GEN-20190730). In addition, authorities also promote compliance in newly emerging fields of business in the context of tightening

96 For details on this concept, see Section 2.5 and Edelman and Suchman (1997).

regulations, for example in internet finance (e.g. peer-to-peer lending) and online ride-hailing (GEN-20160327, GEN-20160513, GEN-20180419, GEN-20180917). In this context, compliance is conceptualized as an economic measure (经济手段) and contrasted with its counterpart, market supervision (市场监管) (GEN-20101209).

With regard to enforcement instruments, the official documents show three trends that emerged over time: First, the topic of self-regulation has gained importance, e.g. by setting up new self-regulatory organizations[97] in new business areas such as internet finance (GEN-20160327) and by stressing the importance of industries' as well as businesses' internal compliance and self-regulatory capacities (合规自律内功; GEN-20160513, GEN-20161212, GEN-20170315). Second, authorities have increasingly adopted network instruments[98], both for portraying positive and negative compliance behavior. For instance, authorities in Ningxia published information on environmental projects that were not in compliance with local regulations (GEN-20111130), whereas authorities in Tianjin praised compliant private schools (GEN-20120712). In addition, compliance-related company ratings have gained importance (e.g. GEN-20200509). Third, authorities have started to rely on digital tools to improve enforcement. For instance, consumers can use a tool integrated in WeChat to search for compliance information on drivers active in the online car-hailing market (GEN-20210325) or use government complaint platforms for different industries (e.g. GEN-20170315). Moreover, businesses can now report non-compliance incidents in the tender-bidding process via the State Council's 'Internet plus Supervision' platform[99] ('互联网+督查', GEN-20210107) and check their compliance status with regard to personal information protection via an app (GEN-20190730). The emergence of these trends in the compliance and regulatory enforcement context resonates with the Chinese government's larger project of establishing the SCS as a new enforcement tool, which incorporates all new approaches[100].

97 A self-regulatory organization possesses a certain amount of authority over a sector or a profession (e.g. securities firms). Such organizations can substitute or complement government regulations and enforcement, depending on the administrative set-up. Their factual level of independence from state agencies varies accordingly.

98 For details on the different types of enforcement instruments, refer to Section 2.4.1.2.

99 Individuals can also report problems via this platform.

100 For a more detailed discussion of the SCS and its impact on compliance, refer to Section 5.

In parallel with these developments, the SASAC has also paid increasing attention to compliance since 2014. The authority made the internal legal institutionalization of central SOEs (法制央企建设) a key priority for the five-year period 2015 to 2019, which explicitly includes the improvement of compliance management capabilities as a measure ("提升合规管理能力", GEN-20141225). Already in 2016, the SASAC started to build compliance management systems in five central SOEs (PetroChina Company Limited, China Mobile, Dongfang Electric Corporation, China Merchants Group Limited and China Railway Group Limited) via pilots (GEN-20210604). The efforts culminated in the release of the 'Guidelines on Compliance Management for Central SOEs (for Trial Implementation)' ('SOE Compliance Guidelines' in the following) and the 'Guidelines for Compliance Management of Companies' Overseas Operations' ('Overseas Compliance Guidelines' in the following) in 2018 (GEN-20181102, GEN-20181231(1)).

The 'SOE Compliance Guidelines' is the first regulatory document from the Party-state to lay down concrete requirements for compliance management targeting companies outside the financial sector, specifically central SOEs. Therefore, the document provides additional valuable insights into the current construction of compliance. Specifically, the 'SOE Compliance Guidelines' outline the motivation for prescribing compliance management, the meaning of compliance and required compliance management practices. In all these areas, the 'SOE Compliance Guidelines' build on the way compliance was constructed in documents targeting the financial sector and slightly enhance the previous concept: With regard to the motivation for strengthening compliance management in SOEs, this document mimics the guidelines released in the financial sector by emphasizing the importance of compliance for a healthy market development and Chinese companies' internationalization efforts. However, the scope of Chinese companies' compliance management has broadened: While the 'SOE Compliance Guidelines' still mention Chinese firms' own adherence to the local regulations overseas as a success factor for operations, they now also include the importance of Chinese SOEs to manage compliance of international companies they have invested in ("强化海外投资经营行为的合规管理", GEN-20181102).

Similarly, the meaning of compliance that is constructed in the 'SOE Compliance Guidelines' builds on the broad notion of compliance and the strong prominence of risk mitigation introduced in previous guidelines in the financial sector. Yet, the concept of compliance is extended in two ways. First, the already broad scope of rules that companies need to adhere to now explicitly includes international treaties, a further emphasis on the international dimension of compliance. Second, the guidelines mention employees' role and compliance practices in the context of compliance management. Nevertheless, the focus on the top-down implementation of compliance management still dominates.

Lastly, as in the documents from the financial sector, the required compliance practices outlined in the 'SOE Compliance Guidelines' are in line with international best practices, e.g. including common compliance areas, such as anti-money laundering, and prescribing compliance management systems to contain, among others, trainings and audits. Still, the document also mentions several aspects, which were not emphasized before. For instance, companies are supposed to set up information technology to improve process management ("通过信息化手段优化管理流程"), collect and store related information ("记录和保存相关信息") and use big data to control compliance risks ("运用大数据等工具"). In addition, integrity plays a more prominent role in compliance management: On the one hand, employees' compliance awareness and integrity is to be raised by compliance management activities, such as letting employees sign compliance commitments (合规承诺). On the other hand, companies are supposed to set up a self-regulation and integrity system (自律诚信体系) to ensure compliance in market transactions. Even though the document does not detail the nature of this system, the name suggests it should help companies go beyond self-restraint and also foster ethical conduct. Moreover, the close relationship between SOEs and authorities is highlighted, e.g. by requiring companies to report big compliance risks directly to the SASAC and other relevant departments ("重大合规风险事件应当向国资委和有关部门报告"). Finally, the document also stresses compliance management in the context of third-party management and thereby extends the scope of compliance management. For example, SOEs should inspect important business partners and require them to sign compliance commitments.

The 'Overseas Compliance Guidelines', which were published nearly one and a half months after the 'SOE Compliance Guidelines' adopt the same conceptualization of compliance. Thus, both documents lay out detailed requirements for compliance management. This codification of compliance management specifics in government regulations shows that compliance management is increasingly institutionalized and institutional isomorphism perpetuated in China.

In addition, the release of these compliance guidelines has not only directed SOEs' attention to compliance management, but also resulted in a heightened attention to compliance generally. Overall, internet searches with the keyword 'compliance' (合规) almost doubled between 2013 and 2018 (see Figure 18[101]).

With respect to SOEs, an increasing amount of compliance-related documents were released after the issuance of the SASAC's compliance guidelines. On the one hand, SOEs have posted open compliance-related positions via the SASAC's website (e.g. GEN-20200915, GEN-20201202). On the other hand, the SASAC itself has also published further compliance-related documents, such as compliance management case studies of successful central SOEs and further compliance-requirements (e.g. GEN-20200812, GEN-20210513). Moreover, local SASAC branches have issued their own compliance management guidelines for local SOEs based on the SASAC's blueprint from 2018[102] (e.g. GEN-20200227, GEN-20200918, GEN-20210517).

Figure 18: Baidu index for the keyword '合规' (compliance) from 2011 to 2020 (Baidu, 2021)

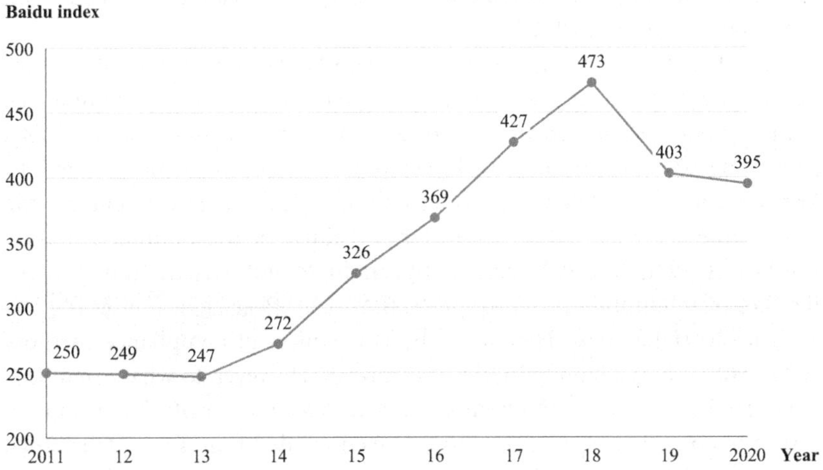

101 The Baidu index calculation algorithm is not published by Baidu, but the company explains that it is based on the total amount of searches for a keyword and the total amount of searches in a set period of time (Baidu, 2021).

102 The 'SOE Compliance Guidelines' explicitly mention that local SASAC branches can refer to this document when promoting compliance-related work in local com-

Based on these developments, the Supreme People's Procuratorate (最高人民检察院), in collaboration with eight other authorities, including the SASAC, is now establishing pilots for a new supervision and evaluation mechanism for compliance commitments of companies that are involved in legal cases (GEN-20210604, Supreme People Procuratorate, 2021). The mechanism includes inspections of and improvement requirements for companies' compliance management systems. For the first time in China, companies are being incentivized to set up compliance programs via such programs' impact on lawsuits. Specifically, courts may take the existence and shape of compliance management systems into consideration when passing sentence and determining the severity of a penalty.

The implementation of these pilots since the crackdown on internet companies in 2020/2021 sheds light on the increased importance attributed to compliant behavior. This crackdown targeted big internet companies, such as Alibaba, for unfair competition practices, namely forcing businesses using platform services to exclusively choose one platform to operate from ('pick one of two', 二选一) (SAMR, 2021e). In this context, 34 targeted platform businesses were required to publish 'Commitments of Legally Compliant Operations' (依法合规经营承诺) (SAMR, 2021a,b,c). Several insights regarding the construction of compliance can be gleaned from these statements (SAMR, 2021a,b,c).

First, the 34 commitments are very similar both in terms of content covered (e.g. promising abidance to regulations, setting up compliance management systems, ensuring product and personal information safety, protecting consumers), but also in terms of the wording of the statements. While none of the statements are exactly identical, many of them use the exact same sentence parts. For instance, "abuse of the dominant market position" ("滥用市场支配地位") appears in 24 and "strictly fulfill the obligation of intellectual property protection" ("严格履行知识产权保护义务") in 20 statements. Therefore, the conception of compliance in these statements shows a high level of isomorphism. However, to what extent this isomorphism in the commitments also translates into institutional isomorphism in compliance practices cannot be concluded from these statements, since the drafting process of the statements (e.g. whether companies received help from authorities or even collaborated) is not made transparent

panies ("地方国有资产监督管理机构可以参照本指引，积极推进所出资企业合规管理工作") (GEN-20181102).

and the detailed compliance practices of these companies are not revealed in the documents.

Second, the commitments themselves serve as a new network enforcement instrument. Many of the commitments state that companies are supposed to be monitored by society (社会监督) based on their promises regarding compliance and ethics. On the one hand, this indicates an increasing responsibilization of businesses (see Parker and Nielsen, 2009, p. 48ff), because they are made to carry a moral responsibility towards society and have to implement measures for self-regulation. On the other hand, it intimates that compliance management is no longer a business function with a strongly internal orientation, but rather needs to engage in close dialogue with the population and societal actors at large.

Third, the notion of credit (信用) has become an element of compliance. Several companies commit to adhering to the "basic principles of credit, namely voluntariness, equality, fairness and honesty" ("自愿、平等、公平、诚实信用基本原则") in the context of compliance. In such an understanding, compliance becomes dependent on how credit is conceptualized and firms' credit levels affect compliance levels[103].

Overall, this overview of the genesis of the compliance concept in Chinese official discourse shows how the understanding of compliance has gained depth and breadth over time. This trend is also reflected in the way experts and business representatives conceptualize compliance in interviews. Even though they are aware of the existence of both a broad and a narrow conceptualization of compliance (EXP21-04, BUS21-13, BUS21-24)[104], the majority of interviewees adopts a broad notion of compliance (e.g. BUS19-04, BUS21-05, BUS21-09, BUS21-10, BUS21-11, BUS21-14, BUS21-19, BUS21-20, BUS21-21):

> "You do not only abide by external rules, you also abide by internal rules" ("你不只遵守外规，你也遵守内规", BUS21-07).

103 An in-depth analysis of how these two concepts interplay can be found in sub-case one on the Social Credit System's influence on compliance (Chapter 5).

104 Interestingly, those interviewees that explicitly mention the difference between the broad and the narrow understanding of compliance, apply the two concepts in reverse meaning compared to the theoretical definition as explained in Section 2.2.2: For them, the narrow notion of compliance refers to the adherence to company-internal rules only, while the broad notion also contains external regulations (EXP21-04, BUS21-13, BUS21-24).

In addition, several interviewees mirror the ethical notion of compliance used in the official discourse about compliance. Two business representatives regarded fostering morality in employees' conduct as vital for compliant behavior (BUS19-14, BUS21-12). Another interviewee considered understanding the supervisor's intention (e.g. the person's attitude), rather than only documented actions, as a significant component of compliance investigations (BUS21-10). One compliance manager even resonated with the broad compliance understanding promoted by the 34 compliance commitments when she called compliance itself a "means to supervise the market and society" ("监管市场和社会的方式", BUS21-19).

Notwithstanding the congruence of business representatives' compliance construction with the official discourse, interviewees' compliance understanding also provides additional nuance to the way compliance is conceptualized in China. First, interviewees pointed to the potential differences in how a rather general compliance concept is implemented depending on the industry and even the business department within one company (BUS21-09, BUS21-11, BUS21-24).

Second, they highlighted the importance of the individual, both in the understanding of compliance and the implementation of compliance management. One compliance manager stated:

> "Everyone's understanding of compliance is different" ("每个人对合规的理解是不一样的", BUS21-23).

She then continued to describe how even within the compliance department in her company, there are disagreements on what behavior classifies as non-compliant. Therefore, some interviewees regarded compliance as dependent on the personal attitude to rule adherence (BUS21-02, BUS21-05).

Third, compliance is constructed as a status that is triggered by external pressures and is thus not necessarily intrinsically motivated. For example, the government's requirements and supervision in the context of the campaign to Govern the Country According to the Law constitute an extrinsic compliance motivation for Chinese companies and SOEs (BUS21-15, BUS21-23). Moreover, interviewees conceptualized compliance as the 'bottom line' (底线) and the only basis on which companies can operate (BUS19-03, BUS21-11, EXP21-01, PO21-ON).

Fourth, interviewees distinguished between the roles of the compliance department and the discipline inspection department (纪检部门), a branch of the Party organization within companies, which, similar to compliance, is supposed to conduct inspections and raise awareness for rules. According to one interviewee who had worked in both the compliance and discipline inspection department in an automotive company, compliance has a rather positive notion, because it also promotes benefits (BUS21-22). Instead, discipline inspections possess a more negative connotation, since they mostly focus on working against something, e.g. against corruption in the anti-corruption work (BUS21-22). Hence, discipline inspection work is not as comprehensive and systemic as compliance management (BUS19-05)[105].

Similar to the construction of the meaning of compliance, the functions which interviewees attributed to the concept mostly mirror the official discourse: Interviewees stressed the importance of compliance for successful business operations and growth (e.g. increasing standardization and efficiency) (BUS21-08, BUS21-14, BUS21-15, BUS21-19, BUS21-24, EXP21-01). One representative from a startup even claimed compliance to be her company's development direction (BUS21-03). Moreover, company representatives highlighted compliance's risk mitigation function (BUS21-12, BUS21-13). They regard compliance as a means to prevent legal violations and mistakes in general: Compliance management is necessary "to not let the business make mistakes" ("不让业务犯错误", BUS21-23). Therefore, interviewees described the protective function of compliance, both for companies and employees (BUS21-01, BUS21-14, BUS21-18). A proactive preventative approach in business management via compliance not only avoids the threats to a company's existence and business success, but also protects the national economy and society (as a whole) from harm (BUS21-06, BUS21-12).

Despite all these benefits, some interviewees also emphasized the pressures and limits of compliance. From this perspective, compliance does not possess a 'positive value' ("正面价值"), but is only measured by its 'negative value' ("负面价值") (BUS21-10), i.e. in costs of violations that happen rather than the value it adds. A lawyer corroborated this point by claiming that Chinese enterprises consider compliance often purely as a cost factor (EXP19-01). According to him, companies therefore only set up compliance management on paper, but do not truly pursue its essence (EXP19-01). An example for this compliance understanding is calculated non-compliance

105 For more details about the differences between these two departments in practice, refer to Sections 4.5.2, 6.1.5 and 6.2.5.

incidents, i.e. violations of regulations that are intentionally tolerated as they are cheaper than actually complying with the regulations (EXP19-01). The CEO of an SOE provided an example for this kind of thinking, when he shared his behavior related to the 'Eight-Point Regulation' (八项规定)[106]: Normally, his company's reception desk arranges business dinners according to these rules. But in some cases, when a business partner is especially important, the CEO nevertheless orders the expensive dishes which exceed the allowed budget. He then pays for them via his personal account in order to avoid these orders from being listed as company expenses. He considered this personal investment worthwhile, since he would indirectly be reimbursed for this personal expense at the end of the year with a higher bonus if he successfully landed a big contract (BUS19-10).

The existence of such calculative thinking with regard to compliance coexisting with the ethical and social functions of compliance in China reflects the way compliance has been constructed in the international discourse. Hence, the general conceptualization of compliance in China is largely in line with what is discussed internationally.

Yet, from the elements discussed above, three are emphasized particularly, especially in comparison to the international construction: The link between compliance and credit levels, the proactive attribution of a societal supervision function to compliance and the prescription of concrete compliance management practices to certain corporate actors (firms in the financial sector or SOEs) by the Party-state. The fact that the official discourse, interviewed experts and business representatives in China agree on this construction of the meaning of compliance hints at a high level of institutional isomorphism. The following chapters go more in depth on how this understanding of compliance manifests itself in practice by first providing an overview of the influences on compliance (Section 4.4) before detailing compliance practices in China (Section 4.5).

106 This set of rules aims to foster discipline among Party members and, among many other points, calls upon them to practice thrift (e.g. in meetings, meals and accommodation).

4.4 Influences on corporate compliance

4.4.1 External factors

4.4.1.1 Social, economic and political environments

Social environment

In general, a trend towards an increasing awareness for compliance can be discerned across society in China (BUS19-01, BUS19-08, BUS19-20, BUS21-22). This awareness becomes evident in a variety of phenomena, including customers' increased knowledge about and changing attitudes towards regulations (BUS21-09). Other examples are societal condemnation of child labor (EXP19-10, EXP19-13) and a stronger awareness about data protection (EXP19-05). One lawyer specializing in the field of data protection claimed that the government's stricter data protection regulations went hand in hand with a change in the public's opinion on this topic (EXP19-05). Hence, companies are now being monitored from both authorities and society (EXP19-05).

Despite these improvements, some interviewees also pointed out the limitations of societal supervision. For instance, one interviewee referred to the complexity of business operations in certain fields, which may hinder societal actors (e.g. consumers, shareholders) from identifying rule violations (BUS19-14). He concluded that at times it suffices for firms to make their stakeholders think they comply without actually abiding by the rules (BUS19-14). This risk of creative compliance was also raised by other interviewees, especially in the context of a lacking internalization of rule-compliance by individuals (BUS21-25, EXP19-01). One government official provided an example for this problem from Shanghai (GOV19-02): When the government limited married couples from buying more than one apartment in the city, many couples got divorced only to buy a second apartment before re-marrying. Thus, the city of Shanghai had to adapt the regulation to avoid such behavior (Bloomberg News, 2021a). She concluded that this example from the private realm shows that Chinese people are willing to find regulatory loopholes and evade regulations, also in the economic realm, to make a profit (GOV19-02). This is facilitated, she claimed, by insufficient enforcement of regulations and the trend that topics which were traditionally handled via personal relations are today regulated by official legal processes (GOV19-02). This two-sided depiction of the overall compliance awareness across society shows that compliance has not yet fully turned into a cultural and normative institution in China, even though there are signs that the institutionalization of compliance is progressing.

Nevertheless, business actors already notice impacts of increased compliance and rule awareness in society on their businesses in four ways (BUS21-09). First, customer complaints have become a common practice. Customers use companies' official customer complaint hotlines, but also complaint platforms run by the state[107], such as the central 12315 platform (12315.cn) and its local variants (e.g. Guangzhou's gz12345.gz.gov.cn or Shanghai's sh12345.gov.cn) (BUS21-09). On these platforms, customers can both complain about commercial transactions (投诉) and report legal violations of natural and legal persons (举报) (SAMR, 2021d).

Second, local society exerts pressure on companies in case they notice non-compliance incidents or see their rights violated. For example, one business representative described his enterprise's difficult relationship with local residents due to factory emissions (BUS19-10). The government had received complaints about his company despite his factories being compliant with emission limits (BUS19-10). He concluded from this incident that he needs to invest more efforts in communication with local actors about his measures to improve the situation (BUS19-10) – a sign that local residents actually have an influence on companies' compliance management[108].

Third, the media's reporting of non-compliance incidents compels companies to pay attention to compliance. Despite a lack of free press in China, which could suggest the media to only play a minor role in influencing compliance (Graafland and Zhang, 2014, p. 44), the interviews attest that the media, especially social media, has a strong influence on compliance (BUS21-02, BUS21-08, BUS21-10, BUS21-11, BUS21-24). One business representative even stated that her company is "subject to the media's supervision" ("受到媒体的监督", BUS21-02). Media outlets at times successfully uncover non-compliance incidents, e.g. regarding food safety (EXP19-04), which often trigger strong reactions by the public and ultimately raise businesses' costs for non-compliance incidents (EXP19-01, BUS19-17). Social

107 The installation of complaint websites is one element of the 'Internet plus Government Services' (互联网+政务服务) project, an initiative that forms part of the larger 'Internet Plus' strategy (Government of the People's Republic of China, 2017).

108 Based on the coopted state of Chinese civil society as a whole, it can be assumed that such actions by local civil society actors are only tolerated to the degree that they are not directed against the Party-state as a whole, e.g. questioning its legitimacy (Howell, 2015).

media platforms, such as WeChat and Weibo, play important roles in public outcries about non-compliance incidents, especially because of their rapid dissemination of news (BUS19-06, BUS19-14). In addition, such platforms provide consumers with opportunities to rate companies, products and services (e.g. restaurants) and bad ratings or comments can affect a company's business negatively (BUS19-20). One interviewee claimed that this impact is particularly strong for bigger and listed companies, since they receive more media attention in total (BUS19-15). Overall, the increasing pace of content generation and information distribution via social media seems to pose a challenge to companies' compliance management (BUS19-14). Because they fear reputational impacts and stricter enforcement due to uncovered legal violation, many firms immediately react to media reports, even when they do not refer to their own company (BUS21-02, BUS21-22). Responses include improving the issue that was detected in case of a non-compliance incident or learning from the mistakes of other companies (BUS21-08, BUS21-21). Yet, two interviewees also saw an opportunity in this increasing influence of the media, since (social) media can also serve as a channel to promote their companies (BUS19-10, BUS19-11).

Fourth, third-party enforcers influence compliance management. Both, bouncers[109] and chaperons[110] could be identified in the interview process. For instance, one interviewed third-party accounting service provider refused to wrongly report her client's income in government forms because the client wanted to continue to receive government subsidies (BUS19-16). Instead, the service provider turned the client down and that way acted as a gatekeeper for compliance (bouncer) (BUS19-16). In addition, a great variety of chaperons support companies in their compliance efforts, e.g. (international) professional accounting firms (EXP19-04, EXP19-04, EXP19-15, EXP21-04) and consultancies which check clients' business partner compliance (EXP19-10, EXP19-13). Through their monitoring and other services, they influence companies' compliance management.

With all these mechanisms in place, the social environment's role in the construction of compliance seems to have increased.

109 They refuse collaboration in case of legal violations (see Section 2.4.1.2 and Oded, 2013, p. 206f).

110 They monitor companies and possess compliance-related information (see Section 2.4.1.2 and Oded, 2013, p. 109f).

Economic environment

The economic environment impacts compliance in China on the macro-, meso- and micro-level, thereby mirroring the academic discourse. However, in detail, the intricacies of these influences diverge from the points that are raised in the academic literature.

On the macro-level, the findings from China resonate with the academic discourse to the extent that the economic climate affects compliance practices, i.e. a negative economic climate leads to less investments into compliance management. For instance, two compliance managers reported that their compliance department is short-staffed, but due to the overall economic outlook, especially in times of the COVID-19 pandemic, as well as their companies' economic difficulties, no new staff is being hired (BUS19-19, BUS21-05). Moreover, the expert interviews underscore the idea of compliance as a cost factor, especially for smaller companies in China (EXP10-05, EXP19-13, EXP21-01). But the business representatives also seemed to adhere to this kind of thinking, for example, when they made cost calculations in the compliance context (compliance investment versus avoided opportunity costs; BUS21-01), highlight managers' compliance dilemmas by juxtaposing compliance with profits (BUS19-01) or illustrated the company-internal conflicts between compliance departments and business units' operations (BUS19-16, BUS21-23). One interviewee even directly stated that because of the limited regulatory supervision in his sector and in light of the companies' current economic situation, his firm is not willing to invest in compliance (BUS21-21). The representatives from startups echoed this calculative thinking, when they described their businesses' pure focus on growth and high cost pressures in the early phase of founding the company, which, in consequence, led to less investments in compliance (BUS19-09, BUS19-20). Still, they also highlighted the opportunities and benefits they gained from paying more attention to compliance at a later point in time (e.g. better access to funding) (BUS19-09, BUS19-20).

The economic pressure seems to be particularly high for SMEs because they are caught in the middle of the Chinese economic transformation from the workbench of the world (low-price strategy) to an economy producing higher-quality, innovative, internationally competitive products and services (EXP19-12). One CEO of an SME illustrated this problem, when he described how, in order to stay competitive, his manufacturing company changed its strategy away from only selling products to providing additional innovative services (BUS19-11). He explained this transformation with increasing cost pressures, including for compliance, which do neither allow his company to compete on price with bigger enterprises, such as SOEs, nor with other SMEs, which violate regulations (BUS19-11). Another factor leading to increasing cost pressures are compliance-related requirements from foreign MNEs towards their supply chain partners in China (EXP19-13).

Yet, the interviews also illustrated that a positive economic climate is not an automatic guarantor of high levels of compliance. Interviewed experts see a cause of deficient compliance levels in China in the fast economic development after opening up: Because companies focused on short-term profit alone, they did not pay attention to compliance (EXP19-01, EXP19-05). Firms "did as they pleased" ("随意的态度") with regard to compliance (BUS21-16). According to one interviewee from a private equity firm, only when markets were regulated and supervised more strictly by the government, did businesses start to improve their compliance (BUS21-16).

Other business representatives from the insurance and automotive sector described the same trend: Enterprises' compliance management practices tend to improve with markets becoming more mature[111] (e.g. greater market size, higher number of competitors, increasing familiarity with products) (BUS19-03, BUS19-10, BUS21-13). Hence, a highly dynamic economic climate and immature markets appear to have negative impacts on compliance, especially due to laxer market supervision.

On the meso-level and in line with the academic discourse, the stock market is an important factor influencing compliance. According to the interviews, the prerequisites for being listed, including the listing process itself, as well as the requirements for companies after being listed (e.g. publication of environmental, social and corporate governance reports) foster compliance awareness and practices (BUS19-05, BUS19-15, BUS21-01, BUS21-02, EXP19-11, EXP19-12). In addition, listed companies face stricter supervision, both from authorities and controlling shareholders (BUS21-09, BUS21-19). Nevertheless, fraud is apparently not always uncovered and therefore compliance mechanisms still need to be improved (BUS19-14, BUS19-16).

111 Yet, even though compliance-related practices improve, this does not automatically mean that fewer non-compliance incidents are detected at these companies as compliance practices can but do not always automatically protect against non-compliant behavior.

Similarly, the Chinese case also underpins previous findings regarding the business-to-business relationships' conduciveness to compliance. For instance, foreign MNEs that collaborate with or have a significant share in the ownership of domestic companies have apparently introduced the concept and the importance of compliance to these companies (BUS19-01, BUS21-19, BUS21-22). Other examples from the interviews are SOEs in the same industry conducting compliance trainings for smaller firms, shareholding companies providing compliance suggestions and private companies sharing their best practices proactively with others (BUS21-06, BUS21-09, BUS21-20). Furthermore, exchange on compliance is fostered by professional networks, e.g. via seminars, workshops and events with compliance experts (BUS21-05, BUS21-25). They are organized by industry associations, consulting companies or even the World Bank (BUS21-06, BUS21-15, BUS21-22). Beyond these formal events, informal exchanges within the networks occur via WeChat groups, compliance employees changing their employer and former colleagues informally discussing this topic (BUS21-19, BUS21-23, BUS21-25).

The findings from the interviews also show the influences of competition and industry concentration on compliance. Interviewees described higher levels of competition caused by increasing industry concentration as triggers for improvements in companies' compliance practices because of stricter supervision by authorities (BUS19-03, BUS21-16). An important reason for this effect is the fact that competitors do not only seem to pressure each other into adopting a greater consciousness on compliance by setting higher standards, but they also collaborate in the context of compliance. For instance, Siemens was not only mentioned as a best-in-class compliance example in interviews, but the company's extensive collaborative efforts to improve the compliance levels within its industry and China as a whole were highlighted (BUS19-01, BUS21-22). In addition, an interviewee from a tech firm described an alliance for integrity among big internet firms has formed (BUS21-04). This alliance does not only exchange on compliance practices, but also shares information on blacklisted employees, i.e. staff that has violated regulations and was therefore dismissed (BUS21-04). Such close collaboration between competitors with regard to compliance has not yet been mentioned by the existing compliance literature.

Another aspect impacting compliance in China that could not be found in the existing academic discourse, is the strategic importance of an industry for the national economy and society. Sectors of high strategic importance are regulated and monitored with much greater rigor (e.g. financial sector) because they pose a higher systemic risk (BUS21-02, BUS21-03, BUS21-13, EXP19-08, EXP21-01, EXP21-04). This does not only pertain to the regulation and enforcement in the sectors as a whole, but also to specific topics, e.g. data protection, which is regulated much stricter in sectors of high strategic significance compared to others (EXP19-05). High levels of regulation and enforcement, in turn, require bigger investments in compliance by the companies in the sector. Hence, the strategic importance of a sector influences the manifestation of compliance management by firms operating therein.

On the micro-economic level, this research identified additional influencing factors to those mentioned in the existing literature: The types of products or services offered by a company as well as employee turnover affect businesses' compliance, e.g. a lower employee turnover, is generally conducive to compliance (BUS19-13, BUS19-14, BUS21-25). Moreover, a firm's location also plays a role, since the strictness of regulations and enforcement rigor vary across the country (BUS19-11). Specifically, more developed regions in China (e.g. on the east coast) tend to apply a higher level of rigor compared to regions with a lower development status (e.g. provinces located in the west of China) (BUS19-11). Lastly, the pace of change in a sector and the companies' level of adaptiveness affect compliance (BUS21-06). For example, in the internet sector, both technology and regulations are changing comparatively quickly and influence how companies practice compliance, by providing entirely new opportunities for detecting incidents with the help of big data (BUS21-06).

Overall, this discussion shows that the economic environment in China significantly influences the way compliance is constructed and practiced.

Political environment

From the interviews, three main factors in the political environment in China that affect compliance can be gleaned. First, there is a strong political will to implement rules-based systems across society. While corruption and enforcement problems still allow non-compliant actors to benefit, the government is attempting to improve its rules-based governance approach (EXP19-12). Among others, the government also targets the bureaucratic apparatus with its measures in order to gain credibility in its efforts (EXP19-06, EXP19-05). For instance, officials' compensation is linked to policy implementation success and the anti-corruption campaign turns corruption into a high-risk behavior for officials (EXP19-06, EXP19-05). In addition, businesses are involved in the supervision of the bureaucracy via opinion seeking systems, where they can complain about the practices of authorities, for instance during inspections (BUS21-22). This effort to institutionalize rules-based governance has also spread to the state-business relationship, where the idea of compliance as a red-line has gained in importance (EXP19-06, EXP21-01). Yet, the fact that the Party stands above the law means that a certain level of ambiguity and arbitrariness exists in the government's governance approach, e.g. in decisions on priority topics and the adoption of campaign-style enforcement approaches (EXP19-01, EXP19-06).

Second, differences between regions within China persist. Due to the different development status across different regions, the political focus stills differs (EXP19-08). For example, in western provinces with lower levels of economic development, the focus remains on economic development, whereas politicians in eastern highly developed provinces pay more attention to compliance-related topics (EXP19-08, EXP19-11). While some businesses regard these regional variances as unfair, a Chinese expert explained the inevitability of differences in strictness in which regulatory and enforcement mechanisms are applied based on the diverging necessities in different regions (BUS19-11, EXP19-14).

Third, the government aims to improve the Chinese business environment both for domestic firms and in order to attract international enterprises (BUS21-11). One key goal in this context is to increase firms' convenience in administrative procedures, e.g. via a one-stop-shop approach (EXP19-06, EXP19-09). The reform 'Run at Most Once' (最多跑一次) in the context of the 'Internet Plus' strategy ('Internet plus Government Services') aims to make it possible for businesses to handle all their administrative issues (e.g. diverse approvals) at one window ("一窗受理") in administrative service centers (行政服务中心) or convenience centers (便民中心) (Zhejiang Daily, 2018, EXP19-06, EXP19-09). For such reforms to be successful, data silos between different authorities involved in the process need to be torn down. However, this turns out to be a difficult endeavor due to power struggles and a lack of trust between involved authorities (EXP19-06). Therefore, these reforms are still ongoing.

All these factors affect companies' and their compliance management in different ways, both by restraining them and providing opportunities.

Nevertheless, regardless of the consequences for the individual business, these measures and the compliance-related repercussions seem to enjoy legitimacy in the business community: When asked about the reasonability of the government's actions related to compliance, interviewees provided logical reasoning for the measures' adequacy[112]. For instance, business representatives explained stricter government measures that may be unfavorable for their own companies with the bigger picture, e.g. the need for market stability in their industry, avoiding systemic risks or even the overarching national economic strategy, for which individual economic actors need to make sacrifices (BUS19-03, BUS19-13, BUS19-18). In addition, interviewees argued that the government's actions have a protective function for businesses and society as a whole, because the political leadership takes actions against wrongdoings and closes loopholes, which certain actors had been taking advantage of at the expense of others (BUS19-18, BUS19-14). One interviewee even compared the government to a mother who tells her children (i.e. businesses) what to do (EXP19-04).

Still, the ambiguity and arbitrariness inherent in the authoritarian political system contributes a certain degree of nervousness or even fear (BUS19-01, EXP19-01). This is especially the case in the international business community and results in preemptive obedience, i.e. stricter compliance measures taken by companies than the regulations would actually necessitate (BUS19-01, EXP19-01). Hence, in China, not only the political legitimacy of compliance-related measures, but also systemic ambiguity influence compliance in a positive manner.

4.4.1.2 Regulation and enforcement

Regulation

The phenomenon of increasing amounts of regulations described by scholars of regulatory capitalism for modern capitalist economies (see Section

112 None of the interviewees openly criticized the government or labeled its measures as unreasonable. This could be a consequence of the interviewees' fear of discussing politically sensitive opinions, especially in an online setting. Therefore, it cannot be concluded from the data that all government actions with regard to compliance are fully supported by the business community. However, the detailed explanations provided by some interviewees for their government support at least intimate a certain level of legitimacy.

3.2 and Levi-Faur, 2005) can also be observed in China: While the total amount of regulations in China is difficult to determine, the amount of regulations[113] released by the central authorities annually shows a steep increase starting from the mid-2000s (see Figure 19) (Peking University, 2021).

This trend is also reflected in the interviews. Interviewees consistently described that in the early 2000s, businesses were regulated rather loosely, which resulted in fraud and scandals (e.g. the Lantian stock fraud[114]) (BUS21-01, EXP19-16). Since the mid-2000s, however, the interviewees have witnessed an increase in the amount and strictness of regulations (BUS19-01, BUS19-02, BUS19-03, BUS19-05, BUS19-10, BUS19-11, BUS19-13, BUS19-14, BUS19-15, BUS19-18, BUS21-08, BUS21-13, BUS21-19, EXP19-04, EXP19-08, EXP19-10, EXP19-12, EXP19-15). One expert explained this phenomenon with a strengthening of rule-based management within the government, which automatically affected the way the government regulates enterprises (EXP19-06).

Figure 19: Amount of regulations released by central authorities in China annually according to PKU Law (Peking University, 2021)

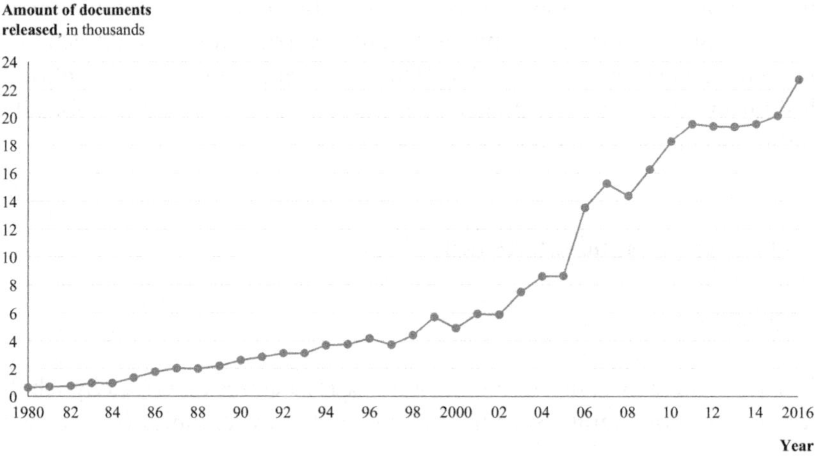

113 Regulations in this context include laws (法律), administrative regulations (行政法规), judicial interpretations (司法解释), departmental rules (部门规章), military regulations (军事法规规章), Party regulations (党内法规制度), industry regulations (行业规定) and group provisions (团体规定) (Peking University, 2021).

114 Lantian Stock was involved in misreporting and accounting fraud. For further details, see Lau et al. (2009).

Simultaneously, the interviews have identified a broad range of regulators. On the one hand, a multitude of traditional Party-state institutions are involved in the regulatory process:

- Central agencies on the ministry level such as the PBoC, the MIIT, the SAMR, the CSRC, the General Administration of Customs (GAC, 海关总署), etc., as well as their local branches (e.g. BUS21-01, BUS21-02, BUS21-04, BUS21-05, BUS21-08, BUS21-10, BUS21-11, BUS21-18, BUS21-19, BUS21-25, EXP21-01);
- Local governments and their agencies (e.g. BUS19-11, BUS19-18, BUS21-04, BUS21-15, BUS21-16, EXP19-14);
- The SASAC and its local branches (e.g. BUS19-10, BUS21-15, BUS21-24, EXP21-04);
- The CCDI (e.g. BUS19-10, BUS21-07).

Due to the many regulatory actors involved, the supervision process was described as scattered (BUS21-05).

On the other hand, new actors have joined the ranks of regulators; both actors directly associated with the Party-state and players outside of the Party-state. Actors associated with the Party-state are, for instance, the stock exchanges and industry associations, which are supposed to function as self-regulatory organizations (e.g. BUS19-20, BUS21-01, BUS21-02, BUS21-10, BUS21-13, BUS21-16, BUS21-23, EXP21-01). But SOEs also possess a regulatory capacity, e.g. when they require their business partners to fulfill certain requirements as prerequisites for collaboration (BUS19-04). In a similar manner, both business partners in general and international supply chain partners in particular act as regulators (e.g. BUS19-08, BUS19-11, EXP19-05, EXP19-08, EXP19-12). Furthermore, international regulators active in China are international investors and foreign MNEs with Joint Ventures (JVs) or affiliated firms in China (e.g. BUS19-10, BUS21-19, BUS21-24, EXP19-11, EXP19-13), international standardization organizations, such as ISO (e.g. BUS21-22, EXP21-01), regulators in other nations where Chinese firms are active (EXP19-08) as well as international organizations (e.g. the World Bank) and consultancies who not only advise businesses, but also the government in China (e.g. BUS21-07, BUS21-22, EXP21-01). In addition, domestic investors, shareholders as well as compliance auditors and advisers act in this capacity (BUS19-02, BUS19-05, EXP19-08, BUS19-14, BUS21-08, BUS21-19, EXP19-10, EXP19-13). Lastly, the interviews reflect what the official discourse on compliance suggests, namely that society takes on the role of a regulator (BUS19-10, EXP19-05). Not only do customers use means, such as company ratings on social media platforms or complaint platforms, to regulate businesses (BUS19-06, BUS21-08, BUS21-09, BUS21-11, GOV19-02), business are also subject to regulation and supervision by the media ("受到媒体的监督", BUS21-02), e.g. they identify non-compliance incidents and create transparency about compliance (BUS19-20, BUS21-11, BUS21-12, BUS21-24). Overall, this shows that the spectrum of regulators both directly affiliated with and outside the Party-state in China is rather broad, a development that regulatory capitalism also describes (see Section 3.2 and Levi-Faur, 2005). Both the greater number of regulators and regulations result in high complexity for regulatees in their compliance-related efforts, which potentially translates into higher costs (EXP19-04, EXP19-15).

The costs caused by regulations, however, not only depend on the number of regulators involved or the absolute amount of guidelines, but also their characteristics, specifically the degree of leeway regulations provide companies during implementation. In this regard, the interviews show that the nature of regulations varies between industries and topics (BUS19-03, BUS19-16, EXP19-01, EXP19-04). In some areas, interviewees described regulations that only provide vague and broad principles (e.g. interviewees from manufacturing businesses), whereas in others the regulations prescribe businesses' actions in a very detailed fashion (e.g. in the insurance industry) (BUS19-03, BUS19-07, BUS21-05). Especially in the financial sector and regarding corporate governance, Chinese authorities seem to be more prescriptive in their regulations compared to other regions such as the EU and the US (EXP19-04). Hence, business representatives complained about regulatory strictness causing efficiency losses in their business operations, which at times may be avoided in the US thanks to the stronger market-orientation (BUS19-02, BUS19-03, BUS19-18). In cases where the authorities only provide principles, one interviewee also explained, that the industry associations step in and provide more detailed guidance on the implementation of stated principles (BUS21-07). In yet other fields, companies even rely entirely on international regulations to set up their compliance management as a basis for cooperation with other companies because China's regulation in these areas is still underdeveloped (e.g. maritime law, crypto-currencies) (BUS19-16, BUS21-03).

Another important aspect to consider with regard to compliance costs is changes in regulations. Interviewees stated that they bear a high risk related to changes in regulations, as such modifications are often hard to predict and require the company to update its entire compliance management system (e.g. updating equipment to meet new standards) (BUS19-12, BUS21-06, BUS21-16, BUS21-21, BUS21-22). The amount and intensity of regulatory fluctuations appear to be related to the maturity of the market or field being regulated: In some sectors, interviewees reported rather stable regulations with adaptions every three to ten years (e.g. pharmaceutical sector) (BUS19-04, BUS19-16, BUS21-16), whereas constant changes in regulations are reported in other sectors, such as the internet and the securities industries, or new business fields such as data protection and peer-to-peer lending (e.g. BUS19-14, BUS19-15, BUS19-17, BUS21-06, EXP19-04).

The interviewees explained these fluctuations on the one hand by referencing market volatility and authorities' reaction to it (BUS19-03, BUS19-18, BUS21-08). On the other hand, the changes were also interpreted as the authorities' learning processes with regard to regulation: The Party-state's knowledge and capacities to regulate and supervise evolves along with an industry's development and the strictness of regulations levels out at a reasonable degree over time (BUS19-02, BUS19-15). Requirements that were originally hazy become updated and are increasingly standardized (BUS19-03, BUS21-10, BUS21-21). An important channel through which authorities improve their regulatory capacity are international influences: Chinese regulators learn from their counterparts in countries with more mature markets, such as the US, and base domestic rules on international regulations (e.g. Basel 2 and 3 in the financial sector) (BUS21-07, BUS21-10, EXP19-04). However, with improved regulatory capacities, Chinese regulators no longer directly adopt international practices. Instead, China has started to set its own standards and even shape the way international standards are set (EXP19-04, Weithmann, 2018). An example for China-specific standards is data protection, where China does not simply copy the EU's regulations, but develops its own based on local conditions, namely the need to exempt the state from data protection for the purpose of national security (EXP19-05, Zhao and Feng, 2021, p. 4f). An area, where China has started to proactively influence international standard setting, is, for instance, in technical requirements for electric vehicles (Weithmann, 2018, p. 333ff).

The incremental improvement process in regulations not only affects compliance costs, but also has businesses gradually improve their compliance management, i.e. learning compliance from the rules that are released (BUS21-08, BUS21-10, EXP21-01). One business representative, for instance, described how he learned about the negative effects of bribery only via related regulations and enforcement actions, because before he had regarded bribery as a common, acceptable practice (BUS19-15). In addition, Chinese firms learn and adapt their compliance management to the requirements they face as business partners to international companies and when operating abroad (BUS21-22, PO21-ON). In cases where Chinese regulations are not yet well developed, Chinese firms also study the regulations in other countries directly and build their operating model on that basis, for example in the case of crypto-currencies (BUS21-03).

On this journey of regulatory learning, the interactions between state and businesses have a significant influence. Concretely, they contribute to the managerialization of law, the legalization of organizations and the flow of organizational and management logic into the regulatory field (concepts proposed by Edelman, 2007) via three types of interactions. First, the authorities actively involve businesses in the drafting process of regulations to ensure support for proposed rules. The authorities invite selected firm representatives, consultants (e.g. from law and accounting firms) and other experts to support the drafting process of regulations via expert committees (BUS19-03, BUS19-10, BUS21-02, BUS21-10, BUS21-23, EXP21-01). Especially for regulations that address entirely new topics, the authorities rely on advice from these types of panels (BUS19-17, BUS21-04, BUS21-18)[115]. While this kind of influence on regulations is limited to selected experts, often from big and state-owned enterprises (BUS19-02, BUS21-01, BUS21-23, EXP19-04), every company gets the chance to provide feedback in the so-called 'opinion seeking' phase (征求意见) (BUS19-15, BUS21-02, BUS21-07, BUS21-08, BUS21-19, BUS21-22, BUS21-23, BUS21-25, EXP21-01). Business representatives see this as a good opportunity to influence regulations and trust in the approach, particularly because the process is transparent: The authorities consolidate the feedback and respond to it (BUS21-08, BUS21-10). One interviewee has even seen his firm's suggestions be implemented in final regulations several times (BUS21-08). Overall, this process can not only improve the content of regulations, but also contributes to the managerialization of regulations and the flow of management logic into the legal sphere, because feedback from businesses is, by nature, rooted in managerial thinking.

Second, businesses and authorities interact in the implementation process after regulations are passed. While many company representatives stated that regulations are generally very clear, especially when they are pre-

115 For further details on how companies lobby for their interests, especially in technology-intensive industries, refer to Lüdtke (2017).

scriptive (BUS19-14, BUS21-01, BUS21-02, BUS21-04, BUS21-06, BUS21-11, BUS21-12, BUS21-13, BUS21-15, BUS21-21, BUS21-25), they also explained that they consult the responsible authorities in case they have questions about specific rules (BUS19-07, BUS21-01, BUS21-06, BUS21-07, BUS21-23). Especially in areas which are newly regulated, more interaction with the authorities is necessary to understand desired behavior and where there is leeway for businesses in implementation (BUS21-10, BUS21-22). Despite the opportunities that vague rules can provide, companies seem to prefer concrete guidelines and standards, because they help ensure compliance more easily (BUS19-07, BUS21-10, EXP19-05). The fact, that interviewees regarded regulatory criteria as sufficiently clear in many fields (e.g. provision for air pressure in certain manufacturing processes, standards for electric vehicle batteries or investment proportions for funds), intimates that the interaction and negotiation processes between the two sides result in mutual influences, i.e. the managerialization of law and the legalization of business organizations (BUS19-10, BUS19-12, BUS21-08).

Third, authorities and enterprises mutually influence each other regarding the long-term regulatory direction. Business representatives explained that they regularly interact with authorities that supervise them and use this channel to provide feedback on regulations (BUS21-06). While changes in regulations after their release are much harder to achieve, businesses can still report problems they face in their compliance efforts (BUS21-08). In cases where many companies report similar issues, the government may react (BUS21-08). Especially the fact, that many regulations are passed as pilots initially, leaves the door open for regulatory updates (EXP19-04). Additionally, some businesses are invited to meetings with authorities to discuss a broad range of topics (BUS21-07, BUS21-16). These meetings are not dedicated to regulatory discussions, but nevertheless serve as a platform to voice improvement suggestions for regulations (BUS21-07, BUS21-16).

All these state-business interactions support Edelman's (2007) conception of the endogeneity of the law and the mutual influences between the legal and the organizational realm. However, they also challenge the linearity of the process loop outlined by Edelman (2007): The various interaction points between the Party-state and enterprises discussed above show on the one hand, that mutual influences between the two realms are not limited to the moments, when businesses start to implement regulations and when they claim their rights. Instead, the interaction processes and thereby the mutual influences between the two realms happen constantly. On the other hand, the Chinese case shows that the legalization of organization and the flow of organizational and management logic into the regulatory field are not only by-products of compliance-related interactions, but also result from proactive negotiation processes between the regulators and regulatees.

Enforcement

The interviews show that all categories of enforcement instruments described in the academic literature (legal, communicative, economic and network instruments) are adopted in the regulation of enterprises in China. Yet, some of the instruments described by interviewees nevertheless shape the construction of compliance in China in a distinctive fashion.

Traditional legal instruments are clearly laid down in regulations and are consequently predictable for companies (BUS19-03, BUS21-14). For example, one CEO described in detail the different levels of administrative and political (via the Party's disciplinary system) warnings and punishments (BUS19-10). The most commonly adopted legal instruments in China are warnings, official notices for offenses and, in cases where companies commit serious violations or do not improve, different types of punishments (BUS10-01, BUS19-03, BUS19-10, BUS19-13, BUS19-18, BUS21-07, BUS21-10, BUS21–16, BUS21-25). One of the most common punishments are fines (BUS19-03, BUS19-07, BUS19-09, BUS19-10, BUS19-11, BUS19-14, BUS19-18, BUS21-15, BUS21-17, BUS21-20, BUS21-21, BUS21-23, EXP19-16). Some companies even have to pay fines every year because the requirements for factories have changed and they have no means to upgrade their factories to meet these changed standards (BUS19-12).

But despite the financial losses that fines cause, companies seem to fear other punishments more. Several business representatives worry about restrictions to their business operations: This can be in the form of a temporary withdrawal of a license, a ban from certain business fields, the closing of selected factories or, in the worst case, the shutdown of a company for good (BUS19-03, BUS19-07, BUS19-14, BUS19-15, BUS19-18, BUS21-10, BUS21-20, BUS21-21, EXP19-11, EXP19-16). Another legal instrument that deters companies from non-compliance incidents is the restriction from going public or the delisting of companies that are not operating in full compliance (BUS19-05, BUS19-14, EXP19-05, EXP19-12). While previously only financial criteria were considered in Initial Public Offer (IPO) decisions, the set of criteria has been broadened to also include other compliance-areas, such as environmental protection (EXP19-12).

A noteworthy aspect in the legal enforcement instruments adopted by authorities, which motivates businesses to ensure compliance, is that punishments do not only target companies, but also individuals (e.g. legal representatives, managers) (e.g. BUS21-16, BUS21-20). In case of non-compliance incidents, responsible individuals may be punished with individual fines, (temporary) bans from the industry, the withdrawal of their personal qualification license for their position or industry and in the worst case imprisonment (BUS19-10, BUS19-11, BUS19-14, BUS19-15, EXP19-10, EXP19-12, EXP19-16). This connection between consequences for the business and its managers has more recently been further reinforced by the SCS, as detailed in Chapter 5.

Another deterrent that is strengthened by the SCS (and discussed in depth in Chapter 5) is the negative impact of non-compliance incidents on business ratings (BUS21-20). One business representative that has experienced a drop of his company's rating saw this as one of the most problematic punishments a company can face, because low ratings or the appearance on blacklists (for enterprises with a deficient compliance record) affect future business operations negatively (BUS21-20, EXP19-12). For instance, negative ratings restrict bidding for government tenders, turn away potential customers and business partners and increase the difficulties to access loans or government subsidies (BUS19-10, BUS21-17, GOV19-01).

While these two mechanisms, the restrictions due to bad ratings and the connected enforcement between firms and responsible individuals are not entirely new legal instruments per se, they do play a distinctive role for compliance and its enforcement in China. Specifically, they enhance existing enforcement instruments and trigger new motives for compliance (see the discussion on motives in Section 4.4.2.2). In addition, they foster the perception of increasingly strict and comprehensive enforcement, which shapes the social practices of compliance, e.g. by evoking reflection on compliance practices and more preventative compliance approaches (BUS19-19, BUS21-20).

With regard to communicative instruments, interviewees mention a variety of common mechanisms adopted by authorities: First, compliance-related trainings, conferences and meetings are used as a way to teach businesses about compliance practices and details on specific regulations, as well as to foster exchange between professionals (BUS19-03, BUS19-06, BUS19-07, BUS19-13, BUS19-14, BUS19-17, BUS21-07, BUS21-02, BUS21-10, BUS21-23, BUS21-25, EXP19-04, EXP19-12). Through such events and the release of regulations requiring certain compliance management practices (e.g. by the SASAC in 2018), the Party-state is propagating the concept of compliance in business communities, but also society as a whole (EXP19-08, EXP19-14, EXP21-04). In addition, other regulators such as industry associations, NGOs, consultancies and foreign MNEs promote compliance best practices (BUS19-01, BUS21-07, BUS21-13, BUS21-20, EXP19-12).

Second, the authorities provide businesses with explanations about new policies and regulations, e.g. written announcements on the release of new rules or details on their implementation (BUS19-06, BUS19-07, BUS19-11, BUS19-18, BUS21-16, BUS21-20, BUS21-23, BUS21-25, EXP19-04). This kind of information is supposed to support companies in their efforts to comply with new regulations. The authorities also appear to give enterprises time to implement certain new regulations, e.g. by excluding the new requirements in their onsite inspections for a certain amount of time after they are passed (BUS21-25).

Third, the regular contact between firms and authorities supports businesses in learning about compliance. Business representatives explained that they regularly consult their contact persons in relevant authorities to clarify questions about regulations (BUS19-17, BUS19-18, BUS21-01, BUS21-04, BUS21-05 BUS21-07, BUS21-10, BUS21-19, BUS21-25). Furthermore, when the authorities were not satisfied with certain aspects in the businesses' operations, they would give them the chance and guidance to improve before imposing punishments (BUS19-11, BUS21-08, BUS21-17, BUS21-18, BUS21-21, BUS21-23). These types of exchanges in the process of implementing regulations ultimately contribute to companies' education on expected compliance practices. Hence, learning by doing has been a common practice that has improved firms' compliance management in China (BUS21-11, BUS21-12).

Fourth, the authorities indirectly foster businesses' compliance capacities by formulating qualification requirements for certain industries and positions (BUS19-11, BUS19-13, BUS21-08, BUS21-10). For example, one CEO of an SME described that, as the legal representative of his company, he has to attend regular trainings organized by the authorities (e.g. about safety, environmental protection) and pass exams to keep his operations certified, a prerequisite for doing business (BUS19-11). In addition, certain industries, such as the securities sector, require professionals to pass a qualification test before individuals can work in the industry (BUS19-13, BUS19-14). While this is not a new communicative instrument, in certain areas in China, the measure is taken to new extremes, by allowing authorities to become involved in staffing decisions for compliance officers (e.g. the securities sector, see Section 6.1.3).

With respect to the economic instruments adopted in the Chinese business context, the interviews only provide limited insights. There are three likely reasons for this. First, interviewees may think of financial incentives in the context of compliance less often, since most understand the concept of compliance as a prerequisite for operations (as described in Section 4.3). In other words, in a context where compliance is not dominantly constructed as an opportunity, but rather a means to mitigate risks, economic opportunities may not be present in the interviewees' minds. Second, knowledge on subsidies and other financial incentives may not be as widespread, especially across smaller companies, as one expert from an industry association reported (EXP21-05). Third, the government may simply not use economic instruments as frequently as other means for enforcement.

Nevertheless, a few interviewees described government subsidies, government tenders and the cooperation with SOEs, i.e. economic enforcement instruments (BUS19-04, BUS19-20, EXP19-12, GOV19-01). The general approach is always the same: If a company wants to obtain access to these opportunities, it needs to fulfill certain requirements. For instance, government subsidies and loans for SMEs are tied to compliance in business operations (BUS19-20). In order for small companies to achieve the required level of compliance, local governments may even subsidize legal trainings and services, because the authorities are aware of the financial pressure these firms are exposed to (GOV19-01). In the case of government tenders and SOE cooperation, there are also certain red-lines with regard to compliance that companies cannot cross (e.g. being blacklisted) (see Chapter 5). Firms that meet these minimal requirements used to compete for a tender in areas such as pricing and product/service quality. More recently, companies' compliance and integrity management practices beyond the legal bottom line have become new areas of competition in this context (BUS19-04). While the interviews do not show that compliance is predominantly constructed as a competitive advantage (see Section 4.3 and Section 4.4.2), this phenomenon has the potential to contribute to a change in enterprises' compliance understanding over time. This is especially likely, since consultancies promote this notion of compliance in their events (PO19-BJ).

Lastly, Chinese authorities adopt various network instruments to ensure compliance. Traditional means to achieve transparency on business operations, such as business performance and compliance reports, come into effect (BUS19-18, BUS21-01, BUS21-02, BUS21-04, BUS21-07, BUS21-09, BUS21-10, BUS21-15, BUS21-19, EXP19-09). At times, the information is self-reported, at times external reviewers either from the authorities or third-party auditors (e.g. accounting or consulting firms) collect the data (BUS21-13, BUS21-19, EXP21-01). A certain amount of the collected information is then shared with the public, for instance, via communication channels from the authorities and SCS platforms. The latter do not only provide general business information, but also black- and redlists[116] as well as ratings (e.g. BUS19-15, BUS21-08, BUS21-09, BUS21-11). Hence, publicly available business-related information has increased, become more easily accessible and moved from being descriptive to more evaluative. With regard to the official communication on corporate compliance levels, businesses have also noticed the increase in naming-and-shaming activities, as described in Section 4.3. They described, for example, that both non-compliance incidents, as well as punishments are published by the authorities (BUS19-03, BUS21-07, BUS21-10). This awareness intimates that such publications actually impact firms and their decision-making and that the societal supervision, which the government aims to promote, is working.

The interviews reveal two more mechanisms of societal supervision. First, interviewees elaborated on the extensive use of customer complaint mechanisms to both identify businesses' non-compliance incidents and collectively shame them (BUS21-07, BUS21-09 BUS21-11, BUS21-13, BUS21-14, BUS21-15, BUS21-22). Not only the firms themselves, but also various authorities have implemented customer complaint platforms which collect and at times publish customer complaints online (e.g. local 12345-websites inspired by the complaint hotline '12345'). For this reason, business representatives in customer-facing industries reported a high attentiveness to customer complaints and high motivation for compliance (see also Section 4.4.2) (BUS21-07, BUS21-09 BUS21-11, BUS21-13, BUS21-14, BUS21-15, BUS21-22). While customer complaints are a common phenomenon in business management, the instrumentalization for regulatory enforcement in the Chinese case has not been addressed in the compliance literature. This approach can be understood as an attempt to create a functional equivalent for the role that free press and civil society play in the compliance context of democratic systems.

116 Blacklisted companies are listed due to blameworthy behavior, redlisted companies are listed because they acted praiseworthily.

Second, interviewees described monitoring-mechanisms between businesses (e.g. BUS19-03, BUS19-04, BUS21-11, BUS21-16). It is no longer only foreign MNEs that monitor their Chinese supply chain partners' compliance due to pressure from customers in their home country. Instead, all types of companies operating in China use the increased transparency to select and monitor their business partners (e.g. BUS19-03, BUS19-04, BUS21-11, BUS21-15, BUS21-16; for more details, refer to Chapter 5). This can go as far as SOEs requiring their business partners to sign compliance commitments and to check the adherence to these promises (BUS19-04).

One key block upon which the above described network instruments are built is the excessive use of technology in enforcement. In the context of the 'Internet Plus' strategy, authorities have already developed a number of tools to benefit from technology in their enforcement practices. For instance, authorities have implemented real-time emission monitoring in factories with color-coded ratings that are published online (BUS19-10, BUS19-11, BUS21-21, EXP19-09, EXP19-11, EXP19-12). But Party-state agencies have also installed other equipment for live-monitoring; for example, a representative from an SME mentioned that the authorities set up cameras in his factories to oversee compliance with safety regulations (BUS19-12). In addition, the CSRC has direct access to certain elements of securities firms' IT-systems to monitor their actions in real-time (BUS21-01, BUS21-20). Beyond live-monitoring, authorities also use technology in their post-event compliance checks. The tax authorities' new IT-system to control the authenticity of invoices, which was set up in the context of the 'Golden Tax Project' (金税工程)[117], seems to leave businesses significantly less leeway for fraud (BUS19-01, EXP19-12, EXP19-16). Overall though, in the context of adopting technology for enforcement, the SCS constitutes the biggest government endeavor, since the system serves as an overarching instrument that connects all other efforts, as discussed in Section 5.2.4.

The above elaborations show that companies in China face smart regulation as an enforcement approach: Regulators, both within (e.g. government officials, bureaucrats) and outside of the Party-state (e.g. business partners and consumers), adopt the broad mix of enforcement instruments that are escalated in accordance with the situation. Consequently, businesses face a

117 The 'Golden Tax Project' aims to adopt information technologies to improve tax compliance in China. The third phase of the project started in 2009 and included the creation of a value-added tax invoice system, which uses artificial intelligence to monitor value-added tax invoice compliance (Liu and Chen, 2020).

high level of complexity in managing a broad set of stakeholders and adhering to all the regulatory requirements. In this context, technology plays a central role. On the one hand, the set-up of the SCS allows the Party-state to increasingly act as a facilitator in the supervision and enforcement process. On the other hand, the transparency gained via SCS mechanisms mitigates complexity in business transactions to a certain extent.

Despite the increasing facilitation role in enforcement, the Party-state still gets involved directly in supervision and enforcement via inspections[118]. In this context, the interviewees paint a picture that mirrors the contradictions which need to be bridged for successful enforcement as previously identified in the academic discourse: Discretion versus formalism, dialogue versus sanctions and relationship versus distance. Indeed, the Chinese regulators appear to be moving away from a discretionary, dialogue-focused and relationship-based inspection system. Specifically, interviewees agreed that overall inspections have become more rigorous, e.g. in their frequency and strictness (BUS19-04, BUS19-10, BUS19-11, BUS19-14, BUS19-17, BUS19-19, BUS21-07, BUS21-08, BUS21-12, BUS21-13, BUS21-16, BUS21-19, BUS21-20, BUS21-22, EXP19-10, EXP19-13, EXP19-16). They consistently listed four types of inspections they face: Regular announced on-site inspections, regular remote inspections via IT-systems or the revision of materials provided by the business, event-based on-site or remote inspections, and unannounced on-site inspections (e.g. BUS19-10, BUS21-10, BUS21-15, BUS21-16, BUS21-17, BUS21-23, BUS21-25).

Regular, announced on-site inspections vary in frequency depending on the industry as well as the size and type of a company. For example, non-compliance incidents in certain sectors, such as the finance, food or pharmaceutical sectors, pose a high risk for society as a whole and therefore companies in this sector are supervised more strictly (BUS19-03, BUS21-02, BUS21-15, EXP19-08, EXP21-04). Moreover, experts and business representatives had the impression that larger-sized companies and SOEs are inspected more frequently (BUS19-06, BUS19-20, BUS21-11, BUS21-19, PO20-ON). For instance, interviewees argued that SOEs face more inspections, because they face controls from the CCDI and other Party institutions in addition to those from state departments (BUS19-10, BUS19-13, BUS19-15, BUS21-14, BUS21-24). No matter whether this impression reflects the actual

118 The elaborations in this section focus on the inspection by authorities, whereas inspections by business partners and accounting firms are addressed in Section 4.5.2.

situation or not, it nevertheless constructs a narrative, in which larger companies, including SOEs, need to pay more attention to compliance.

Furthermore, business representatives described regular remote inspections as a common phenomenon (BUS19-07, BUS19-13, BUS19-18, BUS21-05, BUS21-10, BUS21-15, BUS21-22, BUS21-23, BUS21-25). Since this inspection mode is predictable, one business even considered this type of interaction with the authorities as helpful and necessary: The interviewee argued that regular remote inspections help them to identify problems early and avoid big regulatory infringements from happening (BUS21-08).

Next, event-based inspections refer to all types of inspection that are triggered by an incident. Interviewees consistently mentioned three types of triggers. First, inspectors visit them in case of major customer complaints (BUS21-07, BUS21-10, BUS21-11, BUS21-13, BUS21-15, BUS21-17). Second, a non-compliance incident in one company has authorities inspect similar firms (e.g. in the same sector) to ensure the same problem does not occur again; a type of campaign-style enforcement (BUS19-01, BUS21-06, BU21-07, BUS21-15, BUS21-18). One business representative described this mode as a continuous improvement process, where supervision becomes stricter after an incident, which then triggers changes in compliance management until the next incident (BUS21-13). Third, authorities inspect companies when the latter apply for certain benefits, such as government loans, subsidies or government tenders (BUS19-09, GOV19-01).

Lastly, authorities conduct unannounced on-site inspections in an increasingly randomized fashion (BUS19-11, BUS21-17, BUS21-19, BUS21-21, EXP19-10). For example, one consultant observed that his clients were now not only randomly inspected during regular working hours, but also at the weekends and during the night (EXP19-10). This high level of uncertainty in the authorities' enforcement approach has even made companies that are not regularly inspected vigilant about potential inspections (BUS19-02, BUS19-07, BUS19-19, BUS21-04, BUS21-06).

While the inspection frequency and unpredictability has increased, progress has also been made in the formalization of inspections: One expert pointed to the 'double random, one disclosure' inspection mechanism (双随机、一公开)[119], which was set up in an effort to prevent close guanxi

119 'Double random' refers to the random selection of the inspector and the company inspected, 'one disclosure' requires the open publication of inspection results (Economic Times, 2016). The implementation of this mechanism started in 2015 (Economic Times, 2016).

between inspectors and inspected enterprises (EXP19-07, Economic Times, 2016). In line with this, business representatives describe that they often do not know the inspectors and therefore can rely less on personal relationships than before (BUS19-07, BUS21-20). Moreover, when asked about leeway for negotiation in the context of inspections, several interviewees pointed to the strictness of the inspection, where they had to follow the instructions of the inspector and saw fewer opportunities for negotiation (BUS21-05, BUS21-11, BUS21-20). In addition, one interviewee explained that businesses can only have criticism by the authorities' inspections dropped if the companies can provide evidence that it is incorrect (BUS19-03).

In spite of these improvements regarding inspection frequency and strictness, the interviews nevertheless show that elements of discretion, relationships and dialogue persist. For instance, interviewees claim that despite becoming less relevant in the compliance context, guanxi is still an important element which prevents stringent enforcement (EXP19-10, GOV19-02). In addition, business representatives and experts described elements of negotiation in the inspection process (BUS19-13, BUS21-10, BUS21-22, BUS21-25, EXP19-10). One business representative shared that in his company, the management discusses the topics that come up during an inspection with the company's lawyers, who get in touch with the government to object to criticism and defend the firm (BUS21-22). Similarly, another interviewee explained that the final inspection report needs to be signed by the business and in this context adjustments can be discussed (BUS19-13). While the consequences of an unlawful action itself cannot be negotiated, because specific enforcement measures are prescribed for different legal infringements by regulations, the definition of an action is up for discussion (BUS21-10). Specifically, this business representative stated that his company can discuss with inspectors whether a non-compliant action was purposefully undertaken, how easily it could be mitigated, etc. (BUS21-10). Based on these criteria, the incident is then classified and consequences differ (BUS21-10). Therefore, negotiations on the classification can make a big difference. This description resonates with the phenomenon of embedded autonomy in the context of the regulatory state of the Global South, where negotiations on the substance of issues co-exist with adherence to procedural rules. As a result, compliance officers need soft skills (e.g. networking, negotiation and communication skills) in their interactions with the authorities, especially during inspections, where these skills can influence the rigor that inspectors apply (EXP19-04, EXP21-01).

The administration does not only continue to use its discretionary power with regard to inspections; more generally, the enforcement of consequences due to non-compliance incidents is also often not practiced consistently. Experts alluded to persisting loopholes for businesses at the same time as they mentioned improvements in enforcement (EXP19-12, EXP19-14, EXP19-16). Several interviews with business representatives support this evaluation. The CEO of an SOE, for instance, described an incident where his enterprise's factory emissions were too high and he called local authorities to get this emission data removed from the systems on the quiet, an illicit action (BUS19-10). Thereby, the negative record was not only removed from the government-internal databases, but also from the publicly accessible emissions website (BUS19-10). Moreover, interviewees elaborated on differences in the enforcement rigor based on locations (BUS19-10, BUS19-15, EXP19-08). Specifically, less developed regions that still mainly focus on economic growth at times do not enforce environmental and social regulations as strictly, because they fear negative economic consequences and unemployment in case of factory closures (EXP19-13). Finally, in one of the participant observations, the presenters claimed that authorities are more lenient with big companies, because these actors have established a certain level of trust and reputation as compared to smaller firms (PO20-ON). True or not, such narratives reinforce the notion that relationships play an important role in compliance management and discretion is still omnipresent. One business representative summarized the situation bluntly by stating that enforcement is political and if authorities want to find a problem, they will be able to (BUS19-16).

All in all, these elaborations nevertheless show that inspections, which used to be highly discretionary, dialogue- and relationship-based, are increasingly formalized. So far, this development has not yet led to fully formalized inspection and enforcement processes that could be executed from a distance. Consequently, businesses still have a certain level of leeway and flexibility with regard to compliance, especially when they possess a good reputation and sufficient guanxi. In such cases, creative compliance seems to be a reasonable path forward. Nevertheless, just as the ambiguity in regulations, the uncertainty surrounding inspection and enforcement campaigns has some companies taking preventative compliance measures to avoid risks. Hence, the external enforcement environment fosters contrasting compliance conceptions, one of formalism and creative compliance and one of substantive and preventative compliance.

4.4.2 Internal factors

4.4.2.1 Organizational capacities and characteristics

The interviews show that organizational capacities and characteristics affect the construction of compliance in companies in China. The identified topics are generally in line with the factors mentioned by the academic discourse on compliance. But similar to the manifestation of external influences in China, certain details nevertheless differ or further specify what has previously been found.

As the academic discourse posits, managerial capacity also affects compliance and compliance management in China. This, for example, manifests itself in those interviews that highlighted the importance of the tone from the top in compliance management (e.g. BUS19-01, BUS21-05, BUS21-10, BUS21-24). In addition, interviewees recognized the contribution of compliance management to the improvement of managerial capacities (e.g. professionalism, standardization, efficiency) (e.g. BUS21-01, BUS21-14, BUS21-16, BUS21-22). This shows that the influence of compliance management and managerial capacities is reciprocal and not just unidirectional.

With regard to compliance-related knowledge, interviewees considered legal and compliance management expertise paired with general management skills as important for success (BUS21-20, EXP19-10, EXP21-04). Overall, they saw an improvement in compliance staff's expertise over time: For instance, one interviewee described how, originally, positions in the compliance department were filled with staff from business units who were previously not familiar with compliance (BUS21-10). Today, the same company hires employees that are specialized in compliance directly (BUS21-10). Other business representatives added to this point by mentioning the appointment of highly experienced compliance staff as a means to acquire compliance-related know-how and improve their compliance management (BUS21-04, BUS21-06). In addition, a company's previous non-compliance incidents as well as those of other firms serve as learning opportunities to improve compliance-related knowledge (BUS19-01, BUS19-04, BUS19-09, BUS19-10, BUS19-14, BUS19-15, BUS21-05, BUS21-13, BUS21-16, BUS21-21, BUS21-25). Furthermore, in certain sectors the regulator prescribes qualification requirements for employees and compliance managers to ensure a certain level of knowledge (e.g. in the securities industry) (BUS19-13, BUS19-14).

Nevertheless, companies still face problems with regard to compliance-related knowledge. Experts criticized missing compliance capabilities despite companies having set up compliance management systems (EXP19-10, EXP21-04, EXP21-05). This resonates with compliance managers who complained about the absence of compliance knowledge and awareness among employees on top of missing staff in compliance departments (BUS19-04, BUS19-16, BUS21-05, BUS21-13). The compliance staff shortage is attributed to the lack of financial means on the one hand, and the difficulties in hiring compliance experts on the other[120] (BUS19-02, BUS21-04, BUS21-05, BUS21-13). Reasons for the difficulties mentioned are the location of the company, the limited amount of highly qualified professionals as well as the attractiveness of the company as an employer (e.g. salary, size) (BUS19-02, BUS21-01, BUS21-04, BUS21-13). Some companies compensate for this problem with hiring professional service companies, such as accounting firms (BUS19-16).

Overall, lacking compliance staff and related compensation mechanisms shape compliance management practices in China. Specifically, the outsourcing to professional service firms and the adoption of digital technologies foster institutional isomorphism (further details in Section 4.5.2). Thereby, these factors influence the construction of compliance.

With regard to organizational complexity, the Chinese case also mirrors the academic discourse to a certain extent: Interviewees acknowledged that increased organizational complexity makes compliance more difficult (e.g. BUS19-02, BUS19-09, BUS21-15). However, the complexity in the Chinese case seems to stem more from the company size than from the level of decentralization: According to the interviews, larger-sized companies have a greater need for systemic compliance management and standardized control mechanisms compared to smaller ones (BUS19-02, BUS21-15).

Chinese companies do not only try to mitigate organizational complexity with compliance management systems, but they also stress the importance of compliance awareness among employees to lessen organizational complexity and prevent unintentional non-compliance incidents: They argued that compliance awareness and ethical conduct of employees reduce risks and benefit compliance irrespective of the specific compliance management practices that are adopted (BUS19-14, BUS21-07, BUS21-22). Therefore, the

120 Only few interviewees explicitly stated that they do not face problems with compliance-related staffing (BUS19-12, BUS21-16).

level of compliance awareness among employees also constitutes an important organizational characteristic that affects compliance.

In the case of China, interviewees reported increasing levels of compliance awareness among the staff thanks to the consistent implementation of compliance management (e.g. via trainings, information provision, audits) (BUS19-09, BUS19-17, BUS21-07, BUS21-10, BUS21-14, BUS21-15, BUS21-16, BUS21-20, BUS21-22, BUS21-25, EXP19-10, EXP19-11, EXP21-04). These actions have provided positive results, e.g. staff that did not know about waste separation before are now familiar with and implementing desired practices (EXP19-10). Furthermore, interviewees described that employees now proactively seek advice from their firms' compliance departments, which was not the case before compliance was managed actively for several years (BUS21-18, BUS21-22, BUS21-23, BUS21-24, EXP19-08).

Interviewees named several factors and measures that improve compliance awareness: Strict regulations and supervision by authorities (e.g. regular inspections) (BUS21-08, BUS21-14, BUS21- 16, EXP19-04), non-compliance incidents (BUS21-13), influences from foreign MNEs (BUS21-25, EXP19-16), as well as the inclusion of compliance as a performance evaluation criterion (BUS21-02). One company has even run campaigns where employees collaborated for more compliance, e.g. reminding each other of the topic (BUS19-07).

Nonetheless, some interviewees still regarded compliance awareness as low (BUS21-21, EXP19-01) or at least a subject that needs improvement (BUS19-19, BUS21-05, BUS21-06, BUS21-15, BUS21-20, BUS21-23). For example, one CEO of an SME explained that his employees' compliance awareness is only strong in areas that benefit them personally (e.g. workers' safety), but not others, such as environmental protection (BUS19-12). Another interviewee saw the cause for missing compliance awareness in the high employee turnover in his company which means that the compliance department has to explain compliance basics to new recruits in order to ensure a minimal compliance level repeatedly (BUS21-01). Hence, similar to managerial capacities, compliance awareness also stands in a reciprocal relationship with compliance management: Compliance management reinforces compliance awareness, but compliance awareness also fosters compliance practices and improves compliance management.

Furthermore, the interviews also resonate with the academic discourse in identifying a firm's economic pressure as a factor influencing compliance. On the one hand, business representatives explained that in times where their company is not doing well, there are less resources available for compliance (BUS21-05, BUS21-21). In this context, they referred to macroeconomic trends in the economic environment (e.g. the COVID-19 pandemic) and losses from non-compliance incidents as reasons for financial squeezes (BUS21-05). On the other hand, if the losses from non-compliance incidents are not too high, previous incidents and related enforcement measures can also lead to increasing investments in compliance management thereafter (BUS21-25). Especially because hiring compliance professionals is costly, having sufficient financial resources for compliance management at hand is an important factor that affects compliance levels (BUS21-04). In addition, larger companies can also invest in and develop sophisticated (digital) compliance tools and practices, since such investments have a proportionally lower effect on profits (BUS21-04, BUS21-08, EXP19-12). One interviewee even went as far as regarding higher regulatory pressure from authorities as a necessary evil for smaller companies to ensure compliance, because considering the financial pressure they generally face these firms would otherwise not be willing to invest in compliance (BUS21-20). This elaboration shows that in line with insights from the economic environment (Section 2.4.1.1), companies' willingness to implement compliance management is to a large extent contingent upon their financial situation.

In contrast, the precise influence of firm size on compliance in China is difficult to determine. On the one hand, experts stressed that larger companies are more attentive to and professional in their compliance management (EXP19-10, EXP19-11, EXP19-16). This is consistent with the findings from a compliance-related survey in China (CICLA et al., 2019, p. 72, 75). On the other hand, according to that survey, larger companies are subject to more enforcement actions by authorities than smaller firms (CICLA et al., 2019, p. 64). This phenomenon suggests that either larger companies possess worse compliance levels or that smaller companies are targeted by authorities less. Moreover, smaller businesses may simply need less sophisticated compliance management due to lower organizational complexity as discussed above.

In any case, there are two observations related to company size that deserve mentioning. First, company size seems to influence the subjective compliance pressure businesses experience.

The representatives from larger companies did not mention compliance-related requirements and enforcement as explicit pressures, whereas SMEs complained about the increasingly strict regulations that may even threaten their existence (e.g. BUS19-11, BUS19-12). SMEs seem to be in a difficult sandwich position with regard to compliance, in which they do not possess the same economic resources for professional compliance management as larger enterprises, yet face increasingly strict supervision.

Second, size is not an isolated factor that compliance deviations can be attributed to. Other factors, such as ownership type and industry, in combination with size influence the constructed compliance meaning and practices in an enterprise. This is illustrated by the differences in compliance focus topics and the varying compliance motives across companies, both of similar and deviating sizes (e.g. BUS19-06, BUS19-11, BUS19-12, BUS19-10, BUS19-17, BUS21-03, BUS21-04, BUS21-25).

Besides these organizational factors that originate from the academic discourse, the Chinese case points to another important organizational factor influencing compliance: Company culture. While compliance best practices simply tout a compliance culture as a feasible means to improve compliance management, this research shows that a strong company culture as a whole can also affect compliance. For instance, companies that are more conservative, i.e. risk-averse, and focus on long-term success rather than short-term profit, also paid close attention to compliance (e.g. BUS19-19, BUS21-02, BUS21-08, BUS21-10, BUS21-12, BUS21-13). Similarly, certain values were mentioned as corporate values closely related to compliance, such as transparency (BUS19-02, BUS21-11), openness to learning (BUS21-04, BUS21-06, BUS21-12, BUS21-15, BUS21-17, BUS21-18), unity among firm members (BUS19-03, BUS19-10, BUS19-19) and integrity (BUS19-02, BUS21-04 BUS21-07, BUS21-18, BUS21-22, EXP19-14). But also very pragmatic, business-oriented corporate cultures can foster compliance, when they regard business success as a result of rule-adherence (BUS19-15).

In order to build a corporate culture supportive of compliance or to foster a compliance culture itself, businesses actively run campaigns, e.g. a digital campaign via a company's WeChat account or traditionally by putting up posters that promote certain values (BUS19-02, BUS19-07). Yet, business representatives still see leeway to improving their compliance culture (BUS19-02, BUS19-19, BUS21-05). Overall, the existing corporate culture can either foster or hamper compliance. Consequently, ensuring that the existing corporate culture matches with a culture of compliance is a concern for businesses in the same way as other organizational factors mentioned by the academic compliance literature.

4.4.2.2 Motives

With regard to compliance motivations, economic motives appear to be dominating in China. Six sub-categories could be identified, which economically motivate companies to comply. First, meeting Chinese authorities' requirements is an important economic motive for compliance in China mentioned by most interviewees. The main drivers for compliance interviewees stated in this context are the avoidance of losses (e.g. direct financial sanctions by the government) which limit firms' growth potential (BUS21-02, BUS21-06, BUS21-07, BUS21-09, BUS21-10, BUS21-19, EXP21-04) as well as the simple fact that compliance is a prerequisite for businesses' survival (BUS19-15, BUS21-02, BUS21-03, BUS21-06, BUS21-11, BUS21-12, BUS21-16, BUS21-19, EXP19-15, EXP21-01). Specifically, individuals fear being banned from their industry, for example in the financial sector (BUS19-14), while businesses are afraid of losing their general business license or licenses for certain business fields, e.g. the government shutting down specific factories because they do not respect environmental regulations (BUS21-07, BUS21-20, EXP19-10). Hence, companies essentially see the need to adopt compliance as a means to avoid punishments (BUS21-07, EXP19-08), especially since their perception of authorities' supervision is strict (BUS19-13, BUS21-02, BUS21-09, BUS21-10, BUS21-12, BUS21-15, BUS21-19, EXP19-16, EXP21-01). But not only strict supervision seems to trigger compliance, unpredictability in the authorities' regulation and enforcement was also mentioned as a reason for setting up compliance management systems (BUS19-19). Lastly, in the case of SOEs, the government as a shareholder directly requires the establishment of compliance management systems and compliance reports (BUS19-10).

Second, international compliance requirements also motivate Chinese firms to focus on this topic. For instance, international mother companies demand certain compliance levels in China and foreign companies and investors may make compliance a prerequisite for cooperation, e.g. certain product certificates (BUS19-07, BUS21-20, EXP19-04, EXP19-08). Moreover, the wish for international expansion fosters compliance, because regulations in other countries may be stricter or more rigorously enforced (BUS21-02, BUS21-09, EXP21-04). This especially applies to SOEs, who can no longer rely on guanxi to avoid punishments for non-compliance incidents abroad (EXP21-04).

Third, demands from customers drive firms towards a higher attention to compliance: With an increasing awareness of rights among the general population, customers actively speak out about compliance-related problems (e.g. product quality) and raise demands (BUS19-10, BUS21-11, BUS21-24, EXP19-10). Enterprises react with improvements in their processes and standards, because they worry they may lose customers and receive low ratings on online platforms (BUS19-04, BUS21-09, BUS21-21). Hence, customers' trust, which is nurtured by compliance, is important for companies to remain competitive (BUS19-10, BUS19-18).

Fourth, another economic reason for compliance is maintaining or achieving a good reputation, because it ultimately helps to increase profits (BUS19-10, EXP19-16, BUS21-19). Some interviewees regarded it as possible to improve their companies' reputation via compliance management (BUS21-14, BUS21-16). But at the same time, others act upon compliance more out of fear for their reputation (e.g. negative press or low ratings) (BUS21-06, BUS21-10, BUS21-16, BUS21-24 EXP21-04). In addition, compliance can support brand building and thereby provide advantages in several areas, such as talent acquisition (BUS19-11, EXP19-08, BUS19-15, BUS21-09) and customer retention (BUS19-18).

Fifth, increased professionalism motivates companies to invest in compliance management (BUS21-01, BUS21-15). Specifically, business representatives named an improved control environment (BUS19-02, BUS21-04), higher levels of standardization (BUS21-14, BUS21-17) and transparency (BUS19-02, BUS21-06) as well as increases in management efficiency in general (BUS21-11, BUS21-15, BUS21-16, BUS21-22, BUS21-24) as key incentives to implement compliance. Thus, in interviewees' opinion, compliance management contributes to smooth and stable business operations, a reduction in risks and ultimately healthy growth (BUS21-09, BUS21-11, BUS21-13, BUS21-14, BUS21-20, BUS21-22, BUS21-25).

Sixth, from the perspective of some interviewees, compliance is a goal worthwhile pursuing, because it increases their firms' business opportunities (BUS21-11, BUS21-19). For example, a good compliance management is helpful in public tenders (BUS19-09, BUS19-12, BUS21-17), an important aspect considered in the application for IPOs (BUS19-02, EXP19-10) and product approvals (BUS19-07) as well as conducive to obtaining funds (e.g. from private investors) for startups (BUS19-20, BUS21-15). Therefore, some companies even regarded compliance an aspect that can generate a competitive advantage (BUS21-16, EXP21-04).

Besides these economic motives, business representatives also mentioned social and normative motives. For instance, interviewees described compliance in society and find it an important trend to follow (BUS19-08,

BUS21-22). One expert even highlighted the societal consensus on certain compliance-related topics, such as the eradication of child labor (EXP19-13). Moreover, businesses are motivated by their responsibility towards society: They want to contribute to society (BUS21-16), they make promises to their external stakeholders and the general public which they do not want to break (BUS21-09) or they want to gain people's respect (BUS19-10).

With regard to normative reasons, interviewees agreed that ethics and moral conduct (especially integrity, 诚信) are important motivations for compliance, because not everything and everyone can be controlled (BUS19-01, BUS19-14, BUS19-16, EXP19-12, EXP19-14). In the interviews, normative motives appear in several cases, e.g. an employee leaving a company due to the misconduct she witnessed there (EXP19-16), a business founder who runs a values-based company and attempts to improve compliance-related problems in his industry via a foundation (BUS19-17) or a CEO who goes beyond regulations in his compliance efforts without promoting it publicly (BUS19-02). However, several interviewed experts also agreed that such examples are rare and that cost-benefit calculations related to compliance are more common (EXP19-15, EXP19-16, EXP21-04).

Spanning these categories, two more motives could be identified. On the one hand, previous compliance incidents seem to drive businesses' compliance. Many business representatives mentioned that their firms' intrinsic motivation for compliance management increased after non-compliance incidents in their company, be it in China or at other locations (BUS19-01, BUS19-04, BUS19-09, BUS19-10, BUS19-14, BUS21-05, BUS21-13, BUS21-25). But even compliance violations by other companies, e.g. in their industry, foster compliance management (BUS19-14, BUS19-15, BUS21-16, BUS21-21, EXP19-08, EXP21-04). For instance, some interviewees specified that if they learn about others' non-compliance incidents, they use these firms as case studies to educate employees (BUS21-06, BUS21-16). In this context, companies also check whether their own processes are designed to prevent the same non-compliance incidents from happening, especially since authorities often pay more attention to this topic in upcoming inspections (BUS21-15, BUS21-22).

On the other hand, several business representatives highlighted the fear of personal implications due to non-compliance incidents as a factor that motivated them to pay attention to compliance. For example, they pointed out that non-compliance incidents can have detrimental effects on individuals' long-term career development in certain industries (e.g. ban from working in the industry) and reduce personal bonuses for managers, which are often directly linked to a company's performance (BUS19-15, BUS21-07). Moreover, one interviewee explained that authorities' punishments for legal violations have become stricter and there is a realistic risk for people in charge to go to prison (BUS19-11). Lastly, in case of non-compliance incidents, individuals' personal freedom may be limited and his/her reputation implicated, especially in the context of the SCS and its restrictions on luxury consumption etc. (BUS21-06, BUS21-19).

Overall, these motives are in line with the way compliance has been constructed in the official discourse in China (Section 4.3): Extrinsic drivers, such as economic factors, dominate, but normative elements are also gaining in importance.

4.5 Corporate compliance practices

The influences on compliance outlined in the previous section shape how compliance management is practiced in China. Therefore, this section discusses the manifestations of compliance management by first introducing the results from an objectivist compliance survey on the status quo in China (Section 4.5.1) and then contextualizing these results based on the qualitative data collected for this study (Section 4.5.2).

4.5.1 Corporate compliance status quo

Since 2018, the China Institute of Corporate Legal Affairs (CICLA, 中国公司法务研究院, a platform established by the CCP's newspaper Legal Daily), the China Council for the Promotion of International Trade's Commercial Legal Service Center (中国国际贸易促进委员会商事法律服务中心) and the law firm Fangda Partners (方达律师事务所) publish China's Annual Corporate Compliance Blue Book. This blue book, on the one hand provides information and practical advice on important compliance-related topics and trends, such as compliance with anti-corruption, data protection and intellectual property regulations. On the other hand, it includes an annual survey about companies' compliance status and related management practices. The company survey for the blue book providing insights for the period 2018 to 2019 ('Blue Book 2019' in the following) was conducted between August 11 and October 20, 2019 (CICLA et al., 2019, p.

57). The results, therefore, reflect the compliance situation at the beginning of this study's field research.

The Blue Book 2019 incorporates compliance-related information on the previous year from 263 respondents, covering a broad spectrum of corporate actors in terms of ownership structure[121], industries[122] and company size[123] (CICLA et al., 2019, p. 57). While the self-reported data from companies operating in China is likely to be subject to biases, the research approach is objectivist and the questions only focus on international compliance management best practices, the Blue Book 2019's results can nevertheless provide a good starting point for understanding the intricacies of compliance construction in China.

A first overview reveals that compliance levels have not improved compared to the previous year: More than 30 percent of the respondents encountered enforcement measures by the Chinese government over the course of the period examined, a similar level as in the previous survey (CICLA et al., 2019, p. 62). Roughly two thirds of the companies who face enforcement measures are confronted with administrative investigations and punishments for the company (CICLA et al., 2019, p. 63). In addition, the government adopts other means, such as criminal investigations and punishments, as well as administrative and criminal punishments targeting employees (see Figure 20).

121 23 percent wholly foreign-owned enterprises, 36 percent domestic private enterprises, 30 percent SOEs, 6 percent JVs and 5 percent other ownership types (CICLA et al., 2019, p. 57).

122 20 percent from the finance and investment ('finance' in the following) sector, 19 percent from the pharmaceutical and healthcare ('pharmaceutical' in the following) sector, 13 percent from the technology, media and telecom sector (including software and information technology), seven percent from the automotive sector and the remaining 41 percent from other sectors (e.g. real estate, energy, transportation, etc.) (CICLA et al., 2019, p. 57).

123 63 percent large companies above 500 employees, 21 percent medium-sized companies with 101-500 employees and 16 percent small companies with 100 employees or less (CICLA et al., 2019, p. 57).

Figure 20: Percentage of occurrence of different types of enforcement measures companies in China faced in 2018/2019 (CICLA et al., 2019, p. 63) (author's design and translation)

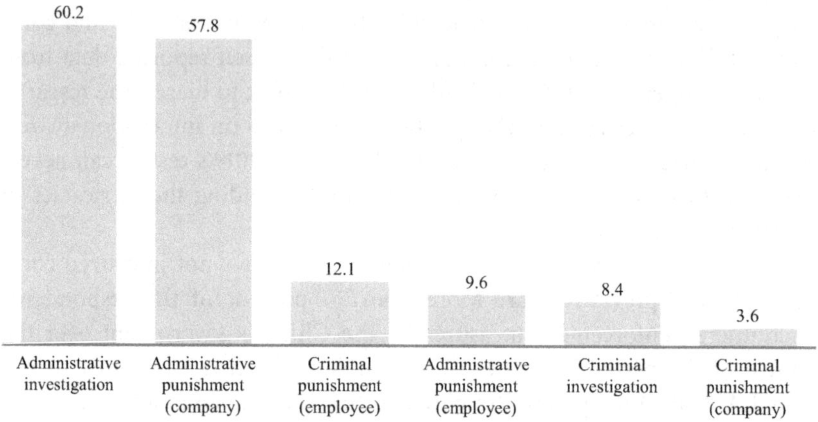

From the analysis of the firms that face enforcement measures, patterns related to company type, industry, company size and reason for enforcement can be gleaned: SOEs are the top target of enforcement measures, followed by domestic private firms, JVs and wholly foreign owned companies in descending order (CICLA et al., 2019, p. 64). In terms of industries, the energy and environmental, real estate and manufacturing (excluding automotive) sectors face most government enforcement, whereas pharmaceutical, automotive and finance sectors are least affected by enforcement measures (CICLA et al., 2019, p. 64). Moreover, the survey shows that the larger a company is, the more it has to be prepared for government scrutiny and enforcement (CICLA et al., 2019, p. 64). The top reasons for enforcement measures are non-compliance with advertisement rules (25 percent) and environmental regulations (24 percent), but also anti-bribery, product quality, (food, drug and medical instrument) safety, tax, anti-monopoly and data protection/cybersecurity regulations are mentioned in 5 to 12 percent of the cases (CICLA et al., 2019, p. 63).

The enforcement situation depicted above is largely reflected by the results of companies' compliance management systems. Sectors, which face the least enforcement measures, invest most efforts into their compliance management systems on average and vice versa: Most companies in the finance and pharmaceutical sectors (89 and 90 percent respectively) have established dedicated compliance departments, whereas only 59 to 65 percent of energy and environmental, real estate and manufacturing (excluding automotive) businesses have done the same (CICLA et al., 2019, p. 72). This trend is also mirrored by the reported levels of importance placed on compliance, the existence of compliance policies, as well as further compliance requirements (e.g. systems to handle non-compliance reports), where firms in the strictly regulated and supervised pharmaceutical and finance sectors score best (CICLA et al., 2019, p. 70, 74 and 75). Only the automotive sector is an outlier as it is comparatively less affected by enforcement measures despite relatively little compliance-related actions: The survey exhibits low shares of firms with dedicated compliance departments (58 percent), compliance policies (68 percent) and other compliance requirements (63 percent) as well as the lowest share of leaders that place importance on compliance in the automotive sector[124] (CICLA et al., 2019, p. 70, 74 and 75).

The same phenomenon as for industries exists for company types (CICLA et al., 2019, p. 70, 74 and 75): SOEs and domestic private companies, which are targeted by government enforcement the most, are least likely to possess a dedicated compliance department, leadership that regards compliance work as important, compliance policies or other compliance requirements. In contrast, the share of firms with dedicated compliance systems in place is high among wholly or at least partially (JVs) foreign-owned firms. This trend corroborates the significant role international influences play in the context of compliance that has already been identified in previous sections. Specifically, this phenomenon intimates the importance of foreign MNEs in the implementation of compliance management.

In contrast, the relationship between company size, enforcement measures and compliance efforts is reversed to the situation described for industries and ownership types (CICLA et al., 2019, p. 72 and 75). This means that the companies least targeted by the government's enforcement measures (small- and medium-sized businesses) are also least likely to have established dedicated compliance departments or defined compliance requirements. At the same time, companies with more than 500 employees are significantly more active with regard to compliance (CICLA et al., 2019, p. 72 and 75). These results support scholars who claim that larger

124 Sub-case three (Section 6.2) provides more context and details on this phenomenon.

companies are more often the target of supervision and enforcement due to their greater economic impact and higher level of business activity, whereas smaller companies stay below the regulators' radar (e.g. Kagan et al., 2011, Gunningham, Thornton and Kagan, 2004). At the same time, these numbers do not provide answers on the quality of smaller companies' compliance management, since smaller companies may simply not need the same level of sophistication in compliance management thanks to more straightforward business operations.

Lastly, the report highlights certain compliance areas that are currently at the center of attention or regarded as future focus topics (CICLA et al., 2019): First, Chinese companies' compliance with international regulations (especially those in the US) takes up a lot of space in the Blue Book 2019, both as a separate sub-chapters in the company survey and in the sections that provide input on regulations and enforcement[125]. While this research focuses on compliance management in China, the fact that international compliance is emphasized a lot in the blue book indicates the international influence on compliance management in Chinese companies and its importance for compliance management in China. In addition, the survey investigated topics of intellectual property and data protection. The results show that companies still have a lot of room for improvement with regard to these topics (e.g. only about 54 percent of surveyed companies possess a compliance system connected to data-related measures) (CICLA et al., 2019, p. 79).

Overall, compliance management measures have improved compared to 2017/18 according to the Blue Book 2019 (CICLA et al., 2019). For instance, the share of companies that have established dedicated compliance departments, has increased by about a quarter in 2018/19 compared to the previous time period and now stands at a level of about 75 percent of surveyed firms (CICLA et al., 2019, p. 72). SOEs have contributed to this rise to a large extent with their significantly increased shares of compliance departments (increase from 32 percent to 73 percent), which coincides with the SASAC's release of the 'SOE Compliance Guidelines' (CICLA et al., 2019, p. 71). In addition, the Blue Book 2019 shows that many companies which did not possess compliance policies or other compliance requirements yet, were in the process of setting them up (CICLA et al., 2019,

125 This fits well to the fact that Chinese companies are quite often subject to enforcement measures abroad and debarred by the World Bank (The World Bank, 2021c, CICLA et al., 2019).

p. 74 and 75). However, these changes do not automatically lead to better compliance levels, especially considering that SOEs still constitute a main target of enforcement measures and that their reaction to compliance risks (e.g. start an investigations) remains below the levels of all other company types (CICLA et al., 2019, p. 64 and 78).

4.5.2 Corporate compliance management practices

The qualitative interview data resonates with the trends described in the section above. As in the survey, interviewees also pointed out differences in compliance management between sectors and company types. The variations in industries are caused by different regulations and enforcement levels as detailed in Section 4.4.1.2 and are discussed in more depth using the example of securities and automotive firms in sub-case two and three (Chapter 6).

With regard to divergences in compliance management approaches between company types the interviews show that SOEs are comprehensively addressing this topic (BUS21-08, BUS21-20, EXP19-08). They are moving away from traditional approaches (with a focus on anti-corruption work) and increasingly converge with Western compliance management practices (EXP19-16). The SASAC's requirements for compliance management from 2018 play an important role in this development (EXP21-04).

In contrast, the situation in POEs is very diverse even though a general trend towards higher attention to compliance management is discernible (EXP19-05, EXP21-04). Listed and bigger POEs show comparably well-established compliance management approaches, whereas smaller firms and those that are not listed tend to invest less in compliance management (BUS21-08, BUS21-15, BUS21-20, EXP19-05, EXP19-08, EXP19-10, EXP19-16, GOV19-01). Foreign MNEs and JVs also tend to possess high compliance levels and rather sophisticated compliance management programs (BUS19-04, BUS21-20, EXP19-08, EXP19-10, EXP21-04). But even among firms of the same type, the spectrum of compliance approaches ranges from very detailed and comprehensive compliance management to high level approaches only focusing on the most important compliance issues (BUS21-13).

In addition, the interviews also mirror improvements in compliance management reported in the survey (BUS19-08, BUS21-25, EXP19-05, EXP19-13, EXP19-16, EXP21-04). One business representative illustrated the development as follows: In the beginning, they needed to teach their staff to differentiate between "what is compliant and what is not" ("是不是合规"), whereas now that everyone knows, employees approach the compliance management staff with the question "What do we need to do to be in compliance?" ("怎么做才是合规?") (BUS21-22).

Overall, there are four pathways to compliance-related learning according to the interviews. First, companies gain compliance awareness and learn how to implement compliance management as they grow (BUS19-09, BUS21-06, BUS21-17). The larger the company becomes, the higher the necessity for compliance management: Larger companies' management is more complex and therefore business representatives mention a management need for compliance (BUS19-02). In the growth context, financing needs also lead to an increased attention on compliance, as many sources of funding are tied to compliance-related prerequisites (e.g. government loans, subsidies and IPOs) (BUS19-09, BUS19-20, BUS21-16, EXP19-12, GOV19-01).

Second, enterprises described an incremental compliance management learning process parallel to authorities' regulatory and enforcement learning. Concretely, as authorities adopt more rigorous regulations and enforcement means, companies gradually implement increasingly comprehensive compliance management measures (BUS21-01, BUS21-08, EXP21-01). In the worst case, detected and sanctioned non-compliance incidents are also part of this learning process (BUS21-20). In this context, one interviewee described the SASAC's release of the 'SOE Compliance Guidelines' as a milestone that set a standard for compliance management across industries (BUS21-22).

Third, businesses in China learn from professional networks. This entails exchange with compliance professionals across companies and industries via formal (e.g. seminars, conferences) and informal platforms (e.g. WeChat groups, friendships) (e.g. BUS19-01, BUS21-02, BUS21-21).

Fourth, firms in and from China improve their compliance in response to international pressures. In this context, international pressure pertains to both pressures exerted on Chinese companies facing strict regulatory regimes in the destination country and influences of international actors on companies operating in China (BUS21-09, EXP19-05). For instance, foreign MNEs provide compliance guidance to their local Chinese branches or JVs (BUS21-05, BUS21-20, BUS21-22, BUS21-24). In addition, Chinese supply chain partners face compliance-related requirements from their international cooperation partners (BUS19-04, BUS19-08, EXP19-08, EXP19-10,

EXP21-04). All these pathways have contributed and still contribute to improvements in compliance management in China.

Besides these details on the corporate learning processes regarding compliance, the interviews also provide an explanation why the increase of compliance management measures across companies in China is not directly related to improvements in compliance. Several interviewees emphasized that the set-up of compliance management systems and measures is not sufficient (BUS19-13, EXP21-04, EXP19-08). Even with the right measures in place, it simply takes time for compliance to permeate a firm's every action (BUS19-13, EXP19-05, EXP19-08). However, as compliance was introduced to China less than 20 years ago and has only become a topic of attention recently, enterprises' internalization of compliance is still ongoing (BUS21-22). The academic discourse on compliance only indirectly addresses this point by including compliance culture and values-based compliance management as success factors for compliance management. However, the interviews add time as a new dimension to this discussion, by pointing out that a certain level of maturity in compliance management is important.

Lastly, the qualitative research provides an additional level of detail to compliance management practices in China, which the survey cannot achieve. The findings from the interviews show that compliance practices in China are largely in line with the six core best practices described in the compliance literature (Section 2.5.2), namely solid formal compliance management structures, embeddedness of compliance management into business practices and IT-systems, good management practices, top-level commitment, a compliance culture and values-based compliance management. First, the interviewees describe solid formal compliance management structures in the form of compliance organizations, clearly defined processes, compliance policies as well as certifications: With the exception of a few business representatives from very small companies (BUS19-11, BUS21-21), all other interviewed firms possess compliance-related organizational structures. The organizational location where compliance work is done varies between dedicated compliance departments, legal, finance or internal audit departments (e.g. BUS19-03, BUS19-16, BUS21-09, BUS21-17, BUS21-18, BUS21-23, BUS21-24, EXP19-16). In some enterprises, compliance management is also spread across different functional departments depending on the content, e.g. product-related compliance is monitored by the product management department, environmental compliance by the environmental department, etc. (BUS19-10, BUS19-12). In foreign MNEs and JVs, the headquarters' compliance department guides the local compliance work (e.g. BUS19-01, BUS19-04, BUS19-07, BUS21-05, BUS21-18, BUS21-19). In addition, the interviews show that, often, compliance personnel or contact persons in the business units support the work from the central compliance function (e.g. BUS21-07, BUS21-19, BUS21-23, BUS21-25). Because of the different organizational set-ups and compliance requirements that firms face, compliance departments also vary in size: Interviewees mention compliance staff numbers from less than five to more than 100 compliance professionals (e.g. BUS19-03, BUS19-04, BUS21-02, BUS21-13, EXP19-15).

These formal organizational structures are mostly supported by operational compliance processes that are clearly and formally defined (e.g. BUS19-01, BUS19-10, BUS19-13, BUS21-12, BUS21-14, BUS21-17). In this context, some interviewees use compliance jargon, such as 'compliance management system' and 'lines of defense'[126], which hints at their congruence with international best practices[127] (e.g. BUS19-03, BUS19-13, BUS19-19, BUS21-12). With regard to compliance policies, interviewees described codes of conduct, employee handbooks, general compliance policies and specific policies for certain target groups within their companies to exist (e.g. BUS19-02, BUS19-07, BUS19-08, BUS19-17, BUS19-19, BUS21-06, BUS21-11, BUS21-16, BUS21-25). These written documents are constantly adapted to the changing regulations and organizational needs (e.g. BUS21-08. BUS21-09, BUS21-13, BUS21-20, BUS21-22, BUS21-24). In some firms, employees even need to sign a compliance commitment or take an annual compliance exam, both of which cover the contents laid down in the compliance policies (BUS19-13, BUS19-14, BUS19-19, BUS21-04, BUS21-15).

In addition, business representatives unanimously described formal control mechanisms in the form of internal audits, both regular announced and random unannounced audits of specific business units and processes as well as the entire compliance management system (e.g. BUS19-02,

126 Three or four lines of defense is a concept, according to which a company protects itself against risks on three or four levels, e.g. for three lines of defense this could be the employees with compliance awareness as the first, managers adopting risk-preventing management approaches as the second and the compliance and risk management functions as a third line of defense.

127 Still, few interviewees mentioned that process standards are not explicitly and formally laid down in their company (BUS19-11, BUS19-16). However, this is not a contradiction to the consistency with international best practice, because the essence of a best practice is to work as an approach that a large share of companies adopts, not as a standard that every enterprise fulfills.

BUS19-11, BUS19-16, BUS19-17, BUS21-03, BUS21-06, BUS21-12, BUS21-14, BUS21-16, BUS21-22, BUS21-23). Often, the audits are conducted in cooperation with the internal audit department (BUS19-08, BUS21-02, BUS21-03, BUS21-19). Some companies take further measures and conduct spot-checks for individuals, e.g. via compliance interviews between managers and employees or by recording phone calls with customers (BUS19-14, BUS21-19).

These solid formal compliance management structures are often reinforced by certifications. Businesses in China use popular international standards, such as ISO14001 for environmental protection, or domestic standards to improve their compliance management, hold evidence for and promote their compliance-related efforts (BUS21-09, BUS21-16, BUS21-24, EXP21-04). Enterprises are also motivated to adopt such standards because the certificates are often a prerequisite for cooperation with international business partners (BUS19-04, BUS19-08, BUS19-10, BUS19-11, BUS19–12, EXP19-04). The international compliance management standard ISO37301 is seemingly not yet adopted in practice so far, since it is neither obligatory nor requested by international business partners (BUS19-02, BUS19-19, EXP21-01). Nevertheless, the formal organizational structures described in this paragraph largely mirror the standards' best practices.

Second, compliance experts in China promote embedding compliance management into business operations (e.g. EXP19-05, EXP19-08), an approach that is also put into practice according to the interviews with business representatives. Interviewees were aware that compliance management needs to be integrated into business processes (e.g. BUS19-03, BUS19-11) and many have already achieved this (e.g. BUS19-10, BUS21-20). Concrete examples for embeddedness are the need for approval from the compliance staff for certain process steps that involve high risks (e.g. BUS19-02, BUS19-10) or the linking of managers' and staff's promotions, bonuses and pay rises to their compliance levels or results in compliance exams (e.g. BUS19-13, BUS19-15, BUS21-02, BUS21-15). Specifically, compliance is included in performance evaluations for employees and entire business departments in the form of key performance indicators (BUS21-02, BUS21-14, BUS21-15, BUS21-20, BUS21-24, BUS21-25). In this context, non-compliance incidents lead to lower ratings, whereas none of the interviewed businesses have a mechanism implemented where positive compliance behavior translates into additional points. The reason mentioned for the exclusion of positive incentives was the difficulty to define and measure praiseworthy behavior in a fair manner (BUS21-07, BUS21-08, BUS21-23).

Furthermore, the interviewed compliance officers noticed a trend where business units reach out to them more proactively for advice on compliance-related matters leading to improved communication processes between the two parties (e.g. BUS19-08, BUS19-18, BUS21-04, BUS21-13, BUS21-23). As discussed above, this type of embeddedness is fostered by the allocation of compliance management staff or contact persons to each business unit, an approach that is implemented by many companies.

Another indicator for embeddedness is the continuation of firm-internal compliance practices in the relationships with external partners. Interviewees described that in the initial cooperation decision, background checks and on-site visits play an important role (e.g. BUS21-08, BUS21-11, BUS21-15, BUS21-19, BUS21-22, BUS21-25). After a positive decision on the cooperation, compliance requirements (e.g. production standards) are included in contracts with business partners (e.g. BUS21-05, BUS21-09, BUS21-11). Based on these agreements, cooperation partners are then allowed to conduct mutual audits (both announced and unannounced) to ensure compliance (BUS21-05, BUS21-15, BUS21-16, BUS21-19, BUS21-23, BUS21-24, BUS21-25, EXP19-10, EXP19-13).

Finally, embeddedness relies on the alignment in compliance-related priorities between the top management and the compliance function as well as the integration of compliance in the IT-infrastructure (e.g. BUS21-06, BUS21-24). Typically, companies embed compliance into the IT-infrastructure via access rights as well as process controls (BUS19-01, BUS19-10, BUS19-18, BUS19-19, BUS21-07, BUS21-14, BUS21-15, BUS21-16, BUS21-17, BUS21-19, BUS21-23). This means that individuals and departments are only allowed to access certain databases and information cannot be transmitted freely within the entire organization (BUS19-02, BUS19-10, BUS21-10, BUS21-12, BUS21-14, BUS21-25). At the same time, IT-systems entail compliance checks at certain process steps, where an employee cannot proceed (without special approvals) or receives compliance-related warnings and information (BUS19-03, BUS21-10, BUS21-25). All these examples show that embeddedness as a compliance best practice has been adopted in China.

Third, the interviewees in China also provided insights into good management practices that foster compliance, namely adequate communication to employees on compliance topics as well as stringency and fairness in compliance procedures. Compliance-related communication manifests itself in four formats according to the interviews: Trainings, events, reports and other information material. Interviewees unanimously described compliance trainings, both online and in person and often including an exam, as a core feature of their compliance management (e.g. BUS 19-02, BUS19-06, BUS19-08, BUS19-11, BUS19-16, BUS21-02, BUS21-06, BUS21-14, BUS21-16, BUS21-18, BUS21-22, BUS21-24). Dependent on the circumstances, trainings are conducted regularly or on demand and for a specific target group (e.g. new hires, certain business departments) or for the entire staff (e.g. BUS19-14, BUS19-16, BUS19-19, BUS21-02, BUS21-03, BUS21-06, BUS21-11, BUS21-17, BUS21-25). But compliance trainings do not only serve as a means to improve employees' knowledge about compliance and foster a corporate compliance culture, they also help compliance managers to understand the compliance status quo on the ground (BUS19-01, BUS21-10, BUS21-25). Hence, they are a means of exchange.

Compliance events (e.g. annual compliance days) work in a similar fashion, i.e. as a platform for exchange and knowledge transmission (BUS21-05, BUS21-15, BUS21-19, BUS21-22, BUS21-24). Compliance-related activities also entail small compliance competitions (e.g. quizzes) where the winners receive small rewards (e.g. coupons) (BUS21-08, BUS21-19). They incentivize employees to become familiar with compliance.

Furthermore, many companies draft reports to promote transparency about compliance; either only to the board of directors (e.g. BUS19-02, BUS19-04, BUS21-03, BUS21-04, BUS21-10, BUS21-12, BUS21-19) or company-internally (BUS21-02). The frequency of report publications varies depending on the sector and business need (e.g. BUS19-01, BUS19-07, BUS21-05, BUS21-13, BUS21-21). Sometimes reports are dedicated only to compliance; often they report business performance in general, including compliance information (embeddedness) (e.g. BUS19-18, BUS21-10, BUS21-12, BUS21-13, BUS21-21). While most firms only ask business units, projects or teams to report information (e.g. BUS19-18, BUS21-14, BUS21-18), one business even requires every employee to submit a compliance report on a monthly basis (BUS21-22). The transparency these reports grant helps enterprises to control risks and therefore constitutes a management practice that improves compliance.

Finally, companies use other information channels and materials to communicate their compliance-related messages to employees, be it via posters in the offices and factories, emails containing compliance content, compliance newsletters or one-on-one interactions on compliance between managers and employees (BUS19-14, BUS19-15, BUS19-16, BUS21-02, BUS21-05, BUS21-14, BUS21-15, BUS21-17, BUS21-18, BUS21-19, BUS21-23, BUS21-24, BUS21-25). Frequency is key in this case, because this type of communication serves as a constant reminder of compliance during day-to-day operations (BUS19-14).

In addition to communication, stringency and fairness are also important components of good management practices. In the Chinese case, interviewees illustrated these qualities of their compliance management when they described their companies' consequence management: Firms adopt standardized and formal procedures to deal with non-compliance incidents (investigations)[128], in which they first identify the people responsible for the issue (e.g. BUS19-01, BUS19-08, BUS19-10, BUS19-19, BUS21-09, BUS21-10, BUS21-13, BUS21-14). In the next step, consequences are determined based on company-internal rules and external regulations (BUS21-06, BUS21-10, BUS21-11). The repercussions vary on a spectrum between warnings and handing over individuals to authorities (e.g. for imprisonment) depending on the gravity of the issue (e.g. BUS19-01, BUS19-13, BUS19-15, BUS19-18, BUS21-05, BUS21-06, BUS21-11, BUS21-20, BUS21-21, BUS21-25).

While some business representatives stated that other than these punishments, no further consequences follow an incident (BUS21-09, BUS21-10, BUS21-12, BUS21-16, BUS21-17), several also provided examples of additional measures to incentivize compliance: For instance, in one business, the compliance department determines 15 percent of business units' budget and thereby motivates managers to focus on the topic (BUS21-10). Other firms provide examples of small financial rewards or presents for employees who portray positive behavior (e.g. participation in compliance events, smooth cooperation with compliance managers, improvement after receiving feedback, whistle-blowing) (BUS21-10, BUS21-19, BUS21-24). Furthermore, some interviewees explained that they shame and praise behavior within the company, be it by publishing non-compliance incidents, including the responsible supervisor and HR officer, or by promoting stories where employees went out of their way to ensure compliance (e.g. reporting a business partner's illegal behavior even though they could benefit from it personally) (BUS21-04, BUS21-19). All these consequences follow certain formalized rules which are a prerequisite for decent management practices[129].

128 Apart from the compliance department, often representatives from other departments, such as HR and the department involved in the incident, participate in the investigation process (BUS19-01, BUS19-19, BUS21-02, BUS21-24).

129 Nevertheless, this study cannot determine whether individual managers exhibit good conduct at all times.

Fourth, interviewees also regarded top-level commitment to compliance as an important success factor for compliance management in their companies (e.g. BUS19-06, BUS19-17, BUS21-15, BUS21-16). Specifically, some stress that the implementation of compliance management depends on the CEO and his/her character (e.g. a cautious attitude fosters compliance) (BUS19-01, BUS19-06, BUS21-17, BUS21-20). Examples for top management commitment from the interviews are frequent compliance-related communication by the CEO and other top managers (e.g. in speeches, at the start of every meeting) and the CEO acting as a role model in compliance questions (BUS19-16, BUS21-03, BUS21-05, BUS21-06, BUS21-17, BUS21-21, BUS21-22, BUS21-24, BUS21-25). This compliance-related action then trickles down to managers at all levels, who reinforce the importance of compliance to ensure that staff internalize the idea (BUS21-07, BUS21-09, BUS21-10, BUS21-13). In this context, interviewees emphasized the power of a clear message, i.e. concrete compliance-related requirements (BUS19-19, BUS21-09, BUS21-17, BUS21-22).

Furthermore, the organizational structures reflect the importance compliance management holds among corporate functions: Compliance officers often directly report to the CEO or dedicated compliance boards, including top managers, who are installed to address compliance-related issues (BUS19-15, BUS21-05, BUS21-24). In this context, business representatives describe monthly top management meetings and the high priority compliance possesses there (BUS19-02, BUS19-03, BUS19-08, BUS21-07, BUS21-19). While interviewees saw a trend towards an increased attention to compliance from the leadership, some still did not believe their top management values the topic sufficiently (BUS19-02, BUS19-04, BUS19-19, BUS21-20). Nevertheless, the topic of top-management commitment has found its way into compliance management discussions in China in the same way as it has done in international best practices.

Fifth, the interviewees stressed the importance of a compliance culture for successful compliance management. While only one interviewee explicitly attached a strong compliance culture to her company (BUS21-14), several others emphasized that their enterprises are currently in the process of establishing a strong compliance culture (BUS19-02, BUS21-19, BUS21-24) or see improvement needs in this regard (BUS19-19, BUS21-01, BUS21-06).

Besides top leadership commitment and communication measures, complaint channels also foster the institutionalization of a compliance culture (BUS19-01). These channels send a signal that everyone plays an important role in achieving the state of compliance. For this reason, the interviewed business representatives unanimously confirmed the existence of this compliance instrument in their companies: Employees can report non-compliance incidents via phone, email or online (intranet, WeChat) anonymously (e.g. BUS19-04, BUS19-05, BUS19-08, BUS19-18, BUS21-13, BUS21-18, BUS21-22, BUS21-25). Some firms incentivize non-anonymous reporting via monetary rewards (BUS19-02, BUS19-14). Employees' adoption of these channels, however, varies between companies with frequent (e.g. BUS19-19, BUS21-19, BUS21-22) and rare usage (e.g. BUS21-08, BUS21-10), which reflects the picture the interviews portray about compliance culture overall.

Importantly, interviewees also discussed complaint channels for other stakeholders, such as customers and suppliers (e.g. BUS19-13, BUS21-09, BUS21-14, BUS21-16). For example, one business representative highlighted that contracts with suppliers contain "clauses related to honesty and uprightness" ("廉政的条款") from both sides and complaint hotlines are necessary to ensure adherence to them (BUS21-15). This statement corroborates that compliance is constructed as a concept that extends beyond the confines of the company. A culture of compliance becomes a promise to stakeholders, but also an idea that is exported to other business relationships.

This concept follows international best practices and efforts by foreign MNEs to improve compliance in their supply chains. Yet, the idea of setting compliance standards for business partners still seems to be in its early stages of implementation in China, since cultural changes, i.e. changes in individuals' mindset and behavior, take time (EXP19-08).

Sixth, companies in China further emulate international best practices in their aspiration to pursue a values-based compliance management approach. One interviewee specifically argued that instilling ethics among employees is key for achieving compliance, because not every action can be controlled (BUS19-14). Overall, the interviews intimate that companies in China are becoming increasingly proactive in values-based compliance management and preventative in their measures (e.g. BUS19-01, BUS19-19, BUS21-01, BUS21-08, BUS21-16, BUS21-18, BUS21-20, EXP21-04). Some business representatives already saw improvements in cases, for instance, when employees proactively approach compliance managers to ensure their behavior and decisions abide by regulations (BUS21-05, BUS21-07, BUS21-23, BUS21-25). In addition, companies mention their CSR practices to highlight their ethics and contribution to society (e.g. BUS19-02, BUS19-03, BUS19-11, BUS19-17, BUS19-18).

Yet, a values-based approach still appears to be a goal which companies aspire to. Some interviewees highlighted the differences in depth of compliance management between their employer and other companies (BUS21-01, BUS21-07, BUS21-19). For example, one business representative shared how his company follows a values-based approach by setting up stricter controls internally than those they face from the authorities (BUS21-08). He also provided an example of how his company differs from its competitors (BUS21-08): With regard to contracts, his company upholds the attitude that anything that is not specified is not allowed, whereas other businesses consider unspecified aspects of contracts as loopholes that can be exploited. Nevertheless, a values-based approach has not become a commonplace phenomenon (EXP21-01). Some interviewees criticize their companies for not being sufficiently proactive with regard to compliance beyond the minimal regulatory requirements, e.g. they see a need to improve compliance risk prediction (BUS19-01, BUS19-03, BUS19-16, BUS21-06, BUS21-07). One business representative even described conflicts between the business unit and the compliance department that erupt when compliance management places 'excessive' limits on business units (BUS21-23). Hence, a values-based approach has not been successfully implemented yet. Both the implementation of a values-based approach and the related limitations show that a discourse on this topic exists and that the idea of a values-based approach is an element of the constructed understanding of compliance in China.

Taken together, all these parallels between the concept and practices of compliance derived from the academic discourse, the details provided in the interviews for the Chinese case as well as the similarities between the companies in China in this regard are signs of institutional isomorphism in compliance management. According to the interviews, this institutional isomorphism is significantly fostered by two key factors, namely the cooperation with external service providers and international influences. The hiring of external service providers contributes to institutional isomorphism, specifically normative and mimetic isomorphism. The interviews show that most companies rely on external services in the context of compliance. While some smaller firms only work with legal advisers or make it an exception to hire accounting firms and consultancies due to their limited resources[130] (e.g. BUS19-04, BUS19-11, BUS19-19, BUS21-15, BUS21-21),

130 One interviewee from the government explained that her department supports startups by subsidizing legal and accounting services from external providers, be-

most interviewees commonly cooperate with law firms, consultancies and accounting firms (e.g. BUS19-01, BUS19-03, BUS21-05, BUS21-06, BUS21-08, BUS21-11, BUS21-12, BUS21-25). Both domestic and international service providers are mentioned, including the Big Four[131] (e.g. BUS19-11, BUS19-13, BUS21-07, BUS21-10, BUS21-13, BUS21-18, BUS21-22, BUS21-23). Law firms support companies with legal advice as well as in litigation cases (BUS19-03, BUS21-04, BUS21-06, BUS21-14, BUS21-19, BUS21-20). Consultancies are hired to help companies set up entire compliance management systems (including related IT-systems) and teach innovative management approaches (BUS21-02, BUS21-06, BUS21-09, BUS21-20, BUS21-25, EXP21-04). Accounting firms, on the other hand, mostly serve as external auditors to provide compliance reviews, including improvement suggestions for companies (BUS19-01, BUS19-05, BUS19-17, BUS19-18, BUS19-19, BUS21-10, EXP21-01). Moreover, all the external service providers conduct compliance related trainings (BUS19-17, BUS21-20, BUS21-25, EXP19-08, EXP19-10, EXP21-04).

Beyond the support on a regular basis, companies access the skills of third parties in the compliance context in certain circumstances. For instance, some consultancies help businesses to improve their compliance management during the process of going public (BUS19-09, BUS19-15, EXP19-12). Furthermore, manufacturers hire specialized auditing firms to check environmental, social and safety standards in factories they cooperate with (BUS21-05, BUS21-15, EXP19-10, EXP19-13). Small companies often rely on compliance-related trainings for specific topics from the local government or industry associations (EXP21-05, GOV19-01). At times, companies also decide to hire individual compliance experts to support their internal compliance work and provide advice (BUS21-17, BUS21-20). One company even asked an external service provider to conduct background checks on potential future employees (BUS21-04). These are all examples of the high influence of service providers on compliance management in China, a typical source of normative institutional isomorphism. But previous elaborations have also illustrated the vivid exchange between compliance professionals that emerges from these collaborations (e.g. on compliance-related events), which fosters mimetic institutional isomorphism.

---

cause startups cannot afford high-quality services otherwise, even though they are dependent on the help for sustainable development (GOV19-01).

131 The Big Four is a term to describe the four biggest accounting firms worldwide (Deloitte, Ernst & Young, KPMG and PricewaterhouseCoopers).

In addition, international influences have been an important driver for the increase in compliance management efforts in China. Typically, international actors promote compliance management practices in their own Chinese branches and industries (BUS19-19, BUS21-05, BUS21-18, BUS21-25). The textbook example for this influence, mentioned by several interviewees (e.g. BUS19-01, EXP21-04), is Siemens, who not only set up a comprehensive compliance management system, but also provides exchange platforms (conferences, etc.) for mutual compliance-related learning. In addition, foreign MNEs influence Chinese compliance management practices as shareholders in local firms, e.g. JVs (e.g. BUS21-02, BUS21-05, BUS21-18, BUS21-22, BUS21-25). In this context, one interviewee pointed out:

> "Our international mother company introduced the notion of compliance to us, and we thought it was very interesting" ("母公司带来了合规这个理念，我们觉得很有意思") (BUS21-22).

This trigger caused the implementation of compliance management in said firm (BUS21-22). In the initial phase of setting up compliance management systems, foreign MNEs also sent compliance experts to China for support (BUS19-02, BUS21-05, BUS21-24). The exchange has been kept up via compliance trainings at the international headquarters with international compliance staff, including the Chinese compliance managers, as well as regular (online) international compliance staff meetings (BUS19-02, BUS21-05, BUS21-24).

Moreover, Chinese actors are exposed to international compliance requirements and best practices when they do business abroad (BUS21-09, EXP19-05). One business representative illustrated how her company had improved its compliance management via its exporting business to the US, including a litigation case (BUS21-09). In this context, seminars on compliance management offered by consultancies and law firms reinforce international compliance management standards (BUS21-02, PO21-ON).

These influences have led to a convergence with already rather homogeneous international compliance best practices and therefore caused institutional isomorphism. Depending on a company's situation, the type of institutional isomorphism that is triggered varies; it can be both coercive (e.g. foreign MNEs issuing demands to their supply chain partners or JVs) and mimetic (e.g. Chinese POEs emulating Siemens' compliance practices for success).

Despite the congruence between compliance management in China and internationally propagated compliance best practices, the interviews also revealed several idiosyncrasies of compliance management in China. The most ostentatious idiosyncrasy is the CCP's discipline system, which exists in parallel to compliance management. Traditionally, many Chinese companies, especially SOEs, only had a discipline inspection department, which was responsible for compliance-related topics (BUS21-22). Today, many companies have compliance departments in addition to discipline inspection departments (e.g. BUS21-05, BUS-19, BUS21-22). According to the interviews, the responsibility between these two departments is clearly separated (BUS21-01, BUS21-02, BUS21-10, BUS21-12, BUS21-19): The discipline inspection department is responsible for ensuring employees' compliance with Party-internal rules and propagating Party ideology, whereas the compliance department focuses on ensuring business process compliance with state authorities' regulations (BUS21-02, BUS21-08, BUS21-12, BUS21-15, BUS21-16, BUS21-17, BUS21-19, BUS21-20, BUS21-24). In practice, however, there are overlaps in these two departments' anti-corruption work, resulting in their cooperation (e.g. joint investigations) (BUS21-05, BUS21-10, BUS21-15, BUS21-24).

The importance of the discipline inspection department and a company's Party branch seems to vary between enterprises: For instance, one business representative saw little influence of the Party on his firm's employees, who are not Party members, whereas another interviewee considered the entire staff, Party member or not, subject to discipline inspections (BUS21-05, BUS21-08). Especially in JVs the duplication of structures can become a source of conflicts, as one of the interviewees recounted (BUS21-05): From the beginning, the discipline inspection department's leader, who was installed by the Chinese majority shareholder, was allocated a higher organizational level than the compliance department's head, who was supported by the foreign MNE (BUS21-05). Because of a conflict between the two shareholders, the board of directors ultimately removed the compliance department and had the discipline inspection department take over compliance management (BUS21-05). This shows that the strong role of the Party increases the complexity of compliance management in China.

In addition, IT plays an important role in Chinese firms' compliance management. As mentioned above, firms in China embed compliance management in their IT-systems in the same manner as international practices suggest. However, many of the interviewed Chinese firms go beyond recommended practices in their application of technology for the purpose of compliance. The most basic extension mentioned, is the creation of a dedicated compliance app, IT-system or WeChat account, which provides compliance materials, promotes the topic among employees and can be consulted in case of compliance-related questions (e.g. BUS19-02, BUS19-10, BUS21-02, BUS21-12, BUS21-14, BUS21-25, EXP21-04). But some companies go one step further to adopt smart systems, including the use of artificial intelligence, to ensure compliance. For example, some businesses use screening and approval systems that automatically flag problems in contracts; or software, which uses big data to identify risks (e.g. in finance, related to expense fraud) (BUS19-04, BUS21-04, BUS21-08, BUS21-10, BUS21-11, BUS21-12 BUS21-13, BUS21-15). While some interviewees still saw potential in the adoption of more intelligent systems (e.g. BUS19-18, EXP19-12), others provided examples of how their companies develop their own tools to address specific compliance challenges (BUS19-10, BUS21-04, BUS21-06). For example, one internet company active in the education sector developed a tool to scan video material from lessons to automatically identify non-compliant behavior among teachers (e.g. bad language, inappropriate clothes) (BUS21-06). Another interviewee, this time from the automotive sector, presented his company's vehicle lock system to ensure customer compliance (BUS19-10). In case customers do not settle their invoice for a purchase, they receive a warning via the system (BUS19-10). If they still do not pay, they are informed that the driving distance of their vehicle will be limited to a certain radius starting the next day (BUS19-10). The vehicle is locked completely only in case the customer continues to refuse to pay the required amount (BUS19-10). While such examples do not seem to be the norm yet, the government's overall encouragement of technology-adoption in all areas (e.g. via the 'Internet Plus' strategy) supports these developments.

Lastly, the interviews show that transparency and rating mechanisms play a prominent role in compliance management in China (e.g. BUS21-04, BUS21-19, BUS21-22). This is a development directly linked to the set-up of the SCS in the Chinese business environment and is therefore discussed in depth in Chapter 5.

4.6 Consequences for the construction of corporate compliance

After a literature review and an introduction to the Chinese political economy, this chapter has provided an overview of the manifestation of compliance in China, touching upon the conceptualization of compliance over time, influencing factors on compliance as well as compliance practices.

While the findings generally resonate with the international and China-specific compliance discourse, this chapter provided additional nuance to the influences on and social practices of compliance. With regard to the influences, the elaborations have shown that the social environment is gaining importance thanks to increased societal awareness of compliance, which triggers among others customer complaints, media reports and local civil society activism. This rise in significance of societal actors in the compliance context illustrates the overall increase in regulators besides the Party-state. Yet, as previous research has shown, the political sphere, with the Party-state's high legitimacy levels, still controls the social sphere in the context of compliance (Van Rooij, 2006, p. 222).

Nevertheless, this guidance does not always manifest itself in limitations as previously assumed (e.g. by Van Rooij, 2006, p. 222), but can also lead to the active encouragement of social supervision by the Party-state. Specifically, the increasingly rules-based political environment mobilizes individuals and organizations to become self-regulating regulatees as well as regulators at the same time by providing more convenience to praiseworthy actors in administrative procedures. In the context of self-regulation, systemic ambiguity in the regulatory system can act as a driver for additional compliance efforts.

While previous studies have attested a higher importance either to the economic environment or the regulatory context of compliance respectively (e.g. Yee et al., 2016, Van Rooij, 2006), this chapter has shown that these two spheres of influence actually act in concert in China. For instance, the economic maturity of a business field is closely tied to the stringency of regulations and enforcement, which both affect compliance. In addition, the strategic importance of an industry, a sector's products and services as well as its innovation capacities and dynamism influence the way this industry is overseen and consequently the way companies react and implement compliance management (for two differing examples, refer to Chapter 6).

Consequently, the impacts of the economic and regulatory environments on compliance appear to be more complex than previously portrayed in the literature. This proves to be particularly true with respect to the endogeneity of law, i.e. the mutual influence of the legal and the managerial sphere resulting in a legalization of organization and a managerialization of the law. The discussion of the empirical findings above shows that this reciprocal relationship is not characterized by selective points of influences happening in a predefined order of sequence, which trigger legalization and managerialization in the respective realms, but rather a constant process which the involved actors proactively bring about in various interactions in parallel.

The prevailing managerial logic in enforcement is corroborated by the approaches adopted; for example, the increasing application of naming and shaming, ratings and customer complaint mechanisms. Paired with powerful technological tools, these instruments affect businesses in a significant and distinct manner, especially their compliance management. The epitome of this development, the SCS, with its influence on compliance is discussed in Chapter 5 in more detail.

With respect to internal influences, company culture and general compliance awareness are additional organizational characteristics that affect compliance. When including these two aspects into compliance-related considerations, time emerges as an important dimension affecting compliance. Concretely, the interviews illustrated that even with formal structures in place and compliance knowledge transmitted, the passage of a certain period of time is necessary for actors to internalize compliance and behave accordingly. Both cultural change and awareness raising are processes that take time.

Similarly, ethical considerations in compliance decisions need time to develop. This is portrayed in the still predominantly economic motives for compliance that interviewees expressed. Nevertheless, social and normative motives also start to play an increasing role, in addition to overarching motives, such as personal implications and the experience of previous compliance incidents.

Spanning all these internal and external factors are international influences, which have significantly shaped the construction and social practices of compliance in China. Yet, this aspect has so far not received dedicated attention in the academic compliance discourse. However, especially in the context of China and other countries of the Global South, where compliance has been imported from abroad, this factor deserves greater scrutiny. Therefore, the two industry case studies in Chapter 6 shed light on the specific types of international influences by delineating the transfer processes of the concept of compliance to China.

International influences have also been one of four pathways of compliance management learning this study has identified. Specifically, the regulations Chinese companies operating abroad face, as well as the requirements international actors pose on domestic actors (e.g. via their supply chain management) have fostered compliance-related improvements. The other pathways for compliance management improvement have been companies' growth and the ensuing management complexity, professional networks as well as the regulatory process itself, i.e. learning from prescriptive compliance management regulations offered by authorities. All in all, these learning processes have resulted in a high level of institutional isomorphism regarding compliance management. The interviews illustrated that compliance management practices in China (attempt to) mirror the core best practices of compliance management mentioned by the international compliance discourse.

Yet, based on the specific influencing factors for compliance in China, the research also identified several features in compliance management practices in China beyond what has been addressed in the international discourse. On the one hand, compliance management is adapted to the Chinese environment, especially to the distinct role of the CCP in the Chinese regulatory system. Hence, Party discipline inspections play an important role in the Chinese context and increase the level of complexity for compliance management. This is especially the case where compliance and discipline inspection functions coexist, cooperate and compete. On the other hand, companies expedite the use of technology as well as rating and transparency mechanisms in the context of compliance management in China; fairly new trends that have not received scholarly attention so far.

Against this backdrop, a compliance notion has been constructed in China that is based on the internationally accepted broad definition of compliance and exhibits a strong focus on risk mitigation and top-down management. With differences in risks across sectors, locations and company types, the compliance narrative in China connects compliance levels with economic development and modernization. Consequently, two constructs of compliance coexist: One based on formalism and prescriptive compliance regulations which entails the risk that firms react with creative compliance; and one propagating substantive and preventative compliance practices based on normative motives as the ideal state. Taken together, these two constructs foster embedded autonomy, where regulators and regulatees follow procedural rules, yet negotiate the substance of compliance issues.

At the same time, recent developments, such as the increased adoption of network instruments and digital technology in the context of the SCS, have extended the scope of compliance beyond the confines of the firm. Specifically, third-party management is constructed as a component of compliance management, thereby attributing a societal supervision function to compliance. Furthermore, compliance is closely linked to the concept of credit, e.g. via credit commitments as a means for compliance management. In this context, a new trend in the compliance discourse has emerged, which constructs compliance as an opportunity (e.g. for more convenience) and a competitive advantage. This conceptualization stands in contrast to the currently predominant notion of compliance as a bottom-line. It has to be seen whether this idea will prevail.

Overall, this chapter has shown that compliance in China exhibits characteristics that are in line with international best practices, but also possesses idiosyncratic features, which deserve further scrutiny. Thus, the following two chapters investigate two distinct aspects that influence the China-specific manifestation of compliance, which this chapter has identified. Chapter 5 examines how the Chinese trend of increasingly adopting information technologies to address regulatory problems across society (NDRC, 2020, State Council China, 2015) affects compliance by investigating the impacts of the SCS on businesses. Then, Chapter 6 investigates in more depth how corporate compliance manifests differently across industries, since variations between industries in one country can be greater than those between the same industry in different countries (Levi-Faur, 2006, p. 368). Thereby, the comparison addresses the fact that compliance in China has been largely influenced by international actors; it provides additional detail on how the international influences and the resulting manifestations of compliance understanding as well as practices vary across sectors.

5 The Social Credit System's impact on corporate compliance in China

The previous chapter identified a movement in the Chinese regulatory environment to increasingly adopt network instruments and technology to improve enforcement, with the SCS as the epitome of this trend. Therefore, this chapter discusses the SCS's impact on the construction and social practices of compliance, by first providing an overview of literature related to the SCS (Section 5.1) and the SCS's set-up (Section 5.2), including the system's goals and scope, elements and distinctive enforcement approach. On this basis, Section 5.3 discusses the relationship between the SCS and compliance, followed by insights into the SCS's impacts on the corporate sector (Section 5.4). Section 5.5 concludes by highlighting the SCS's impact on compliance construction in China.

5.1 Literature review

As mentioned in the introduction, the Chinese government has been building the SCS as a new enforcement approach since 2014 in an effort to strengthen rule-based governance across the country (Meissner, 2017, p. 2). Specifically, the SCS is a socio-technical system that aims to improve trustworthiness across all realms of society (Krause and Fischer, 2020, p. 438ff). This sublime goal, however, already indicates the complexity, which characterizes the SCS. Hence, academic literature so far has predominantly discussed the theoretical foundation and conceptualization of the SCS as well as its set-up.

The theoretical discussions about the SCS date back to the early 2000s, when Chinese academics started to conduct credit-related research more intensively (Lin, 2012, p. 2). Lin Junyue can be considered the SCS's trailblazer, as he discusses principles of a SCS in his book 'Principles of a Social Credit System' as early as 2003 (Lin, 2003). Theoretical discussions on the substance of credit and the right credit reporting model for China followed (e.g. Yu, 2018, 2016, Ye, 2015, Lin, 2012, 2011a). Besides Lin Junyue, the most influential Chinese thinkers in this context are Wu Jingmei, whose theory about the three dimensions of credit (Wu, 2020b, 2013) contributed greatly to conceptualizing the SCS, as well as Wu Weihai, who considers credit an important feature of great powers and advocates for an export of the Chinese SCS (Wu, 2018, Wu and Zhang, 2017).

After the establishment of the SCS started in 2014, the attention of the Chinese-language literature shifted to focus on the implementation status of the SCS, remaining problems and improvement suggestions (e.g. He, 2021, Wu, 2020a, Shi and Wang, 2018, Wu, 2018). In this context, the need for social credit regulation (e.g. He, 2021, Wang, 2021, Zhou and Zhang, 2020) and the development of credit service organizations (e.g. Wu, 2019a, Wu and Liu, 2017) have been topics of high importance. However, these works mostly do not contain empirical research.

The English-speaking literature picked up on the SCS only after Rogier Creemers (2015) published an opinion piece on the SCS in 2015. Due to the SCS's complexity, the focus has so far also been on explaining the system's set-up (e.g. Honghai and Bi, 2021, Jakob, 2021, Werbach, 2021, Heberer, 2020, Von Blomberg, 2020, Chen et al., 2018). Most of this work, however, has revolved around the branch of the SCS that targets individuals (e.g. Chen and Grossklags, 2020, Kostka and Antoine, 2020, Knight, 2018, Liang et al., 2018).

The discussion on the corporate arm of the SCS only started after Meissner's (2017) piece on the SCS as an instrument for market regulation for the think tank MERICS as well as the report "The Digital Hand: How China's Corporate Social Credit System Conditions Market Actors" jointly written by the consulting firm Sinolytics and the EU's Chamber of Commerce in China in 2019. This research gap is surprising, since the SCS branch targeting the corporate sector has been implemented with great force, whereas the branch targeting individuals remains in the pilot phase. With the business community recognizing the importance of the SCS, further publications on the role of the SCS for the economy and its impact on corporate actors followed (e.g. Krause et al., 2022, Serrano et al., 2022, Fischer, 2021, Kessler and Jin, 2020, Krause and Fischer, 2020, Pache, 2020). However, these contributions remained conceptual in nature.

Therefore, only few empirical studies on the SCS exist so far. Kostka (2018) collected data on the Chinese population's opinion on the SCS[132], whereas Engelmann et al. (2019, 2021) examined the characteristics of the SCS's black- and redlists and Knight and Creemers (2021) analyzed the adaptation of the SCS to the consequences of the COVID-19 pandemic. In addition, several studies investigated local SCS pilots (e.g. Lin and Milhaupt, 2021, Tsai et al., 2021). While some of these empirical studies also provide important insights for the corporate sector (e.g. Krause et al., 2022, Serrano et al., 2022), there is still a lack of dedicated empirical work on the SCS's impact on businesses, a gap this chapter addresses.

5.2 Overview of the Social Credit System

5.2.1 Historical development

The concept of social credit (社会信用), including the plan to establish the SCS, originated from the notion of financial credit and has evolved in four phases since China's reform and opening in 1978. In the first phase (1979 – 1990), the need for controlling and improving loan-lending activities in

132 The results from this study are contested due to shortcomings in the empirical method. For instance, data collection took place at a very early stage of SCS implementation and many Chinese respondents had not been in contact with the SCS and did not know what the system entailed. Opinions on topics, however, are highly dependent on the exposure to and experience with a tool or measure. Hence, the validity of the presented results can be questioned.

commerce and finance emerged (Chorzempa et al., 2018, p. 3). Back then, the government focused on expediting the transition to a market economy via extensive economic reforms in order to achieve growth and development. This transition created financial problems for the newly established market economy, such as fraud and excess borrowing (Chorzempa et al., 2018, p. 3). One of the causes for these problems was the fact that China, at that time, did not possess a credit system or data sharing mechanisms between lenders[133] (Chorzempa et al., 2018, p. 3). Hence, in 1990, the idea of credit, specifically social credit, was mentioned for the first time in the 'Notice of the State Council on Launching the Work of Clearing "Triangular Debts" across the Country' (State Council China, 1990). However, this document neither defined nor discussed the concept in depth. It simply stated, as a problem definition in the first sentence, that the current high amount of debt owed by Chinese enterprises is a serious issue which harms social credit among others (State Council China, 1990). Thus, in this initial phase, it seems that only the notions of financial and commercial loans were linked to the concept of social credit.

The second phase spans from 1991 to 1998; a period when market reforms were deepened and the government's countermeasures to the arising problems, such as environmental degradation, were initiated. A broader awareness for credit-related topics arose among enterprises, investors and banks, since the increasing modernization of the economy with transactions between strangers showed these actors the need for a financial credit system (Yu, 2016, p. 50f). At this point, the debate was still purely focused on financial issues rather than the inclusion of social aspects into a credit system. Consequently, the first private financial and commercial credit systems, rating schemes and risk management activities that emerged focused on purely financial indicators for creditworthiness (Shi and Wang, 2018, Yu, 2016, p. 51). However, at that time, no nationwide all-encompassing credit system was established.

In the third phase (1999 – 2011) the Chinese government undertook the first concerted efforts towards establishing a national credit reporting system. These measures were still focused on financial creditworthiness, specifically on resolving information asymmetries between creditors and borrowers in order to allow for a risk-reduced and effective lending process.

133 No such system had been necessary in the pre-reform era, where banks' lending activities had been limited to the state and SOEs (Chorzempa et al., 2018, p. 3).

In 1999, after the Shenzhen-based female entrepreneur Huang Wenyun publicly called for measures to ensure a market environment which allows for safe credit transactions, the Chinese government asked the Chinese Academy of Social Sciences to establish the first credit-related research project (Yu, 2016, p. 51). The project, named 'Establishing a National Credit Management System' (建立国家信用管理体系), focused on a comparative analysis of credit systems and related infrastructure. It laid the foundation for the set-up of a Chinese credit system and started the Chinese discourse on credit as an academic discipline[134] (Lin, 2012, p. 2). At the same time, international credit service companies, such as Fitch, Coface and Dun & Bradstreet entered the Chinese market (Wu, 2018, p. 59). Furthermore, pilots for credit institutions emerged in cities and municipalities, such as Shanghai and Beijing and provinces, such as Guangdong and the building of a SCS was advanced at the 16th Party Congress by Jiang Zemin in 2002 (Jiang, 2002).

At that time, however, the SCS as a concept turned out to be identical with financial credit systems in other countries, i.e. the SCS focused on increasing economic efficiency and competitiveness by providing financial information on economic actors (Chorzempa et al., 2018, p. 3). It is likely that the word 'social' was added to the term 'credit system' only to better integrate the concept into the ideological discourse. Such a terminology seemed more suitable in a system that designates itself as 'socialism with Chinese characteristics' (中国特色社会主义), where it could join the ranks of similar terms, such as the 'social market economy' (社会市场经济) (Chorzempa et al., 2018, p. 3).

All these developments culminated in the launch of two institutions: First, the PBoC's Credit Reference Center (征信中心), an independent and nationwide financial credit scoring institution, in 2004; and second, the Inter-Ministerial Joint Conference on the Construction of the Social Credit System[135] (社会信用体系建设部际联席会议) in 2007, which later became one of the most influential institutions in building the SCS and passing social credit policies (Knight, 2018, p. 12).

The fourth phase (2012 – 2020) marked a turn in the discourse and understanding of social credit. From this point onward, social credit was no

134 For a detailed record on how the academic discourse about credit has evolved since 1999, refer to Lin (2012).

135 Based on a Leading Small Group composed of the five largest national banks and 17 ministries of the government.

longer equated with financial credit and the SCS was not defined as congruent with credit schemes in other countries anymore. The word 'social' in the term 'social credit' was filled with meaning, as the Chinese government decided to adopt a broad notion of credit (Shi and Wang, 2018). This idea culminated in the 'State Council's Outline for Issuing the Plan for Building a Social Credit System (2014 – 2020)' ('Outline' in the following) in 2014 (State Council China, 2014); the main policy document explaining the Chinese central government's goals, scope and implementation plan for building the SCS.

In this publication on the SCS, the terms '(社会)信用' and '诚信' are central[136] and provide insights into the new conceptualization of social credit in the context of the SCS. '信用' is a complex term with several meanings (Shi, 2020, p. 23). On the one hand, it is translated as 'trustworthiness', i.e. that actors actually do what they promise to do (Shi, 2020, p. 23). On the other hand, '信用' means 'credit(worthiness)', i.e. to what extent someone is suitable for obtaining financial credit (e.g. loans) (Shi, 2020, p. 23). The term 'creditworthiness' differs from 'trustworthiness' in one aspect: The former is related to the financial realm, while the latter is a broad social and relational term. At the same time, both meanings refer to a quality that is attributed to someone by others, potentially based on an actor's previous behavior. This amalgamation of social and technical financial qualities in the term '信用' is reemphasized in the concept of social credit (社会信用)[137]. Social credit essentially extends the judgment of an actor's financial status to a judgment of the same actor's overall status in society, which is equated with trustworthiness.

However, the SCS attempts to go beyond merely attributing qualities, but aims to change social behavior. This is where the term '诚信', often translated as 'integrity and honesty', comes into play. '诚信' enhances the SCS's scope by adding a moral component. The term entails an ethical element in character, attitude and behavior and thereby raises the standards for trustworthiness: While people can also act trustworthily for personal gain (calculative orientation), '诚信' requires a true sense of morality (moral

136 In contrast, '征信', which also translates as 'credit' is predominantly used for the narrow notion of financial credit, e.g. in publications by the PBoC.

137 This research translates the term '信用' as 'credit', 'creditworthiness' or 'trustworthiness' depending on the context and refers to '社会信用' as 'social credit' in the following.

orientation) and thus results in the highest level of trustworthiness, where a person commits to acting based on ethical values[138] (Etzioni, 1975, p. 9f).

Thus, compared to a narrow concept of credit, which focuses only on the field of finance and economics as in Western countries, the SCS's broad credit concept also includes societal morals and ethical behaviors (Ye, 2015, p. 25). Based on this broad understanding of credit, the key indicators businesses and individuals are judged against, in addition to their financial situation, are their levels of compliance to general laws and regulations, as well as their levels of behavioral integrity (Ye, 2015, p. 25). Therefore, the SCS is regarded as a tool that is based on the existing corpus of law and helps to achieve healthy social and economic development (Ye, 2015, p. 25). The Chinese social credit theory specifies this improvement mechanism: By fostering integrity, morals and ethics among the population via the SCS, people's self-restraint, and therefore their social credit, will increase, which again motivates 'good' behavior – a reinforcing cycle (Ye, 2015, p. 32).

Interestingly, this development of the conception of credit in China – from a narrow focus on evaluating financial aspects to a broader moral notion – is contrary to the way the notion of credit emerged in the West, such as in the US and Germany: There, credit originally had a dominant educational purpose and included social and ethical factors in its evaluation, but only later became the strong financial and seemingly objective concept that it is today (Lipartito, 2013, Berghoff, 2008, Guinnane, 2001).

The greater moral orientation of social credit and the SCS, as compared to previous credit-related institutions, matches traditions in Chinese political theory, which attribute a strong role to the government in moral governance. For instance, Confucian rule by virtue stresses the moral guidance the sage ruler provides to the population (e.g. Deng, 2007). Accordingly, the Chinese ruling class is regarded as the judge of what is ethical or moral and is therefore permitted to make normative decisions (Thornton, 2007, p. 14f). Practical manifestations of this idea of governance in Chinese history are, for example, the Song dynasty's 'baojia' (保甲) system[139] and the book 'Ledgers of Merit and Demerit'[140], which was popular during the transition from the Ming to the Qing dynasty (Creemers, 2018, Brokaw, 2014).

138 For the purpose of simplicity, this research refers to the term '诚信' as 'integrity' in the following.

139 A community-based system for law enforcement.

140 A Neo-Confucian morality handbook including a point system for (im)moral deeds and resulting punishments and rewards.

But the CCP has also held up the idea of providing moral governance to and morally educating the population, for example, via concepts such as 'moral construction' (道德建设) and 'social engineering' (社会工程), educational propaganda campaigns, such as the 'suzhi' (素质) discourse[141], and 'personnel files' (档案), which record information on every Chinese citizen and play a crucial role in career advancement in the public sector (Jiang, 2020, p. 3f). The SCS, as a socio-technical instrument to guide actors' behavior, therefore represents the epitome of the CCP's combination of these moral obligations as a ruler with its technocratic government style.

The SCS has been forcefully implemented since the release of the 'Outline' in 2014. For instance, the importance of this system was underscored by the Chinese government's decision to install the NDRC as a co-lead in the Inter-Ministerial Joint Conference on the Construction of the Social Credit System (Knight, 2018, p. 16). This move provided the NDRC with the necessary resources and power to implement the mammoth project quickly. This did not only include the set-up of entirely new databases and platforms (e.g. Credit China), but also the integration of previously existing scoring mechanisms into the scope of the SCS (e.g. firms' customs ratings).

With the completion of the initial phase of establishing the SCS in 2020, the fifth and still ongoing phase of the evolution of social credit has started. While the implementation of the SCS was significantly advanced since its set-up (e.g. creation of nationwide databases, installment of listing- and scoring-systems, definition of joint punishment and reward mechanisms), the work on the system is nevertheless nowhere near being completed. Thus, the State Council released the 'Opinion on Further Improving Systems for Restraining the Untrustworthy and Building Mechanisms for Building Creditworthiness that have Long-term Effect' ('Opinion' in the following) as a document to specify the focus for the implementation and improvement of the SCS after 2020 (State Council China, 2020). The dominating theme throughout this document is nationwide standardization, e.g. of credit information, repair mechanisms, punishments and information sharing (State Council China, 2020).

Since the release of the 'Opinion', the NDRC, the PBoC and the Inter-Ministerial Joint Conference on the Construction of the Social Credit System have already pressed ahead with their efforts for national standard-

141 Suzhi can be translated as 'quality' or 'character'. The suzhi discourse in China uses the notion of human quality to cultivate sophisticated and civil citizens (Kipnis, 2007, p. 384).

ization, for instance by releasing draft guidelines (opinion seeking phase) on which information counts as credit information ('National Catalog of Basic Public Credit Information') and allowed punishments for lost credit ('National List of Basic Penalty Measures for Untrustworthiness') in 2021 (NDRC, 2021). Moreover, several provinces have passed laws and regulations dedicated to social credit (e.g. Shandong, Guangdong), which intend to clarify the legal status of the SCS and its mechanisms (Guangdong Province, 2021, Shandong Province, 2020). Discussions about a national social credit law have started; however, the authorities have not yet released a first draft (Trivium, 2019).

Still, these standardization efforts cannot belie the fact that the development direction of the SCS is contested. An article released by Caixin in 2020 illustrated the disagreements between the NDRC and the PBoC, the two most powerful authorities in the context of the SCS (Caixin, 2020): While the NDRC insists on a broad notion of credit (represented by the term '信用'), which results in the combination of financial data with other behavioral data for credit evaluations, the PBoC, as a financial institution, calls for the adoption of a narrow understanding of credit (reflected in the term '征信'[142]) and opposes fully connecting its financial databases with the databases built by the NDRC in the context of the SCS (Caixin, 2020, EXP19-02). The reason for the PBoC's stance is likely that the bank does not control the non-financial aspects of credit, yet wants to retain its power in the credit reporting realm (Wu, 2019b).

But the conflicts extend beyond these two authorities: Connecting databases of authorities across the country is challenging and data sharing at times inefficient (BUS19-09). The mistrust between authorities (e.g. questioning of data quality from other departments) even goes so far that some authorities prefer purchasing data from private data platforms (e.g. Qichacha and Tianyancha) or build their own databases, instead of directly using another department's data (BUS19-09, GOV19-01). Despite these implementation challenges, major elements of the SCS have already been up and running for several years. The following sections first elaborate on the overarching goals and scope of the SCS, before delineating its set-up.

142 征信 also translates as 'credit' and is predominantly used for the narrow notion of financial credit.

5.2.2 Goals and scope of the Social Credit System

The 'Outline', as the initial and main policy document on the SCS, provides key information on the goals the Chinese central government pursues in building the SCS and the scope this system is supposed to cover. This document defines the SCS's overarching goal in the first section as the following:

> "The goal is to increase the entire society's awareness for integrity and its trustworthiness levels" ("目的是提高全社会的诚信意识和信用水平") (State Council China, 2014).

This means that the SCS targets trustworthiness based on an honest and upright moral orientation, not only in financial transactions, but in any type of social interaction.

The Chinese government draws out three steps to achieve this goal in their motto 'Know trust, keep trust, employ trust' (知信，守信，用信) (NDRC and PBoC, 2018): First, to know what trust means, i.e. at the individual's cognitive level; second, to act in a trustworthy manner by keeping your word, i.e. at the individual's behavioral level; third, to employ trust in one's interactions with others, i.e. at the societal level.

This overarching goal breaks down into three specific realms to be addressed by the SCS in order to ensure China's further development and success. First, integrity and trustworthiness need to be improved between citizens in order to foster a civilized culture necessary for positive societal development (State Council China, 2014). This goal can be regarded as a reaction to a dominant discourse in China on the so-called 'moral crisis' of the Chinese society (Krause and Fischer, 2020, p. 438). Whether a moral crisis exists or not, trust deficits appear to occur in all realms of society, for example among individuals: According to the World Value Survey, only 11 percent of the surveyed Chinese believe that people they do not know can be completely or somewhat trusted, only half of the average level identified across all surveyed countries (22 percent), and at the same level as in Azerbaijan (10 percent) or Colombia (12 percent) (World Value Survey Association, 2014). Incidents, such as people helping fellow citizens, only to find themselves being sued by the person they aided (The Guardian, 2011), further fuel the mistrust towards strangers.

Chinese scholars have identified reasons that led to this moral crisis: Sociologists, such as Fei Xiaotong (1992), have described China as an 'acquaintance society' (熟人社会) that is held together by guanxi and family ties in a traditional Chinese hierarchy. According to this line of argument, Chinese society has always exhibited high trust levels within families and networks of guanxi, but lacked trust towards strangers. In today's modern society the mistrust towards people outside the personal network has simply become more prominent, because interactions and exchange more often extend beyond the family and existing guanxi relationships (e.g. business interactions with unknown firms). Other scholars attribute the trust problem to the rapid economic development that China has undergone since the reform and opening in 1978: Ye (2015, p. 25) considered loss of trust a natural side-effect of fast economic growth, which is comparable to the social challenges developed nations, such as the UK, Germany or Japan, faced right after the industrial revolution. Since these nations have already overcome similar challenges and built societal trust, they do not need to include social aspects in their credit systems (Ye, 2015, p. 27). Other scholars specify development's side-effects as a loss of collective identity and moral agency that gives rise to corruption, individualism and inequalities in Chinese society (e.g. Ci, 2014, Steinmüller, 2013, Oxfeld, 2010). So far, the Chinese government's efforts to increase trust-levels by introducing mechanisms connected to rule by law seem to have not produced the desired results, for instance, due to the authoritarian nature of the political system and low levels of faith in the legal system (e.g. Pia, 2016, Cai et al., 2010, Gallagher, 2006). Against this background, the SCS looks like a new attempt to overcome these obstacles and strengthen law enforcement.

Second, the SCS aims to improve integrity and trustworthiness in the economic realm. The 'Outline' explicitly mentions the need to increase the competitiveness of the Chinese economy, e.g. by reducing economic risks and trade costs, improving allocation of resources, reducing administrative interventions in the economy and increasing domestic demand (State Council China, 2014). Moreover, the 'Outline' emphasizes that the credit service market needs to be further developed, because no comprehensive credit reporting system covering the entire Chinese society existed and the credit service market was underdeveloped before the set-up of the SCS (State Council China, 2014).

Without such a system, acting in an untrustworthy manner in financial interactions came at comparably low costs and credit risks were higher, which ultimately led to an erosion of trust in the corporate sector (Krause and Fischer, 2020, p. 447). For example, many corporate scandals in recent years, such as the melamine-tainted milk-powder problem in 2008, the financial frauds by Wanfu Biotech and the vaccine scandal in Shandong in 2016, harmed Chinese consumers' image of the corporate sector (Dong et al., 2018, p. 543). At the same time, companies themselves developed mistrust towards the government. On the one hand, the center's lack of control over local governments in the fragmented Chinese bureaucratic system and the encouragement of local experiments by the central government after 1978 have given local cadres leeway to interpret central policies as they see fit (Mertha, 2009, Landry, 2008). This has led to deficits regarding predictability and transparency for companies and induced corruption. Even though Xi Jinping initiated an anti-corruption campaign in 2012 that was unprecedented in its scope, methods and duration, China still ranks 78th out of 180 countries on the Corruption Perceptions Index of Transparency International[143] (Transparency International, 2020). On the other hand, the central government has also caused problems related to trustworthiness: Its autocratic rule can at times lead to arbitrariness, which harms businesses. In the past, the centrally controlled media have, for example, only targeted foreign MNEs with negative campaigns selectively, which resulted in significant image and thus economic losses (Yang and Jiang, 2015, p. 103f).

However, trust in the corporate sector is especially important. High levels of trust are directly related to performance, both on the firm-level and the level of the national economy. On the firm-level, trust helps to reduce transaction costs in several ways, e.g. by decreasing the complexity in setting up contracts and the time needed for negotiations (e.g. Dyer and Chu, 2003, Zaheer et al., 1998, Chiles and Mcmackin, 1996). Moreover, in relationships of trust, counterparts need to engage in monitoring less while collaboration and information sharing work better (e.g. Cai et al., 2010, Dyer and Chu, 2003, Pollitt, 2002). On the national level, reduced transaction costs of key economic players as a consequence of improved levels of trust can accumulate and produce significant benefits for a country's economic growth (e.g. Beugelsdijk et al., 2004, Zak and Knack, 2001). In turn, a low-trust environment characterized, for example, by a lack of judicial efficiency, bureaucratic quality and tax compliance, is a main cause for underdevelopment and economic stagnation (Dasgupta, 2000, p. 365f). Hence, the government has an interest to increase trust-levels in Chinese society to reap economic benefits (Krause and Fischer, 2020).

---

143 For a comparison, Germany ranks 9th and the US 25th (Transparency International, 2020).

Third, the Chinese government even goes one step further by positioning the SCS as a tool to improve its standing in the international community. The 'Outline' characterizes modern market economies as 'credit economies' (信用经济, State Council China, 2014). With the SCS, the Chinese government not only wants to meet the economy's demands, but also wishes to set a new standard for credit rating systems internationally (State Council China, 2014). Hence, the SCS is supposed to help deepen international collaboration, strengthen the country's international reputation and ultimately increase China's soft power in the international community (State Council China, 2014).

In Western industrialized democratic countries, however, the SCS seems to have fostered the exact opposite reaction, namely strong criticism and damage to the Chinese reputation. This is most prominently manifested in the international press, which, without distinction between the corporate and individual arm of the system, portray the SCS as the epitome of the Orwellian surveillance state in the context of discussions on the threats of big data and artificial intelligence (e.g. "Beijing Pioneering Citizens' 'Points' System Critics Brand 'Orwellian'", The New York Times, 2018; "China is taking digital control of its people to unprecedented and chilling lengths", Naughton, 2018). Thus, the objectives regarding the SCS's international impact appear to not have been reached.

However, the 'Outline' does not specify the countries China wants to influence internationally. Thus, (autocratic) countries of the Global South may be the target group instead of advanced industrialized nations (Fischer, 2021). China has already sold technological solutions, such as smart identity cards, to some of these countries (e.g. Venezuela, Berwick, 2018) and could aim to strengthen relationships by exporting the SCS as a tool for economic development.

These elaborations show that the SCS is to serve as a "cure-all solution to a multitude of disparate societal and economic problems" that emerged in Chinese society (Ohlberg et al., 2017, p. 2). To achieve this ambitious goal, the SCS targets four realms: The government, the judicial system, businesses and society (State Council China, 2014). The 'Outline' describes the targeted measures in all four areas. These include initiatives explicitly listed as targeting businesses, but also selected measures in the society realm that address the corporate sector (see Table 4): In the business realm, the 'Outline' lists 14 aspects to be improved via the SCS, in the society realm six aspects affect corporations.

Table 4: SCS measures impacting the corporate sector from the 'Outline's' description of the business and society realm (State Council China, 2014)

Realm	Aspect	Exemplary measures
Business	Production	Improve production safety in coal mines, hazardous chemical production and other high-risk sectors
	Logistics	Strengthen anti-trust enforcement, the prosecution of false propaganda and bribery; construct credit in wholesale, retail, accommodation and other logistics industries; establish a tracking system for goods
	Finances	Introduce new financial credit products and better financial services; safeguard the security of personal information of financial consumers; strengthen the punishment of financial fraud, insider trading, etc.
	Taxation	Establish cross-departmental exchange of tax-related information; improve the tax payment ranking system
	Pricing	Implement measures for pricing inspections and against price monopolies; strengthen self-discipline in pricing; strengthen businesses' internal price management
	Construction projects	Punish enterprises with major quality and safety accidents; dismantle illegal subcontracting and late payment of migrant workers' salaries in the construction field
	Government procurement	Prohibit government contracts to untrustworthy companies for a certain period of time; construct a unified national government procurement management system
	Tenders	Set up a comprehensive and standardized electronic tendering and bidding system; use basic credit information in the bidding process
	Traffic & transportation	Set up a consistent assessment and evaluation system across bodies in the transportation sector, including the definition of consistent assessment standards; encourage all work units to purchase from high-credit transportation companies
	E-commerce	Set up customer credit ratings; improve quality inspections for online shop products; punish false advertising, counterfeit products, etc.
	Statistics	Strengthen investigation of false statistics; set standards for integrity in enterprises' statistical analysis; link statistical credit records with corporate finance, government subsidies, commercial registration, etc.
	Intermediary services	Strengthen the credit management for intermediary organizations, such as consultancies, accounting enterprises, monitoring businesses, law firms, etc.
	Events & ads	Punish all kinds of false advertising; promote trustworthy event management with sincere service contracts
	Enterprises credit management	Create positions for credit supervisors; encourage enterprises' credit self-construction and credit management; promote model cases of trustworthy and trust-breaking enterprises

Realm	Aspect	Exemplary measures
Society	Healthcare	Ensure drug safety; promote creditworthy hospitals, pharmacies, etc.; punish bribery
	Employ-ment	Publicize unlawful acts by employers (e.g. labor guarantees); standard-ize employment activities
	Culture, sports & tourism	Establish credit evaluations for businesses in the cultural sector; set up a third-party assessment system for travel agencies, hotels, etc.
	Intel. prop-erty	Raise awareness on intellectual property protection; prosecute intellec-tual property infringements
	Environ-mental pro-tection & energy sav-ing	Establish structures for businesses' self-monitoring regarding pollution, publishing results and improvement measures; establish credit evalu-ation mechanisms for businesses' environmental behavior; link bank and insurance services with pollution data; strengthen energy audits and reporting mechanisms
	Internet	Establish credit rating mechanisms for internet companies; collect on-line credit information

Judging from the elaborateness and length of descriptions in the 'Outline', as well as the implementation status, the SCS's focus lies on the corporate sector: In stark contrast to the Western debates about the SCS, where the monitoring and rating of individuals takes center stage (see Section 5.1), the individual rating system is only one of ten aspects in the 'Outline's' society realm. While the 'Outline' only lays the foundations, the actual implementation practices are also skewed towards the corporate sector as the main target group of the SCS. The individual arm of the system still remains in the pilot phase, whereas the SCS's corporate arm has been running for several years (Schaefer and Yin, 2019).

5.2.3 The set-up of the Social Credit System

The set-up of the SCS certainly reflects the complexity of the central government's goals. In contrast to (often oversimplified) illustrations in the media (e.g. Reuters, 2018, The New York Times, 2018), to date, no one central comprehensive score per (natural or legal) person exists from which points are deducted for misbehavior and to which points are added for exemplary conduct. Instead, an intricate system of various elements addressing different target groups and adopting a range of enforcement instruments has been created and is still in the process of being refined.

This section provides an overview of the main elements of the SCS that directly or indirectly affect the corporate sector[144].

The key components of the SCS all build on one central data platform, the National Credit Information Sharing Platform (NCISP, 全国信用信息共享平台). All the other elements can then be clustered according to the main target group they address (individuals or companies) and the type of provider who runs this platform (public or private) (see Figure 21). The following subsections first describe the NCISP, followed by elaborations on the elements targeting companies (upper and lower fields on the left in Figure 21) and individuals (upper and lower fields on the right in Figure 21).

Figure 21: Overview of the SCS's key elements (author's design)

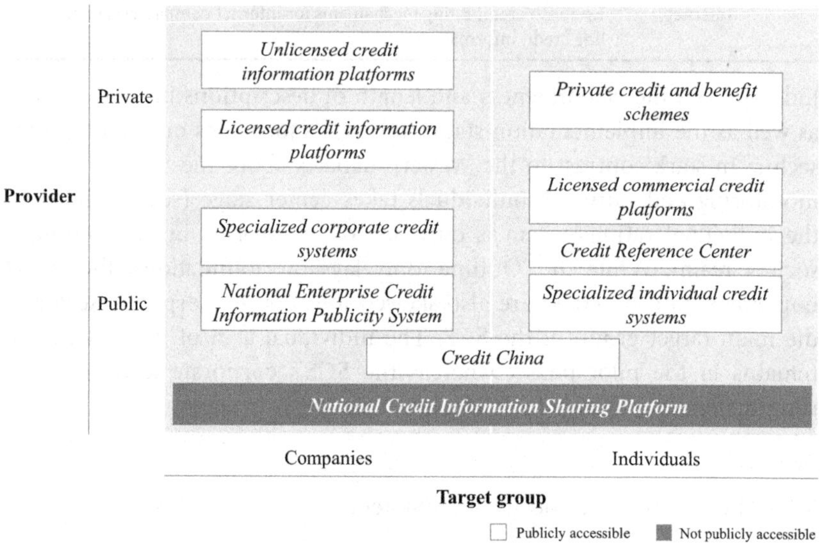

144 Since the SCS is a mammoth project, it is necessary to focus on the key elements of the system. However, further elements beyond what is described exist or are under development, for instance elements targeting NGOs or research institutions (Ministry of Civil Affairs, 2021, Central Committee of the CCP and State Council China, 2018).

The National Credit Information Sharing Platform

One of the first undertakings following the decision to build the SCS, was the creation of one centralized database as the back end of the entire system, the NCISP[145] (Meissner, 2017, p. 6). The purpose of this platform is to consolidate existing administrative data from authorities across the country (e.g. central ministries, local administrations). The NDRC drives this effort and acts as a data administrator, i.e. is responsible for compiling, standardizing and – for certain data sets – publishing the information (Schaefer, 2020, p. 17). The NDRC does not create these pieces of information itself, but collects existing data points from within the administration. As these data-points originate from authorities across the country, they can be considered 'second-hand' information. This means that processed information, instead of raw data, is compiled via the NCISP (e.g. the information on a fine due to speeding, rather than the video recording of the speeding) (EXP19-09). Often the generation of these types of information is not (fully) automatized and humans are involved (EXP19-09); a potential gateway for corruption, manipulation, gaming and mistakes[146].

The data consolidation on this platform is a huge endeavor, since many different actors need to cooperate and share information. One of the first steps to achieve this goal, was to create nationwide unified social credit codes (统一社会信用代码)[147] (Chen et al., 2018, p. 10). The 18-digit codes for all natural and legal persons aggregate information on these actors that used to be listed under several different identification numbers (e.g. for natural persons the tax identification number, social welfare identification number...) in one account per (natural/legal) person (Chen et al., 2018, p. 10). Hence, the unified social credit code has an administrative function for consolidating dispersed data and providing transparency in a similar manner as the Legal Entity Identifier (LEI) provides the key reference information on companies participating in financial transactions globally in one profile[148] (Global Legal Entity Identifier Foundation, 2021a).

145 The platform went live at the end of 2015 (Guangming Daily, 2018).

146 While fully automatized data collection process can also be manipulated and subject to biases, they still possess one less gateway for mistakes (the human factor).

147 The China Organization Data Service is responsible for managing the system of unified social credit codes (China Organization Data Service, 2020).

148 The LEI was initiated by the Group of 20 as a reaction to the financial crisis in order to provide additional transparency about global financial transactions and prevent fraud. This international project is run by the Global Legal Entity Identifier

In addition, there are ongoing efforts to connect databases from authorities across the country to the NCISP. However, this is an intricate process, since decisions on the sensitivity and confidentiality of data have to be made and data quality needs to be ensured (EXP19-09). There appear to be limits on departments' willingness to share data (e.g. financial data from the PBoC) as well as to the mutual trust among authorities with regard to data quality (EXP19-02, GOV19-01). Nevertheless, as of May 2018, the platform had already connected 44 government/administrative departments and 32 provincial-level credit platforms, as well as gathered over 17 billion pieces of credit information (Guangming Daily, 2018).

In addition, initiatives in which state agencies from different regions are cooperating to improve the business environment and service quality have been reported; for instance the announcement of data sharing (in total 268 government service-related data sets) related to topics such as industry access and qualifications between Beijing, Tianjin and Guangzhou in August 2021 (Cyberspace Affairs Commission, 2021). This shows that the process of collecting data and improving the database is ongoing.

While some of the gathered data is published via other SCS platforms, such as Credit China (信用中国), the NCISP itself is not publicly accessible. Meissner (2017, p. 6) estimated that about 75 percent of the data on the platform are publicly available (公开) and the rest is classified as data for limited (有限共享) or inter-governmental sharing (政务共享).

Elements targeting companies

The main platform for publishing data from the NCISP is Credit China; a website initiated by the NDRC and the PBoC (NDRC and PBoC, 2021). Credit China constitutes the central communication platform for all information related to the SCS and therefore includes a broad spectrum of information on the SCS (e.g. regulations, news, reports). In addition, the website lists other actors in the context of the SCS (specialized credit systems, accredited credit service providers, etc.). While the information is not limited to corporate actors[149], the website nevertheless has a section dedicated to information on industry credit (行业信用). Moreover, the

Foundation, a non-profit organization (Global Legal Entity Identifier Foundation, 2021b).

149 Credit China also includes information on the SCS branches targeting individuals and other actors, such as cities and education institutions.

platform possesses a search function, with the help of which profiles of legal and natural persons can be accessed. The company profiles on this platform provide basic company information (e.g. legal representative, founding date, company type, licenses) as well as information related to the businesses' social credit, such as administrative punishments, rewards for trustworthy behavior, punishments for untrustworthy behavior, points of special attention, qualifications and risk prompts (see Figure 22 for an example). The so-called 'double publication' (双公示) mechanism, which was instated in 2015, ensures that information is up to date, because it requires authorities to publish social credit information on the internet within seven working days from the day an administrative decision is made (NDRC, 2018a).

Figure 22: Screenshot of Huawei's company profile on Credit China (2021g) (information categories highlighted by the black frame)

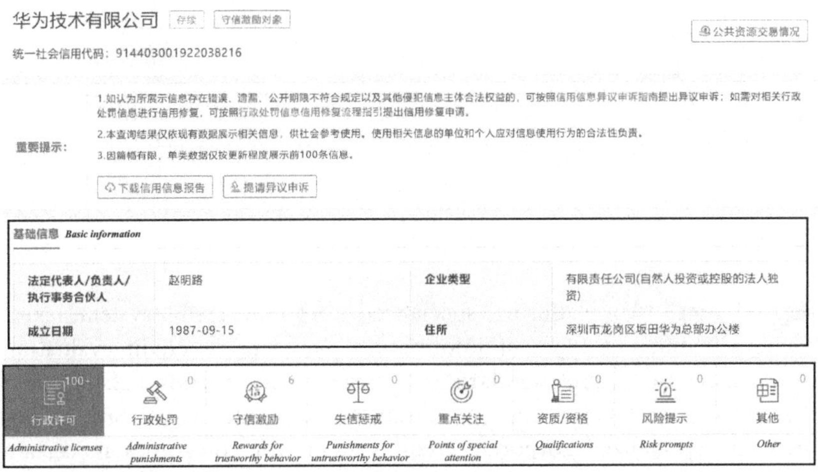

A similar set of information can be accessed on the National Enterprise Credit Information Publicity System (国家企业信用信息公示系统, NECIPS), which the SAMR has been operating since October 2015 (Chen et al., 2018, p. 12). This is a comprehensive national database exclusively focusing on the corporate sector. Similar to Credit China, the NECIPS includes any type of business with an operating license in China regardless of size, industry, shareholders and location of the mother company, etc.[150]. Since NECIPS company profiles are based on the same set of data as information on Credit China, the published information overlaps to a large extent (see Figure 23 for an example). Yet, the company profile information on the NECIPS is more comprehensive with regard to general business information (e.g. provision of annual reports, names of board members and information on intellectual property).

Figure 23: Screenshot of Huawei's company profile on the NECIPS (2021) (information categories highlighted by the black frame)

Beyond these two platforms, specialized corporate credit systems exist. These are different types of information platforms or credit evaluation mechanisms that adopt standard SCS mechanisms (Section 5.2.4 for further details) and target certain subsets of corporate actors. Specifically, there are specialized corporate credit systems for companies in certain localities, for firms operating in certain industries or addressing particular regulatory topics. An example of a local corporate credit system is the case of Zhejiang province, one of the few places, where companies receive one comprehensive credit rating (Lin and Milhaupt, 2021, p. 8f). Beyond that, there are also black- and redlists from local authorities for companies in their jurisdiction. With regard to systems that are specialized on industries, firm rating systems in the financial sector are prominent examples, e.g. securities firms' ratings (for further details on this system, refer to Section

150 For each branch of a company that is registered separately, a distinct company profile exists.

6.1.3). Moreover, the transport and the tax rating systems are cases of specialized corporate credit systems, where certain regulators, in this case the Ministry of Transport (交通运输部) and the State Taxation Administration (国家税务总局), address particular topics in their areas of responsibility (Schaefer, 2020, p. 36). Some of these specialized corporate credit systems, such as the system in Zhejiang, have been newly built in the context of the SCS, whereas others, e.g. the securities firm ratings, predate the SCS and were later integrated into, and at times adapted to, the context of the SCS (Lin and Milhaupt, 2021, Schaefer, 2020).

In addition to these efforts from public providers, private actors have also developed credit information platforms that are publicly accessible, with some information provided for free and certain details requiring a fee. Over 130 private firms have received a license from the PBoC as credit reporting organizations, among which the most popular providers are Qichacha (企查查) and Tianyancha (天眼查) (PBoC, 2021, Qichacha, 2021g, Credit China, 2019d). These licensed credit information platforms combine a very comprehensive overview of companies with a convenient user interface. A previous study has shown that these databases provide the highest level of transparency on companies in China[151], even when compared to international counterparts (e.g. reports from private credit reporting firms, such as Dun & Bradstreet) (Krause et al., 2022). Taking the example of Qichacha[152], the data portrayed consists of basic company information (e.g. business information, such as ownership structure, financial information), but also extends to categories for risk evaluation (including information from the public social credit providers) (see Figure 24 for an example). For instance, the category 'own risk' (自身风险) provides information on lawsuits the company is involved in and the category 'sensitive public sentiment' (敏

151 Some of the credit information platforms, such as Qichacha (2021h), have already launched international versions, where users are also supposed to find information in English and on companies in other countries. However, the information provided on the international company profiles is very basic and the database of companies not comprehensive yet.

152 Tianyancha has not been accessible from Germany during the entire research process. However, when checked during the field work in China in November and December 2019, Tianyancha's content and interface were similar to what can be found on Qichacha.

感輿情) reports on sensitive media coverage of a firm (related to losses, non-compliance incidents, etc.).

Figure 24: Screenshot of Huawei's company profile on Qichacha (2021e) (information categories highlighted by the black frame)

The distinguishing feature of these private platforms compared to the public ones, are the greater amount of data on the searched company as well as the category 'relational risk' (关联风险). This section lists risk information of companies or individuals (e.g. management personnel, owners) that the searched firm is linked to and thereby underpins that the understanding of credit constructed on these platforms extends beyond the confines of the single enterprise.

In addition to these licensed private providers, further unlicensed private credit information platforms have emerged (e.g. the Alibaba corporate integrity system, 阿里巴巴企业诚信体系).

However, they seem to not play a significant role for companies in the sample, since none of the interviewees mentioned these platforms.

Overall, the sheer number of private providers – licensed or not – shows that the burgeoning market for credit reporting organizations in China is still immature. It has to be seen, which of the private credit reporting firms will ultimately survive.

Elements targeting individuals

Even though this study focuses on corporations, some of the SCS elements targeting individuals nevertheless play an important role for businesses. On the one hand, one of the SCS's design features is to establish a connection between natural and legal persons. This means that actions of individuals in their personal lives can, under certain circumstances, impact the company they work for and vice versa (for more details on these mechanisms, refer to Section 5.2.4). On the other hand, firms may have an interest in the credit levels of their customers, which, in the case of business-to-customer companies, are individuals. Therefore, firms can use the SCS elements targeting individuals in customer-related business decisions and processes. In addition, the credit information on individuals can also provide insights into potential new employees. For these reasons, the individual arm of the SCS also needs to be considered in the corporate context.

Just as the corporate arm of the SCS, Credit China constitutes the basis and key resource for SCS-related information on individuals from public providers. However, since the SCS's individual arm is still in the pilot phase and has not been uniformly implemented nationwide, Credit China does not provide credit information on every individual. Instead, it aggregates certain, but not all, information from specialized individual credit systems, such as local blacklists. In addition, it provides links and information on specialized individual credit systems and therefore can be considered as a starting point on quests for credit information on individuals.

The category 'specialized individual credit systems' then subsumes both the local SCS pilots, as well as nationwide systems that focus on particular topics. The government started with 41 local pilot cities, most of which are located in the eastern or central provinces of China (see Figure 25) (NDRC and PBoC, 2021). In January 2018, the Chinese government announced twelve of these pilot cities as model cities, because they most successfully implemented all the required components of the SCS according to the government's evaluation (NDRC, 2018b).

However, none of these or other pilots have, to date, been consistently rolled out nationwide. In their research on one of the pilot cities, Tsai et al. (2021) found that the development of the SCS's individual arm is hampered by risk calculations among local officials, who consider the risks of implementing individual credit systems as much higher compared to the risks of implementing the SCS's corporate arm. Beyond this reason, path dependencies related to already existing corporate SCS elements and higher economic incentives stemming from the implementation of the SCS's corporate arm are also likely to play a role. Irrespective of the reasons, the stagnation of the individual arm's implementation leads to a comparatively low level of impact of these pilots for businesses beyond the local context.

Figure 25: Original SCS pilot and model cities (author's design based on NDRC and PBoC, 2021, NDRC, 2018b)

In contrast to local pilots, there is one nationwide specialized credit list targeting individuals which has gained significant importance: The Supreme People's Court (最高人民法院) defaulter list (Supreme People's Court, 2021). This is a website which lists natural and legal persons that have failed to comply with court judgments (Supreme People's Court, 2017). Because being listed by the Supreme People's Court usually results in a high level of shaming, e.g. by business partners, colleagues and on social media, as well as significant additional punishments (refer to Section 5.2.4 for further details), this specialized individual credit system has received considerable attention (e.g. Botsman, 2017, The Economist, 2016).

In addition to the elements targeting individuals from public providers that were newly set up in the SCS context, the PBoC's Credit Reference Center has been a provider of financial credit information since 2004. Originally, this platform was supposed to enable the assessment of borrowers' creditworthiness nationwide, in a similar manner as the Schufa score in Germany or the FICO score in the US (What's on Weibo, 2018). In contrast to the schemes initiated after 2014, it focuses on a narrow notion of credit limited to financial aspects. However, in 2014, after ten years of operation, the Credit Reference Center had only managed to encompass 25 percent of the Chinese population (Yang, 2017b).

In order to achieve a higher coverage of the population, in 2015, the PBoC picked eight private companies to run pilots for commercial credit schemes that could potentially develop into a nationwide commercial credit system (PBoC, 2015): Zhima Credit (芝麻信用), Tencent Credit (腾讯征信), Intellicredit (中智诚征信), Kaola Credit (考拉征信), Pengyuan Credit (鹏元征信), Sinoway Credit (华道征信), Qianhai Credit Services (深圳前海征信) and China Chengxin Credit (中诚信征信). These private credit schemes were set up slightly differently, but what they had in common was the generation of publicly available user scores based on both users' online track record (e.g. payment of loans, postings on social media) and certain information publicly accessible from public providers (What's on Weibo, 2018). However, the algorithms and exact criteria for score generation were not made transparent to the user. In 2018, discord between the private operators and the government prevented all these schemes from receiving official licenses for operation as a nationwide commercial credit system (Credit China, 2018). The officially announced causes were deficient data management and data security, missing independence and the existence of isolated islands of non-shared data, which likely meant a lack of transparency towards the government (Credit China, 2018).

Instead of providing a license to one of the eight firms, the government coopted the schemes by setting up Baihang Credit (百行征信) as the first licensed commercial credit platform (Credit China, 2018). Baihang Credit is owned by the government-backed National Internet Finance Association (中国互联网金融协会) (36 percent of the shares) and the eight pilot companies (each 8 percent of the shares) (Credit China, 2018).

In this restructuring effort, some elements of the eight piloted credit schemes related to credit ratings targeting individuals were incorporated into Baihang Credit, while the remaining elements could be kept in operation independently, e.g. Sesame Credit's research on commercial credit services (What's on Weibo, 2018). This has de facto downgraded the eight firms' remaining systems to voluntary customer benefit schemes, where certain behaviors (e.g. early payment of loans) provide users with benefits in other areas of the respective ecosystem (e.g. free bike rental in certain cities). Other contributions of the eight companies to Baihang Credit are technology and data sharing. Furthermore, representatives from the eight companies fill positions on the board of directors and the board of supervisors at Baihang Credit (What's on Weibo, 2018). However, since then, not much progress in the implementation of a nationwide scoring mechanism has been recorded. This may be due to the discord between the shareholders, for example with regard to data sharing[153] (Yang and Liu, 2019). In the meantime, one more actor has received the same type of license as Baihang Credit, namely Pudao Credit (朴道征信)[154] (Faridi, 2020). Furthermore, Ant Group plans to set up a JV with several state-backed partners, which aims to be the third licensed commercial credit platform (Yang and Yu, 2021, Zhu, 2021). As these have been rather recent developments, it has to be seen how the newly licensed commercial credit platforms will interpret their role and implement credit scoring.

All in all, this overview of the SCS's elements, which affect the corporate sector, shows that companies face a high level of complexity in dealing with the SCS, since the system consists of a large variety of different sub-systems. This complexity is twofold: On the one hand, it pertains to the many platforms that enterprises need to check for information on other actors and where they need to ensure that their own company is portrayed correctly. On the other hand, firms face complexity with respect to the SCS's actors that are involved. Besides private providers, many Party-state agencies play a role in the SCS, e.g. the NDRC, PBoC, SAMR, CSRC, State Tax Administration as well as local governments. This illustrative list shows that, except for the local governments, all of these authorities are, at least on paper, positioned at the same hierarchical level in the Party-state, which bears the threat of inter-ministerial conflicts. Hence, even though there are efforts to standardize and integrate SCS mechanisms, it remains to be seen to what degree these endeavors will be successful in the face of diverging vested

153 Officially, Baihang Credit's license was granted for three years and therefore expired in 2021. So far, it is unclear how the authorities will proceed.

154 This company's biggest shareholder is Beijing Financial Holdings Group, a state-managed enterprise (35 percent), followed by JD Digits (JD.com's digital commerce platform) with 25 percent and Xiaomi with 17.5 percent (Faridi, 2020).

interests at play (e.g. the conflicts between NDRC and PBoC described in Section 5.2.1). Notwithstanding existing differences, there are several basic mechanisms that are adopted across all SCS elements and agencies, as described in the following section.

5.2.4 The Social Credit System's enforcement approach

In order to achieve the goals mentioned above with the SCS elements described, the SCS combines a number of different mechanisms. These mechanisms range across all discussed categories of enforcement instruments (network, legal, economic and communicative enforcement instruments) and together form the SCS's unique enforcement approach (Table 5).

Table 5: The enforcement instruments included in the SCS

Network instruments	Legal instruments	Economic instruments	Communicative instruments
- Profiles - Blacklists - Redlists - Scores	- Joint punishments	- Joint rewards	- Credit repair - Educational campaigns

At the core of the SCS's enforcement approach lie three network instruments: Profiles, lists and scores that provide information and transparency about corporate actors; both natural (e.g. business managers and owners) and legal persons (e.g. companies). As shown in the previous section, profiles vary in the amount and type of information they portray as well as the layout, which depends on the platform. But what they all have in common is that they increase transparency by making additional information on actors accessible, which the person searching could otherwise not have retrieved as easily. To increase convenience, the most popular platforms, such as Qichacha and Tianyancha, provide a wide range of different information to minimize the need for persons looking for information to conduct additional searches. Thus, profiles are a constant network instrument, i.e. not one that is used only under certain circumstances: Profiles exists on a permanent basis and information on them is updated continuously. Consequently, profiles constitute the starting point for information retrieval.

One piece of information typically included on profiles is a notice on the entry of an actor to a black- or redlist. These lists are published by different Party-state agencies and therefore cover many different topics, such as taxes, social and environmental behavior, volunteering and intellectual property (Chen et al., 2018, p. 15f). Generally, they focus on the enforcement of court orders and industry regulations (Engelmann et al., 2021). By naming actors that are particularly good (redlists) or have acted badly (blacklists)[155], they provide transparency (Chen et al., 2018, p. 14ff). However, research has found that the share, comprehensiveness and elaborateness of blacklists is much higher compared to redlists (Engelmann et al., 2019). This suggests that the current focus of the government lies in achieving legal compliance. Since starting to use black- and redlists, the NDRC, PBoC as well as other authorities responsible for the specific lists have made efforts to standardize, which regulators are allowed to use black- and redlists, which data points are to be considered in listing decisions and what kind of behavior leads to a list entry (e.g. NDRC, 2021, Creemers, 2018, NDRC and PBoC, 2017).

In a similar vein, certain regulators apply scores as network instruments. Scores provide transparency by communicating an evaluation of a subject against a set of standards. In the case of scores from public providers, e.g. the CSRC, companies know which criteria they are judged against, because the calculation approach is published in regulatory documents (e.g. SEC-20170707). With regard to private providers, the algorithms for score calculation are not disclosed. Contrary to assumptions in Western media, no nationwide comprehensive scoring mechanism for all natural and legal persons is publicly available at the moment. Even though the NDRC released information on efforts to comprehensively evaluate companies' public credit (公共信用综合评价) in 2019, neither information on the progress of the scoring nor the scores themselves has been published for all companies across industries and regions (NDRC, 2019). At this point, the scoring mechanisms are less commonly adopted as compared to lists. The key difference between scores and lists is that scores allow for a more nuanced approach, since gradual evaluation results are possible instead of a dichotomous yes-no decision. Overall, all three mechanisms (profiles, lists and scores) increase transparency and thereby allow more stakeholders (e.g. business partners, investors, customers) to monitor firms and base their decisions and behavior on the newly gained information,

155 The only actors listed are those located at both ends of a spectrum, whereas the large majority of actors with moderate behavior remain unlisted (Chen et al., 2018).

i.e. stakeholders can become involved as regulators themselves. In this way, these mechanisms levy their force as network instruments.

In addition to network enforcement instruments, the SCS adopts legal and economic instruments according to the same principle: Based on the black- and redlists, authorities administer joint punishments (legal enforcement instrument) and rewards (economic enforcement instrument). The guiding principle and innovative element of these punishments and rewards is cross-departmental collaboration following the motto 'trust-breaking here, restrictions everywhere' (一处失信，处处受限) (Chen et al., 2018, p. 17). Specifically, different Party-state agencies have signed and implemented Memoranda of Understanding (MoUs, 合作备忘录) that prescribe additional consequences for highly untrustworthy or trustworthy behaviors (Chen et al., 2018, p. 18).

MoUs focus on different fields, such as tax matters, food safety, environmental protection, accounting and intellectual property (for a detailed list, refer to Chinalawtranslate, 2021). They describe which and how other authorities than the ones that detected an actor's non-compliance or praiseworthy behavior additionally punish or reward an actor[156]. For instance, the MoU on 'Joint Disciplinary Actions against Seriously Untrustworthy Enterprises and Related Personnel in the Field of Social Insurance' (关于对社会保险领域严重失信企业及其有关人员实施联合惩戒的合作备忘录) was signed by over 28 departments in total, including the NDRC, the PBoC, the Central Propaganda Department (中央宣传部), the Ministry of Transport and the Medical Insurance Bureau (医保局) (Government of the People's Republic of China, 2018). The MoU determines that companies that do not correctly report the social insurance fee base for employees face additional punishments, such as restricting the untrustworthy enterprise's applications for financial subsidies from the state (Government of the People's Republic of China, 2018). Other common punishments for businesses are an increase in authorities' monitoring intensity and frequency, as well as lower chances in government tenders (Chen et al., 2018, p. 17f). Moreover, the punishments for misconduct may not only affect the company as a legal entity, but also the legal representatives personally (Chen et al., 2018, p. 30). In that case, joint punishments for individuals, such as restrictions on luxury consumption (e.g. for vacations, cars or real estate)

156 Based on the manifestation of black- and redlists, the focus in the MoUs also seems to lie on punishments rather than rewards. Hence, the dominant mechanism here is deterrence as compared to providing incentives.

and stalling individuals' career prospects in certain areas (e.g. denying them the possibility to obtain qualifications or licenses) are applied (Chen et al., 2018, p. 19).

In comparison, a typical reward related to the corporate sector is that businesses run by deserving volunteers receive faster access to certain administrative procedures (Chen et al., 2018, p. 15). Therefore, joint rewards can lead to virtuous cycles, where 'good' companies receive benefits that allow them to run their business even more successfully. In contrast, joint punishments bear the risk of triggering vicious cycles, i.e. companies being burdened by punishments to the extent that they lack the means to improve and resort to more negative behavior to survive. If detected and enforced consistently, this negative spiral may ultimately lead to the closure of the company. In order to prevent such an escalation, the SCS also adopts a communicative enforcement instrument, which helps blacklisted actors to improve: Credit repair (信用修复). Actors can restore their credit after being blacklisted and punished via standardized procedures[157] (Credit China, 2021h, 2019c). Depending on the gravity of the legal violation, credit repair is possible after different periods of time (e.g. three or six months after being listed) and requires actors to undergo a variety of procedures (e.g. trainings, drafting credit reports, signing credit repair commitments[158]) (Credit China, 2019c, 2021h). Credit China provides process charts and lists with accredited credit service organizations that conduct credit repair seminars and/or issue credit reports (Credit China, 2021a,b). Thus, the credit repair mechanism allows actors to learn from their mistakes and improve their behavior. Only in case of severe non-compliance incidents is credit repair not possible[159] (Credit China, 2019c, 2021h).

157 Credit repair, the restoration of credit after a violation of regulations, is not to be confused with information correction mechanisms, which actors can deploy in case of wrong credit information on their profile (Credit China, 2021f).

158 Credit (repair) commitments (诚信(修复)承诺书) are promises made by actors (e.g. businesses) to the respective authority about future trustworthy behavior. These commitments can not only contribute to credit repair, but in certain cases also be used to speed up administrative procedures (Credit China, 2021h,i).

159 The credit repair mechanism, however, does not fill the existing legal gaps in insolvency procedures, namely the lack of personal insolvency laws (Parry et al., 2021, p. 518f).

Finally, the SCS possesses one additional communicative instrument, namely its educational campaigns. With the core aim to raise awareness for trustworthiness, integrity and credit in society, the campaigns prominently place these topics in the public discourse and thereby educate the population. The propaganda apparatus is already working in full swing to promote SCS-related values, such as trustworthiness, honesty and integrity. The campaigns are generally targeted at individuals and feature topics, such as integrity and trustworthiness, rather than promoting the SCS as an instrument itself[160]. Examples of propaganda are a popular song about integrity featuring famous Chinese stars, such as Roy Wang, Timmy Xu and Crystal Zhang (What's on Weibo, 2019), as well as publicly displayed posters reminding citizens of the importance of trustworthy behavior (see Figure 26 for an example). In addition, the educational campaigns feature narratives on 'praiseworthy' as well as 'blameworthy' behavior to provide role models and negative examples (Chen et al., 2022). One major achievement of the educational campaigns has been the branding of the term 'laolai' (老赖), which describes actors who refuse to pay debts (Engelmann et al., 2019).

All these efforts contribute to an increased awareness on trustworthiness, integrity and credit across the population, which in turn affects individuals' behaviors in all spheres of their lives, including at work, be it in a company, a Party-state agency or any other organization. Hence, this communicative instrument does not address actors who have violated the law specifically, but instead constantly influences people's mindset and thereby indirectly their actions by shaping the public discourse (nudging).

The above descriptions do not only illustrate that the SCS adopts all existing types of enforcement instruments, but also shows that the different instruments build on each other and are escalated depending on actors' behavior: Based on the transparency provided in profiles and scores on a permanent basis, natural or legal persons may be listed in case of exceptionally good or bad behavior. If listed, these actors receive rewards or punishments that adequately sanction the related behavior. This kind of

160 While a significant amount of publications about the SCS as a system itself can be found on the Credit China website, these contents are mostly related to technical, legal as well as corporate issues and therefore address professionals rather than the general public.

escalation mechanism classifies as the enforcement approach responsive regulation, i.e. an enforcement pyramid[161].

Figure 26: Poster in the Beijing subway, which calls on passengers to avoid certain behaviors (e.g. eating, playing music aloud) because otherwise their credit records would be negatively impacted (author's picture)

However, there are certain features of the SCS's enforcement approach that exceed the definition of responsive regulation and are added to the enforcement pyramid, yet these features do not coincide with other enforcement approaches, such as smart or meta regulation (see Figure 27). First, in addition to a negative escalation mechanism (blacklists, punishments), the SCS possesses a parallel positive reinforcement option via redlist entries and rewards for commendable behavior (e.g. rule compliance or positive

161 For details on the different enforcement approaches, incl. responsive regulation and the enforcement pyramid, refer to Section 2.4.1.2, Gunningham (2011), Braithwaite (2006) and Ayres and Braithwaite (1992).

behavior beyond compliance, such as volunteering). Despite this reinforcement mechanism being less widespread, it still makes compliance more worthwhile and can even incentivize firms to lever compliance as a competitive advantage.

Figure 27: The SCS's enforcement approach (author's design)

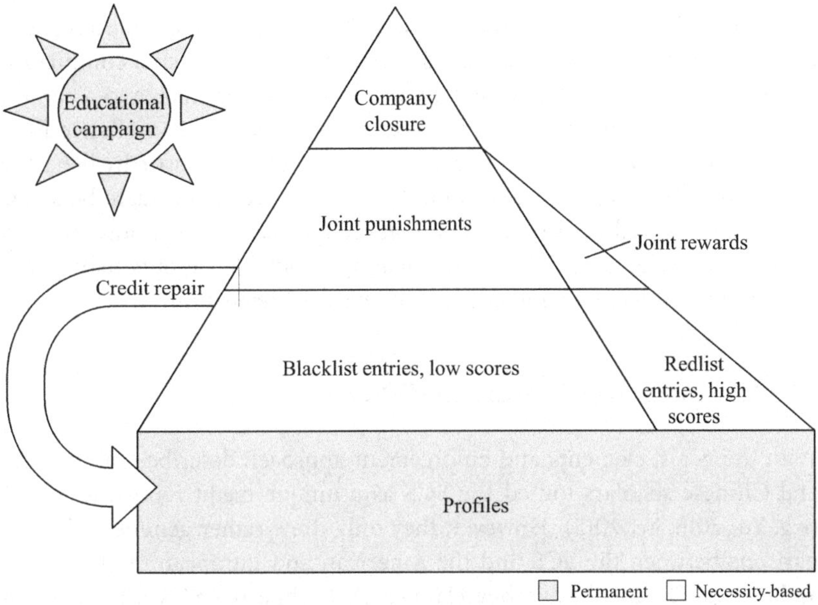

Second, the concept of scores turns compliance from an either-or decision into a question of degree. While this resonates with the social constructionist perspective of compliance, at the same time it also makes compliance a strategic decision with an increased number of options to consider.

Third, the SCS is a learning system by design, thanks to its option for credit repair and educational campaigns. While responsive regulation generally also attempts to educate via its escalation steps and that way prevents legal violations, the credit repair function allows the system to reset an actor's records after a non-compliance incident. In addition, the educational campaigns shape the public discourse and aim to generally raise awareness for this topic.

Fourth, the entire SCS is an enforcement approach that is added on top of the already existing enforcement mechanisms that form part of the regulatory system, rather than replacing or modifying this system itself. This add-on is designed as a self-enforcing system, which the regulator, by defining the rules, operates at a distance. Only once the system is set up, does it become a form of regulation; a post hoc legalization.

In essence, these characteristics exhibit a managerial logic, be it the incentives for compliance via rewards or the option to undo previously bad actions via credit repair. Specifically, the fact that a company can repair its credit, i.e. its compliance status, simply by paying for and attending dedicated credit repair trainings, creates a new market, on which a compliance status can be purchased, and thereby commodifies compliance to a certain extent. Similarly, commodification of integrity, trust and compliance happens in cases, where the SCS attaches a price tag to praiseworthy behavior via (financial) rewards. In addition, the use of scores to evaluate behavior reflects managerial performance evaluation approaches. Therefore, besides being responsive, the SCS's enforcement approach also adopts managerial logic and can thus be characterized as managerial regulation.

5.2.5 Idiosyncrasies of the Social Credit System

With the goals, elements and enforcement approach described above, several Chinese scholars touted the SCS as a unique credit reporting model (e.g. Yu, 2016, Ye, 2015). However, they only drew rather generalized comparisons between the SCS and the American and European credit system archetypes. On this basis, they claimed that while the SCS mimics these systems in certain features (e.g. company profiles, scores), the Chinese system is nevertheless distinct and therefore constitutes a new archetype (Yu, 2016, Ye, 2015). Specifically, they highlighted the broad notion of credit, as well as the dominant role of the state as idiosyncrasies of the Chinese credit reporting model (Ye, 2015, p. 27). To substantiate these claims, Krause et al. (2022) set out to compare the Chinese corporate credit reporting system[162] with its counterparts in the US and Germany. This comparison does not only corroborate the notable role the SCS plays in shaping the Chinese corporate credit reporting model, it also concretizes the distinctive features in the set-up of the SCS.

162 Miller (2003, p. 27) defined a credit reporting system as "the broader institutional framework for credit reporting in an economy". Consequently, the corporate credit reporting system is the part of the institutional framework for credit reporting which targets the corporate sector.

First and in line with Chinese scholars' theses, the Chinese Party-state's influence in the Chinese corporate credit reporting system is considerably stronger than in other countries, such as the US and Germany. Not only did the Chinese government initiate the creation of corporate credit reporting actors as well as the SCS (see Section 5.2.1), the Party-state also dominates implementation, as the descriptions of public providers in Section 5.2.3 illustrate. Moreover, if the Chinese government's efforts to draft a national Social Credit Law succeed (Trivium, 2019), the Chinese government gains additional control over this system. In contrast to this top-down process, the US and German corporate credit reporting systems emerged bottom-up and no singular comprehensive regulation laying down the systems' features and functioning exists (Krause et al., 2022, p. 5). In addition, the dominant role of the Chinese state in its corporate credit reporting system is intimated by the difference in how the notion of credit is conceptualized: The understanding of credit in Western countries, such as the US and Germany, which originally possessed a strong and explicit moral and educational connotation, emerged bottom-up. Only later, in a negotiation process between the credit reporting industry and the government, did it turn into the current narrow notion of credit (Lipartito, 2013, Berghoff, 2008, Guinnane, 2001). The opposite has been the case in China, where the government has held the prerogative of defining the notion of credit from the start. By linking credit to trustworthiness in the context of the SCS, the Chinese government proactively defines the substance of societal and economic trust, including the mechanisms of how trust can be built. This level of dominance over both the SCS's discourse and the implementation by the Party-state is unprecedented.

Second and directly connected to the previous point, the Chinese corporate credit reporting system's information infrastructure is more centralized than in the US and Germany (Krause et al., 2022, p. 12). This is exemplified by the creation of the NCIPS as a central database for the SCS, from which both public and private SCS providers draw. This way, the Chinese government exerts sovereignty over data and information and can steer actors in the corporate credit system (both public and private providers as well as companies) at a distance. Comparable centralization efforts do not exist in the US and Germany. The differences in information infrastructure have direct consequences for companies, for example with regard to information correction procedures. While companies in the US and Germany submit their information to public credit information platforms and thereby have control over which information is shared on the respective platform beyond what is legally required, in China, this decision lies in the hands of public providers, i.e. Party-state agencies: The responsible authority upholds the decision on the type of information that is disclosed on the platform as well as the timing and format of release. Only after publication can businesses apply for data correction in case of mistakes (Credit China, 2021f).

Third, Krause et al.'s (2022, p. 12) comparison of company profiles on publicly and privately run credit information platforms, including Credit China and Qichacha for the Chinese case, shows that levels of transparency between private and public platforms in China are reversed to those in the US and Germany. On the one hand, Qichacha shows a significantly higher level of transparency than its counterparts in the US and Germany. In China's highly opaque business environment, it seems reasonable to leverage the publicly accessible information from the NCISP as well as technologies to accumulate additional information on companies from the World Wide Web to the maximum: These two means generate high transparency levels at relatively low costs and thereby provide opportunities for companies to reduce their transaction costs. In contrast, countries, such as the US and Germany, which operate under the rule of law, do not seem to necessitate such high levels of transparency for smooth business transactions (Fischer, 2021). In fact, higher levels of transparency may not even be desirable for companies in these countries, as increased disclosure is also accompanied by business risks (e.g. publication of company secrets).

On the other hand, Credit China is the least transparent of all the public platforms and does not even contain standard corporate credit information, as provided on the respective platforms in the US and Germany (Krause et al., 2022, p. 13). Instead, Credit China emphasizes legal enforcement by providing information on topics, such as business licenses and court sentences. Rather than compete with each other, as is the case among providers in the US and Germany, Credit China and Qichacha complement each other in their information provision. This hints at an intent to establish a more collaborative relationship between the Party-state and the credit service industry in China; an approach the Party-state adopts in other realms of society as well, e.g. in the cooptation of civil society for service delivery in China (Howell, 2012).

Fourth, compared to the corporate credit reporting systems in the US and Germany, corporate credit reporting's legal enforcement function is extended via the SCS in China (Krause et al., 2022, p. 12): In the US and Germany, corporate credit reporting does not only serve the purpose of mitigating information asymmetries, but is also utilized in legal enforcement, e.g. when authorities require certain credit ratings as prerequisites for receiving licenses. The Chinese corporate credit reporting system originally also only possessed these functions, until the SCS's distinct enforcement approach was added. Hence, the SCS's features, such as the enhanced punishments and rewards via MoUs and the option for credit repair, provide the Party-state with further enforcement means. Thereby, the SCS increases the importance of credit information for companies' overall business operations.

With such unique features, the impact of the SCS on businesses cannot simply be deduced from the effects corporate credit reporting systems have in other countries, but has to be investigated in a dedicated examination. Consequently, the following section discusses the SCS's connection to compliance according to the official discourse (Section 5.3) before Section 5.4 describes the system's impact on companies.

5.3 The relationship between the Social Credit System and corporate compliance

Chinese academics already discussed the relationship between the notion of credit and compliance before the SCS's set-up started in 2014: Wu Jingmei, a professor at Renmin University's School of Finance, who was also involved in the drafting of the 'Outline', had a major influence on the conceptualization of the SCS with her 'three-dimensional credit theory' (三维信用理论) (Renmin University of China, 2021, Wu, 2013). This theory adopts a broad credit understanding and details three dimensions incorporated in credit, namely integrity (诚信), compliance (合规) and contract fulfillment (践约). Integrity as the first dimension refers to a cultural and moral issue, which the government can solve by providing moral guidance via propaganda and education. The second dimension, compliance, is concerned with the behavioral level, e.g. basic societal relationships and standards of behavior. The government's role in this context, according to Wu, is to define administrative rules, supervise actors and punish or reward behavior where necessary. The third and narrowest dimension entailed in Wu's idea of credit is contract fulfillment, because she regards this dimension as an exclusively economic issue. This dimension is closest related to the narrow notion of credit which focuses on financial aspects. According to Wu, the government needs to define economic principles and measures for credit exchange on a macro-level in order to foster healthy market development

(Wu, 2013). Hence the idea of credit covers the realm between the requirements posed by regulations at the bottom and the societal ideal of morality at the top (Wu, 2020b). With compliance constituting a key component of credit, the SCS, as the main institution addressing credit, also influences the social construction and practices of corporate compliance directly.

Specifics on the SCS's relationship to the notion of compliance can be gleaned from both the official SCS discourse related to compliance on the Credit China website and descriptions of the SCS by experts. The official discourse on credit and compliance originally[163] focused on the financial sector. This manifests itself in the dominance of the term '征信' in earlier documents (e.g. SCS-20170915(1), SCS-20170915(08), SCS-20171122), which only gradually shifted to '信用' in late 2017/early 2018 (e.g. SCS-20171212, SCS-20180511). Furthermore, the early documents addressing credit and compliance in the sample of documents analyzed predominantly address the finance sector, e.g. insurance companies, banks or trust companies, before articles on other sectors started to appear (e.g. SCS-20170915(1), SCS-20170915(2), SCS-20170915(7), SCS-20170915(9), SCS-20170922(2)).

The relationship drawn between credit and compliance in these documents goes beyond what is described in Wu's theory (Wu, 2013). Compliance is not only an important factor for a company's credit level (SCS-20170915(8), SCS-20180710), but credit management at the same time also supports compliance (SCS-20170915(1)), i.e. a reciprocal relationship. This is illustrated, for example, by a document on the China Securities Investment Fund Association (中国证券投资基金业协会) (SCS-20180511): On the one hand, it outlines four dimensions, which determine private investment fund managers' credit levels, namely "compliance, stability, professionalism and transparency" ("合规性、稳定度、专业度和透明度", SCS-20180511). This underscores Wu's (2013) thesis regarding compliance as a vital element for credit. On the other hand, the document links the establishment of a credit search platform to private investment funds' compliance-related improvements. Beyond this reciprocal relationship on the business level, compliance and credit also mutually reinforce one another on a systemic level: Improvements in compliance regulation foster the building of the SCS and the SCS promotes compliance and raises compliance levels overall via its measures, such as punishments, credit commit-

163 The earliest documents including credit and compliance on the Credit China website date back to 2017 (see Appendix C, which is available digitally on www.nomos-shop.de.).

ments and credit ratings (SCS-20190506, SCS-20190920, SCS-20191203, SCS-20200702, BUS19-09). Shenzhen's Bao'an district even "regards compliance construction as an extension of Bao'an's credit system construction" ("将合规建设作为宝安信用体系建设的延伸", SCS-20210406).

This intricate relationship between credit and compliance has affected the construction of compliance in several ways. First, compliance has received increased attention, because the government has expedited the set-up of the SCS and the promotion of credit in public discourse (SCS-20201224). The broad range of sectors and topics that address both credit and compliance after the initial focus on finance illustrate this point: Examples are the pharmaceutical, basic materials, real estate, internet platform and electricity sectors; topics addressed are, for instance, big data, audits and transparency on the stock market (SCS-20180126, SCS-20180710, SCS-20190129, SCS-20190320, SCS-20190322, SCS-20190424, SCS-20200108, SCS-20210621). Moreover, compliance has been explicitly and closely related to integrity in business operations (合规诚信经营) in the context of the SCS (SCS-20190130, SCS-20200702, SCS-20210331(2)).

Next, compliance has become dependent on credit-related supervision. Specifically, the official discourse as well as experts regard credit as the basis of a new supervision model (新型监管模式), i.e. the way it has been conceptualized in the context of the SCS (SCS-20201026, SCS-20201224). In this new model, societal supervision is prominent and "the government only possesses a guiding role" ("政府只有引导的作用") (EXP21-03), i.e. a more indirect, yet targeted means of intervention (EXP19-09, PO19-BJ). Thus, firms' compliance management has to consider this new supervision mechanism in the set-up of compliance management systems. Concretely, the SCS emphasizes corporate self-regulation as well as proactive information management (e.g. information disclosure) (SCS-20201224, SCS-20210112). Such means to manage compliance have become more worthwhile, because the additional supervision generally increases compliance pressure for companies (EXP19-03, EXP19-14).

Lastly, the connection of credit and compliance has changed the understanding of compliance fundamentally. From an objectivist perspective, the question of compliance is binary (yes or no) and only from a social constructionist perspective, has compliance been regarded as a gradual phenomenon. In the context of credit, which is generally evaluated on a spectrum between the highest and the lowest possible score, compliance turns into a question of degree, even from an objectivist perspective. An expected consequence of this shift is that compliance management may become more competitive, i.e. compliance may be exploited as a competitive advantage (EXP19-08, PO19-BJ).

In addition to these influences on compliance caused by its connection to credit, the official discourse also explicitly broadened the scope of compliance, when it described the transition from the so-called 'credit 1.0 era' (征信 1.0 时代) to the 'credit 2.0 era' (征信 2.0 时代) (SCS-20170915(8)). While in the credit 1.0 era the company's own credit report was the focus of attention, suppliers' compliance has become increasingly important in the current credit 2.0 era (SCS-20170915(8)):

> "For a company, its compliance refers not only to its own, but also to the compliance of its partners, customers, suppliers, and other third parties. This is a unique feature of the credit 2.0 era" ("对一家企业而言，它的合规不仅仅指其自身，还包括合作伙伴、客户、供应商、还有其他第三方的合规性。这是征信 2.0 时代独有的特色").

Hence, in the context of the SCS, compliance (management) is supposed to incorporate compliance levels of actors outside of the examined organization, a de facto extension of the scope of compliance. This requirement was, for example, translated in a regulation for insurance firms, which prohibits them from providing credit insurance to online sales platforms, and the set-up of blacklists to identify actors with compliance problems that insurance companies should not collaborate with (SCS-20170922(1), SCS-20171227).

All in all, the SCS, with its impacts on compliance and the high level of digitization, is supposed to improve the general business environment, be it via its transparency mechanisms, risk mitigation or higher convenience in the interaction with authorities (EXP19-09, EXP21-03). Yet, the high fragmentation of the system and the myriad authorities involved also require higher compliance investments from and pose additional risks to companies, e.g. overlooking SCS-related requirements in the tangled mass of dispersed SCS-related rules (EXP21-03). Thus, the following section moves on to analyze how exactly the SCS affects the corporate sector in practice.

5.4 The Social Credit System's impact on the corporate sector

This section comprehensively discusses the influences of the SCS on the corporate sector based on interviews with business representatives and experts in China. Therefore, it does not only look at the effects of the SCS on companies (Section 5.4.1), but also how companies proactively exploit the SCS for their own purposes (Section 5.4.2). To complete the picture, Section 5.4.3 describes the SCS's impact on professional service organizations, such as law firms, consultancies and accounting firms, who support companies in their compliance management efforts.

5.4.1 The Social Credit System's impact on companies

Generally, the interviews show that the SCS's impact on companies can be classified into three categories: Compliance awareness, risks and benefits. According to the interviews, the SCS's educational campaigns have raised the awareness for compliance both across society and specifically in the corporate sector (BUS19-09, BUS19-10, EXP19-10). This change has triggered different reactions, ranging from confidence in actors' own abilities and a positive perception of the SCS, to worries about the system and its implications: Most of the interviewed business representatives have not felt negative consequences of the SCS yet and therefore do not voice concerns about the system (e.g. BUS19-17, BUS19-19, BUS21-17, BUS21-09, BUS21-18). At the same time, they are also confident that they do not have to worry about the SCS because of their companies' good compliance levels and even exploit the SCS for their own benefits (e.g. BUS19-17, BUS19-18, BUS21-17, BUS21-18). In this context, one interviewee highlighted that he welcomes the SCS, because people, who violated the rules and negatively affected other businesses, receive adequate punishment (BUS19-10). Other interviewees' views on the SCS are rather pragmatic and neutral; they explained that their awareness for compliance has increased and that they are now more vigilant in order to make sure they follow the rules and avoid being punished, both as individuals (restricted consumption) and as part of their company (e.g. BUS19-06, BUS19-09, BUS19-10, BUS19-12, BUS21-21). Yet others voiced concern about the negative impacts of the SCS, e.g. joint punishments (e.g. BUS19-01, BUS19-11, EXP19-02, EXP19-11, PO19-BJ).

Interestingly, foreign MNEs, who generally possess rather high compliance levels in China, were most nervous about the SCS and its implications

(BUS19-01, BUS21-05, EXP19-07, PO19-BJ, PO20-ON). These worries did not only arise during the participant observations of SCS-related events targeted at foreign MNEs (PO19-BJ, PO19-SH, PO20-ON), but experts also confirmed this impression based on their own observations (EXP19-03, EXP19-05, EXP19-07, EXP19-14). The main reason for the insecurity is the insufficient knowledge about the system and its impacts, which has been reinforced by the Western media reception of the SCS (e.g. EXP19-03, PO19-BJ, Reuters, 2018, The New York Times, 2018, Denyer, 2016, The Economist, 2016), as well as professional service organizations' initial depiction of the system (refer to Section 5.4.3 for further details).

Complaints about the system are related to the varying regional implementation of the SCS across China, which supposedly results in higher pressure for companies in eastern regions (BUS19-11, EXP19-02). While there are indeed regional divergences in the implementation of the SCS, these differences generally correlate with the levels of economic development (EXP19-14). Therefore, experts state that they have not found evidence of unfair treatment and consider the regional variations as justified, even necessary (EXP19-02, EXP19-14). Yet, one interviewee, a CEO from an SOE, provided evidence that the SCS may not always be applied to all companies equally: He described that his company received a fine for environmental and fire protection violations several years ago and asked the government not to publish this fine, because of negative reputational impacts (BUS19-10). The authorities ultimately did not publish the fine online (BUS19-10). How often which types of firms actually ask for such interventions and to what extent their requests are fulfilled by authorities remains unclear. However, as an SOE, with close ties to the government, preferential treatment and a certain level of protection can be well envisaged. Nevertheless, even this interviewee expressed that there is an increasing awareness of compliance in his company because of the SCS (BUS19-10). Hence, despite a certain level of manipulation in the system, the SCS still appears to have an educational effect.

Similarly, the risk of punishment and negative publicity due to blacklist entries and low ratings proves influential. With respect to general blacklists, business representatives mentioned restricted market access and reputational implications, which can cause difficulties in finding intermediaries for cooperation, as the main risks (BUS19-04, BUS21-16, EXP19-15). In order to avoid such scenarios, interviewees emphasized that they need to improve quickly in case of warnings from authorities (BUS19-12, BUS19-18). Moreover, several business representatives were highly aware of the Supreme People's Court's defaulter list for individuals (BUS19-06, BUS19-10, BUS19-11). This list appears to not only have a deterrence effect on business people in reaction to potential consumption restrictions (luxury goods, flights, high-speed trains, etc.), but also due to the negative impact an individual's record can have on the company (BUS19-10). Even though none of the interviewees had been subject to such measures, some of them knew people that were affected or had heard of examples via word of mouth (BUS19-11). This shows that the deterrence effect works. One more type of lists mentioned in the interviews are lists for dishonest people in dedicated industries, such as the insurance or securities sectors (BUS19-03, BUS21-01). An entry on these lists effectively means a ban from the industry, because applicants with related entries are automatically rejected (BUS19-03). However, to be listed, a person, often on the management level, needs to have committed a major legal violation (BUS21-01). Since this rarely happens, these lists do not seem to be as prominent as the other blacklists mentioned above.

The risks businesses perceive and their reactions to negative ratings from public providers are similar to those of blacklists. Independent from the type of rating, interviewees voiced concerns over low ratings due to potential market access restrictions, difficulties in collaborating with third parties (e.g. finding business partners, acquiring customers) as well as financial implications (e.g. higher interest rates for loans, limited access to government funds and equity-based finance) (e.g. BUS19-03, BUS19-14, BUS21-02, BUS21-16, GOV19-01). Specifically mentioned in the context of customs rating was the worry about higher workload, due to increased random inspections by the authorities (BUS21-05). Because of the importance of the ratings, two companies in the sample employ staff dedicated to managing ratings (BUS19-11, BUS21-05).

The perception of and experience with ratings varies among interviewees. Several business representatives commended the public ratings for their transparent requirements that allow companies to adapt compliance management and business processes accordingly (BUS19-03, BUS21-02, BUS21-07). Still, several business representatives had already experienced their firm's rating drop and other negative implications because of non-compliance incidents (BUS19-10, BUS19-14, BUS21-20). In addition, an expert on small businesses' accounting described the case of one of her clients, who, completely unaware of the requirement to file taxes, had received a bad tax rating (EXP19-16). All of the companies are still operating and have slowly improved their ratings ex post via dedicated internal management measures, yet only some had achieved the same rating level as before the drop (BUS19-10, BUS19-14, BUS21-20). In one of these cases, the business representative considered the acquisition of his company by another, better rated firm in the sector as a convenient opportunity to relieve his business of the negative rating (BUS19-14).

In addition to these particular risks emerging from blacklists and ratings, business representatives also saw overarching risks emerging from the SCS's combined enforcement mechanisms, such as the risk of losing access to government tenders, being barred from the stock market or even having to shut down operations completely (BUS19-09, BUS19-10, BUS19-20, BUS19-15, BUS21-17). Especially for companies with a large share of government contracts, being restricted from tender applications is considered a high risk (BUS19-10, BUS19-15, BUS21-17). Because of the MoUs and the potential negative impact business partners on a project could have on the tender application, these firms did not only highlight the importance of ensuring their own compliance, but also of being able to prove the compliance of their business partners (BUS21-17).

Facing all these risks, one interviewee explicitly expressed her relief, when she heard of the existence of credit repair opportunities (BUS19-01). The examples of two blacklisted companies, one which has repaired its credit entry and one which has not, shows the impact of this mechanism. The news reported that several China United Property Insurance (中华联合财产保险股份有限公司) branches had been blacklisted and punished multiple times, e.g. the company's branch in Zibo, which was blacklisted because of missing insurance compensation in a traffic accident in 2019 (Tencent, 2021a, Credit China, 2019a, Haibao News, 2019, Luwang, 2019). On both the branch's and the headquarter's Credit China company profiles, however, entries about these incidents could not be found (Credit China, 2021d,c). Instead, the company profiles feature a prominent badge for trustworthiness, thanks to having been an A-rated taxpayer for several years (see Figure 28) (Credit China, 2021d,c). On Qichacha, the information on the previous lawsuits can still be found under historical risk; however, the blacklist entry is not specifically mentioned in this context. Hence, while court information has not been deleted, the negative consequences from a blacklist entry can be partially mitigated via credit repair (e.g. stop of punishments). Yet, articles in the news on blacklist entries keep existing. Consequently, a full redemption is not possible, since the previously published information can still negatively influence firms' reputation way beyond the time of the removal of the blacklist entry on SCS platforms.

Figure 28: Screenshot of China United Property Insurance's company profile on Credit China (2021d) (trustworthy entity batch highlighted by the black frame)

In contrast, CITIC Guo'an Group (中信国安集团有限公司) caused bonds to default and did not pay back outstanding loans in time in 2019 (Credit China, 2019b, Sohu, 2019). Because of the severity of this incident, credit repair was apparently not permitted in the short-term. Consequently, CITIC Guo'an Group is still prominently listed as an untrustworthy entity on Credit China (see Figure 29), even though the company's profile also features one entry as an A-rated tax payer in addition to the blacklist entry (Credit China, 2021e). Similarly, Qichacha features the negative information prominently on the company profile (see Figure 30) (Qichacha, 2021d). As company profiles have become a key source of information for actors in the corporate realm, credit repair can indeed help companies to mitigate the negative reputational implications of blacklist entries.

Figure 29: Screenshot of CITIC Guo'an Group's company profile on Credit China (2021e) (untrustworthy entity batch highlighted by the black frame)

Figure 30: Screenshot of CITIC Guo'an Group's company profile on Qichacha (2021d) (untrustworthy entity batch highlighted by the black frame)

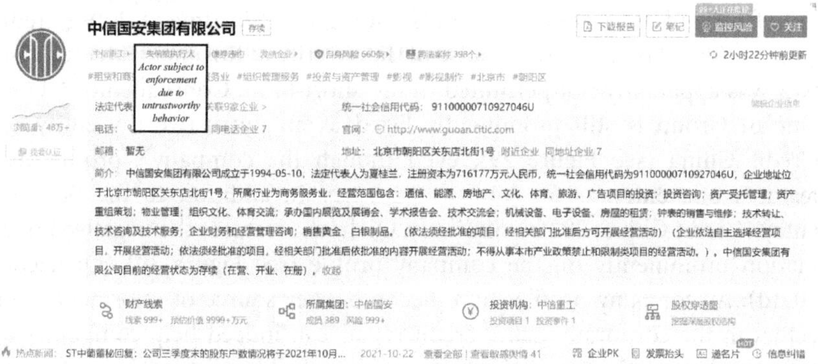

The example of China United Property Insurance, however, also indicates that this mechanism does not necessarily prevent future non-compliance incidents via awareness building: Several of the company's branches have been fined again in the years after 2019 (Tencent, 2021b). Companies may simply include credit repair as a factor in credit risk calculations and tolerate small, easily repairable incidents.

In contrast to awareness and risks, the impact of benefits related to the SCS appears to be negligible. Companies do not perceive direct benefits from the supposed praise of being on a redlist or related rewards. Despite experts promulgating the benefits firms can obtain from the system, such as lower thresholds for loan approvals, faster administrative service delivery and brand building (e.g. EXP19-03, EXP19-14, EXP21-03, PO19-SH, PO20-ON), businesses do not regard redlists and related rewards as important and do not actively strive to be redlisted (e.g. BUS19-02, BUS19-11, BUS21-17). When reminding one business representative of his company's entry on a redlist because of its exemplary tax record (A-rated tax payer), he simply stated that they receive a certificate from the tax authorities every year, as if this was nothing noteworthy or new to him (BUS19-19). Another interviewee explained that the rewards are simply not attractive enough (BUS19-11); a problem which is hard to mitigate, since there are limits on how much incentives a government can afford to provide (EXP19-02). In addition, one interviewee remarked that negative news travels quickly, whereas positive information does not (BUS19-09). This is especially problematic when information provided by SCS platforms is incorrect, a situation which has been reported in the news for Qichacha and Tianyancha[164] (Sina Finance, 2020). Consequently, only few businesses focus on the opportunities of high ratings. Two business representatives considered ratings as a good means to promote firms' reputation as a whole (BUS19-03, BUS21-12). Another interviewee explained the benefits her company gains from its high customs ratings (BUS21-05).

Overall, the above elaborations show that the SCS influences company's compliance awareness and compliance risk perception significantly, whereas the benefits that can be retrieved from redlists, good ratings and rewards are less important. These results resonate with Engelmann et al.'s (2019) findings on the lower importance of redlists as compared to blacklists. As a reaction to these influences, companies strengthen their internal management, in particular their compliance management (e.g. more rigorous compliance audits) (BUS19-10, BUS19-14, BUS21-07). One expert

164 One expert, who helped her clients get wrong information in the SCS databases corrected, described this process as smooth (EXP19-14). Yet, these were rather minor corrections that had no reputational implications (EXP19-14). Overall, the design of the SCS's credit correction system, where corrections can only be made after the disclosure of information, remains a high risk for businesses.

even described how a few large foreign MNE clients of hers have set up dedicated databases to track the SCS's development in order to take action accordingly (EXP19-08). While such cases are the exceptions, one business representative also pointed to potential future (cost) pressures to perfect his firm's compliance management in order to remain competitive (BUS19-10).

But presently, companies' focus on the SCS lies in risk mitigation via compliance management rather than competing with other firms for the system's rewards. Hence, the SCS's legal, communicative and network instruments have a greater impact than the economic instrument of rewards. With respect to SCS elements, private providers' credit evaluation mechanisms (e.g. Alibaba's corporate integrity system) play the least significant role among the interviewed sample of businesses, as they are not mentioned by interviewed business representatives at all. In contrast, the impact of public providers' platforms and systems on businesses dominates; for instance via specialized corporate credit systems, such as customs and tax ratings, the Supreme People's Court's defaulter list as a specialized individual credit system, as well as Credit China and the NECIPS for transparency about blacklists. In addition, licensed credit information platforms from private providers are important with regard to transparency. Yet, they play an even more important role in companies' exploitation of the SCS, which is discussed in the following section.

5.4.2 Companies' utilization of the Social Credit System

In addition to companies' passive reaction to the SCS, the collected data also presents ways in which companies proactively engage with the SCS and exploit the opportunities the system provides. The following paragraphs elaborate on this phenomenon.

The main area in which companies utilize the SCS proactively is in their third-party management. Specifically, businesses benefit from the increased transparency about corporate actors that the system provides. The most popular instruments among the interviewees in this context are the licensed credit information platforms Qichacha and Tianyancha, which enterprises across the board consult for background checks on third parties, be it suppliers, investors, customers or competitors (e.g. BUS19-04, BUS19-15, BUS19-16, BUS19-18, BUS19-19, BUS21-03, BUS21-05, BUS21-11, BUS21-16, BUS21-18). In addition, some business representatives also use data bases from public providers, such as the NECIPS or the Supreme People's Court's defaulters list[165] (e.g. BUS19-01, BUS19-04, BUS19-16, BUS21-10, BUS21-13, BUS21-22, BUS21-25). Table 6 lists the third-party information interviewees commonly check on these websites.

Table 6: Third-party information on SCS websites checked by interviewees

Information category	**Interviews mentioning the category**
Basic information, e.g. company size, legal representative	BUS19-11, BUS19-18, BUS21-05, BUS21-06, BUS21-08, BUS21-09, BUS21-10, BUS21-11, BUS21-23
Business registration information and licenses	BUS21-05, BUS21-15, BUS21-16, BUS21-25
Ownership structure as well as firms and individuals linked to the company	BUS19-01, BUS19-02, BUS19-04, BUS19-08, BUS19-15, BUS19-19, BUS19-20, BUS21-03, BUS21-05, BUS21-08, BUS21-13, BUS21-16, BUS21-17, BUS21-20, BUS21-21, BUS21-22, BUS21-23
The company's financial situation	BUS19-20, BUS21-06, BUS21-08, BUS21-11, BUS21-15, BUS21-17, BUS21-25
Lawsuits the company was or is involved in	BUS19-10, BUS19-11, BUS19-20, BUS21-05, BUS21-06, BUS21-13, BUS21-15, BUS21-17, BUS21-18, BUS21-21, BUS21-22, BUS21-25
Non-compliance incidents in general	BUS19-14, BUS19-20, BUS21-03, BUS21-11, BUS21-15, BUS21-19, BUS21-21, BUS21-23, BUS21-24
Specifically blacklist entries	BUS19-02, BUS19-11, BUS19-14, BUS19-18, BUS19-19, BUS21-11, BUS21-15, BUS21-19, BUS21-20, BUS21-23, BUS21-25
Specifically punishments	BUS19-18, BUS19-19, BUS21-20, BUS21-22, BUS21-23, BUS21-25

These information categories show that the theoretical conception of credit, which includes compliance in addition to the financial dimension, also manifests itself in practice: Companies do not only collect insights into non-compliance incidents that already happened, but also assess the risk of problems a company may potentially run into via information on lawsuits. Firms that check the ownership structure and information on related actors

165 Only one business representative explained that they check customers' financial credit history (征信记录) to determine the payment conditions in contracts (BUS21-21). Hence the usage of the Credit Reference Center and licensed commercial credit platforms seems comparably limited.

further corroborate this finding, since these checks are, for example, a means to identify conflicts of interest (BUS19-01, BUS19-19, BUS21-24). Moreover, the interest in the relationships of a company as well as the use of the SCS for third-party management itself demonstrate that companies actually put the extension of the meaning of compliance via credit, that has been conceptualized in theory and the official discourse, into practice.

Concretely, companies use the newly gained transparency for compliance risk evaluations of third parties (BUS19-10, BUS21-03, BUS21-11). While some companies may exclusively rely on the information they find on SCS databases, several interviewees explained that the information from the SCS serves for the pre-selection of potential business partners or as one among several information sources in the decision-making process (e.g. BUS19-08, BUS19-10, BUS21-04, BUS21-15). For instance, some companies conduct on-site visits and interviews to evaluate third parties based on the information they find on SCS platform[166] (BUS19-01, BUS19-08, BUS19-10, BUS21-15, BUS21-19, BUS21-25). Other business representatives described that they combine the information from the SCS databases with other information in their internal business partner databases (BUS21-04, BUS21-14, BUS21-15, BUS21-19). At times, the internal databases automatically integrate information from the SCS platforms for more convenience, i.e. employees do not need to conduct external searches anymore, but have the information from different sources on a (potential) business partner in one database (BUS21-04). Additionally, companies consult data they collected on a third party separately (e.g. via interviews or visits), historical data on previous collaborations, information from other company databases (e.g. World Compliance) and additional details on companies' financial credit history[167] (BUS21-05, BUS21-14, BUS21-19, BUS21-21, BUS21-25).

Based on the accumulated information, firms then evaluate third parties to identify the best possible business partner. Many companies expressed that they have not determined fixed standards that every company they work with has to meet, but that the management makes individual decisions based on the specific case (BUS19-02, BUS19-16, BUS19-18, BUS21-02, BUS21-11, BUS21-16, BUS21-20). For instance, one interviewee

166 Several interviewees stated that on-site visits, e.g. random inspections, continue even after the selection of a business partner in order to continuously ensure compliance (e.g. BUS19-04, BUS19-10, BUS19-13, BUS21-25).

167 This refers to additional information on the financial situation of a third party, which companies directly receive from the third party's bank upon the third party's consent (BUS21-25).

explained that in addition to the risk a company poses, the availability of alternative business partners and the third party's willingness to collaborate also play a role (BUS21-25). To illustrate this, she used the example of a cooperative business partner who seemed to pose comparably high risks, but was willing to provide further information and accepted additional regular audits (BUS21-25). Under these circumstances, the company agreed to collaborate with this third party (BUS21-25). In another case, the company already cooperated with a business partner that turned out to expose the firm to high risks (BUS21-25). Due to a lack of alternatives, the contract was kept for another six months, a period in which the business unit that cooperated with that partner was confident they could find an alternative company to fulfill their business needs (BUS21-25).

Nevertheless, for most interviewees, one cause for an automatic refusal to cooperate exists: The appearance of a third party on a SCS blacklist (BUS19-02, BUS19-04, BUS19-11, BUS19-12, BUS19-15, BUS19-15, BUS19-16, BUS19-18, BUS21-05, BUS21-14, BUS21-16, BUS21-17, BUS21-19, BUS21-22). The reasons stated for this clear denial to collaborate are the high risks that such cooperation entail[168], the reputational implications considering the fast spread of negative information online and the potential negative implications on the chances of winning government tenders (e.g. BUS19-11, BUS19-15, BUS21-16, BUS21-17, EXP21-04). Since tenders constitute a sensitive issue, even the involvement in too many lawsuits may be an exclusion criterion for business partner choice (BUS21-17).

Overall, in the context of third-party management, four specific phenomena described by business representatives exhibit noteworthy resemblances with SCS mechanisms. First, despite the complex evaluation processes for business partners outlined above, several companies use internal rating systems to evaluate third parties and decide on a cooperation and contract terms (BUS19-01, BUS19-08, BUS19-19, BUS21-04, BUS21-14, BUS21-15, BUS21-19, BUS21-25). Second, one SOE in the construction sector with an internal rating system for suppliers provides additional benefits to suppliers that achieve the highest rating[169], such as reduced fees for

168 Fully aware of the risks collaborations with blacklisted firms pose, one business representative nevertheless did not refuse the cooperation with blacklisted firms per se, rather he suggested his company "needs to prepare mentally beforehand" in case it decides on a collaboration ("之前要做心理上的一些准备", BUS21-21).

169 In total, the company applies three rating categories (A, B and C) with A being the highest level (BUS21-15).

tender applications (BUS21-15). Third, some businesses use internal blacklists for third parties they do not wish to cooperate with[170] (BUS19-15, BUS21-03, BUS21-04, BUS21-05, BUS21-06, BUS21-07). Tencent even publishes these lists on its WeChat account, thereby likely causing reputational impacts to the listed companies (PO21-ON, Tencent Anti-Fraud Investigation Department, 2021). Fourth, the CEO of one SOE instrumentalizes the SCS as a deterrent to enforce his company's rights. Specifically, he threatens to sue customers that do not pay their debt, with the aim of getting them listed on the defaulter list and consequently having their luxury consumption restricted (BUS19-10). This concrete pressure has, at times, helped him to obtain payments[171] (BUS19-10).

All these mechanisms allow companies to enforce their cooperation requirements for third parties more consistently. In cases where the third party is another company, this automatically means that companies are exposed to strict enforcement regimes by their business partners. For instance, one business representative from a Chinese POE described the rating procedure of his company's business partners, all of whom are foreign MNEs (BUS21-17). While every foreign MNE poses different requirements, normally it is sufficient to pass a certain rating threshold to be accepted as a business partner, i.e. companies do not have to have an excellent rating in every aspect (BUS21-17). Yet another interviewee described the importance of good evaluations from business partners (e.g. entering a redlist when fully compliant) in order to receive preferential treatment during cooperation (BUS19-16). Companies that are located downstream in the supply chain generally tend to pose more stringent requirements on their suppliers compared to companies upstream in the supply chain. Hence, the former are more likely to intensively exploit the SCS in the above-described fashion.

In addition to exploiting the SCS for third-party management, the interviews illustrated that selected companies utilize the SCS in two more areas: Recruitment and internal management. In recruitment, several companies use the information provided by the SCS on individuals, such as the Supreme People's Court's defaulter list or sector specific personal files

170 One interviewee confirmed that his company has only used this blacklist since 2018, i.e. after the SCS was set up (BUS21-06).

171 Interviewees, however, also described that they have come across few cases of individuals that do not worry about these personal punishments and find work-arounds instead (e.g. transferring all their money to their wives and getting divorced) (BUS19-10, BUS19-11, GOV19-02). But these cases are framed as exceptions.

in their staffing processes (e.g. the integrity files in the securities sector; BUS19-18, BUS21-01, BUS21-07, BUS21-16; for more details, refer to Section 6.1.3 and 6.1.5). This, however, mostly pertains to the hiring of personnel in leadership positions (BUS19-08).

With respect to internal management, companies use the SCS in their internal control systems, such as compliance management. For instance, one compliance manager explained that information from the SCS on individuals was helpful in internal investigations (BUS19-01). Another company mirrors the SCS within its own organization by setting up an internal compliance risk database and rating the compliance levels of business units and key processes (BUS21-22). Yet, the resemblance of internal management practices and the SCS has been taken to the extreme by one large IT company. This company possesses an internal integrity rating system, where employees' values are evaluated (价值观评估) (BUS21-04). A-ratings, the highest level, are attributed to employees with outstanding actions, e.g. saving a person's life, and the recipients' stories are published firm-internally (BUS21-04). While the other ratings are not made public, the company still announces the names of employees who have received punishments, including the details of their offenses, the financial costs of the non-compliance as well as the name of the offenders' supervisors and HR officers (BUS21-04). Hence, the announcement does not only affect the employees themselves, but also the managers responsible for them; just as the SCS also establishes a link between individuals and companies as well as cooperating companies. Moreover, this company set up an alliance with other major tech companies in 2015/16 for the purpose of promoting integrity. This alliance not only meets regularly and discusses best practices in integrity management, but also shares employee blacklists within the alliance to prevent untrustworthy individuals from being hired in the industry again (BUS21-04). This private-sector cooperation closely resembles the integrity files adopted by public actors in other sectors, such as the securities sector, both in name and action.

Overall, these elaborations show that the increased transparency the SCS provides offers companies a high level of flexibility, certainty and ultimately convenience, especially in their third-party management (BUS19-01, BUS19-09, BUS19-14, BUS19-15, BUS21-02, BUS21-05, BUS21-13, BUS21-15, EXP21-04). A comparison with the way firms accessed comparable information before the existence of the SCS corroborates this finding: Some businesses purchased company reports from third parties, such as credit rating agencies (BUS21-05, BUS21-08, EXP19-16, EXP21-04). Others collected information from the many official public information sources across which the data was spread (e.g. government websites, prospectuses) (BUS19-19, BUS21-05, BUS21-08). However, some of the information that is now available was still nowhere to be found (BUS21-05). Yet another business representative explained that his company had to rely on word-of-mouth reporting before (BUS19-14).

One main benefit from the newly gained transparency for businesses is transaction cost savings. Specifically, companies that used to check a multitude of sources before, now save time, which can translate into cost savings (BUS21-15), whereas firms that purchased company reports directly save money, because of the low costs at which information is provided on SCS platforms[172]. Even some government departments purchase information from Qichacha and Tianyancha for convenience purposes, instead of requesting the information from other government departments, which may not even be willing to share their data with other administrative units (BUS19-09, GOV19-01). This way, the departments in need of information receive the data faster and pre-processed, which they ultimately considered more efficient (BUS19-09, GOV19-01). While the SCS to date has limited effect on inter-departmental data sharing, the system at least provides a workaround.

The benefits from the increased transparency seemingly outweigh some of the difficulties interviewees experienced when using the databases. The few problems mentioned concern data quality. For example, one business representative elaborated on the challenges of identifying conflicts of interest via these websites: While the information is helpful for understanding relationships between actors, persons with fraudulent intent tend to register their activities under the guise of friends' or extended family members' names in order to cover up existing conflicts of interest (BUS21-24). Therefore, disguised conflicts of interest can only be detected in cases where a company is able to identify other unreasonable information on the respective company profile (e.g. unusually high profits for a very small company with few employees) (BUS21-24). Another interviewee stated that information on the platforms is not up to date at times (BUS21-17). For

172 The databases from public providers, such as Credit China or the NECIPS, offer information free of charge. Private providers, in contrast, require a small fee for additional information. For instance, an annual pass for one person to access all information on Qichacha costs 360 RMB, but cheaper offers are also available (e.g. access for two/three years or entire teams) (Qichacha, 2021a). This is a price that traditional companies, which charge for individual credit reports, cannot beat.

this reason, his company, as several others, has resorted to the strategy of comparing information on different SCS platforms or, in important cases, consulting additional sources (e.g. accounting firms, own data collection efforts); meaning that they only use the SCS as a starting point for an inquiry to pre-select potential candidates (e.g. BUS21-04, BUS21-13, BUS21-17). In addition, one business representative from the IT sector was concerned with data security, because he himself still saw a lot of loopholes and risks in the information infrastructure the government is building (BUS19-17). Finally, interviewees were uncertain of the data quality on the databases beyond the information on their own company (BUS21-17, EXP19-10). Specifically, one interviewee explained that he feels more at ease retrieving information from other third parties for this reason:

> "In fact, we could also search for this kind of information on Qichacha and Tianyancha, but we do not know whether the information is accurate" ("其实，我们查企查查、天眼查这些也可以查得到，不过我们不知道他们的信息是不是准确的", BUS21-17).

Most interviewees, however, did not raise these concerns or even explicitly expressed trust in the platforms and data quality (e.g. BUS21-05, EXP19-15).

In sum, the research findings show that the SCS plays a key role in companies' third-party management. In addition, the interview data indicates several patterns in the SCS's impact on companies[173]. First, since third-party management is especially important in industries with high procurement activities, long supply chains and complex networks of business partners, the exploitation of the SCS's mechanisms plays a dominant role in such sectors, e.g. manufacturing (e.g. BUS19-19, BUS21-11, BUS21-24, BUS21-25). It seems only logical, and is reflected in the interview data, that companies with a stronger position in the market (e.g. foreign MNEs, large Chinese SOEs or large domestic POEs) in these industries exploit the SCS to a greater extent than smaller companies, which act as suppliers and may feel the impact of this behavior more strongly (e.g. BUS21-25 versus BUS21-17). Sections 6.2.4 and 6.2.5 describe this phenomenon in more detail for the automotive sector. Second, and in contrast, service-oriented sectors, such as the securities and insurance industries, focus more on the impact of the SCS on themselves, e.g. achieving optimal ratings, as de-

173 As applicable to all patterns identified in this study, these types of structural features need to be validated by quantitative research with a sufficiently large sample to be generalizable.

scribed in Sections 6.1.4 and 6.1.5. Third, not all elements and enforcement instruments of the SCS appear to be equally important to companies. With respect to SCS elements, Credit China, NECIPS, specialized corporate credit systems as well as licensed information platforms, such as Qichacha and Tianyancha, affect companies the most, whereas unlicensed credit information platforms as well as private credit and benefit schemes were not mentioned at all. The Supreme People's Court's defaulter list as a specialized individual credit system as well as providers of commercial credit (the Credit Reference Center and licensed commercial credit platforms) play a limited role for companies (e.g. consumer-oriented companies seeking inquiries on consumers' credit history, e.g. BUS21-21). In terms of enforcement instruments, network instruments are the dominant SCS features that companies both utilize and are affected by, whereas all other instruments are not exploited to the same extent.

The fact that businesses welcome increased transparency shows that the self-regulatory effects which the designers of the SCS intended to create have manifested themselves in practice. Companies do not only restrict their own behavior and increasingly focus on compliance management because of the SCS's impacts on them, but they also mirror the SCS's structures themselves.

This is reflected in their third-party and internal management mechanisms. In addition, the SCS's adoption in third-party management means that every company and individual now has the means to act as a regulator for the corporate actors it is related to, a broadening of the set of regulators involved in the regulatory regime.

5.4.3 The Social Credit System's impact on the credit service industry

In addition to the influences of the SCS on companies described above, both the official and the academic discourses define the development of the credit service industry as one of the main objectives of the SCS (e.g. Wu and Liu, 2017, State Council China, 2014). This research shows that the set-up of the SCS has two effects on the credit service industry, the creation of new markets and changes in the existing service provision.

The SCS set-up provides entirely new business opportunities for a number of different types of firms. On the one hand, the creation and maintenance of the SCS's infrastructure has become a market for IT companies. All across the country, companies support authorities to consolidate databases (BUS19-19, EXP19-09). Connecting data sets from different authorities does not only entail setting up the underlying technological infrastructure, but is also an intricate conceptual task: Decisions on data access rights internally and externally have to be made, data quality has to be ensured, etc. (EXP19-09). The IT providers involved in setting up the SCS infrastructure support these processes (EXP19-09).

On the other hand, the SCS has created markets for service providers that cater to the SCS's elements and enforcement mechanisms. First, the PBoC has provided over 130 companies with licenses to become credit reporting firms, with Qichacha and Tianyancha being the most popular examples (China Association of Small and Medium Sized Enterprises, 2021). In addition, there are non-licensed providers competing in the same market, such as Alibaba (see Section 5.2.3). The business model of these firms is to consolidate existing (publicly available) information on corporate actors, process the data to increase its informational content (e.g. providing graphs with results of analyses or scores) and provide it to customers at a comparatively small fee. The unique selling point of these platforms is their superior user interface compared to government websites, as well as the low costs at which information is provided. As a comparatively new and immature market, which has emerged since the initiation of the SCS, both large IT companies, such as Alibaba (Alibaba corporate integrity system) and Baidu (Aiqicha, 爱企查), as well as entirely new actors, e.g. Qichacha Technology Company Limited (企查查科技有限公司) and Beijing Jindi Technology Company Limited (北京金堤科技有限公司) who operates Tianyancha, currently compete for market shares.

Second, a market for commercial credit providers has emerged. So far, the government has only handed licenses for this service to JVs (e.g. Baihang Credit). Some of the big IT firms have therefore joined forces with public actors to access this market (e.g. JD.com and Xiaomi are involved in Pudao Credit and Ant Group also plans to set up a JV, Yang and Yu, 2021, Zhu, 2021, Faridi, 2020). This way, not only data from authorities, but also user data from large IT ecosystems can be leveraged in the computation of scores for individuals' commercial creditworthiness. The use of these alternative data points for credit scoring can serve as a means to make loans accessible to hitherto unbanked segments of society (Aggarwal, 2019). In addition to this market for commercial credit with rather strict access restrictions, private IT firms also use credit rating mechanisms within their ecosystems, be it for simple benefit schemes or for credit evaluations for their own payment services (Zhima Credit, 2021, WeChat, 2020). For instance, Zhima Credit by Ant Group uses social media interactions and purchases recorded in the Alibaba ecosystem, as well as payments via Alipay mobile wallet, as a basis for providing privileges on e-commerce sites within their own ecosystem (Zhima Credit, 2021). Tencent has launched a similar system in 2020 (WeChat, 2020).

Third, the installment of the credit repair mechanism has created demand for credit-related seminars and credit reports, i.e. created a market for credit repair providers. To prevent credit repair scams, the Credit China website provides lists with licensed credit repair institutions (Credit China, 2021a,b). 63 percent of these credit repair providers already existed before the SCS was launched, whereas 37 percent were founded after the initiation of the SCS (e.g. Aisino Credit Information Company Limited in 2015) (see Figure 31[174]). Hence, the SCS attracted both existing and newly-founded companies to enter this market. Since the large majority of credit repair providers (81 percent), including all of the providers established in 2014 or later, belong to the credit service industry, it is likely that the establishment of new companies was triggered by the SCS and the business opportunities it creates. Moreover, the fact that almost 75 percent of these providers are not state-backed (i.e. none of their main shareholders are state agencies or state-owned entities) shows that the Party-state mainly steers this market via license provision and allows private actors to compete for market shares.

Figure 31: Founding date, enterprise type and industry of licensed credit repair providers

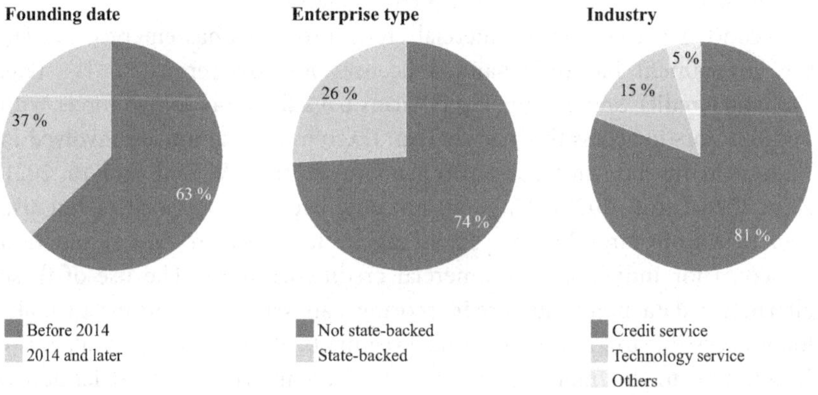

174 The data is based on a Qichacha search of the 62 licensed companies listed on Credit China (2021a, 2021b) on November 9, 2021. For details, contact the author.

With respect to changes in existing service provision, the SCS affects four types of companies that have been providing credit-related services (including compliance) in the broad sense: Credit rating agencies, business networks, law firms and consultancies.

Credit rating agencies existed before the creation of the SCS and the market has been dominated by ten state-backed companies[175] (Lin and Milhaupt, 2017, p. 16). But only recently has the government implemented two fundamental changes in its handling of credit rating agencies. On the one hand, the government opened this market to fully foreign-owned credit rating agencies (e.g. Standard & Poor's) starting from 2019/20 (S&P Global, 2020). On the other hand, the authorities have finally reacted to the long-standing problem of credit rating inflation after several recent bond defaults[176] (Bloomberg News, 2021b). A new regulation passed in August 2021 not only prescribes stricter rules for credit rating models and improvements in rating agencies' internal governance mechanisms, but also connects credit rating agencies with the SCS explicitly (PBoC et al., 2021). It requires "credit rating agencies to launch credit commitments and information disclosure on the "Credit China" website and via other channels in order to strengthen social supervision" ("信用评级机构在"信用中国"网站等渠道开展信用承诺和信息公示，加强社会监督", PBoC et al., 2021). While it remains to be seen how credit rating agencies are integrated into the SCS (which type of information has to be disclosed, etc.), this development towards increased transparency and standardization of credit rating models will certainly impact the operating model and service provision of credit rating agencies[177].

Like credit rating agencies, business networks, such as industry associations, are long-standing actors in the corporate sector. But since the creation of the SCS, industry associations have started to become involved

---

175 China Chengxin International Credit Rating, China Lianhe Credit Rating, Dagong Global Credit Rating, Shanghai Brilliance Credit Rating & Investors Service, China Chengxin Credit Rating, United Credit Ratings, Golden Credit Rating International, Shanghai Far East Credit Rating, Pengyuan Credit, China Bond Rating Company.

176 Chinese credit rating agencies used to provide overly optimistic credit ratings, since they lacked incentives for providing more realistic ratings in a regulatory context where all issued bonds have to be rated and the issuer-paid operating model predominates (Livingston et al., 2018, p. 216).

177 For instance, the new requirements may ultimately cause changes in the currently predominant issuer-paid operating model (Hu et al., 2019, p. 135).

in the credit service industry. For instance, industry associations that had previously acted as self-regulatory organizations (e.g. the Securities Association of China, SAC, 中国证券业协会) now also adopt SCS mechanisms, such as lists and ratings, in their self-regulatory practices. Moreover, business networks also provide service offers related to the SCS to their members, such as seminars and consultations (EXP21-05). Lastly, in some localities, companies can not only apply for a redlist entry themselves, but certain state agencies and industry associations are also allowed to recommend companies to be added to a redlist[178] (e.g. Sichuan Province Bureau of Statistics, 2021, Suzhou Government, 2021, EXP21-05). A representative from an industry association explained that he provides the names of around ten praiseworthy companies from their association to the authorities every year (EXP21-05). He chooses companies based on their performance, but also on guanxi (EXP21-05). The final decision on the redlist entry, however, is made by the authority and cannot be influenced by the industry association, according to the interviewee (EXP21-05).

Furthermore, law firms receive new types of service requests and can broaden their service offering because of the SCS. Representatives from law firms not only mentioned that companies inquire about the SCS, but some clients also approach them with concrete cases (EXP19-01, EXP19-14). Law firms address the inquiries with seminars on the SCS to increase their clients' knowledge on the topic (e.g. EXP19-14, PO19-SH, PO20-ON). Cases where law firms actively consult their clients with regard to the SCS are, for example, wrong company information on the SCS websites that caused entries on blacklists or companies aiming to have another actor added to a blacklist via a litigation (EXP19-01, EXP19-14). Moreover, the increased regulatory complexity, which the SCS creates (e.g. via the MoUs), makes it more difficult for companies to handle legal issues themselves. Therefore, law firms may even acquire new customers thanks to the SCS.

Lastly, the SCS affects the service offering from consultancies (e.g. accounting firms, policy consultancies). On the one hand, the SCS makes some of their services redundant or less attractive. For example, some accounting firms provide integrity evaluations on their clients' (potential) business partners and help them set integrity standards for cooperation (EXP19-08). Since the SCS serves as a helpful tool in third-party management and the government defines integrity standards via this system,

178 No official document confirming this procedure could be found. Therefore, it is considered an informal practice explained by an interviewee (EXP21-05).

the demand for these kind of services will likely decrease (EXP19-08). Thus, consultancies need to adapt their service offering to changing circumstances. They can, for example, include the SCS as an aspect they consider in their evaluations on how to set up and improve clients' compliance management systems, e.g. via dedicated SCS monitoring (EXP19-07, EXP19-08, PO20-ON). Hence, consultancies now already provide seminars and information material about the SCS to position themselves as experts on this topic (e.g. PO19-BJ, PO20-ON, Schaefer and Yin, 2019, Sinolytics and European Union Chamber of Commerce in China, 2019).

On the other hand, consultancies apparently consider the SCS as a new business opportunity both to support clients in mitigating the negative effects of the SCS (e.g. blacklist entries) and to fully leverage the system's benefits (e.g. rewards) (EXP19-08, PO19-BJ). The focus appears to have shifted from the former to the latter. For example, one consultancy presented at two SCS-related events that were twelve months apart and which are both included in this study's sample of non-participant observations (PO19-BJ, PO20-ON). The presenters at the first workshop focused mostly on the risks that the SCS potentially entails and how their company could help clients to navigate them (PO19-BJ). In contrast, the second presentation placed greater emphasis on promoting opportunities the SCS can provide for businesses (PO20-ON).

While this shift has not manifested itself in companies' reaction to and utilization of the SCS (yet) (see Section 5.4.1 and 5.4.2), such presentations nevertheless influence the public discourse on the SCS, especially when other consultancies join in on promoting the opportunities the SCS provides. For instance, several representatives from consultancies linked companies' integrity and compliance to their overall competitiveness (EXP19-08, EXP21-03, PO19-SH, PO20-ON). In this context, they encouraged companies to leverage compliance management as a competitive advantage, since the SCS allows firms to distinguish themselves via top ratings, credit commitments and redlist entries (EXP19-08, EXP21-03, PO19-SH, PO20-ON). Hence, these consultancies call on companies to act more strategically with regard to compliance (EXP19-14, PO20-ON). Furthermore, they placed the SCS and its benefits in the context of the government's overall goal to improve the business environment via informatization, e.g. by highlighting concrete benefits for companies, such as fast lanes for administrative services and easier access to loans (EXP19-09, EXP21-03). This emphasis on competitiveness and opportunities with regard to compliance in the SCS context may impact the construction of compliance in the long run, which has so far mostly been shaped by the avoidance of punishments and risk mitigation.

5.5 Consequences for the construction of corporate compliance

This chapter has introduced the SCS with a focus on its impacts on the corporate sector. The analysis of the SCS elements and mechanisms has identified the system's unique enforcement approach, which combines responsive regulation with managerial elements. Thereby, the SCS commodifies compliance (e.g. via the credit repair process and rewards) and ultimately economic trust. Set up this way, the SCS affects the construction of both the meaning of compliance and its social practices.

The theoretical conceptualization of the notion of credit incorporates and thereby directly affects the meaning of compliance. The reciprocal relationship between credit and compliance constructed in the official discourse influences the understanding of compliance in China in three main ways. First, the gradual nature of credit evaluations has influenced compliance, which is no longer exclusively thought of as a dichotomous decision. Second, credit-related supervision by authorities aims to improve compliance as well as aspects covered by the notion of credit (e.g. integrity, financial factors), which automatically become elements to be considered in compliance decisions and actions. Especially via concrete lists of compliance requirements (e.g. for public scores), the SCS sets compliance standards and thereby fosters institutional isomorphism in the context of compliance. Third, the SCS's relational approach extends the scope of compliance, i.e. the importance of third parties' credit and compliance behavior for a company, for example in the context of tender bidding processes.

These effects also manifest themselves in practice, where companies not only react to the SCS, but also proactively exploit the system's benefits[179]. First, the SCS has raised awareness for compliance in companies. On the one hand, compliance risks have become more preeminent because of the greater negative consequences the SCS caused. Here, key concerns are grave

179 The phenomena identified in this study are not representative of every business operating in China. They describe a comparatively pronounced impact of the SCS on the corporate sector, which may not reflect current reality across China, especially in light of regional differences. Hence, the elaborations provide an idea of the development direction of the SCS's impact on the corporate sector.

reputational ramifications, restricted access to finance and operational limitations (market access, tenders, etc.). These risks are underscored by the fact that the credit repair mechanism as a learning and redemption approach for compliance does not always bear fruits. On the other hand, the exploitation of opportunities with respect to transparency that the SCS provides has become a common practice. Firms use information on the SCS platforms in their third-party management and to strengthen their compliance management. This corroborates companies' role as regulators via their third-party management[180] and shows that the self-regulatory approach promoted by the SCS has been put into practice. Consequently, businesses are not only a target group, but also active multipliers of the SCS.

Second, several companies have internal management structures in place that are very similar to the SCS (e.g. ratings, blacklists). Some predate the SCS, some were installed after the SCS was initiated. This hints at mutual influences between companies and the SCS and ultimately fosters the legalization and institutionalization in businesses as well as the managerialization of the legal sphere.

Third, the idea of a gradual notion of compliance based on the concept of credit has been taken up by the credit service industry, which promotes the opportunities of the SCS for businesses and actively constructs compliance as a competitive advantage. While these attempts may influence the construction of compliance in the long-run, the gradual notion of compliance is still underrepresented among the interviewed business representatives. This is, among others, reflected in the importance of different SCS mechanisms for enterprises. While network (except redlists), legal and communicative instruments play a comparatively important role, the positive cycle of the SCS's enforcement approach via redlists and rewards remains negligible. In addition to this new trend promoted by the credit service industry, the discussion above has shown that the government has triggered changes in the operating models of existing credit service providers and created entirely new markets via the SCS (e.g. the credit repair market). By adapting to the new circumstances the SCS has set,

180 Foreign MNEs had adopted the practice of checking local supply chain partners (for the most part) voluntarily in the context of CSR before the existence of the SCS (e.g. EXP19-10, EXP19-13). The SCS further fosters this voluntary behavior, while at the same time also making it mandatory under certain circumstances (e.g. tender applications).

specifically by aiming to profit from the system, these companies act as disseminators of the notion of compliance that the SCS constructs.

Overall, this summary shows that the SCS has proven conducive to compliance by reinforcing, standardizing and extending the meaning and social practices of compliance. Nevertheless, several problems with respect to the SCS and compliance have been identified. For instance, the interview sample includes anecdotal evidence on the manipulation of the SCS (e.g. the deletion of negative data for an SOE); also the system's data quality and reliability is questioned by interviewees occasionally. In addition, the COVID-19 pandemic has shown that the SCS is not applied consistently under all circumstances (Knight and Creemers, 2021, Supreme People's Court, 2020). A certain level of flexibility can be an advantage, e.g. when protecting businesses during an exceptional crisis, as the government has done via its exceptions for SMEs related to SCS punishments during the COVID-19 pandemic (Supreme People's Court, 2020). Yet, this malleability also illustrates the lack of neutrality of the SCS, resulting in a risk of abuse inherent in this system, which could be deployed for political purposes by the Party-state. Consequently, the ethical concerns of one powerful actor (the Chinese government) collecting, centralizing and controlling huge amounts of data on companies and individuals with minimal checks and balances need to be considered in an overall evaluation of and lesson drawing from this system.

6 Corporate compliance in different industries in China

Having provided an overview of compliance in China, including the specific impacts the SCS has on this institution, this chapter discusses the construction of compliance in two specific industries, the securities sector (sub-case two, Section 6.1) and the automotive sector (sub-case three, Section 6.2), as compared to the cross-sectoral trends. This way, the chapter attends to the fact that cross-country influences within sectors are significant and often lead to strong variations between sectors within one country (Levi-Faur, 2006, p. 368). Hence, the following elaborations capture two different ways of how compliance was introduced to China and the resulting diversity in the constructed meaning of, influences on and social practices of compliance.

6.1 Corporate compliance in the securities sector in China

This first industry sub-case investigates compliance in securities firms. After a literature review (Section 6.1.1) and an overview of the securities sector's regulatory approach (Section 6.1.2), this sub-case examines the genesis of the concept of compliance in China (Section 6.1.3). On this basis, Section 6.1.4 and 6.1.5 discuss the particular manifestation of compliance in the securities sector by outlining the influences on compliance in this industry and the compliance practices of securities firms in China respectively[181]. The sub-case concludes with a discussion of the consequences of the findings on compliance construction.

6.1.1 Literature review

Generally, academic research on compliance in the securities sector is scarce, with two strands of literature addressing the issue. On the one hand, scholars discuss the regulatory regime in the Chinese securities sector and thereby indirectly provide insights into factors that influence securities firms' compliance (e.g. He, 2018, Xi and Pan, 2017, Wang, 2011). Often, these discussions focus on the historical development after the Chinese reform process started in 1978 and track the transformation of the financial sector in China, including the securities sector (e.g. Zhang et al., 2019, Collins and Gottwald, 2011, Hsueh, 2011, Pearson, 2005). Some of the literature on the Chinese stock market also provides insights into securities firms and the regulatory regime they are exposed to (e.g. Allen et al., 2020, Li et al., 2020). Moreover, scholars discuss the Chinese developments in the international context, e.g. by analyzing international policy learning by the CSRC or the influence of international standards (e.g. Basel II) on the Chinese regulatory model (e.g. Zhang et al., 2021, Collins and Gottwald, 2011). Some studies also compare the Chinese securities market to other countries, be it Western nations with mature financial systems, such as the US (Wei, 2005) or to other emerging markets (Ma et al., 2010).

On the other hand, a strand of Chinese-speaking literature discusses Chinese securities companies' compliance management (e.g. Niu, 2020, Chen and Fan, 2012, Zhou and Cheng, 2011). For instance, some scholars

181 The findings are mainly based on 12 interviews with representatives from the securities sector, which amount to ca. 18 percent of the total number of interviews conducted to understand compliance trends in China overall.

analyze problems securities companies face in their compliance management, such as a lack of compliance culture, gaps in compliance monitoring as well as the insufficient use of IT in compliance management, and propose countermeasures (e.g. Gao, 2020, Wang et al., 2017, Wu, 2012). Others draw from international examples to identify learnings for Chinese companies (e.g. Wu, 2015, Zhou and Cheng, 2011). However, these publications are conceptual in nature and do not provide evidence from empirical research. This chapter closes the gap by examining both official documents and qualitative interview data on compliance in securities firms in China, after providing an overview of the securities sector's regulatory regime.

6.1.2 Overview of the securities sector's regulatory approach

6.1.2.1 Historical development

Before the People's Republic of China was founded in 1949, the Shanghai Stock Exchange was the largest stock market in Asia. However, the restructuring to a centrally-planned economy led to the elimination of all types of private ownership, the stock exchanges and the securities market (Wei, 2005, p. 488). Only after the reform and opening in 1978, did the securities sector start to develop again. Initially, the innovation and entrepreneurial spirit set free by the reforms contributed greatly to this development. Hence, market participants and local government authorities were in the driving seat (Wang, 2011, p. 233). For example, in 1984, the first public share offering was made and in 1986, the PBoC authorized the first over-the-counter market in Shenyang (Wei, 2005, p. 488). While banking still dominated the financial service sector, over time, more and more securities brokerages were established, such as Anshan Securities in 1988 (Hsueh, 2011, p. 197). In 1990, national stock exchanges were established in Shanghai and Shenzhen. They were subject to a complex regulatory set-up with many powerful authorities, such as the PBoC, the State Council, the Ministry of Finance and city governments, being involved. As the owner of these stock exchanges and many securities firms, the Chinese government has essentially acted as both the owner and the regulator of the securities sector ever since its establishment (Ma et al., 2010, p. 159).

The high complexity in the securities sector, due to the above described initial bottom-up development and the many regulators involved, resulted in several serious scandals, such as the August 10 riot[182]. Consequently, the central government started to establish a nationally coherent regulatory framework for this sector in the 1990s (Wang, 2011, p. 237). First, the SAC was founded as the securities industry's self-regulatory organization in 1991 (CSRC, 2008, p. 160). Another major milestone in this context was the establishment of the CSRC and the Securities Committee by the State Council in 1992 (CSRC, 2008, p. 164). However, at that time, the authority of the CSRC was still limited and responsibilities among different actors were not delineated clearly: The CSRC was responsible for overseeing listed companies, supervising securities firms' trading activities, controlling the overseas listing of domestic companies and developing market regulations. But its scope overlapped with the PBoC, which was responsible for the supervision of securities firms, and the State Council's Securities Committee, which drafted laws as well as regulations for the securities market and supervised market activities (CSRC, 2008, p. 164).

In the late 1990s and early 2000s, the position of the CSRC was further strengthened; an initiative that aimed to end the turf war between the different regulatory authorities. Other challenges the Chinese Party-state faced during this phase were the Asian financial crisis of 1998[183] and China's WTO accession in 2001 (Yang, 2004, p. 294). Hence, the government initiated several changes in the securities industry's regulatory set-up during this period. First, the government successfully achieved the CSRC's membership in the International Organization of Securities Commission (IOSCO) in 1995. This was followed by the consolidation of regulatory responsibility for the supervision of the two existing stock markets in the hands of the CSRC in 1997, i.e. removing Shenzhen's and Shanghai's municipal governments as stock market regulators (Pearson, 2005, p. 312). Next, in 1998, the State Council Securities Committee merged with the CSRC to strengthen the commission's authority (CSRC, 2008, p. 164). In the following year, the first Securities Law was enacted, defining the CSRC as the sole regulator of securities firms and granting the agency full authority

182 In August 1992, a large number of people queued in front of the stock exchange in Shenzhen for days because they wanted to buy purchasing vouchers for new shares. However, many investors were not able to buy such vouchers and complained about the unfair sales process. In the following, conflicts between these queuing investors and the local police erupted and thus, share prices on both stock exchanges fell sharply (Ma et al., 2010, p. 165).

183 This crisis had underpinned the importance of financial security and thus adequate regulation of this sector (Yang, 2004, p. 294).

over regulating this market nationally in a consistent manner (Wang, 2011, p. 237). Consequently, the CSRC gained ministerial status in 2003, another step underpinning its authority (Hsueh, 2011, p. 197).

Nevertheless, this institutional set-up did not suffice to prevent risks in the securities sector. The rapid initial market development and strong competition led to frequent failures of firms, which had destabilizing effects (CSRC, 2008, p. 214). For instance, a lot of securities firms had missed the opportunity to build sustainable business models, adequate internal control measures and a solid corporate governance system during their fast expansions (CSRC, 2008, p. 214). These firms were found to engage in risky speculations and illegal activities (CSRC, 2008, p. 214). Therefore, a CSRC report concluded:

> "By early 2004, the whole industry was on the brink of bankruptcy with years of risky and sometimes illegal investments and a lack of proper supervision and enforcement" (CSRC, 2008, p. 214).

To address the need for stricter regulation and enforcement in the sector, especially regarding disclosure and anti-fraud rules, the CSRC used campaign-style interventions intensively (Xi and Pan, 2017, p. 94). In addition, the CSRC's strengthened mandate as sole regulator was conducive to further improvements made in the sector. Specifically, the CSRC revised the securities law to accommodate changes in the sector and passed additional regulations (Xi and Pan, 2017, p. 83). For instance, after the securities law amendment in 2005, this legal text contained stricter requirements for securities firms regarding internal control and enhanced CSRC supervision mechanisms (CSRC, 2008, p. 230). At the same time, public disclosure regulations were passed and risk monitoring systems installed, which ensured transparency and provided early warnings (CSRC, 2008, p. 215). Moreover, the CSRC centralized its supervision framework, for example by reorganizing its regional supervision offices to provincial supervisory bureaus and by better coordinating its supervision work with local governments in 2004 (CSRC, 2008, p. 174). This led to the development of a centralized enforcement system on the part of the CSRC in 2007, which included a "Sanction Committee, Chief Enforcement Office and the Law Enforcement Task Force in its headquarters and [...] Enforcement Offices with a larger workforce at local supervisory offices" (CSRC, 2008, p. 175).

At the same time, the CSRC implemented several market-oriented reforms in order to meet international standards. For example, a greater number of stock indices were published to help investors, and an ownership structure reform finally allowed SOEs to circulate state-owned shares on the stock market (Ma et al., 2010, p. 166). In addition, regulations regarding information disclosure were passed to improve transparency and further strengthen investors' rights on the Chinese securities market (Ma et al., 2010, p. 166).

These market-oriented reforms went hand in hand with a slow opening up of the market to the international community. Hence, by 2007, China already had seven Sino-foreign securities firms (JVs) (CSRC, 2008, p. 185). In addition, the CSRC increased international cooperation during that time, for example by signing MoUs with other securities regulators internationally. In 2006, the CSRC's chairman was even elected as the vice-chairman of IOSCO's executive committee (CSRC, 2008, p. 187). The CSRC continued gradual opening up in the following years, a process that is best illustrated by the cap on foreign capital in securities firms' JVs: In 2012, the CSRC increased the limit from previously 33 to 49 percent and abolished this requirement in 2018 entirely (Zhang et al., 2019, p. 278ff).

These internalization efforts in the securities industry were part of a general trend towards liberalization in the Chinese financial sector, which aimed to spur industry innovation (e.g. in financial products and business practices) and to relax administrative controls; in the case of securities firms especially in relation to business scope (Li et al., 2020, p. 7f). This trend was disrupted by two crises: The global financial crisis of 2007/08, which did not affect China to the same degree as Western nations, but nevertheless had Chinese regulators on edge (Huang, 2010); and the Chinese stock market crisis of 2015/16, which was triggered by tightened regulations of the CSRC due to increasingly problematic practices, such as shadow banking (Li et al., 2020, p. 9). Nevertheless, the main regulatory framework remained the same and was enhanced, e.g. by the recent opening of a third stock market in Beijing in 2021 as a primary platform for SMEs (Beijing Stock Exchange, 2021).

This review of the historical development in the securities sector shows that even though this market initially emerged thanks to market forces and local governments' initiatives, the Chinese central government eventually coopted these developments and set up a centralized regulatory and institutional framework to govern the sector. But not only did the Chinese government majorly affect the development of the securities sector, research also hints at a significant influence of US securities institutions and regulations on Chinese development (Xi and Pan, 2017, p. 81f): An international advisory council provided foreign input at the time when the

CSRC and its enforcement program were set up. In addition, individuals educated in the US were placed in influential positions in the CSRC early on, which fostered the knowledge transfer of US securities regulations and enforcement practices to China. For instance, Gao Xiqing and Laura Cha served as the CSRC's vice-chair(wo)men (from 1999 to 2003 and 2001 to 2004 respectively); both of them attained a legal degree in the US (Xi and Pan, 2017, p. 82).

This balancing act between an emulation of US practices on the one hand, and perpetuating the traditional Chinese regulatory practice of strong Party-state guidance and involvement in the market on the other, has led to the current regulatory set-up in the securities sector, which is described in more detail in the following section.

6.1.2.2 Regulatory framework

The current regulatory framework in the securities sector consists of eight main institutions, two targeting the securities sector from a macro-economic perspective and the remaining six directly regulating and supervising securities firms: The Central Finance and Economic Affairs Commission (中央财经委员会), the NDRC, the PBoC, the CSRC, the three stock exchanges and the SAC (see Figure 32[184]).

Figure 32: Schematic overview of the regulatory set-up in the securities sector (author's design)

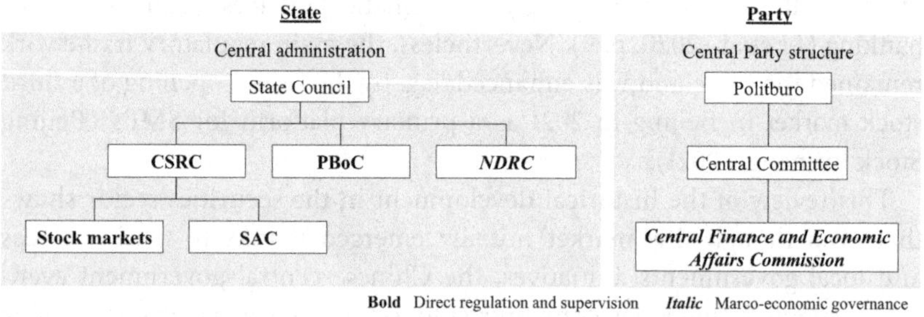

184 This summary does not claim to be exhaustive, but rather combines a general overview with more details on the organizations that are most important for the following elaborations on compliance. The focus in this figure is placed on the

The Central Finance and Economic Affairs Commission[185] is part of the CCP's Central Committee and the highest body managing and supervising economic work, including finance- and economy-related policy-making, in the Chinese Party-state, i.e. in both the CCP's Central Committee and the State Council (Grünberg, 2021, Grünberg and Drinhausen, 2019, p. 5). The Central Finance and Economic Affairs Commission closely collaborates with the NDRC, the state agency under the State Council responsible for macro-economic planning (Heilmann, 2016, p. 77f). However, both of these commissions focus on macro-economic governance and are not directly involved in the regulation and supervision of securities firm. Yet, their decisions and steering affect the securities sector.

This high-level guidance is reflected in concrete regulations and supervision by two state agencies. The PBoC monitors securities firms with respect to anti-money laundering and the CSRC supervises all other aspects concerning the securities sector. Hence, as the main regulator for securities firms, the CSRC holds a powerful position, especially compared to regulatory organizations in other industrial sectors (Pearson, 2005, p. 310ff). It is a public institution (事业单位) under the control of the State Council, meaning it is not part of the state administration, yet is granted the status of a ministry (Pearson, 2007, p. 723). On the one hand, this organizational set-up can lead to challenges to the commission's power, since its de facto ministerial status is not reflected in its official organizational rank. On the other hand, as a public institution, the CSRC benefits from fewer bureaucratic restrictions compared to institutions within the state administration (Pearson, 2007, p. 723). The key responsibility of the CSRC is the supervision of the securities sector, including securities companies, the approval of corporate bond listings and the control of stock issuing and trading (International Monetary Fund and World Bank, 2017, p. 8f). Being at least partially modeled after a US's regulatory institution, i.e. the US Securities and Exchange Commission (SEC) and often staffed with Western-trained leadership, the CSRC, as a regulator, has shown high levels of market-orientation compared to other Chinese regulators and is strongly affected by international financial market discipline (Pearson, 2005, p. 312).

---

actors in the central administration, since the local administrations only seem to play a minor role for securities firms' compliance.

185 This commission was formerly known as the Finance and Economic Leading Small Group (中央财经领导小组) and reorganized to become the Central Finance and Economic Affairs Commission in 2018 in the context of administrative reforms (Central Committee of the CCP, 2018).

Nevertheless, the CSRC interferes with the market more directly than its US counterpart. This can be illustrated by the control the CSRC holds over the stock exchanges and the SAC and which limits these organizations' self-regulatory capacities. The stock exchanges are regulators directly under the umbrella of the CSRC[186]. They can be regarded as the CSRC's executive organs, since they do not have the power to make independent decisions (Ma et al., 2010, p. 159). Therefore, the stock exchanges operationally manage the stock markets and provide additional rules for listed companies that are based on CSRC regulations, but possess a higher level of detail. However, the CSRC has the final say when it comes to changes, e.g. regarding listing or trading rules (He, 2018, p. 51).

With respect to the CSRC's control, the situation of the SAC is similar to the stock exchanges:

The SAC is a non-profit organization under the CSRC that is supposed to act as the securities sector's self-regulatory organization (SAC, 2021, Allen et al., 2020, p. 285). Membership is mandatory for all securities companies (International Monetary Fund and World Bank, 2017, p. 10). As members, securities firms benefit from services the SAC provides, e.g. trainings and specifications of regulatory requirements from the CSRC. This illustrates the two main responsibilities of the SAC in general, namely the development and administration of a qualification system for practitioners in the securities sector as well as the development and monitoring of industry rules (International Monetary Fund and World Bank, 2017, p. 10). The SAC's industry rules are based on the CSRC's regulations for the sector, but provide an additional level of detail and are thereby more concrete and easy to implement for securities firms (International Monetary Fund and World Bank, 2017, p. 10).

186 The Shanghai and Shenzhen Stock Exchanges are institutions directly under the CSRC, whereas the newly established Beijing Stock Exchange is only indirectly controlled by the CSRC: The stock exchange in Beijing is owned by Beijing Stock Exchange Company Limited (北京证券交易所有限责任公司), whose sole shareholder is the National Equities Exchange and Quotations Company (全国中小企业股份转让系统有限责任公司) (Qichacha, 2021b). This organization is majority-owned by the other two stock exchanges and China Securities Depository and Clearing Corporation Limited (中国证券登记结算有限责任公司), which is again owned by the other two stock exchanges (each actor 20 percent of shares) (Qichacha, 2021f,c). Hence, since the stock exchanges in Shanghai and Shenzhen are directly controlled by the CSRC, the Beijing Stock Exchange is indirectly also under this agency's umbrella.

These elaborations highlight the Party-state-controlled and centripetal regulatory institutional set-up in the securities sector via the CSRC. Accordingly, enforcement in the securities sector is dominated by the CSRC, which possesses three investigation pillars: The Inspection Bureau (稽查局), the Inspection Contingent (稽查总队) and enforcement forces in the local CSRC offices (Xi and Pan, 2017, p. 87). The Inspection Bureau has the highest authority and oversees investigations (e.g. initiates new investigations, coordinates investigations of cross-regional cases), but does not conduct investigations itself (Xi and Pan, 2017, p. 87). This responsibility lies in the hands of the Inspection Contingent and the local enforcement forces: The Inspection Contingent focuses on investigation cases that possess a high level of seriousness and importance, whereas the local enforcement forces are responsible for regular inspections (Xi and Pan, 2017, p. 87ff). Besides the CSRC's direct supervision, self-regulation has supposedly emerged as a regulatory practice in the securities sector, e.g. via the SAC (Wei, 2005, p. 503). Since this so-called self-regulatory organization for the Chinese securities sector is, however, under the direct supervision of the CSRC and all securities firms are obliged to become members, actual self-regulation by industry members is limited. In addition, other mechanism that supposedly serve self-regulation were also installed by the CSRC, such as publicly-available scores. Hence, these mechanisms can rather be characterized as indirect means to supervise than self-regulation.

Strong Party-state influence also characterizes ownership structures among securities firms, because securities firms historically emerged as affiliates of banks and government agencies and the securities market has only slowly been privatized and opened to international exposure (Chen et al., 2011, p. 791f). Securities companies are commonly state-backed, be it via direct state ownership or by having SOEs as majority shareholders (He, 2018, p. 57ff). Yet, market liberalization efforts have resulted in a diversification of ownership structures: By 2015, none of the twelve largest securities companies possessed a single state-controlled majority shareholder (Li et al., 2020, p. 6). Hence, despite high levels of state-ownership overall, securities firms have to meet demands from a complex web of shareholders, including state agencies and asset management firms (Li et al., 2020, p. 5).

Independent of ownership type, securities firms in China face strict regulatory constraints (Chen, 2009, p. 577). An important reason for the rigorous controls is the fact that the main sources of revenue for securities firms are trading commissions and interest rates, which make business success highly volatile and dependent on the overall economic climate (Chen, 2009, p. 559). The heavy regulation of the securities market not only leads to high entry barriers for new securities firms, but also regulatory limitations after entering the market (Chen, 2009, p. 577). For instance, if securities firms want to add new branches or business fields to their portfolio[187], they need to apply to and receive approval from the CSRC (Chen, 2009, p. 560). The high levels of regulation, however, bear the risk of stifling innovation and rendering business operations inefficient.

As the elaborations above have shown, the regulatory framework in the securities sector is characterized by strong centralized Party-state control, both via state agencies' supervision, especially the CSRC, and state-ownership (He, 2018, p. 45). This hints at a high national strategic importance attributed to this sector as part of the financial sector (CSRC, 2008, p. 284). Wang (2011, p. 228) even went so far as to claim that "securities regulation is a government-controlled process to rebuild and maintain political legitimacy of the Chinese state". Hence, the regulatory approach in the securities sector can be labeled as dependent on government control based on McNally and Gruin's (2017) categorization and 'deliberate reinforcement in strategic sectors' in Hsueh's (2011, p. 226) sense. Since private and international capital have been introduced to the sector gradually over time, the securities sector can be classified in the category 'government-business integration' according to Liu (2011a). Yet, these descriptions do not take recent trends towards increased self-regulation and securities firms' experience with the regulatory regime via compliance management into consideration. Therefore, the following sections elaborate on the manifestation of compliance in the securities sector.

187 Generally, securities firms in China can be placed in two categories: Comprehensive securities companies, which are active in a broad portfolio of securities-related activities (e.g. brokerage, under-writing, proprietary trading), and brokerage securities companies, which exclusively focus on securities brokerage (Chen et al., 2005, p. 116).

6.1.3 The genesis of the concept of corporate compliance in the securities sector

Process tracing of the term 'compliance' (合规) in Chinese securities sector-related official documents[188] ('official discourse' in the following) reveals a clear-cut development path of the concept of compliance. A key reason for the highly consolidated and focused process towards increasing maturity of compliance in the securities sector is the centralized regulatory regime in this industry, with the CSRC as the main regulator around which all regulatory efforts targeting securities firms revolve. But the fact that compliance was first discussed in the finance sector, including the securities industry, (see Section 4.3) likely has also played an important role. The genesis of the concept of compliance, as depicted in the official discourse, can be broken down into four development phases (see Table 7).

Table 7: Development phases of the concept of compliance in the securities sector

	Phase 1	**Phase 2**	**Phase 3**	**Phase 4**
Period	1994 – 2007	2008 – 2013	2014 – mid-2019	Mid-2019 – present
Description	Emergence of the concept of compliance	Compliance system set-up	Enhancement of compliance concept and measures	Compliance culture-building

Phase 1: Emergence of the concept of compliance (1994 – 2007)

Phase one marks the first appearance of the term compliance in documents from the Chinese securities sector, followed by the construction of a first, rough understanding of compliance. The early documents from the securities sector, including the first document mentioning compliance in 1994, indicate the importance of the international context for the introduction of compliance to the Chinese securities sector (e.g. SEC-19940827, SEC-20071107). For example, some of the early documents mention foreign regulations or requirements for Chinese companies that are internationally listed in the context of compliance (e.g. SEC-19940827, SEC-19990921).

188 For further information on the process tracing, refer to Section 1.3.

This finding is in line with interviews conducted for this research and other sources' findings, which both explain that the CSRC adopted the main regulatory principles from international actors and standards (e.g. the IOSCO, the Basel Accords and the International Financial Reporting Standards) (Collins and Gottwald, 2011, p. 145). With respect to compliance, specifically, the compliance notion dominant in the international banking sector had a major influence on the CSRC (e.g. BUS21-01).

From the start, compliance has been closely connected to the idea of legality in the official discourse. The first documents use the combination '合法合规' (e.g. SEC-19980824, SEC-20000406) or '守法合规' (e.g. SEC-19980824, SEC-20010226) and these expressions are later gradually replaced by '依法合规' (e.g. SEC-20040817, SEC-20050404, SEC-20070409, SEC-20070523), all of which can be translated as 'legal compliance'[189]. Hence, early on, compliance has been constructed as the counterpart to supervision by the Party-state; a reaction to the external controls companies face (e.g. SEC-20050404, SEC-20060723). In line with this narrow understanding of compliance, the early official discourse also constructed compliance as a top-down effort. Evidence of this are documents that considered firms' top management and boards as the target groups for compliance efforts (e.g. SEC-19940827, SEC-19980824, SEC-20000406, SEC-20010226, SEC-20020107, SEC-20061130) as well as an article that called for parent companies to support their subsidiaries in compliance efforts in a top-down fashion (SEC-20071228). Furthermore, the early understanding of compliance is closely linked to companies' internal control and risk management (SEC-20000406, SEC-20010226, SEC-20040817, SEC-20060723, SEC-20071012, SEC-20071228). Hence, in this phase, the need for or the implementation of dedicated independent compliance management systems was not mentioned.

In addition, the initial phase of the official compliance discourse in the securities sector constructed an objective to be achieved via compliance that has dominated the official discourse ever since, namely healthy market development. The earlier documents mentioning compliance discussed this motive from a negative angle; meaning they positioned non-compliance as a hindrance for development (SEC-19940827, SEC-20040817, SEC-20070523). But two documents also emphasized the need for compli-

189 The change in expressions can be attributed to the increasing importance of rules-based governance and the idea of a rule by law (依法治国), which exhibits great resemblance to 依法合规.

ance in order to achieve healthy market development, i.e. a positive angle (SEC-20040817, SEC-20070523). Yet, apparently this does not mean that compliance is already regarded as a mandatory prerequisite for business operations across the board, since one document, a case study of compliance management in an exemplary securities company, positioned the investigated securities company's legal compliance as a noteworthy achievement, despite difficult economic circumstances:

> "Even under the difficult situation of the securities market's continuous downturn in the past three years, [the company] still insisted on operating in compliance with laws and regulations" ("即使在近三年证券市场持续低迷的困难形势下，仍坚持守法合规经营不动摇", SEC-20041201).

This description implies that compliance is not regarded as a must-have for companies' existence, but rather a negotiable condition depending on the economic conditions.

Phase 2: Compliance system set-up (2008 – 2013)

The second phase of compliance development in this sector focused on the set-up of compliance systems in the industry. Several major non-compliance incidents in the securities industry triggered initiatives with regard to compliance (SEC-20081024, SEC-20091016): The CSRC promulgated stricter supervision (e.g. SEC-20091016, SEC-20100420, SEC-20110114), but also implemented a stronger focus on the topic of compliance in its official documents. This approach included the publication of case examples of non-compliant companies for deterrence purposes as an indirect measure (SEC-20100420, SEC-20100608). In addition, the CSRC undertook three direct actions to set up compliance systems in the industry, namely enacting a compliance management regulation for securities firms (SEC-20080714), setting up the annual evaluation of companies via the securities score (SEC-20090526) and introducing competency exams for securities firms' compliance managers ('competency exams' in the following) via the SAC (SEC-20080228).

First, the regulation on compliance management for securities firms, the 'Securities Firm Compliance Management Trial Regulation' ('Securities Compliance Regulation' in the following), was enacted in 2008

(SEC-20080714). Since then, securities firms have been required to possess a dedicated compliance management system; hence compliance has been separated from the notion of internal control and given a stand-alone function (SEC-20080714). The regulation laid the basis for compliance management in securities firms, as it defines compliance and describes the required key components for compliance management systems. In general, the contents are in line with international compliance best practices. For example, in clause three, the document requires compliance management to cover all business units, other departments, employees, policies, etc. and clause five names elements, such as compliance management goals and principles, a compliance department, a non-compliance reporting system, as components of a compliance management system (SEC-20080714). In this context, the CSRC left certain leeway for companies regarding the set-up of specific compliance management systems, e.g. the regulation does not provide details on how the compliance department needs to be organized or its specific scope (SEC-20080714). Yet, in this regulation, as well as other documents from the official discourse in this phase, there is still a pronounced top-down notion of compliance, with the responsibility and focus of measures attributed to securities firms' leadership[190] (e.g. SEC-20080117, SEC-20080714, SEC-20131021(5)). Another regulation released by the CSRC in 2008 on the supervision of securities firms echoed this strong role of the CSRC, by clearly defining measures to be taken in case of securities companies' non-compliance, ranging from an increase in the required frequency of internal compliance audits to suspending business operations (SEC-20080423(1)).

Second, in 2009, shortly after the milestone of releasing the first dedicated compliance management regulation in the securities sector, the CSRC introduced a classification system for securities firms, the securities score (证券公司分类, SEC-20090526), which comprehensively evaluates securities firms:

> "The classification of securities companies is based on the risk management capabilities of securities companies, combined with the firms' market competitiveness and continuous compliance status" ("证券公司分类是指以证券公司风险管理能力为基础，结合公司市场竞争力和持续合规状况", SEC-20090526).

190 International best practices, in contrast, also include, among others, an emphasis on compliance culture-building and employees' compliance awareness.

The score evaluates securities firms annually along fixed dimensions, in which points can be subtracted or added from a base score of 100 points (SEC-20090526). The highest possible theoretical score is AAA and the lowest E[191] (SEC-20090526). Points are, for instance, subtracted for the violation of regulations identified by authorities, punishments received from self-regulatory organizations and in case problems are identified in six focus areas, namely capital adequacy, corporate governance and compliance management, comprehensive risk management, information technology management, customer rights protection and information disclosure (SEC-20090526). As a result, these six areas are in the focus of attention when securities firms set up their management structures. At the same time, companies can receive additional points when they achieve success in business (e.g. asset management business income ranked in the top five of the industry) and decent risk management (e.g. major risk control indicators continue to meet the standards of the last three evaluation periods)[192] (SEC-20090526). Originally, the CSRC did not publish scores, because it intended to only conduct this evaluation for the purpose of internal supervision (e.g. decision on inspection frequency) and securities firms were prohibited to use the scores for marketing purposes, e.g. in advertisement (SEC-20090526). However, already in 2010, the CSRC changed its approach and allowed the publication of securities scores (SEC-20100514). Consequently, since 2010, the annual securities scores are publicly accessible via the CSRC website (SEC-20100714, SEC-20110714, SEC-20120713, SEC-20130712, SEC-20140715, SEC-20150717, SEC-20160715, SEC-20170814, SEC-20180727, SEC-20190726(2), SEC-20200911). While companies are still not allowed to advertise their scores, the mere publication adds a reputational element to this enforcement practice.

---

191 According to the regulation (SEC-20090526), companies with over 100 points receive the scores AAA, AA, A, BBB and BB, firms between 60 and 100 points are rated B, CCC, CC and C. All these scores reflect that companies are operating regularly and have the capacities to manage the risk they are facing, at least to a certain extent. The scores D and E are attributed to companies with less than 60 points, i.e. enterprises that face high risks or where concrete risks have already materialized. Companies with an E-score need to stop operations. However, an analysis of the published securities scores over time shows that AAA and E scores have never been used (SEC-20100714, SEC-20110714, SEC-20120713, SEC-20130712, SEC-20140715, SEC-20150717, SEC-20160715, SEC-20170814, SEC-20180727, SEC-20190726(2), SEC-20200911).

192 However, point additions are not available for companies with too serious problems.

Third, the SAC implemented dedicated competency exams for compliance in a top-down fashion (SEC-20080228). The SAC has held these exams since 2008, as they are a prerequisite for staff to be appointed to the so-called Chief Compliance Officer (CCO, 合规总监) position (SEC-20080324, SEC-20080714). This role is another idiosyncrasy of compliance management in the Chinese securities sector that strengthens the CSRC's influence on securities firms' compliance management. The 'Securities Compliance Regulation' initially defines this position and lays down qualification-related prerequisites for position holders, including passing the SAC's competency exam[193] (SEC-20080714). By confirming the candidates proposed by the securities firms, the CSRC retains the ultimate power over the staffing decision for this key position in firms' compliance management. Furthermore, according to clause 25 of the regulation, the CCO is exempt from responsibility for non-compliance incidents in case the CCO directly and correctly reports malpractices to the CSRC (SEC-20080714). This clause appears to incentivize CCOs' loyalty towards the CSRC and thereby furthers the authority's influence on compliance management in securities firms.

To help examinees in their preparation for the test, the SAC regularly publishes an outline that includes all the topics covered by the exam (e.g. SEC-20080228). Knowledge requirements for testees to pass the test are, for example, an understanding of compliance theory (e.g. the relationship between compliance, risk and internal control) and of certain compliance-related regulations (SEC-20080228). In order to educate and prepare compliance staff for these exams, the SAC started to hold compliance-related seminars across the country from 2009 onward (e.g. SEC-20090309, SEC-20090420, SEC-20100329, SEC-20100824). Similar to the 'Securities Compliance Regulation' and the securities score, this educational effort also constitutes a top-down effort towards strengthening the role of compliance and compliance management in securities firms; meaning that from the start, the CSRC has retained the prerogative of constructing compliance in the securities sector.

The notion of compliance the CSRC established via these measures resonates with the general themes that were established in the first phase (e.g. close connection to the topic of risk, compliance as a means to ensure

193 Other requirements are for candidates to have engaged in securities work for more than five years and possessing a qualification to work as a senior manager in securities firms (SEC-20080714).

healthy economic development) and consequently exhibits similarities with international best practices. At the same time, this second phase is characterized by an enhancement of the constructed meaning of compliance, both in terms of the scope of what compliance entails and with respect to the promulgated motives for compliance: During this phase, the official discourse in the securities sector showed first hints of an ethical notion of compliance, which extended the original compliance understanding that focused only on legal compliance (e.g. SEC-20081024, SEC-20110919, SEC-20131021(1)). For example, a recap of a seminar on securities firms' innovation and development, held in Beijing during this phase, positioned compliance on the same level as honesty and trustworthiness and as part of a companies' social responsibility:

> "Securities companies should also undertake social responsibilities and firmly establish the concepts of honesty and trustworthiness, legal compliance, caring for the country, loving the people, alleviating the poor and environmental protection" ("证券公司更要承担好社会责任，牢固树立诚实守信、依法合规、关心国家、热爱人民、扶贫济困、绿色环保的理念", SEC-20120507).

Other documents also framed compliance in the context of integrity (e.g. SEC-20131021(1)) and the SCS (SEC-20110919). Even though the SCS has only been established since 2014, the CSRC already explicitly drew the connection to credit and the SCS in an article on the creation of a database for so-called integrity files (诚信档案数据库) in 2011 (SEC-20110919). Integrity files (诚信档案) are files with information on organizations or individuals active in the securities sector that securities firm can and at times have to check before making decisions (SEC-20110919). For certain positions, e.g. on the upper management level, securities firms are not allowed to hire individuals with negative entries due to legal violations (EXP21-01). The CSRC started to use these files in 2008 and already in 2011, "in line with the overall planning and requirements of the State Council's SCS construction, the CSRC formed institutional arrangements to connect and share [the integrity file database] with the PBoC's credit reporting system" ("证监会按照国务院社会信用体系建设的总体部署和要求，与中国人民银行就征信系统联网共享形成制度安排", SEC-20110919). While the CSRC has not been in the driver's seat for the SCS set-up, this early effort, which predated the official start of the SCS as implemented today, already reflects the underlying logic of the SCS, namely the connection of databases for the purpose of transparency, the promotion of integrity and the naming and shaming of actors in case of non-compliance.

In addition to the enhancement of the scope of compliance, new compliance motives also surfaced in the official discourse. On the one hand, the discourse now positioned compliance as a prerequisite for business operations. For instance, companies need to be in compliance, in order to tap into new business fields, such as asset management and lending business (SEC-20080423(1), SEC-20081005, SEC-20111027, SEC-20121019, SEC-20130316, SEC-20131021(2), SEC-20131021(6)). On the other hand, the official discourse also motivated securities firms to operate compliantly in order to protect customer and investor rights and interests (SEC-20080423(1)). This also entails the establishment of the CSRC's complaint hotline '12386', another mechanism to gain transparency and motivate securities firms to increase their compliance efforts (SEC-20131114).

Phase 3: Enhancement of compliance concept and measures (2014 – mid 2019)

During the following years the concept of compliance and related measures were enhanced. Besides emphasizing the concept of compliance by a republishing of various compliance-related documents from previous phases in 2014 (e.g. SEC-20140220(1), SEC-20140220(5), SEC-20140220(8)), this phase saw a deepening of the ethical notion of the compliance concept, updates on the three elements of the compliance system in the securities sector ('Securities Compliance Regulation', securities score and compliance exams) as well as the introduction of supporting measures to improve existing efforts towards compliance.

With regard to the ethical notion of compliance, the official compliance discourse in the Chinese securities sector increasingly mentioned compliance in the context of firms' social responsibility, ethics and credit (e.g. SEC-20150417(1), SEC-20160321, SEC-20160612, SEC-20170623, SEC-20171116). In this context, the CSRC's vice chairman coined the term 'compliant integrity' (合规诚信) in a speech in 2016, which has become a commonly used phrase in the securities sector's official discourse on compliance (e.g. SEC-20160612, SEC-20190517(1), SEC-20190517(4)). Moreover, the official discourse showed that the securities sector strengthens its SCS-related efforts: The SAC started to build an integrity information management system based on existing integrity files (诚信信息管理系统)

(SEC-20150105), punishments for non-compliance included entries in the integrity files (e.g. SEC-20161223, SEC-20180126) and the CSRC signed 21 MoUs in the context of the SCS in 2018 to ensure that people with integrity-issues receive punishments in all realms of society (SEC-20190125).

The enhancement of the three elements of the compliance system in the securities sector introduced in the previous phase pertains to the release of a replacement regulation for the 'Securities Compliance Regulation', namely the 'Compliance Measures for Securities Firms and Securities Investment Fund Management Firms' ('Securities Compliance Measures' in the following) in 2017 (SEC-20170606(1)). The 'Securities Compliance Measures' are based on the 'Securities Compliance Regulation', yet provide more precise and prescriptive requirements for securities firms' compliance management. For instance, the regulation includes prescriptions on the minimal number of staff in the compliance department in clause 22, which is calculated according to a percentage of compliance staff as part of the overall head office's headcount[194] (SEC-20170606(1)). Furthermore, the replacement regulation provides details on qualification requirements for compliance staff, not only, as was previously the case, for the CCO (SEC-20170606(1)). At the same time, the 'Securities Compliance Measures' also impose stricter requirements on securities firms with regard to compliance management; for example the prerequisites a person needs to fulfill to be appointed CCO are higher compared to before: In the previous regulation from 2008, the requirement for CCOs was possessing a minimum of five years of experience in the securities sector and having passed compliance competency exam *or* possessing more than eight years of legal experience *or* having worked in the field of securities supervision (e.g. the CSRC) for over eight years (SEC-20080714). In the 2017 update, the three options still exist, yet the work experience for the first option was increased to a minimum of ten years, the second option was changed to a minimum of five years of legal experience in combination with having passed the legal qualification exam and the third option was reduced to five years (SEC-20170606(1)). In addition, the new regulation contains the prerequisite that the CCO must not have been punished by any financial supervision organ in the past three years and that the CSRC has the discretion to define further requirements (SEC-20170606(1)). This shows, on the one hand, that the rules for CCOs from 2017 are stricter and, on the other hand, that the CSRC has gained additional leeway for influencing the staffing

194 According to the document, the SAC determines this percentage (SEC-20170606(1)).

decisions for the CCO position by changing the prerequisite in case the authority does not like a candidate. Moreover, the updated document moved away from only holding the top management to account regarding compliance and spelled out the compliance responsibilities for lower-level managers and employees (SEC-20170606(1)). This indication of a more holistic organizational perspective on compliance was reinforced by a stronger emphasis on soft factors related to compliance management, such as values, a compliance culture and awareness as well as "improving the reputation and professionalization of compliance management staff" ("提升合规管理人员职业荣誉感和专业化", SEC-20170606(1)). In the context of professionalization, self-restrictive capacities were strengthened. This becomes especially obvious in an article on the release of the 'Securities Compliance Measures' on the CSRC website, which described the objective to develop actors' compliance awareness in the securities sector from the notion of "I need to be compliant" ("要我合规") to "I want to be compliant" ("我要合规") (SEC-20170606(2)). The SAC's 'Guidance on the Implementation of Securities Firms' Compliance Management', released as a reaction to the 'Securities Compliance Measures' (SEC-20170908(1)) strengthened these regulatory enhancements. Specifically, the document also emphasized all employees' role in compliance management, active compliance culture-building, professionalism of compliance staff and even prescribed compliance to account for 15 percent in managers' and employees' performance evaluations, i.e. a direct compliance incentive system for employees (SEC-20170908(1)).

Moreover, the CSRC updated the dimensions evaluated in the securities score[195] (SEC-20170706). A comparison of the changes in the regulations governing the securities score illustrates that the basic structure of scoring requirements, methods and use cases for scores have remained the same (SEC-20090526, SEC-20100514, SEC-20170706, SEC-20200710). Yet, over time, the criteria for adding and subtracting points have been significantly specified; especially an additional level of detail in the six focus areas is noteworthy (SEC-20090526, SEC-20100514, SEC-20170706, SEC-20200710). Yet, all versions of the regulation still retain a certain level of leeway for the CSRC's scoring, as it allows the CSRC to add and subtract points beyond the predefined values (maximum of three points for each evaluated item) (SEC-20090526, SEC-20100514, SEC-20170706, SEC-20200710). Furthermore, despite the specification, the six focus areas also still provide flexibility

195 Thereafter, another update followed in 2020 (SEC-20200710).

in interpretation, since their definitions are vaguer compared to other categories (SEC-20090526, SEC-20100514, SEC-20170706, SEC-20200710).

A similar development has also been identified in the improvement of the compliance competency exams' knowledge requirements, which were updated in this phase and afterwards (SEC-20150330, SEC-20191212): While the general direction and topic areas have remained the same, in the area of regulations, an additional level of detail has been added, e.g. by listing more regulations that address specific topics, such as pollution and conflict of interest (SEC-20080228, SEC-20120820, SEC-20150330, SEC-20191212). At the same time, the SAC also added further criteria to existing topics, for example anti-money laundering[196] (SEC-20080228, SEC-20120820, SEC-20150330, SEC-20191212). Lastly, entirely new topics emerge, such as dealing with complaints (SEC-20080228, SEC-20120820, SEC-20150330, SEC-20191212). This shows that the SAC reinforced the meaning and social practices of compliance that the CSRC constructed over time.

According to the official discourse, several additional measures have started to enhance existing structures during this phase. First, the use of technology to support compliance management increasingly appears in the official discourse, e.g. the application of information technology and big data for compliance supervision (SEC-20170606(1), SEC-20170908(1), SEC-20170929(2), SEC-20171204). Second, the CSRC adopted transparency as a network instrument more often to spur compliance. Concretely, in this phase, the authority started to publicly announce measures taken against non-compliant firms and individuals, including their names, details on legal violations and punishments (e.g. SEC-20150402(1), SEC-20150402(2), SEC-20150402(3), SEC-20170727(1), SEC-20170727(2), SEC-20170727(3)) as well as feedback for firms related to their applications with the CSRC (e.g. licenses for new fields of business) (e.g. SEC-20150521, SEC-20181130, SEC-20190329, SEC-20190517(2), SEC-20190517(5)). The official discourse justified this approach, by constructing public attention as a compliance motive and highlighted the role of the media in this context:

> "The healthy development of the capital market is inseparable from the support of the news media at the moment" ("资本市场的健康发展，时刻离不开新闻媒体的支持", SEC-20161227).

196 In areas that provide a more general overview of the regulatory landscape (e.g. criminal law, civil law, administrative law), details were deleted from the document, a sign that the test has become more and more specialized on compliance-related issues (SEC-20080228, SEC-20120820, SEC-20150330, SEC-20191212).

Phase 4: Compliance culture-building (mid-2019 – present)

Following the set-up and enhancement of compliance management structures, the emphasis in the fourth and ongoing phase lies on behavioral elements, i.e. compliance culture-building. In order to achieve this goal, the official discourse ran a culture-building campaign from August 2019 to December 2021 in the securities sector (SEC-20191112, SEC-20191121(1)), which prominently promoted compliance, for example in the following slogan:

> "Outstanding main business, outstanding compliance, outstanding innovation, outstanding stability" ("突出主业、突出合规、突出创新、突出稳健", SEC-20190708).

Furthermore, the CSRC's chairman Yi Huiman named the core values of the culture that is to be built in the securities sector in a speech in November 2019:

> "Compliance, integrity, professionalism, stability" ("合规、诚信、专业、稳健", SEC-20191121(1)).

Since then, the official discourse has featured examples of culture-building in securities firms (e.g. SEC-20191125(1), SEC-20191125(2), SEC-20191202, SEC-20191204, SEC-20191209). These initiatives are supposed to further raise compliance awareness in the securities sector. Internalized compliance automatically leads to self-regulation[197]; a topic the official discourse stresses in this phase (e.g. SEC-20191121(1), SEC-20201218(2)). In this target state, the established compliance culture is supposed to work as a preventative force against legal violations (SEC-20191121(1)).

Until this is achieved, however, strict supervision serves as a means to avoid non-compliance incidents (SEC-20191121(1)). Hence, the CSRC has intensified its approach of using transparency, including naming and shaming, as a way to deter non-compliance and educate securities firms with regard to compliance. For instance, the official discourse has seen a new wave of documents, which publish the names of individuals and firms that received punishments, including the causes for and details on the punishments (e.g. SEC-20200110(1), SEC-20200110(2), SEC-20200210, SEC-20200630). This even entails a new category of documents, so-called 'administrative reconsid-

197 The documents use different terms to describe similar concepts in this context, such as self-regulation (自律), self-governance (自治) and self-restriction (自我约束).

eration decisions' ('行政复议决定书'), which discuss cases where firms or individuals appealed against a decision by the CSRC (e.g. SEC-20200407, SEC-20210527). However, in all of the published documents of this type, the CSRC retained its position and declined the appeal (e.g. SEC-20200407, SEC-20200804, SEC-20200831, SEC-20210527). These documents signal not only a certain rigor and consistency towards securities firms, but also the power in enforcement held by the CSRC, and therefore likely serve as an additional deterrent.

The tracing of the genesis of compliance in the Chinese securities sector in four phases illustrates that the CSRC transferred the idea of compliance from the international financial sector and enacted compliance practices that are in line with international best practices. The top-down transplantation of compliance to the Chinese securities sector with dedicated compliance management regulations to foster compliance (among other measures) is likely to spur a high level of institutional isomorphism. The meaning of compliance constructed in the securities sector has been broadened over time, from originally only focusing on the adherence to legal prescriptions as a prerequisite for survival, to later also incorporating ethical components (values, awareness, culture, etc.). In this context, the official discourse draws a connection to the SCS and the CSRC applies SCS instruments (e.g. transparency via scores as well as naming and shaming). As a result, the topic of self-restriction features prominently in the context of the social practices of compliance. The overarching objective for compliance practices promoted by the official discourse is healthy market development, but topics, such as customer and investor protection, also play a role.

This way of constructing the meaning and social practices of compliance is echoed by the interviewees from the securities sector. One interviewee described the development of compliance in the securities sector as a top-down process guided by the CSRC via regulations (BUS19-13). He further highlighted the importance of the CSRC for compliance, by citing the core values for securities firms' corporate culture from the CSRC chairman Yi Huiman's speech in November 2019 (compliance, integrity, professionalism, stability) (BUS19-13). Because compliance was mentioned first, he emphasized, this topic now has become a key concern in his company (BUS19-13). Beyond this, interviewees in the securities sector also considered compliance as a prerequisite for business operations and in this context referred to the need to adhere to the prescribed regulations from the CSRC (e.g. BUS21-02, BUS21-07, BUS21-10, EXP19-04). In addition to this dominant component of legal compliance, business representatives from the securities sector also stressed the normative notion of compliance (e.g. BUS19-14, BUS21-01, BUS21-12). Specifically, they described compliance as a standard for ethical and values-based behavior (BUS21-01, BUS21-12) as well as an attitude to respect rules (BUS21-02). In this context, one interviewee mentioned the moral conflict employees in the securities sector face between maximizing profits and ethical conduct (BUS19-14). Since total control of employees is not possible, he then concluded that the only solution to ensure compliance under these circumstances is to ingrain ethics into employees' mindset (BUS19-14). Consequently, the interviewees from the securities sector seem to have adopted a broad compliance concept, which goes beyond the adherence to externally prescribed regulations, but also contains obeying sets of rules internal to the business, often including ethical elements. The following sections discuss how this constructed meaning of compliance is translated into practices, by describing the factors that influence compliance practices in the securities sector.

6.1.4 Influences on corporate compliance in the securities sector

6.1.4.1 External factors

As securities firms in China operate under the umbrella of the same political economy and society as companies from other sectors, most of the general trends described in Section 4.4.1 also apply to the securities sector. This is especially the case for social, economic and political environments, which tend to describe general societal, political and economic trends that influence firms. For example, in the social environment, the interviewees from the securities sector also emphasized the high pressure they feel from (social) media, because negative reports could affect firms' reputation (e.g. BUS19-14, BUS19-15, BUS21-02). In the economic environment, the interviews from the securities sector mirrored phenomena, such as the important influence of the stock market on companies' compliance practices (e.g. BUS21-01, BUS21-02, BUS21-10) as well as the compliance risks related to a highly dynamic market situation with rapid growth rates (e.g. BUS21-07, BUS21-10). With regard to the political environment, interviewees from the securities sector also echoed points raised in Section 4.4.1, e.g. the government's agenda to establish a more rules-based order (e.g. BUS19-13, EXP21-01) and justified the government's action with reference to the bigger national picture and the protective function the Party-state possesses with regard to firms (e.g. BUS19-13, BUS19-14, EXP21-01).

Hence, in these categories, only few sector-specific phenomena could be identified for the securities industry based on the interviews. For instance, pressure from local society does not play a role in the securities sector; most likely because the regulatory set-up in the securities industry is highly centralized and as part of the financial service sector, specific local conditions do not carry as much weight as in other sectors, such as manufacturing. For the same reasons, regional development differences were not mentioned as a factor that influences securities firms in the economic environment. At the same time, however, the interviews show that sector-specific circumstances in the economic environment play an important role in influencing compliance, e.g. the high systematic risk the securities industry potentially poses to the monetary system and society as a whole (BUS21-02, EXP19-14, EXP21-01). While being a sector-specific phenomenon, this insight also corroborates the general finding from Section 4.4.1 that the strategic importance of a sector affects compliance management.

In comparison, regulation and enforcement are external factors with more sector-specificity, since dedicated industry regulations, regulators and therefore enforcement practices are essential for successful economic governance overall. Consequently, most cross-sectoral developments appear to apply to the securities industry as well; however, they are complemented by sector-specific manifestations regarding regulation and enforcement, which forge the securities sector's unique regulatory approach. With regard to regulation, a general trend that also manifests itself in the securities sector is, for instance, the breadth of regulators from inside (e.g. the CSRC, the SAC, the stock markets, the PBoC and CCP) and outside the Party-state (e.g. the public, external service providers for audits and private shareholders) (e.g. BUS19-02, BUS19-13, BUS19-14, BUS19-15, BUS21-01, BUS21-07). Yet, the regulators inside the Party-state seem to dominate over those from the outside. Furthermore, regulations in the securities sector have also increased and improved over time (e.g. BUS19-03, BUS19-04). As described in Section 4.4.1, this incremental regulatory learning process has been strongly influenced by international examples, be it via the CSRC's exchange with international securities regulators (e.g. in the US) or the support the commission receives from international consultancies (BUS21-07, BUS21-10, EXP21-01). Lastly, as described for the general development in Section 4.4.1, state-business interactions during the drafting of regulations, their implementation as well as for general exchanges and feedback have played an important role in regulatory learning (e.g. BUS19-02, BUS21-01, BUS21-02, BUS21-07, BUS21-10). Hence, constant interactions also lead to a managerialization of law, a legalization of companies and the flow of organizational logic into the legal sphere, i.e. an endogeneity of law, in the securities sector.

In addition to these aspects that are in line with the general trends, several characteristics of regulations in the securities sector seem to be specific to the sector. First, according to the interviews, regulations in the securities industry are perceived as being very clear, detailed and prescriptive[198] (e.g. BUS19-14, BUS21-01, BUS21-07, EXP19-04). Because of these features, one interviewee explained how easy it is to ensure compliance in most cases, even for non-qualified compliance personnel, as the requirements and their implementation are prescribed concretely and in detail (BUS21-10). Detailed regulations even directly teach companies how to implement compliance management (BUS21-12). In cases where the CSRC's regulations are not as prescriptive, the SAC provides more detailed guidance on implementation (BUS21-07). Second, the rate of change in regulations is rather high, sometimes even monthly, which poses a great challenge for companies to adapt (BUS19-04, BUS19-15, BUS21-07). Third, in the few cases where regulations provide leeway in implementation, companies can discuss adequate ways to comply with the authorities' rules (BUS21-10). However, these discussions need to take place early on, when the new regulations are released, in order to avoid punishments (BUS21-10). After inspections and official notices for non-compliance incidents have been issued, it is too late for negotiations, according to one interviewee (BUS21-10). These sector-specific characteristics of regulations in the securities industry show that the CSRC controls securities companies' actions and compliance management via its prescriptive and strict regulations.

This Party-state dominance also shines through in the enforcement practices in the securities sector: While smart regulation as an enforcement approach with multiple regulators (e.g. the CSRC, SAC, PBoC) is practiced in the securities sector, the CSRC appears to be the dominant enforcement agent. Evidence for this are the passages from the interviews with representatives from the securities sector, which describe the enforcement instruments and inspection approaches applied in the industry: Except for economic enforcement instruments, all other types of enforcement instruments, i.e. legal,

198 Interviewees also compared Chinese regulations with those in the US, which they regarded as more principles-based and market-oriented compared to those in China (BUS19-15, EXP19-04, EXP21-01).

communicative and network instruments, are applied in the securities sector and for the most part by the CSRC. Legal instruments are adopted for deterrence purposes and range from regulatory letters (监管函)[199] over fines and business restrictions to the shutdown of a company, depending on the gravity of a non-compliance incident (e.g. BUS19-13, BUS19-14, BUS19-15, BUS21-20). As described for other sectors (see Section 4.4.1), punishments seem to have become more rigorous and thus, the costs of illegal behavior have increased (BUS19-15, BUS21-10).

In parallel, the CSRC applies communicative instruments to teach securities firms compliance management, e.g. by organizing compliance trainings and annual tests for CCO position holders, promoting integrity via campaigns and holding seminars and meetings for securities firms to exchange on new regulatory developments[200] (BUS19-03, BUS21-01, BUS21-02, BUS21-20).

Moreover, the CSRC adopts network instruments to ensure compliance, however in a sector-specific fashion: In addition to traditional regular reports to the CSRC (non-compliance incidents, business data, etc.) for transparency purposes (e.g. BUS19-14, BUS21-02, BUS21-07) and customer complaint mechanisms (e.g. BUS21-07), the securities score and integrity files also serve as network instruments. According to the interviews, few people are listed in integrity files and usually they leave the industry after being listed, since securities firms check integrity files before hiring new managers (BUS21-01, BUS21-07, BUS21-10). Hence, being listed in an integrity file is equal to an industry ban, as the listed individuals cannot find a job in the securities sector anymore (BUS21-07, BUS21-10). While this mechanism only applies to a small group of people in leadership positions in the securities sector and therefore is not as frequently checked as firm scores, it still seems to be a powerful tool in the staffing process for management positions. Even more important, however, are the securities scores, which make securities firms' risk and compliance levels transparent to the public and therefore have reputational implications. Interviewees from the securities sector mentioned the significance of this instrument across the board (e.g. BUS21-01, BUS21-02, BUS21-07, BUS21-12[201]). While these two tools are exclusively dedicated to the securities sector and already existed prior to the establishment of the SCS, the two

199 Regulatory letters are documents sent to securities firms containing the operational irregularities identified by the CSRC, which serve as a warning to improve behavior (BUS19-13).

200 Similar meetings and seminars are also held by the SAC (BUS21-10, BUS21-20).

201 For more details on how companies react and utilize securities scores, refer to Section 6.1.5.

instruments have, nevertheless, been integrated into the SCS's enforcement approach in the securities sector. Further SCS elements relevant for enforcement in the securities sector are platforms for information retrieval on other companies and blacklists for the choice of business partners, such as Qichacha, Tianyancha and NECIPS (e.g. BUS19-02, BUS19-13, BUS21-12, BUS21-20). However, the interviewees from the securities sector emphasize that the securities score is by far the most important network enforcement instrument in the industry (e.g. BUS21-01, BUS21-02, BUS21-20).

The scores, list entries and other information on company profiles are generated based on data the CSRC collects in inspections. In line with the general trends related to inspections (see Section 4.4.1), different types of inspections exist in the securities sector: Regular, announced on-site inspections of the entire business as well as specific business units[202] depend in their frequency on the compliance level and business activities of a company, i.e. the more risks and compliance issues, the more frequent the inspections (BUS21-02, BUS21-20). Moreover, the CSRC also conducts unannounced on-site inspections of business units, entire businesses and/or firms' governance systems (including compliance management) (BUS21-02, BUS21-20). However, due to low staffing levels at the CSRC (BUS19-14), such on-site visits are not very common ("他们也会来检查，不过不是特别平凡", BUS21-10). Instead, the CSRC conducts regular remote inspections via the IT-system and based on securities firms' continuous reports (BUS21-10, EXP21-01). Specifically, the CSRC has direct access to certain IT-systems in securities firms, which the authority can constantly monitor (e.g. BUS21-01, BUS21-20). The fourth inspection category, event-based on-site or remote inspections, also takes place in the securities industry, for instance, in case of irregularities in reports and complaints about a company (BUS19-13, BUS19-14, BUS19-15, BUS21-07, BUS21-10).

Yet, the CSRC has one more way of accessing company-internal information: The CCO. Since securities firms need to have new candidates for this position approved by the CSRC, the CSRC can ensure the most important company-internal compliance position in securities firms is staffed with individuals that cooperate well with them (EXP21-01). One interviewee even explained that the CSRC itself stresses its need for partners within securities companies, namely CCOs, for supervision purposes ("它一直强调，证券公司内部需要有人对这个合规监管负责", BUS21-10), since the authority is short on staff (BUS21-10).

202 In case of SOEs, these also include regular Party discipline inspections (BUS19-13).

In the inspection context, the interviews with representatives from the securities sector corroborated the manifestation of embedded autonomy, i.e. strict adherence to defined administrative procedures, yet occasional leeway for negotiation on the substance of matters (e.g. BUS19-02, BUS21-10, BUS21-20). Yet, despite the existing negotiation option, one business representative from a securities firm described that the importance of negotiations and therefore guanxi in the compliance context is declining (BUS21-20): While the best candidate for the CCO position used to be a professional transferred from the CSRC because of the guanxi the person has in this regulatory agency, today, the CCO's skill set with regard to risk control and compliance management has become a more significant criterion in the staffing process (BUS21-20). The main reasons for this change, according to the interviewee, are small impacts that can be achieved via negotiation with authorities today, as well as the increasing transparency of business operations (publicly accessible data, such as scores) (BUS21-20). Thus, formal enforcement practices and enforcement stringency seem to have improved and are influencing businesses' compliance management.

Overall, these elaborations on external factors, which influence compliance in the securities industry, have shown that the Party-state, in the form of the CSRC, constitutes the main driving force behind external influences on compliance. But the CSRC does not only adopt traditional approaches to govern the sector, such as regulations, legal enforcement practices and inspections, it also adds managerial elements in their enforcement practices, such as the competitive securities score.

6.1.4.2 Internal factors

The main aspects considered in the category internal factors of influence on compliance are organizational capacities and characteristics as well as compliance motives. The interview data for the securities sub-case shows that the general patterns and characteristics in the securities sector with regard to these two aspects match the overall trends identified across industries in Section 4.4.2.

Concretely, the patterns identified in Section 4.4.2 regarding organizational capacities and characteristic, related to economic resources, legal and technical know-how, managerial capacity, firms' size and corporate culture, also pertain to the securities sub-case. Using the example of SMEs, interviewees confirmed that firms, facing financial pressure in general, only invest in compliance management actively when authorities pressure them (BUS21-20). Otherwise these companies would likely not invest in external service providers' support to improve their compliance management (EXP21-01). This point directly relates to business size as a factor influencing compliance: Interviewees stressed the greater amount of challenges in smaller companies' compliance management, due to more limited financial resources compared to larger enterprises (BUS21-01). For instance, hiring qualified compliance staff becomes more difficult and employee turnover is higher (BUS19-13). This, again, affects the level of legal and technical knowledge within a company; an important organizational capacity related to compliance.

While even more challenging for smaller securities firms, hiring qualified professionals is a general challenge in the securities sector (BUS19-02): One business representative described that her company needed to change its CCO multiple times, because the previous candidates, which had a background in business or previously worked for the CSRC, did not do a satisfactory job (BUS21-20). Only now, according to the interviewee, has her company found a candidate who is able to combine the regulatory and compliance knowledge gained when working for the CSRC, with the necessary flexibility in a fast-paced business environment (BUS21-20). Another example is a business representative's description of his company's process of training compliance experts (BUS21-10): Early on in the set-up of a compliance function, no compliance experts could be hired externally and therefore, staff from business units, which acquired the necessary skills on the job, had to transfer to the newly established compliance department (BUS21-10). These are the company's present employees in the compliance function, who now train newly hired compliance staff (BUS21-10).

Similarly, securities firms considered managerial capacities, such as an adequate tone from the top, vital for successful compliance management (BUS21-10). At the same time, they appreciated the managerial improvements related to professionalism that compliance management provides and thereby corroborate the reciprocal relationship between compliance management and managerial capacities (BUS21-01).

Finally, as outlined in Section 4.4.2, the interviewees from the securities industry also drew a causal relationship between their corporate culture and compliance levels: One interviewee explained that risk and compliance have the highest priority in her firm and guide all actions (BUS21-02). Another business representative saw the reason for his company's high securities score in his firm's conservative corporate culture, which focuses more on stability than on innovation (BUS21-10). Other elements in corporate cultures that business representatives considered conducive to compliance are a focus on providing benefits to customers and the pursuit of excellence in all actions (BUS19-14, BUS19-15).

Despite these similarities between the general patterns in China and the securities sub-case, the impact of the Party-state related to organizational capacities and characteristics seems to be greater compared to other industries. Specifically, Party-state actions significantly affect the internal management of securities firms in general and thereby shape businesses' organizational capacities and characteristics, which in turn affect companies' compliance management. For example, the official discourse by the CSRC seems to affect securities firms' corporate culture: The key components of securities firms' corporate cultures, as emphasized by the CSRC since 2019, (compliance, integrity, professionalism and stability) are values that interviewees mirrored in the description of their companies' culture (BUS19-02, BUS21-07, BUS21-10, BUS21-12).

Moreover, via its regulatory measures (e.g. competency test for employees in the securities industry), the CSRC influences staff's legal and compliance knowledge, leading to an elevated minimal knowledge base compared to other industries (BUS19-14, EXP19-04). This effect is especially strong in the requirements the CSRC imposes on the CCO position, which ultimately contributes to a relatively high compliance awareness in the securities sector (e.g. BUS19-13, BUS21-10, EXP21-01). One interviewee explained that compliance awareness in the industry and his firm has significantly increased since the early 2000s, when the industry was shaken by scandals (BUS21-10). Today's compliance awareness appears to be the result of strict Party-state controls in the securities industry, which firms mirror in their compliance management system (e.g. process controls, trainings, performance evaluations)[203] (BUS19-14, BUS19-15, BUS21-02, BUS21-12). Lastly, organizational complexity was not mentioned to have had an influence on compliance, neither directly nor indirectly; a possible sign for the uniform set-up and practice of compliance management in line with regulations and regardless of organizational specifics.

203 Despite the relatively high level of compliance awareness, some interviewees from the securities industry nevertheless pointed to areas where compliance awareness needs to be improved, e.g. in privately-owned securities firms (as compared to SOEs or JVs) or among employees in business units (as compared to those in other departments in the companies) (BUS21-07, BUS21-20).

In addition to organizational capacities and characteristics, motives for compliance constitute another important internal factor that influences the practices of compliance. Interviews in the securities sector are in line with the general findings related to compliance motives, namely the dominance of extrinsic motives. Similar to the general trend, economic motives are consistently mentioned in interviews across the securities sector (e.g. BUS19-13, BUS19-15, BUS21-02) and the motives newly-identified in Section 4.4.2 (previous non-compliance incidents and personal implications) also exist in the securities industry: For instance, business representatives from the securities sector described how their companies have become more attentive to compliance due to cases of non-compliance incidents, not only in their own company, but also in their industry or even in other industries (BUS19-14, BUS19-15, BUS21-01). In terms of personal implications, interviewees mentioned the importance of a good compliance track record and related self-discipline for long-term career development in the securities sector and for personal financial profit (BUS19-15, BUS21-07). In contrast, social and normative motives seem to play an even smaller role in the securities industry compared to the general trend across sectors: These two motive categories are negligible in the securities sector, since none of the interviewees described social motives and the closest statement to a normative motive in the interviews with representatives from the securities sector was the avoidance of systemic risk for China's monetary system (BUS21-02); i.e. a values-based consideration related to China's national interest that exceeds specific company benefits.

Despite this conformity with the general trends, there are three distinct patterns related to the six sub-categories of economic motives that were outlined in Section 4.4.2: First, there is a very strong propensity for being motivated by authorities' requirements. Across the board, interviewed representatives from the securities sector described the importance of meeting regulatory requirements for business survival, which drives their efforts in compliance management; especially due to strict supervision and punishments from authorities in case of non-compliance incidents (e.g. BUS19-13, BUS19-15, BUS21-02, BUS21-12). Second, maintaining a good reputation, increased professionalism and better business opportunities constitute important compliance motives, yet are not as prevalent as meeting authorities' requirements. With regard to reputation as a driver for compliance, interviewees from the securities sector mentioned the impact compliance has on their brand, especially since the public's attention on this topic is high (BUS19-15, BUS21-02). In this context, achieving a high securities score acts as a motivator for compliance management (BUS21-10). With respect to professionalism, the interviewees argued that compliance management guides their companies' development trajectory, transparency and internal control and is therefore pursued (BUS19-02, BUS21-01). Furthermore, business representatives from the securities sector considered compliance management as a means to ensure growth, develop their business and secure funding (compliance as a prerequisite for an IPO), all indications for being motivated by increased business opportunities (BUS19-02, BUS21-12, BUS21-20). Third, international and customer pressure only plays a role in motivating compliance management for a small number of interviewed companies. For instance, only JVs in the securities sector seem to be motivated by the requirements their international mother companies place on them (BUS21-20). Similarly, the protection of customers' profit is only mentioned in one case (BUS21-07).

Overall, these elaborations on compliance motives as internal influences on compliance practices yet again accentuate the Party-state's strong impact on securities firms' compliance, which continues as a common theme in compliance practices, as is explained in the following section.

6.1.5 Corporate compliance practices in the securities sector

The interviews with representatives from the securities sector show a high level of congruence with the cross-sectoral trends outlined in Section 4.5.2, both with regard to companies' learning process towards successful compliance management and actual compliance management practices.

Among the four pathways of compliance-related learning described in Section 4.5.2[204], the most significant course of compliance-related learning in the securities industry has been businesses' learning parallel to authorities' regulatory learning process. Interviewees describe that their firms started to implement compliance management after the CSRC first began to require such practices in 2008 and then gradually improved their compliance behavior along with the development of the CSRC's regulations (BUS19-13, BUS21-02, BUS21-10, EXP21-01). Even though securities companies started to set up compliance management systems once compliance management structures were required by the CSRC, in the beginning, "most people did not

204 The four pathways are: Learning as the company grows, learning parallel to authorities' regulation and enforcement learning process, learning from professional networks and learning in response to international pressure.

understand what the compliance management department was supposed to do" ("大家也不太清楚,合规部门主要干什么事情", BUS21-10). Over time, this has changed and especially since the update of compliance regulations in 2017, which resulted in more detailed compliance management requirements, compliance management models have become more standardized ("合规管理模式得到了统一", BUS21-10), and led to more proactive compliance management in securities firms (BUS21-10). Hence, over time, compliance management has matured and the difference among securities firms' compliance management mainly lies in efficiency levels (BUS21-10, BUS21-20).

Furthermore, the interviews highlighted international influences as a particularly important trigger for compliance-related learning. Business representatives from the securities sector, for example, explained how they learned both from international players after these entered the Chinese market (via JVs) and from players in the securities industry in other countries, e.g. via meetings and conferences with international experts and business representatives (BUS21-02, BUS21-10). The US played the most dominant role in this context (BUS21-02, BUS21-10). Yet, compared to the general trend of learning from international actors described in Section 4.5.2, the learning in securities companies is caused less by pressure from international firms, but rather Chinese securities firms' proactive emulation in order to perform better. In addition, improvements in compliance management as companies grow and via professional networks (e.g. external service providers) were also mentioned, but are not as dominant (e.g. BUS21-01, BUS21-02, BUS21-20).

The described compliance-related learning is reflected in securities companies' compliance management performance. The securities score can serve as a proxy for securities firms' compliance management conduct[205]. In the period from 2010 to 2020, the securities score average across all rated securities firms increased (see Table 8): Translated into numerics, where 1.0 equals the

205 These data points can be taken as an approximation for the compliance levels in the securities sector, since the constructionist analysis has shown that these are important categories, which influence the construction of the meaning and measurement of compliance. While their quantitative nature would make them objectivist tools, these scores are only used to highlight their effect on the construction of compliance in the specific context as well as to complement and confirm the findings from the fieldwork resulting from a constructionist approach. Changes in scores do not exclusively result from changes in firms' internal management, but are also influenced by changes in rating criteria and supervision rigor over time. Since companies are, however, supposed to respond to these changes adequately in their compliance management, the captured trends in securities scores provide a rough estimation of the constructed compliance levels in the respective sector.

distance between two scoring letters, the average score rose from 7.6 to 8.0, i.e. 0.4 points, with an all-time high of 8.8 in 2015[206]. While this means that the average score across all securities firms remains at BBB, this marginal increase is underscored by the change in distribution of securities scores over time (see Figure 33[207]). The A-level scores increased their total share from ca. 36 to 48 percent over the period from 2010 to 2020 (AA: ~12 to 15 percent, A: ~24 to 33 percent), whereas B- and C-level scores decreased (total B-level scores from ~50 to 40 percent; total C-level scores from ~14 to 10 percent)[208].

Table 8: Average securities score from 2010 to 2020

	2010	2011	2012	2013	2014	2015	2016	2017	2018	2019	2020
Average numeric securities score[209]	7.6	7.7	7.9	7.8	7.9	8.8	8.0	7.9	7.9	7.8	8.0
Average letter securities score	BBB	BBB	BBB	BBB	BBB	A	BBB	BBB	BBB	BBB	BBB

Figure 33: Share of securities score levels over time (in percent)

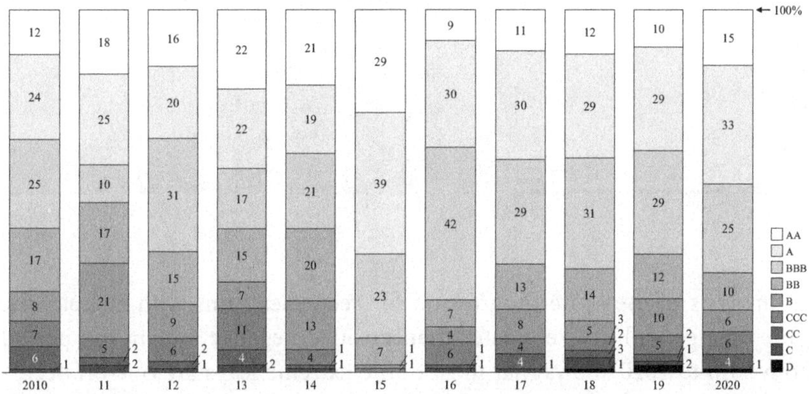

206 A reason for the drop off in the average score between 2015 and 2016 could be the Chinese stock market crisis in 2015/16, which resulted in stricter CSRC supervision.

207 Based on published securities scores between 2010 and 2020: SEC-20100714, SEC-20110714, SEC-20120713, SEC-20130712, SEC-20140715, SEC-20150717, SEC-20160715, SEC-20170814, SEC-20180727, SEC-20190726(2), SEC-20200911.

208 The first D-level score was recorded in 2018, however, the percentages have since remained negligible. A score E has never been issued.

209 Average calculated based on the following, own translation of letter scores into numerical scores (no official translation is publicly available): AAA = 11, AA = 10, A = 9, BBB = 8, BB = 7, B = 6, CCC= 5, CC = 4, C = 3, D = 2, E = 1.

These moderate improvement rates over time are also reflected in individual firms' annual score changes in the period from 2010 to 2020 (see Figure 34 and 35[210]): The majority of all score changes over time were between a drop (-2) and an increase of two points (2) (93 percent), with the highest total share of annual score changes around zero (44 percent or 411 times), i.e. the same score as in the previous year. The greatest leap between scores was a score drop from AA to C (negative seven) between 2013 and 2014 by Guangda Securities (光大证券).

Figure 34: Distribution of annual securities score changes for the period from 2010 to 2020 according to size of score change

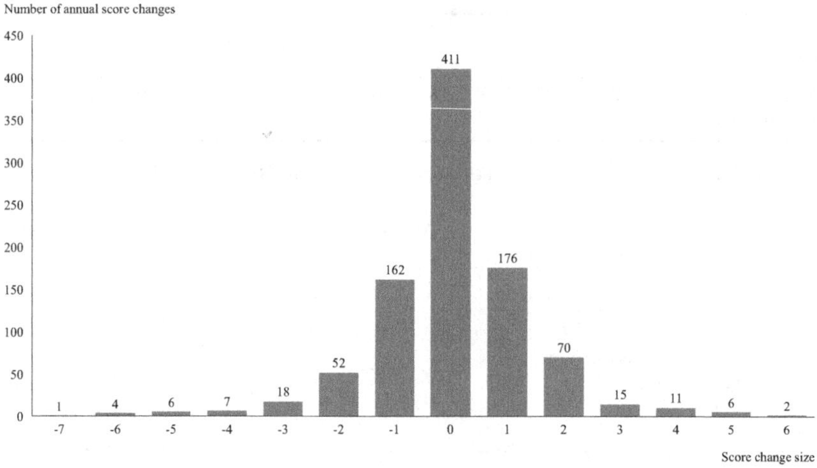

An analysis of the score progression for securities firms with at least one score change with a size greater than positive/negative four in the period from 2010 to 2020 shows that most of the extreme leaps are one-off occurrences (e.g. non-compliance incidents), after which the companies quickly bounce back to a score similar to the original level (eight securities firms, such as Guangda Securities and Southwest Securities, 西南证券). The few remaining score jumps greater than positive/negative four belong to com-

210 For this analysis, letter scores were translated into numerical scores as described in Footnote 207. Based on the numerical scores, the change in size of each securities firm's score for each year was identified via subtraction (score drop resulting in negative, score increase in positive values) (based on published securities scores between 2010 and 2020, see Footnotes 207 & 209).

panies, which regularly exhibited comparably large changes (e.g. Hualin Securities, 华林证券 and Minsheng Securities, 民生证券), a potential sign for immature compliance management. In these cases, the fluctuations often decline over time and the firms' ratings level off at a medium level (e.g. Hualin Securities at a B-score and Minsheng Securities at a BB-score); an indication of potential compliance management learning.

Figure 35: Share of annual securities score change size (absolute values) for the period from 2010 to 2020

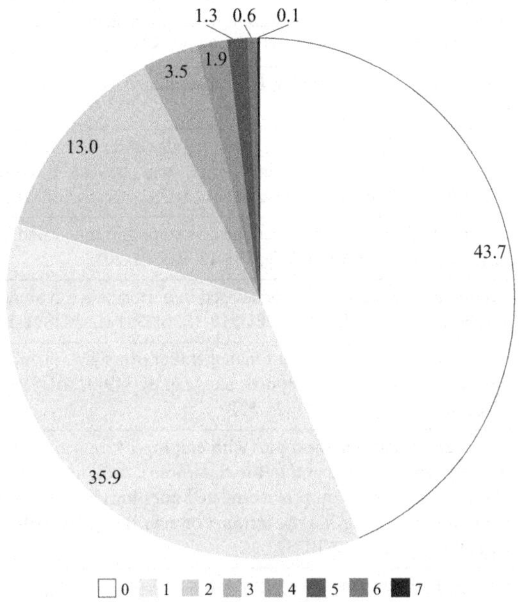

Besides the described learning and improvement processes, securities companies' compliance management practices exhibit further similarities with the general characteristics outlined in Section 4.5.2. In terms of congruence with international best practices, the securities sector's interviewees also describe the six key international best practices in their elaborations on their businesses' compliance management (see Table 9).

Table 9: Examples of manifestations of international best practices for compliance management in the Chinese securities sector

Best practices	Examples from the Chinese securities sector
Solid formal compliance management structures	Independent, central, large compliance departments headed by the CCO as a top-level manager and with compliance staff in the business units (e.g. BUS19-14, BUS21-02, BUS21-07, BUS21-12, BUS21-20)
	A compliance management system set up with three/four lines of defense (see Footnote 124) (BUS19-13, BUS21-12)
	Compliance guidelines and compliance commitments signed by employees integrated in comprehensive compliance management systems (e.g. BUS19-02, BUS19-13, BUS21-07, BUS21-10)
	Process controls and approvals by compliance management (e.g. BUS21-12, BUS21-20)
	Internal compliance monitoring via regular and unannounced audits of business processes, projects, organizational structures and individual behavior (e.g. BUS19-02, BUS19-15, BUS21-02, BUS21-07, BUS21-10, BUS21-20)
Embeddedness	Compliance controls at critical process steps and integrated into the IT-system (e.g. BUS19-02, BUS21-07, BUS21-12, BUS21-20)
	Compliance as a criterion considered in performance evaluations, promotions and bonuses (e.g. BUS19-13, BUS19-15, BUS21-02, BUS21-10)
Good management practices	Comprehensive and constant management oversight via audits, process monitoring, compliance reports, etc. (e.g. BUS19-02, BUS19-14, BUS19-15, BUS21-02, BUS21-10, BUS21-12)
	Dialogue on compliance topics with employees via regular and on demand trainings (both online and in the classroom), compliance staff's consultation of business units in compliance-related questions and compliance-related communication (e.g. via the intranet or email) (e.g. BUS19-02, BUS19-15, BUS19-13, BUS21-07, BUS21-12)
	Stringent consequence management in case of non-compliance incidents via investigations and punishments depending on the gravity of the issue and according to pre-defined criteria (e.g. BUS19-02, BUS19-14, BUS19-15, BUS21-02, BUS21-10)
Top-level commitment	The CCO's participation in top management meetings and discussion of compliance cases, including punishment decisions (e.g. BUS19-13, BUS21-07)
	The frequent communication of compliance-related topics to employees by the management (e.g. BUS21-07, BUS21-10)
	The high position the compliance department and the CCO hold in the organizational hierarchy (e.g. BUS19-15, BUS21-10, BUS21-12)

Best practices	Examples from the Chinese securities sector
A compliance culture	Promotion of the topic of compliance via internal communication and regular trainings, such as trainings for new recruits or monthly seminars for employees (e.g. BUS19-14, BUS21-02, BUS21-10, BUS21-20)
	(Anonymous) complaint and reporting channels (e.g. hotline, email) for non-compliance incidents (e.g. BUS19-02, BUS 21-02, BUS21-10, BUS21-20)
Values-based compliance management	An awareness of the value of compliance actions that surpass the mere legal minimum, especially in larger securities firms (e.g. BUS21-01, BUS21-07, EXP21-01)
	A discourse on nurturing employees' ethics as a preventative compliance management approach (e.g. BUS19-13, BUS19-14)
	Recognition of the protective function of preventative compliance management (e.g. BUS21-12, BUS21-20)

In addition, the interviewees from the securities sector also emphasized the three deviations from international best practices that Section 4.5.2 identified:

- *The impact of the CCP's discipline system:* Interviewees from the securities sector confirmed the influence of the CCP on firms via their discipline system, which mostly becomes manifest in business-internal Party discipline inspection departments (e.g. BUS21-07, BUS21-12). Similar to other sectors, the discipline inspection departments act separately from the compliance department and are only linked in their anti-corruption work (BUS21-10). Interviewees stressed the difference by highlighting that compliance management focuses on business-related issues and is supervised by the CSRC, whereas discipline inspections are triggered by the CCP and focus on Party members' behavior and ideological topics (e.g. BUS21-01, BUS21-02). While the CCO and other leadership positions do not necessarily have to be Party members, installing Party members in key positions is well received and serves as an additional way to influence securities firms (BUS21-02, EXP21-01).
- *Strong use of IT in compliance management*: On the one hand, securities firms use technology for their internal compliance management, for instance, by setting up firewalls between departments that are legally not allowed to share data or via automatic warnings for employees, who attempt to illegally deal shares (BUS21-02, BUS21-10). On the other hand, IT-systems serve as tools for reporting to the CSRC (BUS21-07). Securities companies need to set up certain, compliance-related IT-systems to be compatible with the CSRC's systems, in order for the CSRC to be

able to monitor the firms directly and constantly (BUS21-01, BUS21-10, BUS21-20).

- *Transparency and rating mechanisms:* Securities firms' compliance management is affected by the SCS's transparency and rating mechanisms in a similar manner as described in Section 5.4. While the SCS's rewards play a comparably limited role, interviewees from the securities sector exhibited a high risk awareness with regard to a drop in their companies' securities score or integrity file entries (e.g. BUS21-01, BUS21-02, BUS21-07). For instance, securities firms "pay especial attention to securities scores, because the [scoring] rules are made transparent" ("非常关注这些评级，因为规则是透明的", BUS21-07), which allows securities firms to implement concrete controls and mechanisms to mitigate the risks of low scores. Moreover, interviewees illustrated how score drops (due to non-compliance incidents) have increased their enterprises' compliance awareness (e.g. BUS19-14, BUS21-20). Their companies faced reputational losses and resulting trouble in acquiring customers[211] and business partners, difficulties securing loans and increased financial contributions to the CSRC's risk reserve (风险准备金)[212]. This motivated them to improve their internal management and thereby their securities score as quickly as possible[213] (BUS19-14, BUS21-20). One securities enterprise even stated that the securities score requirements serve as a blueprint for the set-up and improvement of their compliance management system (BUS21-07). Other ways, in which the SCS's transparency mechanisms are exploited in the securities industry are checks of integrity files in staffing decisions for management positions (e.g. BUS21-01, BUS21-07) as well as information retrieval on (potential) business partners, customers and investors via information platforms, such as Qichacha, Tianyancha and NECIPS (e.g. BUS19-02, BUS21-10, BUS21-12, BUS21-20). As in other sectors, interviewees are unlikely to cooperate with blacklisted or low-rated firms (e.g. C- and D-scores). Therefore, scores increasingly

211 Especially in case a company wants to work with SOEs (BUS19-15).

212 The risk reserve are funds established by the stock markets to ensure normal operations and make up for losses cause by unforeseen risks.

213 However, both interviewees admitted that it may actually take a long time to improve the score to the original level: While both firms already saw a score rise after the drop, they have not yet managed to achieve the score level from before the non-compliance incident (BUS19-14, BUS21-20). These statements are in line with the securities score analysis earlier in this section, which shows that great leaps in securities scores are comparably rare.

act as regulatory mechanisms (BUS19-02, BUS19-13, BUS19-14, BUS21-02, BUS21-07). In addition, some securities firms also implement their own transparency and rating systems internally, e.g. one firm possesses files on each employee's compliance performance (similar to the authorities' integrity files) (BUS21-10). Another company has set up an internal rating system for employees and departments, which affects individuals' bonus payments and the resource allocation for departments, with transparent guidelines on reasons for the addition and subtraction of points similar to the securities score (BUS21-07).

Yet, the interviews still pinpointed some sector-specific compliance management features. First, hotlines and certifications as typical compliance management features are of little relevance in the securities sector. While the interviewed securities companies possess hotlines for complaints and whistle-blowing, business representatives at the same time stress that these channels are rarely used (e.g. BUS19-02, BUS19-13, BUS21-10). Instead, problems are identified in other ways, e.g. via audits or direct communication with supervisors (BUS19-14, BUS21-10). With regard to certification, the discussion in Section 4.5.2 highlighted that this feature's application depends on business needs. According to the interviews, the securities sector belongs to those sectors where certification is not necessary for compliance management (BUS19-02, EXP19-04, EXP21-01).

Second, the Party-state has a large influence on compliance management considerations. An example for this phenomenon is the CCO position, which has to be approved by the CSRC, and is oftentimes occupied by Party members and former CSRC staff (BUS21-10, BUS21-20, EXP21-01). By coopting the key compliance management position in securities firms, the Party-state exerts direct influence on compliance management practices. This goes as far as the CCO directly reporting compliance incidents to the CSRC (BUS21-02, BUS21-07, BUS21-10). Moreover, the qualification examinations for employees in the securities sector do not only control the influx of employees into the sector, at the same time, they also ensure a minimal legal and regulatory knowledge (BUS19-15). This way, the Party-state indirectly shapes firms' compliance culture and employees' compliance awareness. Lastly, the CSRC's requirement for securities firms to have an external service provider conduct compliance audits at least every three years increases the compliance service industries' role in securities firms' compliance management (BUS21-07). Not only external consultancies' audits, but also their compliance advice and trainings, which are based on regulatory requirements and international best practices, ultimately lead to the standardization of compliance management efforts in the industry.

Overall, this strong influence of the Party-state has led to a very high level of institutional isomorphism with regard to compliance management in the securities sector; an even higher level than the institutional isomorphism in compliance management identified in general (Section 4.5.2). The description of the respective companies' compliance management practices by business representatives from the securities industry barely show any variation. Few businesses implement compliance management practices beyond prescribed expectations (e.g. through stricter internal compliance rules) (BUS21-01, EXP21-01); at the same time, companies simply react to the CSRC's regulations (e.g. BUS21-07, BUS21-10). This behavior bears the risk of only complying with regulations on paper, but not in substance, and in the worst case results in creative compliance.

6.1.6 Consequences for the construction of corporate compliance in the securities sector

This sub-case has investigated in detail how the meaning and social practices of compliance are constructed in the securities sector. Hence, the elaborations above contribute to a better understanding of the process how the concept of compliance was introduced to the securities sector, the key connotations the constructed meaning of compliance in this industry entails and the features securities firms exhibit in their social practices of compliance.

Overall, the transfer process of compliance to the Chinese securities sector has been affected by international influences and taken place in a top-down manner. However, a deeper look at the insights described above from the perspective of Dolowitz and Marsh's (2000, p. 9) octo-dimensional policy transfer framework yields nuance to this transfer (see Table 10): The concept of compliance, including related best practices, were introduced to the securities sector as a solution to disruptions in the sector in the context of several transfers related to the institutional set-up and policies in the Chinese securities sector (lesson drawing). The deepening international integration of the Chinese economy also demanded the adoption of international standards (international pressure). This rationale already highlights that the transfer process happened from the top down, with government officials and bureaucrats acting as the main transfer agents.

Consultants and think tanks supported the Party-state agents in the transfer process, while at the same time, together with foreign MNEs via JVs, fostering the implementation of the transferred concepts and practices in securities firms. Hence, two transfer paths were identified: Compliance was mainly introduced from the international arena to the Chinese financial sector (cross-national transfer), but also partly from the banking sector (within the nation), since this sector had adopted compliance as a concept slightly faster than the securities sector.

Table 10: Policy transfer framework according to Dolowitz and Marsh (2000, p. 9) with results for the transfer of compliance to the Chinese securities sector

Dimension	Manifestations
Reason for transfer	Mixture of drawing lessons from international examples and (indirectly) international pressure
Transfer agents	Government officials, bureaucrats, consultants, think tanks, MNEs
Transfer object	Compliance as an institution as well as related ideologies, instruments and behavioral standards
Transfer path	Mainly cross-national from governments and international organizations; partly also within the nation from the banking sector
Degree of transfer	Amplification
Constraints on transfer	Lacking cultural proximity and awareness
Demonstration of transfer	Via official regulatory documents, media, reports, conferences, meetings, etc.
Reasons for failure	Incomplete transfer

The transfer of compliance is highly visible in the sector's official discourse, where the concept appears in many different contexts, be it in regulatory documents, media reports, seminars or other events organized by actors in the securities sector, especially the CSRC. These traces of compliance show that the degree of the transfer far exceeds simple copying of the way compliance has been constructed in other countries. The highly prescriptive regulations on compliance management, which are laid down in the securities sector, exceed the outcome-oriented provision of best practices and guidance on compliance management by other international regulatory agencies with regard to rigor[214]. Hence, amplification is the best way to de-

214 In the US and the EU, for instance, regulatory agencies in the financial sector may demand a compliance management function in companies, yet they grant firms

scribe this new degree of transfer. Despite such a strong effort to introduce compliance in the Chinese securities sector, there is still one major constraint to the transfer, which also bears the risk of leading to an incomplete transfer: The cultural setting and awareness. As the elaborations above have shown, the CSRC places increasing emphasis on this topic, since the mere transplantation of structures does not suffice in the context of compliance. Yet, building culture and raising awareness takes time.

This summary shows that the transfer of the concept of compliance to the Chinese securities sector has been a top-down, exogenous process strongly driven by the Chinese Party-state (see Figure 36). Based on international compliance regulations, Chinese officials developed Chinese compliance regulations for the securities sector, which were then implemented in Chinese securities firms from the top down. The emerging compliance understanding and practices in Chinese securities firms, then, triggered the enhancement and refinement of these regulations. The updated regulations again shaped the way the meaning and social practices of compliance were constructed in the securities sector, which could lead to further regulatory adaptions in the future – a continuous development cycle.

The understanding and social practices of compliance that have emerged from this construction process in the securities sector exhibit one key characteristic: They are strongly shaped by the CSRC's top-down control. This control is visible in several phenomena described in this sub-case. First, compliance-related regulations and measures (e.g. securities scores) are highly prescriptive and therefore do not leave a lot of leeway for companies in their implementation. Hence, the level of coercive institutional isomorphism regarding compliance management in the securities sector is extremely high. Second, the CSRC has direct access to securities firms, be it via their influence on the CCO position or the connection between firms' and the CSRC's IT-systems for supervision purposes. Third, representatives from securities firms have unanimously stressed pressure from authorities as the main motive for their compliance efforts, even though the

leeway to implement compliance management in the way the companies see fit (Securities Industry Association, 2005, Securities Industry and Financial Markets Association, 2013, European Union, 2014). Consequently, requirements are less prescriptive and detailed. Instead, the approach is more outcome-oriented, since, for example in the US, enforcement agencies consider the overall compliance efforts of an organization when determining enforcement actions following a legal violation (Securities Industry Association, 2005, Securities Industry and Financial Markets Association, 2013).

official discourse has increasingly and consistently incorporated a strong ethical notion into the concept of compliance and features a culture-building campaign. Fourth and for that reason, the CSRC has intensified its use of network instruments: Besides the securities score and the integrity files, now further transparency is provided via other, non-sector-specific platforms (e.g. Qichacha) as well as the CSRC's publication of various compliance-related cases, a majority of which fall in the category of naming and shaming. This way, the SCS's managerial regulatory approach is introduced to the securities sector. It remains to be seen, however, whether these efforts bear fruit and nurture compliance awareness, culture and normative behaviors in the industry. Otherwise, these highly prescriptive regulations bear the risk of creative compliance.

Figure 36: Schematic transfer process of the concept of compliance to the Chinese securities sector (author's design)

6.2 Corporate compliance in the automotive sector in China

Following the discussion of compliance in the Chinese securities sector, this empirical sub-case focuses on compliance developments in the automotive sector. Despite being of high national strategic importance, this industry possesses a less centralized regulatory set-up compared to the securities sector. Therefore, the automotive sub-case lends itself to comparison in order to answer research sub-question three on the differences in compliance construction between industries.

Building on a literature review (Section 6.2.1) and an overview of the automotive sector's regulatory approach (Section 6.2.2), this sub-case first elaborates on the development of the concept of compliance in Section 6.2.3, then moves on to examine sector-specific influences on as well as practices of compliance (Sections 6.2.4 and 6.2.5)[215] and finally summarizes the findings and their impact on compliance construction in Section 6.2.6.

6.2.1 Literature review

The literature on compliance in the Chinese automotive sector is scarce and does not address compliance from a firm's perspective. Instead, some scholars indirectly touched on compliance in their discussions on the development of the automotive industry since the 1978 reform and opening as well as in their treatises on the regulatory regime in this sector (e.g. Chin, 2017, Tang, 2012, Hsueh, 2011, Chu, 2011, Thun, 2006). For example, Thun (2004) highlighted the Chinese automotive industries' embeddedness in the international economy and its reliance on FDI for development. In comparison, Yeo and Pearson (2008) discussed the decentralized nature of the regulatory regime in the automotive industry and its implications. Lüthje and Tian (2015) built on these two key characteristics of the regulatory set-up in the automotive industry and added a third feature, namely a high polarization between different ownership structures along supply chains, ranging from POEs at the bottom to JVs and SOEs higher up the supply chain.

In addition, one strand of Chinese-speaking literature focuses on compliance in central SOEs from a conceptual standpoint and thereby automatically also targets several SOEs from the automotive sector (e.g. Chen, 2020, Yao, 2017, Song, 2015). The topics raised in this context are, for instance, the problems in SOEs' compliance management (e.g. lacking power and resources of compliance departments) as well as their international exposure, which motivate compliance-related actions (e.g. Chen, 2020, Yao, 2017, Song, 2015). This sub-case builds on this basis and provides first empirical insights into the particularities of compliance-construction in the automotive sector.

215 The findings are mainly based on 10 interviews with representatives from the automotive sector, which amount to ca. 15 percent of the total number of interviews conducted to understand compliance trends in China overall.

6.2.2 Overview of the automotive sector's regulatory approach

6.2.2.1 Historical development

The Chinese automotive sector's development can be traced back to the 1950s and 1960s (Hsueh, 2011, p. 217). Until the economic opening in 1978, however, demand was minimal, focused on trucks and buses and was mainly supplied by imports from the Soviet Union (Hsueh, 2011, p. 217). The economic opening radically changed this situation, because demand for automobiles first gradually increased and then skyrocketed in the mid-1990, when the government allowed the private possession of cars. Initially, the need for vehicles was still met via imports, but gradually, automotive factories mushroomed across the country, with the result, that by the mid-1980s, automotive production facilities existed in nearly all Chinese provinces (Hsueh, 2011, p. 217). In an effort to advance market consolidation in 1988, the government decided to support six companies ('three majors and three minors', 三大三小) out of the multitude of domestic players that existed in the sector at that time: The Shanghai Automotive Industry Corporation, First Automobile Works and Second Automobile Works (later Dongfeng Motor Corporation) as the three majors and firms located in Beijing, Tianjin and Guangzhou as the three minors (Chu, 2011, p. 1243).

Nevertheless, the general trend towards regulatory decentralization in China during that time also took hold of the automotive sector and has remained a key feature of the industry's regulatory framework ever since (Hsueh, 2011, p. 218ff). Not only the active promotion of SOEs by provincial and municipal governments (e.g. Shanghai) throughout the 1990s and 2000s and the existence of 124 state-owned automotive companies in 1993 reflect this development, but the dismantling of the central-level regulators dedicated to the automotive sector by 1993 also marks a milestone in this regard (Hsueh, 2011, p. 218). Originally installed in 1987 in an effort to centrally coordinate collaborations with foreign investors in the automotive sector, the Automobile Leading Group was already disbanded two years later (Hsueh, 2011, p. 218). In 1993, the China National Automotive Industry Cooperation (中国汽车工业总公司), which held central responsibility for planning, technology acquisition and project approval in the automotive sector, was downgraded to an industry association (Hsueh, 2011, p. 218).

Despite the decentralized supervision and ownership of actors in the automotive sector, the central government nevertheless retained certain controls over the market, for instance via the regulation of FDI (Hsueh, 2011, p. 219). Specifically, the central government restricted the investment levels, ownership structures and business scope of FDI, in particular via its industrial policy in 1994 (Eun and Lee, 2002, p. 8ff): Until 1997, for example, foreign companies were only allowed to invest in eight JVs (Hsueh, 2011, p. 219). Even though the amount of FDI increased after this rule was abolished in 1997, two rules kept limiting foreign automotive companies in their engagement in the Chinese market: First, international automotive original equipment manufacturers (OEMs) were only allowed to access the Chinese market via JVs with a maximum of two domestic firms and second, the foreign shares in these JVs were restricted to account for 49 percent at the most (Chen et al., 2017, p. 107). Hence, automotive JVs controlled by Chinese counterparts acted as a vehicle for knowledge transfer and fostered local market development ('market for technology'), since 40 percent of the sourcing for production had to be done locally[216] (Harwit, 2001, p. 656). These rules are only a few examples of how the government actively favored domestic automotive companies[217] to lead in domestic markets and compete internationally.

Until the administrative reforms of 1998, the responsibility for this kind of macro-level steering of the Chinese automotive industry was carried out by two state agencies: The State Planning Commission (国家经济贸易委员会) and the Ministry of Machinery Industry (机械工业部) (both under the State Council) (Yeo and Pearson, 2008, p. 238). During the reforms, however, the NDRC replaced the two state agencies and became the sole authority in charge of long-term planning, technology innovation, industrial policy and investments (Yeo and Pearson, 2008, p. 238). In addition, the SASAC was established in 2003 as a regulator for state assets and strategic central-government SOEs, including those in the automotive sector (Yeo and Pearson, 2008, p. 234).

In the following years, the government steered the development of the automotive industry mainly via industrial policies that focused on strengthening the domestic industry. For instance, the 'Automotive Industry Devel-

216 In addition, higher levels of local sourcing were incentivized: At 60 percent import duty was reduced to 24 percent, and at 80 percent the impact tax was reduced to 16 percent (Harwit, 2001, p. 656).

217 Domestic companies in this case also includes local subsidies of foreign automotive suppliers, which were relieved of obligations to set up JVs early on.

opment Policy' (汽车产业发展政策) issued by the NDRC in 2004 built on the 1994 industrial policy aimed to ensure compliance with WTO obligations and to foster local research and development efforts in order to create indigenous intellectual property in this sector (Li et al., 2015, p. 790; McCaleb, 2015, p. 166). Moreover, this policy as well as the 'Automotive Industry Readjustment and Revitalization Plan' (汽车产业调整和振兴规划), which was passed in 2009 as a reaction to the global financial crisis, had the objective to develop large-scale local automotive enterprises via consolidation and restructuring, i.e. mergers and acquisition (McCaleb, 2015, p. 166). Under Xi Jinping, 'Made in China 2025' as well as the 'Energy Saving and New Energy Auto Industry Plan 2012-2020' (节能与新能源汽车产业发展规划（2012-2020）) have been the main efforts to strengthen the domestic automotive sector by supporting the development of innovative technologies (e.g. battery technologies) in order to become market leaders in new markets, such as e-mobility, especially since catching up on the technology for vehicles with combustion engines had proven difficult (Chen et al., 2017, p. 102f). The massive push towards e-mobility by the government in China has not only strengthened domestic automotive firms and made China competitive in the automotive sector. This Party-state effort also illustrates that, despite the loosening of restrictions in the automotive industry and the important role played by private firms, the Party-state still remains in the driver's seat.

With respect to foreign actors on the Chinese automotive market, the government has continued to relax restrictions, yet still retains its steering capacity. One example for this trend is the 'Foreign Investment Catalog' (外商投资产业指导目录), released by the NDRC together with the MOFCOM, which encourages, permits, restricts and prohibits investments on the Chinese market from abroad (McCaleb, 2015, p. 166f): In the 2011 catalog, automotive investments were removed from the encouraged-category and replaced by electric vehicles, i.e. investments were steered towards the newly emerging market. Furthermore, since 2018, restrictions for foreign actors have gradually been phased out: Ownership restrictions for new energy vehicles manufacturers were removed in 2018, for commercial vehicles producers in 2020 and are to be eliminated for all types of passenger cars companies in 2022 (NDRC and MOFCOM, 2020, 2018). Instead of these restrictions, the Party-state has adopted a more targeted approach to control. For instance, in 2014, a large-scale anti-trust investigation resulted in fines for several domestic and international actors on the automotive market and had international car manufacturers lower car prices immediately (Chen et al., 2017, p. 91).

These elaborations illustrate that, over time, the regulatory approach in the automotive sector altered from a domination of command and control measures to protect the nascent domestic industry from international competition to an introduction and steering of market dynamics in this sector (Chin, 2017, p. 88). This regulatory set-up, which has allowed Chinese automotive companies to better integrate into global value chains and dominate the local electric vehicle market, is described in more depth in the following section (Chin, 2017, p. 88).

6.2.2.2 Regulatory framework

The current regulatory framework targeting firms in the automotive sector is rather decentralized and therefore involves a large number of institutions, each addressing different regulatory topics or actors (see Figure 37[218]).

Figure 37: Schematic overview of the regulatory set-up in the automotive sector (author's design)

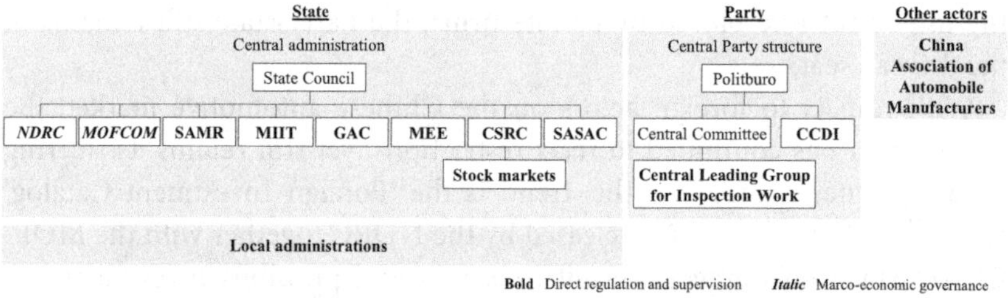

The NDRC and the MOFCOM function as regulators of the automotive sector on a macro-level, e.g. via industrial policies and FDI regulations (Heilmann 2016, p. 77f; Chu 2011, p. 1261). In this context, the NDRC provides guidance on the industry's development (overall macro-economic planning) and the MOFCOM formulates policies related to specific topics, which affect automotive firms, such as import and export, foreign trade, competition and FDI. Neither of the two agencies is involved in the day-to-

218 This summary does not claim to be exhaustive, but rather combines a general overview with more details on the organizations that are most important for the following elaborations on compliance.

day supervision of actors in the automotive sector. Yet, automotive companies receive the chance to interact with authorities in the drafting of new policies, for instance during NDRC-organized conferences or discussion rounds (Yeo and Pearson, 2008, p. 252). This does not only pertain to large central SOEs, but also private automotive firms (Yeo and Pearson, 2008, p. 252). However, the influence of automotive firms on policies still seems to be limited (Yeo and Pearson, 2008, p. 252).

On a micro-economic level, certain state agencies regulate and supervise specific aspects of automotive firms' operations. For example, the SAMR is responsible for topics, such as competition, anti-trust actions and intellectual property, the MIIT sets technological and quality-related standards and the GAC manages imports and exports to and from China (GAC, 2022, SAMR, 2022, MIIT, 2015). Moreover, the MEE focuses on environmental aspects, such as factory emission controls, and the CSRC (including the stock exchanges) passes and enforces regulations dedicated to listed (automotive) companies (MEE, 2022, CSRC, 2021). For SOEs in the automotive sector, two additional regulators exist: On the one hand, the SASAC guides and supervises central SOEs nationwide, irrespective of industrial sector. Therefore, the commission is more involved in the general management and operations of SOEs, such as compliance management, rather than addressing industry-specific topics. On the other hand, the CCP itself acts as a regulator, not only by setting rules and propagating behavioral norms as well as ideologies, but also by actively monitoring and enforcing Party discipline (especially focusing on anti-corruption efforts) (Yeo and Pearson, 2008, p. 233). This is undertaken via the CCDI, the National Supervision Commission (NSC, 国家监察委员会)[219], the Central Leading Group for Inspection Work and their inspection teams' inspection tours in SOEs (Chan and Sun, 2018).

In addition, local Party-state structures play a crucial role as regulators for automotive firms. The lack of functional separation in local institutions, due to local governments' dual role as both owners and external regulators of these companies, creates difficulties to consistently enforce nationwide standards, procedures and regulatory norms (Lüthje and Tian, 2015, p. 260). Nevertheless, local institutions still generally have a strong influence on the performance of locally-owned SOEs (Thun, 2006, p. 28ff).

219 Since its establishment in 2018, the NSC has been co-located/merged with the CCDI. Jointly, these two authorities are responsible for fighting corruption (Chan and Sun, 2018).

Lastly, industry associations complement the regulatory framework in the automotive sector. The China Association of Automobile Manufacturers (CAAM, 中国汽车工业协会), is the main nationwide player in this field (Chu, 2011, p. 1245). With its almost 2700 members from vehicle-related industries, it works as a self-regulatory industry association (CAAM, 2019). For instance, the association provides standards, certifications and trainings to members based on existing regulations, conducts research on automotive-related topics (e.g. technology-related, economic development in the sector) and represents its members' interests in interactions with authorities (CAAM, 2019). Yet, this organization is not independent from the government. Registered as a social organization (社会团体) with the Ministry of Civil Affairs (民政部), it is supervised by the SASAC (CAAM, 2021). Since CAAM is not under the direct control of one Party-state organ, it has been classified under 'other actors' in Figure 37. Other private associations also support actors in the automotive industry, however with comparably shorter reach and often focusing on other topics than compliance. For instance, the China Passenger Car Association (乘用车市场信息联席会) is a group formed by over 100 firms in the automotive sector and serves as a research and information exchange platform, but is not directly involved in regulatory issues (China Passenger Car Association, 2021).

With this highly dispersed and decentralized regulatory framework in place, three features characterize regulatory practices in the automotive sector. First, Chinese regulatory practices are embedded in and influenced by a highly internationalized production regime. This does not only mean that global economic pressures and market dynamics directly impact the Chinese automotive market (Lüthje and Tian, 2015, p. 249). It also leads to domestic regulators' and regulatees' behavior and decision-making becoming affected by international regulatory standards and practices, be it in accounting and financial management or related to product quality (Thun, 2004, p. 472).

Second, standardization constitutes an important regulatory mechanism in the Chinese automotive sector. Since standardization efforts across China were centralized in 2002, automotive products have been required to possess the China Compulsory Certification in order to be sold on the Chinese market (Hsueh, 2011, p. 224f). In addition, China has adopted international standards and developed its own standards, including for the automotive sector. Chinese standards are not only supposed to regulate the Chinese market, but also help the country to become a global power for standard-setting and strengthen China's position in the international community (Weithmann, 2018).

Third, supervision and enforcement vary greatly across different actors in the industry, since the sector is highly polarized along the automotive production and supply chain (Lüthje and Tian, 2015, p. 250). JVs and SOEs mainly act as producers or first tier suppliers and face more supervision compared to POEs or smaller locally-owned SOEs, which cover early stages in the supply chain and have more leeway in their operations and business decisions (Lüthje and Tian, 2015, p. 250). Among other factors, this difference is caused by varying levels of industry concentration: Compared to the rather high industry concentration among producers, OEM suppliers are relatively scattered and can therefore more easily evade supervision (e.g. Lüthje and Tian, 2015, p. 250).

This overview of the regulatory set-up in the automotive sector has highlighted its decentralized and fragmented nature, with regulatory practices varying greatly along the supply chain, from state capitalist controls via ownership of SOEs and JVs that act as producers to less supervision for smaller POEs on lower tiers in the supply chain. At the same time, the automotive sector's strong international embeddedness and related pressure to open the market, as well as efforts to achieve a leading position in the electric vehicle segment globally, are leading to a gradual shift in the focus of the government towards steering market actors at a distance via regulations, monitoring and enforcement.

Hence, the regulatory regime in the automotive sector cannot be classified easily using existing typologies. For instance, Hsueh (2011, p. 226) classified the regulatory regime for automobile producers as 'deliberate reinforcement in strategic sectors', whereas she separately lists suppliers as being midway between 'deliberate reinforcement' and 'decentralized engagement'. Hence, both regulatory modes with dominant government control and modes characterized by networked entrepreneurialism persist (McNally and Gruin, 2017). With respect to Liu's (2011a) typology, the regulatory mode automotive producers face can be described as 'government-business integration', while the lower-tier industry regulation more closely resembles 'government supervision', because of the greater separation of government and business. Especially the more recent relaxations of restrictions for international players show that 'government supervision' as a regulatory mode is gaining importance in the automotive sector. However, few details exist on how the current regulatory approach affects compliance construction and compliance management. The following sections provide empirical insights, by first discussing how the concept of compliance has been constructed, followed by elaborations on the influencing factors and compliance practices in the automotive sector.

6.2.3 The genesis of the concept of corporate compliance in the automotive sector

Process tracing of the term 'compliance' (合规) in Chinese automotive sector-related official documents[220] ('official discourse' in the following) shows that compliance was introduced to the automotive sector's official discourse comparatively late. The term was first mentioned in a document by the MIIT on improving market access management for motorcycle producers in 2009 (AUT-20090325). Specifically, compliance appeared in the context of corporate groups' responsibility to strengthen their subsidiaries' monitoring and urging them to produce in a legally compliant manner ("集团公司应切实加强对子公司（或分公司）的监督管理，督促其依法合规生产", AUT-20090325). Here, the MIIT used the phrasing 'compliance with the law' (依法合规) that has already been identified as a typical combination in Section 6.1.3. After this initial appearance, it took another three years until compliance was first included in the title of an automotive sector-related document, namely the CAAM's announcement that Chang'an Automobile would start internal control and compliance promotion programs and trainings (AUT-20120224). However, compliance only appeared more frequently in automotive sector-related documents from 2014/15 onwards. This increased attention to compliance in the automotive sector coincided with the SASAC's heightened focus on the topic starting from 2016. Further factors influencing this development were Xi Jinping's assumption to power in 2013 and the ensuing anti-corruption campaign, the campaign to 'Comprehensively Govern the Country According to the Law' as well as the Chinese stock market turbulence in 2015/16, which triggered stronger regulation and enforcement for all types of listed companies, including those in the automotive sector (e.g. AUT-20150617, AUT-20150803). More recently, this heightened importance of compliance in the automotive sector has been mirrored in the development plan for the new energy vehicle industry, where improvements in compliance management have been set as a goal for the period from 2021 to 2035 (AUT-20201020).

220 For further information on the process tracing, refer to Section 1.3.

Yet, three features in the official discourse on compliance depict compliance-construction in the automotive industry as much less streamlined and prescriptive compared to the securities sector (see Section 6.1.3). First, a broad range of regulators is involved in the discourse on compliance in the automotive sector and variation in these actors' conceptualization of compliance persists. The MIIT, on the one hand, focuses on (non-)compliance as a result of authorities' supervision and therefore promotes the standardization of supervisory mechanisms to ensure compliance (e.g. AUT-20090414, AUT-20100820, AUT-20111114, AUT-20151019, AUT-20160719, AUT-20170817, AUT-20181102(1)). In this context, the MIIT adopts public condemnation of non-compliant firms and the release of compliance case studies as a means of enforcement (e.g. AUT-20100820, AUT-20110718). Likewise, the CSRC and the stock markets promote information disclosure for listed firms, including automotive companies, as a means to ensure compliance (e.g. the disclosure of non-compliance incidents or feedback on submitted applications for the issuance of shares) (e.g. AUT-20150617, AUT-20150803, AUT-20171204). The SASAC, on the other hand, highlights the importance of compliance awareness and compliance culture-building (e.g. AUT-20150505). Similarly, the CCDI and the CCP, who focus on compliance in the context of anti-corruption work (e.g. AUT-20190425, AUT-20190528, AUT-20191229), take an ideological approach to compliance and thereby extend the notion of compliance beyond the legal context, for instance by including industry ethics, social responsibility and professional virtues in the concept of compliance (e.g. AUT-20150505, AUT-20150916, AUT-20151116). Especially these authorities' later compliance-related documents strongly emphasize the ethical notion of compliance, for instance by stressing the contribution of compliance to international societal common knowledge ("国际社会共识", AUT-20201126, AUT-20201128) and depicting compliance as a traditional Chinese virtue ("中华传统美德", AUT-20201128). In contrast, documents issued by the MOFCOM focus on compliance in the international business context (e.g. import, export, international standards) (e.g. AUT-20160427, AUT-20170719, AUT-20170808, AUT-20180112). These elaborations illustrate that the multiple regulators involved in the automotive sector take different angles on compliance, resulting in a great variety in the compliance discourse and hence a less rigid and uniform understanding of compliance.

Second, no dedicated prescriptive compliance management regulations for the automotive sector exist. Only SOEs in the automotive sector face detailed regulatory guidance on how to implement compliance management, namely the SASAC's 'SOE Compliance Guidelines' and 'Overseas Compliance Guidelines' (e.g. GEN-20181102, GEN-20181231(1))[221]. The analysis shows that these compliance management regulations on the central level triggered compliance-related efforts on the local level, which affected locally-registered automotive SOEs. For instance, local regulators in Zhejiang, Anhui and Shanghai started to convene compliance-related events (forums, trainings, etc.) right after the SASAC's release of its compliance guidelines (e.g. AUT-20181115, AUT-20181211, AUT-20190401, AUT-20190429, AUT-20190505, AUT-20190715, AUT-20191017). Furthermore, local regulators followed the SASAC's direction, by publishing compliance management guidelines for local SOEs, which are largely congruent with the SASAC's 'SOE Compliance Guidelines' and 'Overseas Compliance Guidelines'. For example, the SASAC Shanghai published the 'Guidelines on Compliance Management for SOEs Supervised by SASAC Shanghai (for Trial Implementation)' (AUT-20181228), the SASAC Anhui the 'Guidelines on Compliance Management for SOEs Belonging to the Province (for Trial Implementation)' (AUT-20210513) and the SASAC Jiangsu the 'Guidelines on Compliance Management for SOEs Belonging to the Province (for Trial Implementation)' (AUT-20191108(1), AUT-20191122). The publications from Jiangsu even include a three-year plan for the promotion of compliance in Jiangsu, which closely resembles the central SASAC's approach to piloting compliance management in selected firms, before implementing compliance practices across the nation (see Section 4.3) (AUT-20191122): Starting in November 2019, pilot firms implemented compliance management until the end of 2020; then, compliance management was supposed to have been rolled out to all SOEs in Jiangsu; and from 2022 onward, Jiangsu plans to continuously improve its SOEs' compliance management. Furthermore, these releases were connected to a series of documents published by local authorities, which focus on compliance and refer to the new compliance regulations (e.g. AUT-20191108, AUT-20200117, AUT-20200120, AUT-20200207, AUT-20200514).

The compliance-related documents that target local SOEs, as the only officially dedicated requirements related to the automotive sector's compliance management, however, are less prescriptive as compared to the

221 The CAAM also released the 'Overseas Compliance Guidelines' on its website in 2018 (AUT-20181226(1), AUT-20181226(2)).

detailed compliance management regulations in the securities sector. For instance, the central and local SASAC guidelines mention compliance management elements (e.g. compliance departments, compliance trainings) that have to be set up, but do not provide detailed prescriptions on how these features need to be formed. Moreover, the guidelines feature the principle of appropriateness (适用性原则), meaning that compliance management systems in individual companies are supposed to be adapted to the individual companies' needs ("企业合规管理应从经营范围、组织结构和业务规模等实际出发" (AUT-20181226(2)). This provides a certain level of flexibility in compliance management implementation to automotive SOEs (e.g. AUT-20181226(2)).

Third, instead of posing prescriptive requirements, the various regulators involved in the automotive sector indirectly influence the understanding and social practices of compliance in automotive firms via topic-related stipulations. For instance, compliance is addressed in documents on technical standards, certificates or licenses, product components and materials, information and data management, taxes, anti-trust, consumer protection and third-party management, such as supplier and investor management (e.g. AUT-20141224, AUT-20150112, AUT-20151223, AUT-20160712, AUT-20160823, AUT-20170817, AUT-20190515, AUT-20190709, AUT-20190923, AUT-20200813, AUT-20210622). Hence, compliance is addressed from a variety of different angles in the automotive sector.

Despite these variations, the automotive sector-related documents still embrace several themes that dominate in the overall official discourse on compliance in China (as shown in Section 4.3 and 6.1.3). For example, compliance is conceptualized as the baseline for business operations (e.g. AUT-20151116, AUT-20190102, AUT-20190821), a means to mitigate risks (e.g. AUT-20150505, AUT-20150514, AUT-20170808, AUT-20190516) and a prerequisite for the healthy development of firms, sectors as well as the national economy (e.g. AUT-20150112, AUT-20150312, AUT-20150422, AUT-20190709). Moreover, as in the cross-sectoral and securities sector compliance conceptualization, compliance is often used in the fixed expression 'compliance with the law' (依法合规) (e.g. AUT-20090325, AUT-20100820, AUT-20160712, AUT-20160719) and in the context of governing the country and companies according to the law (依法治国/企) (e.g. AUT-20141208, AUT-20150505, AUT-20210513). This indicates that the official documents focus on legal compliance as well as the construction of compliance management as one tool in the larger context of establishing a rules-based society.

Embeddedness of compliance in the international context is another topic in the official discourse on compliance in the automotive sector that is congruent with the overall construction of compliance in China. However, this topic is emphasized more strongly in the automotive context: Compliance is not only mentioned in the context of the Belt and Road Initiative and the 'Go Out' strategy as explained in Section 4.3 (e.g. AUT-20170817, AUT-20180110, AUT-20190516, AUT-20201128), but international case examples, international product requirements and trade policy compliance in the WTO context also play an important role (e.g. AUT-20140619, AUT-20140722, AUT-20150525, AUT-20180112, AUT-20180912).

Furthermore, the official discourse on compliance in the automotive sector exhibits a feature that has not been identified in the overall and the securities sector's official discourse on compliance, namely a managerial spin on compliance. The managerial logic in the understanding of compliance manifests itself in three ways in the automotive sector-related official discourse: The link between credit and compliance, the commodification and marketization of compliance and the emphasis on constructing compliance as a business opportunity, rather than a cost factor. The link between credit and compliance showed up in the official documents from various regulators, such as the MOFCOM, the NDRC and the SASAC Anhui (AUT-20160427, AUT-20180130, AUT-20190102, AUT-20190516). The MOFCOM conceptualized legal compliance as part of companies' credit status (e.g. "守法合规的信用情况", AUT-20160427, AUT-20180130) and applied this status as a selection criterion for pilot firms in an automotive import program. The NDRC named the strengthening of its credit system in the field of foreign economic cooperation, including the joint punishment system for illegal actions, as an objective that is supposed to improve companies' compliance management abroad by increasing the costs of illegal behavior ("为推动企业加强境外经营合规管理[...]完善违规惩戒机制。加强对外经济合作领域信用体系建设，对违法违规企业和相关责任人实施联合惩戒，提高违规成本", AUT-20190102). Similarly, a discussion of the Blue Book 2019 results, released by the SASAC Anhui, mentioned the recommendation by the National Enterprise Compliance Committee of the China Council for the Promotion of International Trade's deputy secretary-general to incorporate compliance as a factor into the credit system, in order to motivate the entire society to actively comply with regulations (AUT-20190516). These examples show that the regulators active in the automotive sector intend to create an additional economic

Incentive for companies to comply with regulations by connecting compliance to credit.

Commodification and marketization of compliance is the second indicator of the managerial interpretation of compliance in this sector. The key example mentioned in the official discourse in this regard is the compound score for average fuel consumption and new electric vehicles for passenger vehicle companies (乘用车企业平均燃料消耗量与新能源汽车积分) by the MIIT, which indicates whether a company meets the required standards regarding energy saving (AUT-20170928, AUT-20190911, AUT-20200621, AUT-20200622). Companies that surpass the standard can transfer their surplus points to the following year or sell them to other companies that have not met the requirements (AUT-20170928, AUT-20190911). This mechanism grants companies a certain level of flexibility regarding compliance, since they can choose the more economic approach between ensuring compliance themselves and purchasing surplus score points from other companies (AUT-20170928, AUT-20190911). Hence, compliance becomes a commodity that can be sold and bought on the market.

Lastly, managerial logic in the construction of compliance manifests itself in an emphasis on compliance as a business opportunity rather than a cost factor. For instance, a CCDI document on compliance in the context of the Belt and Road Initiative stated that "compliance may increase costs, but compliance will definitely create value" ("合规可能会增加成本，但合规一定会创造价值", AUT-20201128). This notion of compliance creating value was reiterated in the CAAM's article on the China Automobile Forum in 2021 ("合规创造价值", AUT-20210622). Moreover, the CCP promoted the set-up of compliance systems with Chinese characteristics (中国特色的企业合规制度) and regarded "compliance [as] an important aspect for companies' core competitiveness" ("合规是企业核心竞争力的重要方面", AUT-20201228). These examples elucidate that the official discourse has recently started to emphasize the economic benefits companies can gain from compliance in their compliance construction and thereby attempts to trigger economic motives for compliance.

This broad notion of compliance, including its managerial logic, constructed in the automotive sector's official discourse is also reflected in the interviews with business representatives. Across the board, interviewees believed compliance covers both the adherence to external regulations as well as rules internal to businesses (e.g. BUS21-05, BUS21-21) and is essential for a company's survival and growth (e.g. BUS21-11, BUS21-18). At the same time, interviewees recognized the benefits compliance management can provide as well as the importance of employees' compliance awareness and integrity (e.g. BUS21-22, BUS21-25). The fact that the official discourse and the views of business representatives from the automotive sector on the construction of the meaning of compliance are aligned, hints at institutional isomorphism with regard to compliance in the automotive sector. The following sections, which elaborate on how this understanding of compliance manifests itself in practice, further corroborate this finding, but also mirror the themes of variety and managerial logic identified in the notion of compliance as constructed by the official discourse in the automotive sector.

6.2.4 Influences on corporate compliance in the automotive sector

6.2.4.1 External influences

The larger external environment that automotive firms in China operate in is the same as for all other firms in China. Consequently, the overall trends related to external influences on compliance in China (described in Section 4.4.1) also pertain to the automotive sector. This is most evident when investigating influencing factors in automotive companies' social, economic and political environments. For instance, interviewees from the automotive sector described pressure from (social) media (reputational risk in case of negative reporting) and local residents' pressure as important influences on their compliance practices from the social environment (e.g. BUS19-10, BUS21-11, BUS21-22, BUS21-24). Business representatives from the automotive sector also noticed a strong compliance awareness in regions in China with a higher development status, leading to compliance pressure due to, for example, customer complaints (BUS19-10, BUS21-11). With regard to the economic environment, the cross-sectoral themes identified in Section 4.4.1 are also reflected in the automotive sector, e.g. the challenges the dynamic development experience has posed to compliance in the past ten to 20 years (BUS19-10), the consideration of compliance as a cost factor in a highly competitive industry (e.g. BUS19-19, BUS21-05, BUS21-21) and the existence of opportunities to exchange on compliance-related topics with other players in the industry, regardless of competition (BUS21-05, BUS21-22, BUS21-25). In the political environment, interviewees from the automotive sector, similar to business representatives from other sectors, did not challenge the legitimacy of the CCP, acknowledged the improvement towards rule-based governance as well as transparency and considered the larger national context, in which the government operates[222] (BUS21-11, BUS21-21, BUS21-22).

Consequently, the interviews from the automotive sector only exhibit minor sector-specific divergences with regard to the social, economic and political environments. For instance, none of the interviewees from the automotive sector mentioned the stock market as an important factor influencing their compliance practices in China. This is remarkable, since automotive firms listed on the Chinese stock exchanges are certainly influenced by these institutions. Yet, at least for the interviewed firms, this effect did not seem to be noteworthy. Furthermore, the complexity of the value chain in the automotive sector leads to variety in compliance-related approaches that differ between actors, depending on their role: OEMs in the automotive industry seem to manage compliance more proactively compared to suppliers and vehicle dealerships, which tend to only react to regulators' requirements (e.g. BUS21-17, BUS21-21, BUS21-25). At the same time, the level of international exposure also seems to affect compliance behavior, with greater exposure leading to more efforts, especially since interviewees regarded foreign MNEs and international organizations as promoters of compliance in the Chinese automotive sector (e.g. BUS19-19, BUS21-21, BUS21-22).

Similarly, in regulation and enforcement, convergences and divergences with the overall compliance trends identified in China can be found. In line with the cross-sectoral analysis, the interviews in the automotive sector also indicated improvements in regulations, especially in terms of stringency (BUS19-10, BUS21-21), the involvement of a broad spectrum of regulators (e.g. BUS19-10, BUS21-05, BUS21-18) as well as constant interactions between businesses and regulators regarding regulations (feedback in the drafting process, specific consultations, etc.), which reinforce the endogeneity of law (e.g. BUS19-10, BUS21-18, BUS21-22, BUS21-25). Hence, similar to the general trend, the legalization of organizations and the managerialization of the regulations is constantly reinforced in the automotive sector. However, despite this level of congruence with cross-sectoral phenomena, sector-specifics are more prominent in regulation and enforcement, since

222 One interviewee from the automotive sector, for example, stressed the need for China to maintain an attractive business environment for international actors as a justification for the government's actions (BUS21-11).

the regulatory regime varies according to the nature of the industry that is targeted.

The idiosyncrasies center around the theme of regulatory variety. On the one hand, characteristics of regulations targeting the automotive sector exhibit a relatively high degree of variation: Interviewees explained that regulations addressing traditional regulatory topics and business activities have become increasingly mature and hence have reached a rather high degree of clarity over time (e.g. BUS21-05, BUS21-21, BUS21-25). Yet, regulations that target new business areas and address new technologies are characterized by a rapid pace of change and less clarity, leading to the need to interact with authorities in order to ensure an adequate response to regulations (e.g. BUS19-10, BUS21-22). Furthermore, regulations in certain areas, e.g. Party-imposed regulations and technical standards, seem to possess a high level of concreteness, whereas other areas targeted by regulations provide more leeway in implementation (e.g. set-up of compliance management systems) (BUS19-10, BUS21-05). On the other hand, a plethora of regulators is involved in the automotive sector, which exceeds other sectors, including securities. Two aspects related to the automotive sector are noteworthy in this context. First, a large variety of Party-state(-related) regulators are involved in the regulatory process in the automotive sector, such as the MIIT, the GAC, the SASAC and the SAMR (e.g. BUS21-05, BUS21-11, BUS21-17, BUS21-18, BUS21-24). Even though these regulators have different focus areas and are supposed to complement each other, supervision is nevertheless perceived as scattered (BUS21-05). Second, enterprises, particularly foreign MNEs, seem to have assumed the role of regulators, e.g. by imposing requirements on and monitoring business partners or by supporting local firms' compliance-related learning processes (e.g. BUS19-10, BUS21-17, EXP19-10, EXP19-13). This shows that top-down regulation from Party-state agencies is complemented by bottom-up compliance-related regulatory actions from businesses themselves, especially foreign MNEs with compliance experiences from other contexts.

Above regulatory variety is also reflected in the enforcement context. Party-state regulators in the automotive sector adopt smart regulation, i.e. multiple Party-state agencies apply and escalate different types of enforcement instruments depending on the situation: Companies and their leadership face and fear legal enforcement instruments, such as fines, business shutdowns and personal consequences for individual managers in case of severe compliance problems (e.g. BUS19-10, BUS21-21, BUS21-17). However, before such measures are applied, authorities adopt communicative and network instruments to ensure compliant behavior. With regard to communicative instruments, the interviewees from the automotive sector mentioned warnings, consultations and trainings organized by authorities, as well as a grace periods for the adaption of business operations to entirely new regulations (e.g. BUS19-10, BUS21-05, BUS21-25). In addition, several network instruments are relevant in the automotive sector, such as customer complaint platforms, real-life monitoring (and online publication) of emissions data and the SCS's mechanisms described in Section 5.2.4 (e.g. BUS19-10, BUS21-11, BUS21-21, BUS21-22).

In a similar manner as described for other sectors in China, inspections are an important means of information retrieval and control in the automotive sector. For instance, different types of inspections, such as regular and unannounced random on-site visits as well as inspections in case of specific complaints, take place in addition to remote-monitoring (e.g. of factory emissions) (e.g. BUS19-10, BUS21-05, BUS21-11, BUS21-17, BUS21-18, BUS21-25). During inspections, interviewees from the automotive sector confirmed, companies need to cooperate with the inspectors in an observant manner, yet also possess certain leeway for negotiation, as outlined in Section 4.4.1 (BUS21-05, BUS21-11, BUS21-22, BUS21-25).

Specific to the automotive sector, e.g. as compared to the securities sector, is, however, that the supervision intensity a business faces seems to depend on its enterprise type; another sign for variety: JVs and SOEs in the interviewed sample described a significantly greater amount of inspections (e.g. BUS19-10, BUS21-22, BUS21-24) in comparison to domestic POEs or foreign MNEs[223] (e.g. BUS19-19, BUS21-11, BUS21-18).

Besides these enforcement actions on the part of various Party-state agencies, automotive firms also face supervision from business partners, especially foreign MNEs. Specifically, companies exploit the additional and conveniently available transparency provided by the SCS on their business partners in their third-party management (e.g. BUS21-05, BUS21-11, BUS21-22, BUS21-24). Firms escalate different mechanisms in their collaboration with business partners depending on their risk assessment, ranging from increased monitoring (including on-site visits) to adapting contract terms or the decision against further cooperation (e.g. in case of blacklist entries) (e.g. BUS21-05, BUS19-19, BUS21-25). While some automotive firms may consider cooperating with a blacklisted firm under certain circum-

223 One MNE representative even stated that his company is not subjected to regular inspections by authorities at all (BUS19-19).

stances and therefore check every individual case (e.g. BUS21-11, BUS21-25), others consider a blacklist entry as a knock-out criterion (e.g. BUS21-05, BUS21-17):

> "If a company is on the blacklist, you cannot collaborate with it" ("如果一个公司上黑名单，你是没法跟他们合作的", BUS21-17).
> "A reason [for not collaborating with a blacklisted company] is that everyone's assessment of that company is extremely bad" ("一个原因是大家给他们的评价特别差", BUS21-05).

In this context, list entries seem to play a more important role compared to ratings for assessing the risk of a collaboration[224].

Another key influence on automotive companies' third party management is the impact negative SCS information have on government and SOE tenders: A blacklist entry by one's own or a cooperating company can reduce the chances of success in tender bidding processes. Therefore, automotive firms with government/SOE customers attentively check business partners' SCS information (e.g. BUS19-10, BUS21-17). Overall, these elaborations show that the various SCS mechanisms active in the automotive sector, which each pose slightly different requirements, result in an additional layer of complexity automotive firms face in their compliance management.

6.2.4.2 Internal influences

The internal factors influencing compliance in the automotive sector exhibit similar attributes as external influences, namely similarities to the cross-industrial patterns as well as an emphasis on managerial logic and large variety. With regard to organizational capacities and characteristics, certain phenomena identified across industries in Section 4.4.2 also appear in interviews in the automotive sector. For example, interviewees related a smaller firm size to fewer efforts in compliance management, be it because of a lack of resources or a lower level of organizational complexity that does not require elaborate compliance management systems (e.g. BUS21-17,

224 No comprehensive dedicated rating for automotive firms, similar to the securities score, exists. But automotive firms are subject to certain sector-spanning ratings, such as the customs or tax ratings. These ratings play a role for the internal compliance management (BUS21-05), however, based on the interviews, do not appear to be considered in the supervision of business partners.

BUS21-21, EXP19-10). Furthermore, most representatives from the automotive sector described their management's and employees' compliance awareness as on the rise, especially because managers stress compliance in every meeting and employees proactively consult the compliance department in their decisions (e.g. BUS21-17, BUS21-18, BUS21-22). Interviewees appreciated the improved compliance awareness for its contribution to compliance management as well as professionalism in general management (managerial capacities) (e.g. BUS21-17, BUS21-22). With respect to corporate culture, interviewees illustrated how a conservative management approach, transparency and the promotion of values, such as integrity, diligence and openness to learn, contribute to establishing a compliance culture and thereby corroborate the importance of corporate culture as an internal influence on compliance (e.g. BUS21-11, BUS21-17, BUS21-18, BUS21-22). Moreover, interviewees from the automotive sector considered missing legal and technical know-how as a cause for problems in their compliance management in the same vein as their counterparts in other industries (e.g. BUS19-19, BUS21-05, BUS21-25).

At the same time, the significance interviewees from the automotive sector attributed to economic resources stands out in comparison to the general trend and manifestations in the securities sector. The interviews do not only illustrate that investments in compliance are especially scarce in companies facing higher financial pressure, be it due to the COVID-19 pandemic, losses caused by management mistakes and scandals or fierce competition (BUS21-05, BUS21-21, BUS21-25).

But business representatives also drew an explicit link between economic resources and other internal influencing factors, such as legal and technical know-how: The stated cause for lacking compliance-related know-how in automotive POEs is unanimously financial pressure, which leads to a lack of budgeted positions for compliance management (BUS19-19, BUS21-05, BUS21-25). This illustrates the influence of market forces and managerial thinking on compliance in the automotive industry, which is stronger as compared to the securities sector.

Similarly, the motives mentioned by interviewees from the automotive sector exhibit a strong bias towards managerial considerations; a pattern that resonates with the general findings on motives in Section 4.4.2. All the previously identified sub-categories of economic motives also play a role in the automotive industry: Pressure from authorities, e.g. the risk of being inspected and, in case of non-compliance incidents, of business operations being stopped (e.g. BUS19-19, BUS21-11), triggers compliance management alongside pressure from customers (e.g. BUS21-11, BUS21-24) and reputational considerations (e.g. BUS21-17, BUS21-25). Moreover, interviewees from the automotive sector especially recognized the beneficial economic and managerial effects of compliance management, such as increased efficiency and effectiveness in business operations and better opportunities with regard to successful tender participation and business-to-business cooperation (e.g. BUS21-11, BUS21-17, BUS21-22).

Yet, compared to the securities sector, the different sub-categories of economic motives coexist in a relatively balanced manner, without one economic driver being the focal point. Furthermore, categories coexist with the other motives discussed in Section 4.4.2, namely social and normative motives as well as personal implications and previous incidents. For instance, business representatives from the automotive sector explained compliance actions taken with consideration for their companies' social responsibility and role as a corporate citizen (normative motives) as well as the importance society attaches to compliance, which leads to social expectations their businesses strive to meet (social motives) (BUS19-10, BUS21-22). Moreover, business representatives, especially on an executive level, feared personal implications in case of non-compliance incidents (e.g. BUS19-10) and were motivated to implement compliance management with previous incidents in mind, be it problems their own company has experienced or malpractices observed in the industry (e.g. BUS19-19, BUS21-21, BUS21-25). This breadth in motives is another sign for the diversity that exists with regard to the notion of compliance in the automotive sector.

Surprisingly, interviewees from the automotive sector did not list international pressure as a motive for compliance-related actions. It seems as if international compliance influences from other business actors have already been internalized and are no longer perceived as a pressure that triggers compliance practices. The fact that international influences nevertheless play an important role in compliance management is illustrated in the following section on compliance practices in the automotive sector.

6.2.5 Corporate compliance practices in the automotive sector

Similar to the interviews with representatives from the securities sector, the insights gained from interviewees in the automotive sector also resemble the general cross-sectoral trends outlined in Section 4.5.2 to a large extent, both with regard to companies' compliance management learning processes and actual compliance practices.

In terms of compliance-related learning, all of the four pathways outlined in Section 4.5.2[225] appeared in the interviews conducted in the automotive sector. For instance, one interviewee described how his company's CEO introduced compliance management to the company step by step as the firm grew (BUS21-17). Another business representative highlighted compliance-related learning parallel to authorities' regulation and enforcement learning process, when he elaborated on the changes in the automotive sector since 2013/14, when the SASAC started to pay more attention to compliance management (BUS21-22). He recounted that it was around the same time, that compliance became an important consideration in the automotive sector (BUS21-22). Yet, many automotive companies have only started to implement compliance management since the 'SOE Compliance Guidelines' were released in 2018 (BUS21-22). Hence, only since 2018 has compliance become a common consideration for all companies in the automotive sector (BUS21-22). Consequently, compliance management in the automotive sector has not matured yet, especially among domestic Chinese players (BUS21-22).

However, based on the interviews, compliance learning from professional networks and in response to international pressure seem to play a much more important role than the pathways mentioned above. Interviewees described how they have learned to conduct compliance management by hiring external compliance experts as compliance management staff and consulting professional service firms (e.g. law or accounting firms) for compliance audits (e.g. BUS21-05, BUS21-17, BUS21-18). Via the external support from professional compliance experts, automotive companies have not only received regulatory advice and set up adequate local compliance management systems, but also ensured high customs ratings and adequate supervision of their supply chain partners' compliance (BUS19-19, BUS21-05, BUS21-25). Besides learning from professional networks, compliance management learning as a response to international pressure seems to be especially important in the automotive sector. Several business representatives mentioned the dominant influence of their enterprises' international headquarters on their firm's compliance management in China (e.g.

225 The four pathways are learning as the company grows, learning parallel to authorities' regulation and enforcement learning process, learning from professional networks and learning in response to international pressure.

BUS21-05, BUS21-18, BUS21-22, BUS21-25). For example, one interviewee stated that his firm's international "mother company introduced the notion of compliance [to his firm and his company] found it very interesting" ("母公司带来了合规这个理念，我们觉得很有意思", BUS21-22). Other interviewees explained that they receive material and advice from their international headquarters, which they only slightly adapt to the local Chinese conditions (e.g. BUS21-05, BUS21-18, BUS21-25). Furthermore, visits from international leadership to China, regular meetings of compliance officers across the globe and visits to the international headquarters for compliance seminars have fostered the exchange on compliance and thereby compliance-related learning (e.g. BUS19-19, BUS21-24, BUS21-25). In addition, for domestic automotive companies without international shareholders, international product standards, which are higher than those in China, trigger compliance-related improvements (BUS19-10).

These influences have led to a comparatively decent historical compliance performance of firms in the automotive sector. The comparison of a random sample of automotive firms' risk and social credit data from Qichacha with a cross-sectoral sample shows that the average number of entries for historical risks recorded in the automotive sector (44) is significantly lower than across industries (69) (see Table 11[226]). This means that historically, automotive firms have been exposed to a lower number of litigation cases compared to the average across industries; a level similar to the average historical risk, firms in the securities sector have been facing (43), which indicates that in both sectors, compliance levels have historically been above the Chinese average[227].

226 For more details on the recorded categories and the sampling, contact the author.

227 These data points serve as an approximation for the compliance levels, since the constructionist analysis has shown that these are important categories, which influence the construction of the meaning and measurement of compliance (see Section 5.4.2). While their quantitative nature makes them objectivist tools, these proxies are only used to highlight the effect on the construction of compliance in a specific context as well as to complement and confirm the findings from the fieldwork that resulted from a constructionist approach. Changes in values do not exclusively result from changes in firms' internal management, but are potentially also influenced by changes in supervision rigor over time. Since companies are, however, supposed to respond to these changes adequately in their compliance management, the captured trends provide a rough estimation of the constructed compliance levels in the respective sector.

Table 11: Analysis of Qichacha's risk and social credit data

Sample type	Risk data (average number of entries)			Social credit data (share of companies with entries in percent)			
	Own risks	Relational risks	Historical risks	Subject to enforcement due to untrustworthy behavior	Subject to enforcement	Irregular operations	Severe legal violations
Cross-sectoral sample	28	99	69	14.0	15.5	6.0	2.0
Securities sector sample	23	349	43	3.5	5.0	3.5	2.0
Automotive sector sample	31	102	44	17.5	14.0	6.0	1.5

Despite the decent historical performance, the automotive sector's current compliance performance only meets the Chinese average[228], as shown by several indicators: The average number of entries for own risks and relational risks in the automotive sector (31 and 102) are comparable to those in the cross-sectoral sample (28 and 99). The same is true for social credit data, where the share of companies with entries indicating severe legal violations (auto: 1.5 percent, cross-sectoral: 2.0 percent), irregular operations (both 6.0 percent) and subject to enforcement (auto: 14.0 percent, cross-sectoral: 15.5 percent) in the two samples are alike. Only in the share of entities that have been subject to enforcement due to untrustworthy behavior (17.5 percent) does the automotive sector perform worse than the average (14.0 percent); a phenomenon, which does not appear in the interviews, but explains the importance of automotive firms' third-party management, especially in the context of government tenders. The comparison with the current performance of firms in the securities sector shows that this centrally regulated sector with prescriptive compliance management requirements performs better on most indicators. For instance, the

228 The quantitative data cannot explain, whether the Chinese average has improved or the automotive sector's performance has deteriorated over time. But the interview data (see Chapter 4) as well as the Blue Books 2018 and 2019 (CICLA et al., 2019, 2018) indicate that across China, compliance awareness, management and performance have improved. Hence, it is more likely that the Chinese average has increased, than that the automotive industry's compliance has worsened.

securities sector has an average number of own risk entries of 23 as well as significantly lower shares of companies with social credit-related entries than the average and the automotive sector (see Table 11)[229].Against the background of the comparably high level of government enforcement measures the automotive sector faces (CICLA et al., 2019, p. 64), this average compliance performance indicates that automotive companies have implemented at least partially successful means to ensure compliance. Indeed, the elaborations on compliance management practices in the interviews from the automotive sector reflect that the six key international best practices for compliance management are also adopted by businesses in this sector (see Table 12).

Table 12: Examples of manifestations of international best practices for compliance management in the Chinese automotive sector

Best practice	Examples from the Chinese automotive sector
Solid formal compliance management structures	Compliance teams, either as a dedicated compliance department or integrated in other functional teams (e.g. legal or internal audit departments) (e.g. BUS21-05, BUS21-11, BUS21-18, BUS21-22, BUS21-24)
	A top-level compliance committee, which includes managers from different business functions and makes compliance decisions (e.g. BUS21-05, BUS21-24, BUS21-25)
	Compliance guidelines and certifications (e.g. production-related standards) integrated in compliance management systems (e.g. BUS19-19, BUS21-11, BUS21-17, BUS21-18, BUS21-21, BUS21-24)
	Process controls and approvals by the compliance management (e.g. BUS19-10, BUS21-17, BUS21-25)
	Internal compliance monitoring via regular and unannounced audits of business processes and business units (e.g. BUS19-10, BUS21-11, BUS21-17, BUS21-18, BUS21-22)
Embeddedness	Compliance controls at critical process steps and integrated into the IT-system (e.g. BUS19-10, BUS19-19, BUS21-15, BUS21-17)
	Compliance as a criterion for performance evaluations, promotions and bonuses (BUS21-24, BUS21-25)

229 Only the average entry number of relational risks is at 349 and therefore significantly higher in securities as compared to the cross-sector and automotive samples. A potential explanation is the high number of investment activities in businesses and therefore an above-average number of firms that securities companies are related to. For a more comprehensive comparison of the two cases, refer to Section 7.1.3.

Best practice	Examples from the Chinese automotive sector
Good management practices	Comprehensive and constant management oversight via audits, compliance reports, etc. (e.g. BUS19-19, BUS21-05, BUS21-11, BUS21-17, BUS21-18, BUS21-21, BUS21-25)
	Dialog on compliance topics with employees via regular and on-demand trainings, compliance staff's consultation of business units in compliance-related questions, communication (e.g. via the intranet or email) (e.g. BUS21-11, BUS21-12, BUS21-17, BUS21-18, BUS21-25)
	Stringent consequence management in case of non-compliance incidents via investigations and punishments, depending on the gravity of the issue and according to pre-defined criteria (e.g. BUS19-10, BUS19-19, BUS21-11, BUS21-18, BUS21-25)
	Compliance management incentives, e.g. monetary rewards for reporting non-compliance incidents, small presents for the participation in compliance-related activities (BUS21-11, BUS21-24)
Top-level commitment	An increasing amount of resources invested in compliance management by the top management, be it for dedicated compliance events or day-to-day compliance management (BUS19-19, BUS21-22)
	Frequent communication of compliance-related topics to employees by the management, including the CEO (e.g. BUS19-19, BUS21-05, BUS21-17, BUS21-25)
	The top management's role model function and concrete behavioral standards related to compliance from the top, e.g. via compliance commitments signed by employees (BUS21-17, BUS21-21, BUS21-22)
A compliance culture	Promotion of compliance via internal communication, events and regular trainings, e.g. trainings for new recruits or quarterly seminars for employees (e.g. BUS19-10, BUS21-05, BUS21-18, BUS21-22, BUS21-24)
	(Anonymous) complaint and reporting channels (e.g. hotline, email, online system) for non-compliance incidents, both for employees and customers (e.g. BUS19-19, BUS21-11, BUS21-18, BUS21-21, BUS21-25)
Values-based compliance management	Awareness of the value of compliance actions that surpass the legal minimum and risks of business partners' non-compliance incidents (e.g. for the company's reputation) (e.g. BUS19-10, BUS21-17, BIS21-25)
	The promotion of values related to compliance and the benefits of compliance, e.g. via speeches, activities and events (BUS21-05, BUS21-24, BUS21-25)
	Recognition of the protective function of compliance and implementation of preventative measures, e.g. background checks, compliance advice in product development (e.g. BUS19-19, BUS21-18)

At the same time, the interviews from the automotive sector also indicated deviations from international best practices. For instance, the divergences identified in Section 4.5.2 also pertain to the automotive sector:

- *The impact of the CCP's discipline system:* State-backed automotive firms describe the CCP's discipline system as a system that co-exists with compliance management (BUS21-24). They attributed the responsibility to ensure accountability in individuals' conduct to the Party discipline system, whereas compliance management is focused on the identification and prevention of systemic problems (e.g. business process design) (BUS21-24). Hence, the two functions cooperate in cases where responsibilities overlap (BUS21-24). In one firm, initially, staff, whose function was to ensure discipline, was even transferred to the newly established compliance department, since their expertise fit most closely to what was required for compliance management (BUS21-22). While the co-existence of the two systems seems to work in general, one interviewee described a conflict between the compliance department (backed by the foreign shareholder) and the discipline inspection department (backed by the Chinese majority shareholder) in a JV, which ultimately led to the removal of the compliance department, since the Chinese shareholder possessed more power (BUS21-05); a sign of the Party-state's influence on actors in the automotive industry.
- *Strong use of IT in compliance management*: Automotive companies in China use IT both for their internal compliance management and supervision of business partners' compliance. Internally, companies have compliance risk data bases as well as self-developed software tailored to their compliance management needs (e.g. BUS21-11, BUS21-22). Yet, interviews also pointed to the limitations of technology and the importance of human interpretation and contextualization of data (BUS21-11). In terms of the management of business partners' compliance, automotive firms possess data bases for business partner selection and monitoring as a standard feature (e.g. BUS21-25). In addition, the example of an automotive firm that has developed a vehicle lock system in case of missing customer payments (see Section 4.5.2) illustrates that companies in the automotive sector are increasingly creative with regard to the use of technology (BUS19-10).
- *Transparency and rating mechanisms:* As described in Section 5.4 in general, automotive firms are subject to transparency and rating mechanisms in the context of the SCS, but also exploit them in their compliance management. Representatives from automotive firms especially highlighted that the personal implications that individuals face in case of non-compliance incidents as well as the benefits from high ratings (e.g. tax, customs) have heightened their attention of compliance man-

agement (e.g. BUS19-10, BUS21-05, BUS21-21). One automotive firm even employs dedicated staff responsible for maintaining a high customs rating (BUS21-05). While being affected by and reacting to transparency and rating mechanisms of their own business via compliance management, company representatives at the same time also exploit the conveniently gained transparency (including blacklist information) about business partners for their own benefit, e.g. in third-party management (e.g. BUS19-19, BUS21-18, BUS21-24, BUS21-25). In contrast to information transparency, ratings, blacklists and related punishments, redlists and rewards do not seem to influence automotive companies' compliance management (BUS21-17). In addition, some automotive companies reflect the SCS's transparency and rating mechanisms in their internal compliance management in a similar fashion as described in Section 5.4.2, e.g. via setting up internal blacklists and compliance ratings for business partners (BUS21-05, BUS21-17, BUS21-25) as well as incorporating compliance ratings for all business departments and processes in one integrated IT-system (BUS21-22). According to the interviewee, the goal of this transparent rating system is not the rating itself, but rather to use this mechanism with clear and standardized compliance criteria to improve compliance management across the company (BUS21-22).

In addition, compliance management in the automotive sector exhibits two sector-specific features. First, managing business partners' compliance management constitutes a feature of compliance. For instance, companies in the automotive sector impose compliance requirements on their business partners, document them in contracts and supervise each other via background checks and audits (e.g. BUS21-05, BUS21-11, BUS21-24, BUS21-25). In case of compliance-related contract violations, business partners are punished (BUS21-22). While this compliance feature is also prevalent in other types of manufacturing industries (e.g. EXP19-10, EXP19-13), it nevertheless distinguishes compliance practices in the automotive sector from service-oriented sectors, e.g. the securities sector.

Second, the organizational set-up of compliance management across automotive companies exhibits high variations compared to other sectors, such as the securities sector. While some companies possess a dedicated compliance department, at times even with contact persons in each business unit (e.g. BUS21-05, BUS21-24), other firms in the automotive sector allocate compliance-related tasks to other departments, e.g. the legal, internal audit, risk control or finance units (BUS21-11, BUS21-18, BUS21-24).

Some businesses even spread the compliance-related responsibility across different departments over the entire organization, depending on the best possible fit for a respective task (e.g. BUS19-10, BUS21-21). This variation in organizational set-up explains the anomaly identified for the automotive sector in the Blue Book 2019, where automotive firms seem to perform well in their compliance management, while exhibiting comparably low shares of dedicated compliance management departments, policies, etc. (Section 4.5.1 and CICLA et al., 2019, p. 64, 70, 74, 75).

The variability in the organizational set-up shows that compliance management practices in the automotive sector are not as homogeneous as in the securities sector and that compliance can be reached in many ways. The reasons for this difference are likely the centrifugal regulatory set-up in the automotive sector as well as the higher organizational complexity of automotive firms (due to production processes and supply chains). Nevertheless, compliance management in the automotive sector still displays a high similarity to international compliance practices and therefore a high degree of institutional isomorphism, which is mainly caused by interactions with professional compliance networks and international pressure (normative and coercive isomorphism).

6.2.6 Consequences for the construction of corporate compliance in the automotive sector

This sub-case's in-depth investigation has provided insights into the construction of the meaning and social practices of compliance in the automotive industry. Taken together, the empirical results from the process tracing and interviews illustrate the transfer process of the international concept of compliance to the Chinese automotive sector and, based on these findings, the key features of the meaning and social practices of compliance, as constructed in this sector.

As expected, the transfer process of compliance to the Chinese automotive sector has been strongly affected by international influences. However, taking a detailed look at the research insights for the automotive sector from the perspective of Dolowitz and Marsh's (2000, p. 9) octo-dimensional policy transfer framework elicits several nuances of this transfer that deserve mentioning (see Table 13). The empirical data described above has shown that the key actors involved in transferring the institution of compliance to the Chinese automotive sector have been foreign MNEs, compliance experts and consultants. They introduced the meaning and social practices of compliance, as constructed in the international business environment, to automotive firms in China. Agents from the Chinese Party-state (e.g. bureaucrats, government officials) only reacted to the compliance trend that emerged from the bottom up. This reaction entailed the transfer of compliance-related elements from the Chinese financial sector, where the notion of compliance had existed before. However, based on the insights described above, this second transfer pathway seems to have had less influence on the construction of compliance in the automotive sector, as compared to the bottom-up transfer from the international arena.

Table 13: Policy transfer framework according to Dolowitz and Marsh (2000, p. 9) with results for the transfer of compliance to the Chinese automotive sector

Dimension	Manifestations
Reason for transfer	Mixture of drawing lessons from international examples, international pressure, obligations (compliance as a condition attached to business activity) and direct imposition
Transfer agents	MNEs, consultants, think tanks, international organizations, bureaucrats
Transfer object	Compliance as an institution as well as related ideologies, instruments and behavioral standards
Transfer path	Mainly cross-national from international organizations, governments, MNEs and professional networks; partly also within the nation from the financial sector
Degree of transfer	Emulation
Constraints on transfer	Lacking cultural proximity and awareness, structural institutional feasibility, economic climate
Demonstration of transfer	Via official regulatory documents, media, reports, conferences, meetings, etc.
Reasons for failure	Incomplete transfer

Due to the dominance of the bottom-up process, a mixture of reasons for the transfer co-exist in the automotive sector, depending on the actors involved, e.g. direct imposition for Chinese subsidiaries of foreign MNEs, international pressure for Chinese firms going abroad or compliance obligations determined in contracts with business partners. Another consequence of this bottom-up transfer process is the degree of the transfer, namely emulation. Emulation means that the key ideas and concepts related to compliance have been transferred from the bottom up, without any actor or factor requiring Chinese automotive firms to directly copy the best practices and meaning of compliance as constructed internationally. The clearest sign for this flexible bottom-up approach is the variety in the constructed meaning and social practices of compliance, as described above, which stems from the multi-level governance approach in the automotive sector and the ensuing choices companies have in the configuration of their compliance approaches.

Yet, this flexibility with regard to compliance also bears the risk that compliance is neglected in situations of high economic pressure, as the examples of lacking resources for compliance staff have shown; a major constraint to the transfer. Moreover, even when companies are willing to pay attention to compliance, a potential for failure still lies in the need to transfer cultural and behavioral elements related to compliance. These elements are referred to as compliance culture or compliance awareness in the interviews as well as official discourse. Their transfer takes time and has not been achieved throughout the automotive sector, as has been pointed out above. More recently, the Party-state regulators seem to complement the compliance structures that were originally developed from the bottom up with a top-down dissemination of compliance culture and awareness via the SCS and its educational campaigns.

This characterization of the transfer of the concept of compliance to the Chinese automotive sector as a bottom-up, endogenously emerging process strongly driven by private-sector actors (especially foreign MNEs and consultancies) differs considerably from the top-down policy transfers coordinated by bureaucrats and government officials commonly described in the academic discourse (e.g. Prince, 2010, Kwon, 2009, Bulmer et al., 2007, Post, 2005). Hence, the case study of corporate compliance construction in the automotive sector illustrates an additional pathway for policy transfer, namely a habitual, endogenously emerging transfer process (see Figure 38), which has its origin in the existing international compliance understanding and practices that were introduced to actors in the Chinese automotive sector from the bottom up (e.g. via international consultancies and foreign MNEs). Based on this influence, actors in the Chinese automotive sector developed an understanding of compliance and implemented related practices, which were ultimately recognized by actors in the Party-state. These actors consolidated the existing compliance understanding and practices into regulations related to compliance, which then triggered an adaption to these regulations among actors in the automotive industry. The change in practices can, as a consequence, again lead to adjustments in regulations, i.e. trigger a continuous development cycle with regard to compliance.

Figure 38: Schematic transfer process of the concept of compliance to the Chinese automotive sector (author's design)

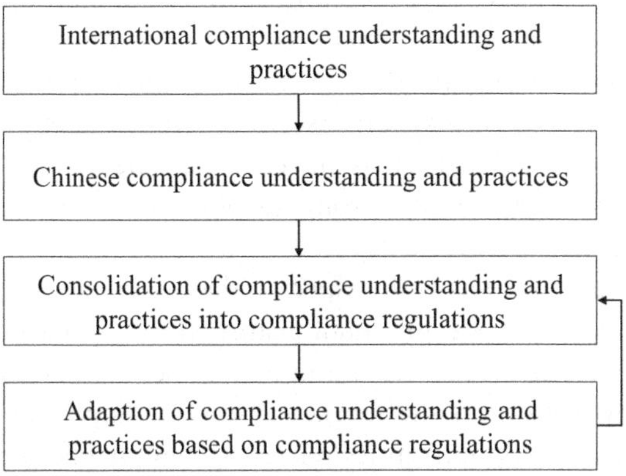

The understanding and social practices of compliance that have emerged from this construction process in the automotive sector exhibit two salient characteristics. First, this research has identified several ways of how a comparatively high level of variety with regard to compliance has manifested itself. For instance, the official compliance-related discourse in the automotive sector does not contain highly prescriptive compliance-related regulations and addresses compliance via a wide range of topics and regulators, each with different focal points. Furthermore, the characteristics of regulations in the automotive sector vary greatly depending on the topic, e.g. between very concrete and detailed rules and vague guidelines as well as between mature and immature regulatory guidance. In addition, the intensity in supervision varies between different firm types (e.g. SOEs and JVs versus domestic POEs and foreign MNEs). These three phenomena can, at times, lead to regulatees' impression of scattered supervision. Another example for the prevailing variety is automotive firms' different approaches to compliance. On the one hand, proactivity levels regarding compliance diverge, depending on companies' location in the automotive value chain, with greater international exposure tending to lead to a more proactive compliance management approach. On the other hand, compliance-related organizational set-ups exhibit a high level of diversity across automotive enterprises. Moreover, motives for compliance are broadly spread across all identified categories and thereby also reflect variety. The fact that this research has identified institutional isomorphism with respect to compliance in the automotive sector (e.g. similarities of compliance management practices to international best practices and a high congruence with regard to the constructed connotations of compliance) does not contradict the variety described, since the identified variations often prevail within the confines of international best practices (e.g. solid formal compliance management structures). In cases where companies overstep these boundaries, the divergences from international best practices also constitute patterns across a larger set of firms and thereby also contribute to institutional isomorphism across the sector (e.g. the role of Party discipline in compliance management, the strong use of IT as well as transparency and rating mechanisms).

Second, managerial logic with respect to the understanding and practices of compliance constitutes a dominant feature in the automotive sector. The official discourse reflects this feature in its link between credit and compliance, the commodification and marketization of compliance as well as the emphasis of business opportunities related to compliance. This managerial way of constructing compliance in the official discourse is mirrored in business representatives' responses, who indicated a dominance of economic compliance motives and a managerial perspective on firm-internal capacities and characteristics with respect to compliance. For instance, resources invested in compliance are highly dependent on the overall economic climate and firms' economic situation. The managerial take on compliance is reinforced by the fact that automotive firms, especially foreign MNEs, act as regulators themselves via their third-party management and thereby complement the scattered top-down regulatory regime institutionalized by the Party-state and – in doing so – add another layer of complexity to compliance management for firms in the automotive sector. The managerial regulation approach innate in the SCS (see Section 5.2.4) further amplifies this tendency of incorporating elements of third-party management into compliance management, e.g. via the SCS's requirements for tender applications and the provision of transparency.

In all, the findings from this sub-case illustrate that the construction of compliance in the automotive sector differs from the securities sector, even though both sub-cases mirror certain general cross-sectoral features. The following Part III places these findings in the context of this study's research questions, compares the findings from the securities and automotive sectors (Section 7.1.3) and thereby highlights this study's research contributions.

Part III Research contributions

7 Discussion

The case study of compliance in China, with its three sub-cases on the SCS, the securities as well as the automotive sectors, has provided insights into the way compliance is constructed in China to deal with the increasing regulatory complexity corporate actors face. This chapter first summarizes and contextualizes how the empirical insights described in Part II answer the first three research sub-questions of this study (Section 7.1), namely:

1. What are the constructed connotations of, influences on and social practices of corporate compliance in China? How do the Chinese manifestations deviate from international best practices?
2. How does the SCS affect corporate compliance construction?
3. How does the construction of corporate compliance differ between industries?

Because of the systemic nature of compliance at the interface between the business and regulatory sphere and the resulting reciprocal influences between the constructed notion of compliance and the regulatory regime, these insights gained into the construction of compliance can also contribute to the understanding of the regulatory regime. Therefore, the chapter then attends to the fourth research sub-question in Section 7.2 that investigates which insights can be deduced from the identified construction of compliance regarding the nature of the Chinese political economy and regulatory regime.

7.1 Discussion of the empirical findings

7.1.1 Corporate compliance in China compared to international best practices

The empirical findings have disclosed the influences on compliance, the prevailing compliance practices and the meaning of the concept of compliance in China in order to attain an understanding of how compliance is constructed. With respect to all of these aspects, the research has yielded notable results relevant to the international compliance discourse.

Regarding influences on compliance, this study has provided evidence that the existing compliance framework (see Figure 4 in Section 2.4) is missing two dimensions, which this research proposes to add: Time and international developments (see Figure 39). On the one hand, the interviews with business representatives and experts highlighted the important influence the factor 'time' has on compliance (e.g. BUS19-13, BUS21-22, EXP19-05). Since compliance as an institution does not only consist of structural elements, but is majorly created by continuously reproduced social patterns, time is an important component. Specifically, the amount of time passed in the implementation of compliance practices affects the way compliance is constructed, i.e. its meaning and social practices. Therefore, even when keeping all other influences stable, compliance possesses a different quality at a later point in time, since the level of internalization and the depth of practices vary. As the passage of time also leads to changes in other influencing factors, e.g. the social, economic and political environments, which then affect compliance, time plays an even more important role as an influence on compliance. Consequently, the factor 'time' has to be added to the compliance framework as an all-encompassing element (see Figure 39).

On the other hand, this study has provided strong evidence regarding the important influence of international developments on the way compliance is constructed nationally. For instance, the process of how compliance was introduced to China has shown that this institution was transferred from the international sphere to China. Moreover, many interviewees emphasized the significance of the international context and international actors for businesses' compliance learning (e.g. BUS19-08, BUS21-09, BUS21-20) and as a compliance motive (e.g. BUS19-17, BUS21-09, BUS21-20). Another sign for the importance of this influence is the fact that overall, compliance practices, as outlined by business representatives in China, are in line with international best practices for compliance management. These examples elucidate that international developments majorly affect the way compliance is constructed on a national level. Thus, this factor needs to be included into the compliance framework as an additional external factor (see Figure 39).

Figure 39: Updated compliance framework based on the research results (author's design)

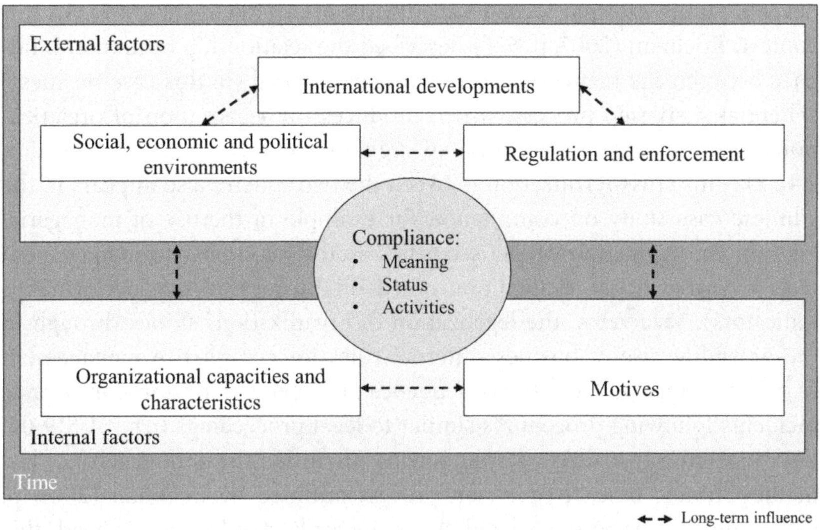

Besides the adaption of the compliance framework itself, the empirical findings also contribute to the understanding of the different influencing factors as well as their relationships to each other. First, the international academic discourse has highlighted the dominance of the political over the social environment, especially in autocratic political settings (e.g. Van Rooij, 2006). However, the example of China shows that while the political sphere certainly controls the social environment to avoid threats to the political leadership's legitimacy, these leaders nevertheless also encourage the social environment to engage in compliance construction within certain limits. The most prominent examples for this phenomenon are the Chinese official discourse's encouragement of self-regulation and mutual regulation between actors in the business sphere (e.g. GEN-20160513, SCS-20170915(8)), as well as the support of society to act as regulators by providing structures, such as complaint hotlines and platforms (e.g. 12315.cn, GEN-20170315), which society can use to report problematic corporate behavior.

Second, the interviews illustrated the complex relationship between the economic and the regulatory environments, with many aspects carrying weight in the construction of compliance, e.g. the strategic importance of an industry and the maturity of a business field (e.g. BUS19-03, BUS19-18, BUS21-13). The close entanglement of these two spheres has been reflected in the concept of the endogeneity of law, which posits that regulations are never a purely external force to an organization (Edelman, 2007). In this context, Edelman (2007, p. 67f) described the relationship of mutual influence between the regulatory and the organizational (in this case business) sphere as a six-step process, which produces the legalization of organizations and the managerialization of regulations (see Figure 6 in Section 2.4.1.2). This cross-fertilization between the two spheres also appears in the Chinese case study on compliance, for example in the use of managerial logic in the regulation of the securities sector's compliance management (e.g. securities score evaluations based on businesses' key performance indicators). Vice versa, the legalization of organizations shines through in the prevailing use of business-internal rules for compliance management (e.g. compliance policies) or consequence management for non-compliance incidents following procedures similar to legal proceedings (e.g. BUS19-02, BUS19-19, BUS21-10). Yet, despite having identified the endogeneity of law in the Chinese case, the six-step process outlined by Edelman (2007, p. 67f) could not be reconstructed chronologically step by step. Instead, this research has found that the endogeneity of law in the Chinese case is a product of constant interactions between the regulatory and the business sphere in the context of compliance. This regular exchange between the two spheres, which takes place via interactions between the two parties' representatives, e.g. at conferences, in day-to-day work and during inspections, leads to the mutual influence.

Third, in the category of organizational capacities and characteristics, this study has identified two aspects that influence compliance in companies in China, namely corporate culture and employees' general compliance awareness. While compliance best practices promote compliance culture-building as an important means to achieve desired compliance levels (e.g. Habisch, 2012, Sokol, 2012), the academic discourse has so far not discussed how the overall corporate culture and general compliance awareness influence this process. Business representatives in China, however, draw a causal relationship between corporate culture, employees' general compliance awareness and companies' compliance levels (e.g. BUS19-03, BUS21-11, BUS21-15). Consequently, these two factors should be included in the list of aspects to consider in the category of organizational capacities and characteristics.

Fourth, based on the interviews, the internal dimension 'motives' can be specified and enhanced. On the one hand, six standard sub-categories for economic motives that dominate in China can be gleaned from the interviews:

- Authorities' requirements (e.g. BUS21-02, BUS21-07, BUS21-10)
- International compliance requirements (e.g. BUS19-07, BUS21-09, BUS21-20)
- Customer demands (e.g. BUS19-10, BUS21-11, BUS21-24)
- Reputation (e.g. BUS21-06, BUS21-16, BUS21-19)
- Professionalism (BUS19-02, BUS21-15, BUS21-17)
- Business opportunities (BUS19-02, BUS19-07, BUS19-09).

On the other hand, this research has identified two motivations for compliance that do not fit the standard categories of economic, social and normative motives as defined by previous research. The first new driver is 'previous incidents', i.e. motivation drawn from a company's experience of a non-compliance incident or the observation of other firms' experience of dealing with a non-compliance incident (e.g. BUS19-01, BUS19-14, BUS21-21). The second motivation, 'personal implications', refers to a firm management's drive to comply with regulations due to the fear of personal implications in case of a non-compliance incident, e.g. reputational loss and personal punishments (e.g. BUS19-11, BUS19-15, BUS21-06). Both of these new motivations consist of a combination of economic, social and normative motives, which the literature highlights (e.g. Lehmann Nielsen and Parker, 2012, Parker and Lehmann Nielsen, 2011c, Gunningham, Thornton and Kagan, 2004), but cannot be exclusively attributed to one category. For instance, in case of a fear of personal implications, a business representative may not only worry about negative effects on the personal income (economic motive), but also a loss of face in social circles (social motive) and a bad conscience (normative motive). Hence, these new motivations for compliance highlight some overarching compliance drivers, which defy allocation into the standard motive categories. An analysis of compliance motives should therefore not be undertaken based on the assumption that the drivers, which trigger actors to behave in a compliant manner, can be exclusively attributed to one type of motive.

Based on a comprehensive analysis of the influences that affect the construction of compliance in China, this research also gained insights into prevailing compliance practices and the meaning of the concept of compliance in China. In this context, the interview data revealed four paths to compliance-related learning in companies: Compliance learning as companies grow, in response to international pressures, via professional networks and parallel to authorities' regulatory learning processes (see Section 4.5.2). While these four ways of compliance learning are not mutually exclusive, they nevertheless highlight the importance of different influencing factors and actors on compliance practices in Chinese firms. They also explain the high level of institutional isomorphism that this study found with regard to compliance management in China. Enterprises do not only adopt compliance management based on international best practices, via the pressure from international actors and professional networks (coercive and normative isomorphism), but in addition, also develop compliance management via authorities' guidance (coercive isomorphism) and model compliance practices after other businesses' examples (mimetic isomorphism). Since the Chinese official discourse's construction of the meaning of compliance is largely in line with international best practices, it is not surprising that compliance practices in China also resemble international best practices to a large extent.

Yet, the analysis has identified three features in the Chinese understanding and practices of compliance that stand out. First, in China, the CCP's discipline inspection system co-exists with compliance management in firms backed by the Party-state. While these two systems are generally clearly separated, overlaps in responsibilities (e.g. with regard to anti-corruption work) and mutual influences (e.g. via staff moving between the two departments) exist (e.g. BUS21-05, BUS21-10, BUS21-24). Furthermore, this research has identified an incident, which illustrates that compliance management in firms, where these two departments co-exist, ultimately possesses less power than the Party discipline inspection department (BUS21-05). Consequently, in companies backed by the Chinese Party-state, compliance management merely constitutes a tool, with the compliance function's existence being at the discretion of the Party-state. Thus, the independence of the compliance function in businesses can be called into question.

In contrast to this China-specific aspect, the following two features are more likely to become international practices: On the one hand, the concept of compliance has been extended in China, especially via the SCS. Compliance is no longer only constructed as the adherence to rules set by the company, but also entails the obligation to monitor business partners' compliance status (e.g. SCS-20170915(8)). Therefore, compliance management does not stop at the confines of the firm, but third-party management with respect to compliance, which internationally has often been defined as an element of CSR (e.g. Epstein, 2018), becomes a central aspect of firms' compliance considerations (e.g. BUS19-10, BUS21-03, BUS21-11). This way, companies obtain the responsibility for supervision and hence act as regulators and regulatees at the same time. On the other hand and related, technology, rating and transparency mechanisms, at times in combination, are intensively used for compliance management in China (e.g. BUS19-10, BUS21-04, BUS21-06). This finding reflects a general trend in China to apply technology, transparency and ratings in order to address a multitude of regulatory issues, e.g. via the 'Internet Plus' strategy (NDRC, 2020, State Council China, 2015). The SCS, as a factor exerting great influence on compliance, constitutes the culmination of this trend and is discussed in more depth in the following section.

7.1.2 The Social Credit System's impact on corporate compliance in China

Chapter 5 has described the SCS's unique enforcement approach, which combines responsive regulation with managerial elements, such as credit repair, ratings and rewards. This way, compliance, conceptualized as an element of credit and economic trust, turns into a commodity that can be exchanged, e.g. by spending money on credit repair trainings to have entries on blacklists (caused by non-compliance incidents) deleted.

But this is not the SCS's only impact on compliance: The SCS with its managerial enforcement approach reinforces, standardizes and extends the constructed meaning and social practices of compliance in China. This is reflected in the increased attention business representatives pay to compliance because of the SCS (e.g. BUS19-06, BUS19-09, BUS21-21). According to this research, the main reasons for this phenomenon are the joint punishments and shaming mechanisms incorporated in the SCS (e.g. BUS19-10, BUS19-11, BUS19-12). Since these mechanisms increase risks and costs related to non-compliance incidents, they trigger businesses' economic motives for compliance and thereby construct compliance as an economic necessity.

The standardization of compliance happens via behavioral requirements, which the SCS defines for credit and thereby for compliance, be it in the different scoring mechanisms (transparent criteria for the addition and subtraction of points), educational campaigns (which promote targeted behaviors) or behavioral thresholds for entries on black- and redlists. Even the transparency mechanism contributes to standardization, as the choice of the pieces of information that are published influences what companies consider in their evaluation of other actors. All these measures draw a rather clear picture of behaviors that are desired (high credit, i.e. high compliance levels) and that are not (low credit, i.e. low compliance levels). Evidence for this standardization are, for instance, companies that set up and adjust their compliance management systems on the basis of scoring requirements in the securities sector (e.g. BUS21-07). One expert made this standardization explicit, when she described that before the SCS, her firm used to consult other firms in defining compliance criteria (e.g. in their collaboration with third parties). However, this field of business has been declining, since the SCS provides a blueprint for how to judge business partners (EXP19-08). Consequently, the SCS further exacerbates institutional isomorphism related to compliance.

Finally, the extension of compliance manifests itself in two ways. On the one hand, the SCS and the related discourse moves away from a dichotomous construction of compliance (i.e. the choice between the two options of being or not being in compliance) to a gradual nature of the concept. Examples for this trend are credit scores and the different stages of credit repair, which represent varying levels of compliance. In such a gradual logic, compliance has the potential to become the subject of competition between actors. For this reason, credit service firms have already started to promote the benefits of compliance and to position compliance as a competitive advantage (e.g. EXP19-08, EXP21-03, PO20-ON). Because this aspect is only starting to burgeon, it remains to be seen whether the trend will prevail in the long-run. In any case, this market-based approach to compliance further corroborates the managerial logic and commodification of compliance in China.

On the other hand, as explained in the previous section, the SCS reinforces the extension of the concept of compliance to also include business partners' compliance. This happens directly via dedicated SCS mechanisms, such as requirements related to business partner compliance in tender bidding processes (e.g. negative implications in case of blacklist entries), which affect businesses' behavior (e.g. BUS19-10, BUS19-15, BUS21-17). At the same time, this phenomenon can also be observed indirectly, via the additional level of transparency provided. SCS platforms are considered highly convenient sources of information to check business partners' compliance levels (e.g. BUS19-01, BUS21-02, BUS21-13). Hence, the information categories provided on SCS platforms become key components in compliance deliberations and foster the supervision of and by third parties. By exploiting the additional transparency and compliance criteria provided by SCS platforms, companies automatically multiply the SCS's enforcement logic and thereby influence the construction of compliance.

This extension of compliance and the importance of information provided by the SCS raises the need to include information governance, i.e. the adequate governance and management of all data- and information-related matters in and for a company, into compliance considerations and practices. Hence, the SCS accelerates the general trend of increasing attention being paid to information governance in business management, which has been triggered by new technologies (e.g. digital technologies, artificial intelligence). Specifically, the massive increase in available information has created business opportunities and turned information into a strategically important resource for companies (e.g. Krause and Fischer, 2021, Gupta et al., 2018, Malecki, 2010). Firms can leverage this resource in many ways, including their compliance management.

In the Chinese context, this results in four key actions companies undertake to address information governance in their compliance management adequately: First, companies self-regulate and thereby ensure that the information presented about them on SCS platforms is positive. Thereby businesses avoid reputational and resulting financial damages (e.g. BUS19-07, BUS21-16). Second, companies need to report required information to authorities on time, but at the same time, also protect their intellectual property and sensitive information (e.g. EXP19-07, PO19-BJ). Third, firms have to check the accuracy of information published about their company on SCS platforms. In case there are mistakes, firms can apply for correction (Credit China, 2021f). Fourth, companies can use the information on other companies provided via the SCS (e.g. information on blacklist entries) in their third-party compliance management to run their business successfully (e.g. BUS19-09, BUS21-02, BUS21-13). In order to manage and exploit information in this context, the SCS fosters the application of technology-driven and transparency-related compliance management approaches by businesses, e.g. business-internal ratings and big data analysis tools for compliance management (e.g. BUS21-04, BUS21-22). While there are variations between industries in the effect of these SCS mechanisms on businesses, the general enforcement approach and businesses' reactions to the SCS are consistent across sectors, as the following section explains in greater depth using the examples of the securities and automotive sectors.

7.1.3 Differences in corporate compliance between industries in China

This study has examined the differences in compliance between industries via two sub-cases that took an in-depth look at compliance in the securities and automotive sectors. Both of these industries are of high strategic importance for the Chinese economy, yet differ in regulatory setup, nature of the business (service versus manufacturing sector) and level of international exposure. This amalgamation of similarities and differences is reflected in the two sectors' approaches to compliance, with regard to compliance transfer and construction processes as well as influences, constructed connotations and social practices of compliance.

The processes how compliance has been introduced to and constructed in the two sectors exhibit some basic similarities, while also displaying major differences. The key similarity is that compliance entered these two sectors via a transfer from the international arena. In this context, a comparison of the main dimensions of the transfers based on Dolowitz and Marsh's (2000, p. 9) policy transfer framework shows further analogies (see Table 14). For instance, the transfer object, the institution of compliance as well as related ideologies, instruments and behavioral standards, have mainly been transferred cross-nationally; a process that has been replicated between industries within China. This has been demonstrated in a multitude of ways, such as in official regulatory documents, reports, via the media, on conferences and meetings. Moreover, in both cases, a mixture of reasons initiated the transfer, with lessons drawn from international examples and international pressures playing important roles. Further similarities can be found in the actors involved in the transfer (in both cases bureaucrats, MNEs, think tanks and consultants), the constraints on the transfers related to cultural proximity and awareness, as well as the risks of failure of the transfer in case of an incomplete transfers, i.e. unsuccessful transfers of ideologies and cultural elements related to compliance, which are needed to ensure the effective implementation of compliance management (e.g. the independence of the compliance function versus the Party discipline inspection).

Table 14: Policy transfer framework according to Dolowitz and Marsh (2000, p. 9) with results for the transfer of compliance to the Chinese securities and automotive sectors

Dimension	Manifestations in the securities sector	Manifestations in the automotive sector
Reason for transfer	Mixture of drawing lessons from international examples and (indirectly) international pressure	Mixture of drawing lessons from international examples, international pressure, obligations (compliance as a condition attached to business activity) and direct imposition
Transfer agents	Government officials, bureaucrats, consultants, think tanks, MNEs[230]	MNEs, consultants, think tanks, international organizations, bureaucrats[231]
Transfer object	Compliance as an institution as well as related ideologies, instruments and behavioral standards	Compliance as an institution as well as related ideologies, instruments and behavioral standards
Transfer path	Mainly cross-national from governments and international organizations; partly also within the nation from the banking sector	Mainly cross-national from international organizations, governments, MNEs and professional networks; partly also within the nation from the financial sector
Degree of transfer	Amplification	Emulation
Constraints on transfer	Lacking cultural proximity and awareness	Lacking cultural proximity and awareness, structural institutional feasibility, economic climate
Demonstration of transfer	Via official regulatory documents, media, reports, conferences, meetings, etc.	Via official regulatory documents, media, reports, conferences, meetings, etc.
Reasons for failure	Incomplete transfer	Incomplete transfer

Despite these similarities, the analysis of the transfer and ensuing construction processes of compliance in the two sectors also revealed fundamental differences. While similar actors are involved in the transfer in both cases, their importance starkly diverges: In the securities sector, government officials and bureaucrats play a key role in adopting the concept and adapting it to the Chinese context, whereas foreign MNEs, who require Chinese firms to adopt compliance practices in collaborations, as well as compliance professionals (consultants, think tanks, etc.) are the main transfer agents in the automotive sector. Consequently, the transfer in the automotive

230 In order of importance from most to least important.
231 In order of importance from most to least important.

sector resembles an emulation, i.e. an adoption of the main ideas related to compliance, yet with leeway for adjustment to the specific context. In contrast, the authorities in the securities sector amplified compliance in China, meaning they did not merely copy international best practices, but reinforced these practices via more stringency, e.g. by enacting dedicated, highly prescriptive compliance management regulations for securities firms.

These profound divergences in the transfers have resulted in contrariant compliance construction processes in the two sectors (see Figure 40). On the one hand, compliance was constructed in a top-down manner in the securities sector: Referring to international compliance regulations, the CSRC drafted Chinese compliance regulations for the securities sector, which securities firms have to adhere to. Thus, securities companies' compliance management was established due to a strong exogenous impetus. Based on the results of the emerging understanding of compliance and related practices in securities firms, compliance regulations were adapted, resulting in changes in securities companies' behavior; potentially a continuous development process. On the other hand, the international understanding of compliance and related practices were adopted by Chinese automotive firms in a bottom-up manner, e.g. via pressure from foreign MNEs. After an understanding of compliance and related practices had emerged endogenously in the Chinese automotive sector, authorities consolidated these efforts into compliance regulations (e.g. the compliance management regulations for SOEs). Companies have had to adapt their compliance behavior to these new regulations, which authorities may react to with changes in compliance regulations; i.e. a continuous development cycle.

The two processes described above, one exogenous and constituted, the other endogenous and habitual, are akin to the processes Buß (1973) outlines for setting up competition regimes and Fischer (2000) has adapted to the Chinese competition regime. In a nutshell, these two processes describe two ways in which institutions are established: Institution-building is either triggered by exogenous factors which prescribe certain norms in order to influence future actions (targeted top-down measure) or institutions are consolidated from existing behavioral norms and actions into an officially prescribed order (spontaneous bottom-up emergence).

Figure 40: Schematic comparison of two types of compliance transfer and construction processes (author's design)

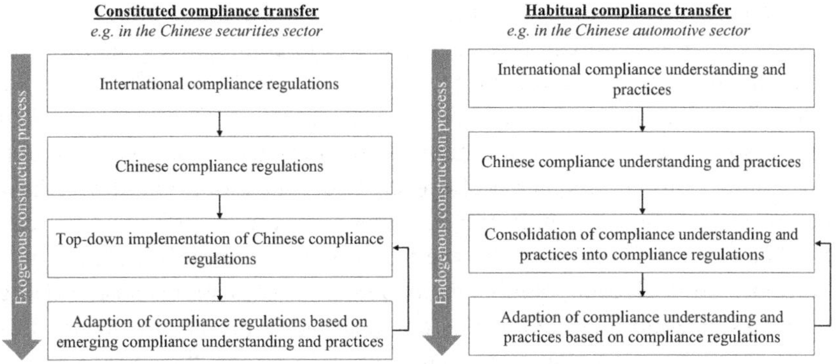

While the question whether the two processes are archetypical for compliance transfers in other sectors, countries or with reference to other transfer objects cannot be answered by this qualitative research, the findings nevertheless provide two valuable insights for policy transfers in general. First, the descriptions highlight that the processes, which were triggered after the institution of compliance was introduced to the Chinese context, have been of great importance for ingraining this transfer object in the new environment. The examination of the developments set off by the transfers gain special significance, when viewing transfer objects as 'irritants' in Teubner's (2001) sense. Yet, as outlined in Section 3.4, the academic literature on policy transfer has predominantly focused on the introduction process of a transfer object and labeling a transfer either a success or failure. Hence, beyond pointing to the need to understand the processes set off by transfers, this research also provides two examples for such developments (see Figure 40). Second, the analysis has highlighted two elements in the transfer process that have so far been understudied. On the one hand, the transfer process in the automotive sector emphasizes the important role of private actors, especially MNEs, for transfers. On the other hand, the process in the securities sector contributes an entirely new degree of transfer: Amplification, i.e. a stronger adoption of the transfer object in the new environment as compared to the environment from which the object has been transferred.

Based on these compliance construction processes, the influences on as well as the social practices and meaning of compliance in the two sectors also exhibit congruence in their basic features and at the same time considerable divergences with regard to details. In both industries, the research has identified a high level of congruence with the international compliance understanding and best practices. Furthermore, both sub-cases display the additional China-specific features in compliance practices that were identified across sectors (see Section 4.5), namely the influence of the Party discipline inspection system, the strong use of IT-systems, as well as transparency and rating mechanisms in compliance management. Yet, the elaborations in Chapter 6 also draw two contrasting pictures of how compliance is constructed. In the securities sector, the CSRC's and thereby the Party-state's hegemony over the institution of compliance stands out: Not only do dedicated compliance management regulations exist, but the measures surrounding compliance are also highly prescriptive (securities score, 'Securities Compliance Measures', etc.). Moreover, the CSRC's power with respect to compliance construction in the securities sector is reflected in the authorities' direct access to securities firms, be it via the CCO position, for which the CSRC has to approve staffing decisions, or firms' IT-systems, which the CSRC can directly connect to for supervision purposes. In case the authority identifies problems, the CSRC seems to resort to increasingly rigorous enforcement mechanisms, as the official discourse and the interviews in the securities sector illustrate (e.g. SEC-20191121(1), BUS19-15, BUS21-10). These include the adoption of more network instruments, be it the publication and shaming of punished individuals and securities companies or the transparency provided on securities firms that apply for administrative procedures (e.g. SEC-20200407, SEC-20200630). The logical consequence of these developments is that the CSRC's pressure on firms constitutes the dominant motive for business representatives in the securities sector to ensure compliance (e.g. BUS19-13, BUS21-02, BUS21-12). These phenomena lead to an extremely high level of coercive institutional isomorphism with regard to compliance, visible, for instance, in the large extent of congruence in compliance management approaches across the interviewed securities firms.

In comparison, the automotive sector displays two salient characteristics with respect to compliance, which profoundly differ from the securities sector: A high level of variety and a strong presence of managerial logic in the influences on as well as the social practices and constructed connotations of compliance. The variety found in the automotive sector in terms of compliance pertains, for instance, to compliance-related regulations, which display differing characteristics, ranging from relatively prescriptive to rather vague rules or which diverge in the regulations' level of maturity (e.g. BUS21-05, BUS21-21, BUS21-22). Furthermore, regulations often address compliance from a topic-focused perspective (e.g. anti-trust, environmental protection) and do not necessarily define the compliance management process in companies in detail (e.g. AUT-20151223, AUT-20160823, AUT-20190821). Additional variety exists in the intensity of supervision, depending on the type of firm and its location in the supply chain and, connected to this, in the level of proactivity related to compliance management practices in automotive firms. Thus, the organizational set-up for compliance management diverges among companies in the automotive sector (e.g. BUS21-05, BUS21-11, BUS21-24). This variety is paired with a strong presence of managerial logic in understanding of compliance and related practices. For instance, the official discourse connects compliance with credit and thereby commodifies compliance (e.g. AUT-20180130, AUT-20190516). Moreover, firms, especially foreign MNEs, constitute important regulators in the automotive sector. This broader set of regulators not only adds another level of complexity in companies' compliance management, but also corroborates managerial approaches in supervision. But managerial logic is not only present in enterprises' external environment, managerial thinking also applies to internal factors. For instance, economic motives for compliance dominate over other types of motives (e.g. BUS19-19, BUS21-24); companies provide compliance incentives to employees (e.g. BUS21-11, BUS21-24) and interviewees from the automotive sector position firms' scope of compliance management as contingent upon their companies' economic situation and the overall economic climate (e.g. BUS21-05, BUS21-25). As a consequence of these two characteristics, institutional isomorphism in the automotive sector does not reach the same level as in the securities sector.

These differences in compliance construction between the two sectors influence how firms in the two industries treat the SCS: In general, SCS enforcement follows general trends and plays an important role for firms in both sectors. But in detail, there are differences that mirror the centralized, Party-state dominated compliance approach in the securities sector, on the one hand, and the higher level of complexity in the automotive sector, on the other hand. Specifically, in the former case, the securities score and the integrity files predominate as the key mechanisms firms pay attention to with respect to their own compliance, while third-party management via newly attained transparency appears to play a subordinate role. In contrast, in the latter, a broader set of mechanisms is considered equally important to business representatives in the automotive sector (e.g. tax and customs scores, blacklist entries, transparency via SCS platforms such as Qichacha). Besides this variety, the handling of the SCS in the automotive sector also reflects the managerial elements depicted above, since the additional information gained on business partners via the SCS databases (e.g. the publicly-run NECIPS or the privately-run Qichacha and Tianyancha) plays an important role in automotive firms' third-party (compliance) management (e.g. BUS19-19, BUS21-18, BUS21-25).

According to the random sample of Qichacha-data analyzed for the two sectors, the two diverging approaches to compliance have resulted in different levels of what has been constructed as compliance: The share of companies with negative social credit-related entries is significantly higher in the automotive sector, e.g. only 3.5 percent of the randomly sampled firms in the securities sector possess entries of 'enforcement due to untrustworthy behavior', as compared to 17.5 percent in the automotive sector (see Table 11 in Section 6.2.5). To what extent these numbers represent substantive compliance in the sense as constructed for the respective industry and to what degree they are a result of formal or creative compliance cannot be told from the collected data. However, the analysis did not attempt to evaluate the efficiency, effectiveness or the overall success of the two compliance regimes. Instead, the findings shed light on two fundamentally different ways of how compliance is constructed under the umbrella of the overall Chinese understanding of compliance and related practices depicted in Chapter 4, and the comparison between the two industry sub-cases indicates the importance for researchers not to stop their analysis and judgments at high-level compliance features, which seem to possess a great degree of resemblance across different settings. To fully understand the construction of compliance and its effect on business, politics and society, an in-depth look at the intricacies of compliance in a specific environment, including external and internal influences, as well as the meaning and social practices of compliance and its development over time is necessary (see updated compliance framework, Figure 39 in Section 7.1.1). Because the continuous habitual repetition of small changes in behavioral patterns potentially accumulate to substantial impacts on the affected actors. Or as Edelman (2007, p. 89) explains:

> "The endogenous construction of social logics is only one process through which social change occurs, and it operates more through constitutive processes such as cultural templates and cognitive schemas than through open contestation, overt political conflict, or direct political

> mobilisation. Perhaps because it operates under the political radar, the endogenous construction of social logics is likely to be an especially powerful source of field structuration and social change".

How the construction of social logics with regard to compliance are reflected in the Chinese political economy and regulatory regime is the subject of discussion in the following section.

7.2 Implications for the Chinese political economy and regulatory regime

The previous section has discussed and contextualized this study's empirical findings on the construction of compliance in China. Because compliance is located at the interface between the business and regulatory spheres, compliance possesses a systemic nature (see Chapter 3). This means that a reciprocal influence exists between the constructed notion of compliance and the regulatory regime and that insights gained into the construction of compliance also contribute to the understanding of the political economy, especially the regulatory regime, and vice versa.

An analysis of the findings from the empirical research through the lens of compliance's systemic nature reinforces characterizations of the Chinese regulatory regime as a regulatory state (e.g. Hsueh, 2011, Pearson, 2005) and the academic discourse on the regulatory state in the Global South (e.g. Lavenex et al., 2021, Dubash and Morgan, 2012). Evidence that supports the label of a regulatory state for China can be found, for instance, in the conspicuous monopoly the Chinese Party-state possesses over rule making, rule monitoring and rule enforcement, be it directly via bureaucratic organs, such as the CSRC, or indirectly via the supervision of other regulators (e.g. self-regulatory organizations and SOEs). Moreover, the interviews showed a trend towards the norm of formal rule-based relations between different actors, be it in a business representative's description of the decreasing importance of guanxi for CCOs (BUS21-20), or several voices pointing to the increasingly limited leeway for negotiation with authorities (e.g. BUS21-05, BUS21-11).

Yet, the research also illustrated that the nature of the regulatory state in China does not resemble the regulatory state of countries in the Global North. The Chinese regulatory regime rather reflects characteristics previously described in the academic discourse on the regulatory state found in countries of the Global South (e.g. Lavenex et al., 2021, Dubash and Morgan, 2012). All of the three key attributes previous research identified for the regulatory state in the Global South, namely embedded autonomy, the co-existence of rules and deals as well as regulatory society, pertain to the Chinese regulatory regime as laid out in the following. Embedded autonomy, i.e. the deep embeddedness of regulatory institutions, which retain the control over rule making, monitoring and enforcement, in their societal and economic contexts, appears at several points in the empirical data: The SASAC is deeply integrated in the economic context via its ownership of central SOEs, but at the same time retains the control over rule making, monitoring and enforcement. For instance, the SASAC has enacted compliance management regulations and monitors SOEs via inspections, a type of supervision that POEs do not face. The research on the securities sector provided further evidence for embedded autonomy in China, e.g. the CCO position, through which the CSRC is embedded in securities firms, or the mandatory membership of securities companies in the SAC, a self-regulatory organization under the umbrella of the CSRC. Moreover, the Party-state is also deeply integrated in the economic context via the Party discipline function, which is a department internal to businesses and, at the same time, embodies the Party as a rule maker, supervisor and enforcer.

The co-existence of rules and deals in regulatory states in the Global South also applies to the Chinese case, as both the interviews and the analysis of compliance-related enforcement measures have highlighted. When discussing the leeway that companies have in the implementation of regulations, business representatives generally confirmed a certain flexibility, especially via negotiation with regulators (e.g. BUS19-13, BUS21-25). However, interviewees also specified that only the substance of a matter is up for negotiation, not the regulatory and enforcement processes themselves: For example, one business representative described that his firm discusses the classification of issues, which are identified in inspections, with the inspectors, but the company does not get the chance to influence enforcement processes that are triggered based on this classification (BUS21-10). Another example is the securities score, which consists of clear definitions regarding point subtractions and additions (e.g. SEC-20090526). But the respective regulations remain comparatively vague regarding evaluation criteria in the different focus areas, such as information technology management, customer rights protection and information disclosure (e.g. SEC-20090526). This provides a certain degree of leeway for negotiation with regard to substance, but clarity on procedural matters. However, the high level of formalism and prescriptive rules regarding compliance, such as in the securities sector, paired with options for deals related to the substance of compliance, bears the risk of creative compliance. For this reason, the focus of authorities has moved towards soft measures, such as compliance culture- and awareness-building as well as campaigns to promote values, such as integrity (e.g. the Social Credit Song, What's on Weibo, 2019). Thus, the case of compliance in China not only underlines the existence of the rules and deals phenomenon (Dubash and Morgan, 2013a), but also the risks that are associated with such a set-up.

The third theme raised in the context of the regulatory state in the Global South is the transition to and impact of a regulatory society. The Chinese case displays signs that this transition is underway: The key feature of a regulatory society is a broadening of regulators, who jointly ensure the maintenance of a rules-based system (Braithwaite, 2006). The analysis of compliance in China has confirmed that, despite of the Party-state's dominance as a regulator, other actors also take on this role, e.g. international organizations, self-regulatory organizations, the media and enterprises. In the context of compliance, international actors, which Braithwaite (2006) highlights as actors in regulatory societies in the Global South, play a particularly important role. For instance, the compliance construction process in the automotive sector has shown that the impetus for the introduction of compliance to this sector came from foreign MNEs and international organizations. But besides international actors, the Chinese case also shows that the Chinese Party-state proactively exploits the mechanisms of a regulatory society domestically to compensate for its legal system's limited enforcement capacities. The SCS is designed to serve exactly this purpose, namely to activate market participants and society to become regulators by providing transparency and evaluations of actors (e.g. list entries, scores). On the one hand, market participants and societal actors can base their decisions on the newly gained information. On the other hand, these actors are also encouraged to report negative behavior to authorities, e.g. via platforms like 12315 (12315.cn) among others. In addition to this delegation of regulatory responsibility to other actors, the Party-state also uses the SCS to pressure companies to increasingly self-regulate, especially via systemic ambiguity and reputational risks. This transformation of businesses into self-regulating regulators, i.e. simultaneously regulatees, who actively restrict themselves, and regulators, who supervise others, is an aspect of regulatory society that has not previously been discussed in the academic discourse.

Beyond these typical characteristics of the regulatory state in the Global South, this research has revealed an additional feature of the regulatory state in China: The constant interaction between the regulatory and the business spheres, that the interviews point to (e.g. BUS21-06, BUS21-16), has not only shaped the particular Chinese construction of compliance. This process also appears to have yielded a new bureaucratic device, namely managerial regulation. By managerial regulation, this study refers to an enforcement approach that features a strong managerial logic. This mechanism can contain all types of enforcement instruments (legal, economic, communicative and network instruments), but designs and combines them based on management logic. The SCS's enforcement approach constitutes the epitome of managerial regulation in the Chinese context, containing managerial mechanisms, such as rewards, complaint channels, ratings, performance indicators for business compliance as well as credit repair as improvement option. Another element of managerial regulation is that this regulatory mode exploits existing market mechanisms. In the Chinese context, this is reflected in the SCS exploiting and coopting bottom-up mechanisms, such as market competition between actors and business partner controls, for the benefit of Party-state supervision. This way, managerial regulation is a means for the Chinese government to step back and steer at a distance. Nevertheless, the low visibility of the state in managerial regulation does not mean a decrease in control. In fact, managerial regulation occurs under the 'shadow of the hierarchy', i.e. it fosters self-regulatory practices, but, if necessary, the Party-state can step in at any time (e.g. by inspecting a company, publishing new information or starting an enforcement campaign). This is possible because the Party-state retains its power via controlling the prerequisites on which managerial regulation is built, namely the regulations and the infrastructure needed for such an approach (Krause et al., 2022). The required infrastructure pertains to technology (e.g. the internet, big data and algorithms) on the one hand, and the information infrastructure (e.g. connected and consolidated databases and data-sets) on the other hand.

But this research has not only identified managerial regulation as an additional regulatory layer that reinforces Party-state control in the Chinese regulatory state, the research also provides insights into this regulatory mode's implementation and effects. Unlike regulatory approaches that scholars previously identified in their analyses of the Chinese regulatory state, such as deliberate reinforcement and decentralized engagement (e.g. Hsueh, 2011), managerial regulation is not limited to selected industries. Instead, this new regulatory mode spans across all industries, only takes slightly different shapes depending on sector-specific circumstances. For instance, the comparison between the securities and automotive sectors showed that the SCS, with its managerial approach, plays an important role in both sectors. Yet, in the securities sector the securities score and the integrity files are the dominant features, whereas in the automotive sector additional transparency, which is used for third-party management, is more prominent. This example visualizes that managerial regulation as a framework that can be filled with substance is malleable and can therefore be flexibly adapted to a broad range of circumstances.

With respect to managerial regulation's effects, a major finding of this study is the additional layer of complexity this regulatory mode adds to business operations: Companies need to consider a broader set of factors in their compliance management and incorporate third-party compliance as well as information governance into the scope of compliance management systems. Furthermore, deliberations on compliance and related decision-making become more difficult, since a more complex web of effects needs to be considered. This makes cost calculations to solve compliance decisions unfeasible and can result in diverging reactions by businesses: Some firms may start to consider compliance as a competitive advantage and optimize their operations to become best in class, as compliance consultancies have started to promote (e.g. EXP21-03, PO19-SH). Others, as a reaction to the systemic ambiguity of the SCS, strengthen their compliance practices in anticipatory obedience, in order to avoid negative consequences (e.g. BUS19-12, BUS19-19). Yet other companies seem to continue business as usual and, in case of negative consequences, make use of the SCS's credit repair mechanism to maintain regular business operations (e.g. China United Property Insurance, see Section 5.4.1). And a last group of firms is pragmatically exploiting the benefits that this new regulatory mode provides (e.g. reduced risks related to third parties) and otherwise maintain their previous compliance management activities (e.g. BUS21-17, BUS21-18). Especially this last group, which actively engages in the role as regulators, further strengthens the managerial logic in regulation and enforcement: These firms, whose essence is managerial thinking, naturally apply managerial means in their supervision and that way may even introduce further managerial devices into the regulatory sphere in the future.

These elaborations go beyond a characterization of the Chinese regulatory regime, they also intimate that the Chinese political economy resembles regulatory capitalism, as all five criteria that Levi-Faur (2005) uses to describe regulatory capitalism apply to the Chinese case:

1. A changed division of labor between the state and society, i.e. regulatory society and the mobilization of businesses as regulators in China;
2. Increased delegation by the state and self-regulatory practices, for instance visible in managerial regulation in China;
3. The proliferation of new technologies that aid regulation, such as the SCS in China;
4. Formalized relations between regulatory actors, in the Chinese case leading to a reduced role of guanxi;
5. Growing influence of experts, especially international networks of experts, e.g. in the transfer and implementation of compliance to China.

Furthermore, the Chinese case of compliance also proves that both regulation *of* and *for* capitalism is practiced by the Chinese Party-state. The ways authorities practice regulation *of* capitalism have already been extensively discussed above. In addition, the example of the SCS illustrates that regulation *for* capitalism takes place in China: The Chinese Party-state commodifies economic trust under the umbrella of credit via the SCS and creates a market for credit, e.g. payments for credit repair trainings in exchange for deleting negative information. Moreover, the analysis of the SCS's implications for the credit service industry has illustrated how the SCS has triggered the establishment of many service firms that are competing on this new market.

Yet, this research refrains from classifying the Chinese manifestation of regulatory capitalism along the dimensions of civil and state regulation, as Levi-Faur (2007, p. 16) proposes, since the line between civil and state regulation is impossible to draw in a regulatory state characterized by embedded autonomy as in China. Instead, the elaborations above suggest that both elements of regulatory capitalism, regulation and capitalism, do not describe the core principles of the Chinese political economy, but merely represent tools adopted by the Chinese Party-state. The Chinese leadership exploits capitalist market logic and regulatory approaches for its own benefit, yet does not subordinate itself to these principles. The concept of managerial regulation epitomizes this phenomenon, because this regulatory mode constitutes a tool to adopt regulatory and managerial logic under the 'shadow of the hierarchy', i.e. this regulatory mode permits the Party-state to retain control over the entire system at a distance and only directly intervene if necessary. Therefore, the Chinese political economy and regulatory regime can be called 'regulatory capitalism under the shadow of the hierarchy' and a 'regulatory state under the shadow of the hierarchy' respectively.

8 Conclusion

The starting point of this book was the effort by the Chinese leadership to build an increasingly rules-based system, which is embedded in a global trend of increasing regulations and government-imposed formalities, i.e. the era of regulatory capitalism. In order to understand related Chinese efforts and their results better, this research adopted the perspective of compliance, an approach that puts the regulatee, i.e. the company, at the center of attention. Specifically, the book set out to answer the question how compliance is constructed in China. After an elaboration on the theoretical foundations of compliance (Chapter 2) and its systemic nature, i.e. regulatory capitalism and the regulatory state (Chapter 3), the case of compliance in China was discussed (Chapter 4). The overview of the constructed meaning of compliance, the influences on and social practices of compliance management was followed by three sub-cases that investigated China-specific developments in more depth. Sub-case one on the SCS (Chapter 5) provided details on how this system, as an epitome of the Chinese trend to adopt information technologies for solving regulatory problems, affects compliance in China. Sub-cases two and three (Chapter 6) discussed and compared compliance in two industries, the securities and automotive sectors. This way, additional insights regarding the industry-specific manifestations of compliance, caused by a combination of sector-specific regulatory set-up and international influences, could be generated. Finally, Chapter 7 discussed this research's empirical findings along the four research sub-questions, i.e. compliance in China compared to international best practices, the SCS's impact on compliance, the differences in compliance between industries and the implications the findings have on characterizing the Chinese political economy and regulatory regime.

What remains to be done is a contextualization of the results by highlighting how the findings contribute to the two objectives laid out in the introduction, namely the furthering of our understanding of China as well as the discussion of the insights' global implications. With respect to China, the research identified Chinese similarities with and divergences from international conceptions of factors that influence compliance, compliance practices and the constructed meaning of compliance. Since the concept of compliance was introduced from the international arena and the implementation strongly influenced by international actors, overall a high level of congruence with international compliance practices exists. Yet, this study also identified Chinese idiosyncrasies. The key divergences from international best practices that were found are the overlap of compliance-related responsibilities between the co-existing compliance management and the CCP's discipline inspection systems, the intensive utilization of technology and transparency mechanisms, including lists and ratings, for compliance management as well as the broadening of the constructed meaning of compliance to also include third-party compliance monitoring. The latter two phenomena are mainly evoked by the SCS; because the system introduces managerial logic to the conception of compliance, e.g. via the gradual rather than dichotomous notion of compliance, which induces compliance-related competition between firms. Moreover, the SCS's contribution to transparency allows and even rewards compliance-related third-party management and encourages firms to self-regulate, e.g. via punishments and transparency as enforcement instruments. One of the ways of self-regulation that firms in China adopt as a reaction is the copying of SCS mechanisms, such as ratings, to company-internal management systems.

Both the congruence with and divergences from international compliance conceptions manifest themselves rather consistently across China, i.e. a high level of institutional isomorphism with respect to compliance prevails. A factor that further strengthens the institutional isomorphism is the SCS with its listing-, rating- and transparency-mechanisms, because these elements provide standardized sets of criteria for the evaluation of businesses and thereby encourage companies to focus on the same topics in their compliance management. Specifically, companies react to and exploit the SCS, e.g. by basing the set-up of their compliance management systems on rating criteria, mimicking SCS mechanism in their internal compliance management and utilizing the additional information provided by the SCS in their third-party management. The industry comparison between the securities and automotive sectors illustrated that, despite divergences in the focus areas of the SCS mechanisms applied in the different sectors, the SCS's core features prevail across industries, irrespective of a sector's strategic importance, international exposure, predominant ownership type or nature of the business. Yet, the industry comparison also showed that the level of institutional isomorphism varies between sectors, depending on the regulatory approach adopted in the sector as well as the sector-specific international influences: Because of a high level of centralization in the regulatory set-up and international influences being transferred via bureaucrats and government officials from the top down, the securities sector exhibits a very high level of institutional isomorphism. In contrast, the comparably decentralized regulatory set-up and the strong international influence on the company-level via JVs, international supply chains, etc. has led to a lower level of institutional isomorphism in the automotive sector. These differences also reflect two fundamentally different ways of how compliance was transferred to and constructed in China: A constituted transfer and exogenous construction process of compliance from the top down in the securities sector versus a habitual transfer and endogenous construction process from the bottom up in the automotive industry.

The findings on China have implications for practitioners both in the economic and the regulatory spheres. For practitioners in the business realm, for example, the findings regarding the expansion of the concept of compliance, especially via the SCS, are of importance. As a consequence of the constructed understanding of compliance in China, companies operating in the country face more complex strategic decisions with regard to compliance, which also contain considerations related to third-party management and their information governance. Firms need to constantly evaluate their compliance-related efforts, not only from the perspective of protecting their company against compliance risks, but also regarding potential opportunities to exploit publicly-accessible information to their benefit. The future development of the SCS, including the information infrastructure created by the Party-state, plays a vital role in this context and should therefore be continuously monitored. While this research has not identified fundamentally different treatments of foreign and domestic firms, the empirical results nevertheless show that, despite a high level of congruence between Chinese compliance and international best practices, international actors nevertheless need to react and conform to China-specific features in order to run successful operations in China; be it the rating- and transparency-mechanisms or the role of the Party-state in compliance management, e.g. in the form of Party discipline inspections in JVs. A potential challenge for firms is the drawing of compliance-related red lines for their business operations, e.g. with regard to the balance between the protection of intellectual property and information transmission to Chinese authorities for the purpose of regulatory monitoring and enforcement.

For practitioners in the regulatory field in China, in contrast, the findings hint at several compliance-related topics that should be addressed. For instance, the knowledge of how businesses react to and exploit the SCS can help regulators to improve the SCS's set-up. Specifically, already effective

SCS mechanisms can be strengthened and implemented across industries (e.g. third-party compliance requirements in government tenders) and loopholes through which firms can still evade the SCS's enforcement mechanisms could be closed (e.g. guanxi with local government officials helping to delete negative entries). That way, the SCS can contribute better to lifting companies' compliance levels and achieving a level playing field for all corporate actors in China. Moreover, the research has shown that there is still room for improving the awareness for compliance and ingraining compliance-related considerations in corporate actors' day-to-day behavior and decision-making in China. To support companies in this development, regulators can draw on the four pathways of compliance-related learning identified from the interviews, namely compliance learning as companies grow, in response to international pressures, via professional networks and parallel to authorities' regulatory learning processes. Depending on the sector-specific characteristics, regulators could, for example, strengthen professional networks and international influences, which promote related compliance approaches. But this example already shows that there is no one right way of regulating the corporate sector to achieve the best possible compliance-related outcomes. The empirical research has shown that not only contextual, but also business internal factors affect compliance. Thus, regulators need to be flexible and responsive to the prevailing conditions when they make regulatory and enforcement decisions. In this context, it is especially important for them to include the level of regulatory complexity into their considerations. The case study on the SCS showed that the complexity companies face related to compliance has significantly increased since the establishment of this system due to the multitude of additional regulatory mechanisms and regulators involved. A further rise bears the risk that the system or the adopted regulatory approaches overall cause more harm than they offer benefit to business operations and economic development.

Beyond the clearer perspective on compliance in China and thanks to the systemic nature of compliance at the interface between the business and regulatory spheres, the study's insights also provide a better understanding of the Chinese political economy and thereby help to contextualize the current efforts towards a more rules-based society in China, especially the increasing adoption of information technologies in regulation, e.g. via the SCS. Specifically, the empirical findings provide evidence of the existence of a regulatory state and regulatory capitalism in China, yet also highlight features previously not discussed in the academic discourse on these topics. The perspective of compliance showed that all features that characterize a regulatory state in the Global South prevail in China, namely, the co-existence of rules and deals, embedded autonomy as well as a regulatory society. With respect to regulatory capitalism, this research only found that the key features characterizing regulatory capitalism apply to China, but also illustrated that in China both regulation *of* and *for* capitalism exists. At the same time, the research suggests that regulatory capitalism and the regulatory state do not fully describe the Chinese political economy and regulatory regime, since the Chinese leadership only seems to instrumentalize this type of set-up for the purpose of economic development. Hence, regulatory capitalism and the regulatory state are rather tools applied under the 'shadow of the hierarchy' than principles that all actors in the Chinese political economy subordinate themselves to. After all, the Party holds the highest position in the Chinese Party-state and can intervene if necessary. Consequently, this study proposes to classify the Chinese political economy as 'regulatory capitalism under the shadow of the hierarchy' and the Chinese regulatory regime as a 'regulatory state under the shadow of the hierarchy'. The newly identified regulatory mode, managerial regulation, reflects this set-up perfectly, since managerial regulation exploits management logic and market mechanisms in enforcement, but still provides sufficient flexibility for the Chinese government to adjust the regulatory direction when needed. In addition, managerial regulation can be regarded as an additional regulatory mode that co-exists with the bifurcated regulatory approach that Hsueh (2011) and McNally and Gruin (2017) identified: In contrast to the previously defined two regulatory modes[232] that are selectively adopted depending on a sector's characteristics, managerial regulation spans across all industries and is only slightly adjusted to industry-specific circumstances. Hence, managerial regulation constitutes an important tool in the Chinese regulators' toolkit that deserves our attention when discussing the Chinese regulatory regime. Only the future can tell, whether this rules-based, yet at times arbitrary regulatory approach with a strong reliance on information technologies by the Chinese leadership will prove successful for further economic development.

With these insights, this research not only contributes to our understanding of China, but the findings also have implications beyond this

232 Strong government control and limited market mechanisms versus lax government control and a strong reliance on market mechanisms.

country. For practitioners from the international business and regulatory spheres (e.g. government officials, bureaucrats and managers), the findings document that the establishment of compliance-related structures does not suffice to change corporate behavior. Instead, decision-makers need to take measures to ensure that the entirety of compliance as an institution prevails in their political economies. Concretely, this means that not only compliance structures, but also normative, cultural and behavioral aspects need to be considered in decision-making related to compliance. In the Chinese context, the Party-state attempts to do so via managerial regulation in the form of the SCS. While the specific Chinese approach may only seem feasible for lesson drawing in political economies with similar structural characteristics as China (e.g. lacking rule of law, limited enforcement capacities) (Fischer, 2021), the insights are also important for political economies that uphold the rule of law and voice ethical concerns in the face of some of the applied mechanisms in China. As the world's second largest economy, China is increasingly exerting influence on the international governance system, be it via international institutions (e.g. Serrano Oswald, 2019, Heldt, 2017) or standard setting (e.g. Weithmann, 2018). Hence, the international community has to deal with the new phenomena identified in China in the global governance context. Specifically, in combination with the global trend of adopting artificial intelligence and exploiting data for a variety of purposes, including regulation (e.g. William et al., 2018), this new Chinese regulatory mode has the potential to significantly affect regulatory approaches internationally; either directly in international governance institutions from the top down or indirectly via implementing the regulatory approach domestically and having actors, who operate globally, such as Chinese MNEs, internalize and habitually transfer these practices to the international arena in a bottom-up process. Thus, practitioners in the sphere of international governance should familiarize themselves with the Chinese political economy regulatory regime, as well as their effects on other countries and global governance.

Moreover, the case study on China has added to theory-building in several strands of academic discourse, namely compliance theory, regulation and enforcement as well as policy transfer. By adopting a social constructionist perspective on compliance in China, this research was able to add two features to the compliance framework by Parker and Nielsen (2011c, p. 5) that was developed mainly based on insights from Western developed and democratic nations: time and international developments (see Figure 39 in Section 7.1.1). These important influences on compliance could be identified because the environment in China, as a country that adopted compliance late and transferred it from the international arena, differed from the countries that previous research scrutinized. Furthermore, the findings from China have added further depth to the manifestation of existing influences on compliance, such as motives as internal factors. The Chinese case, for example, showed that overarching compliance motivations, e.g. personal implications of compliance incidents, exists, which cannot be exclusively categorized as one of the existing motive categories (economic, social, normative motives). Hence, investigations on compliance motives should take overarching compliance-triggers into account. Furthermore, the investigation of the Chinese case adds to theory-building related to regulation and enforcement by providing a new perspective to the discourse that has been dominated by research on the Global North. With respect to regulation, this research questions the universal applicability of the six-step process that leads to the endogeneity of law outlined by Edelman (2007, p. 67f). Instead, it proposes that the endogeneity of law does not only result from this chronological process, but, as the Chinese case illustrates, can also emerge from unplanned and constant non-sequential interactions between the regulatory and the business realms in the context of compliance. Regarding enforcement theory, this research has identified a new enforcement approach, managerial regulation. Lastly, the research has also contributed to our understanding of policy transfers by identifying the exogenous and endogenous transfer processes of compliance to China, as well as a new degree of transfer (amplification) and by emphasizing the role of MNEs as transfer agents. This way, this study has not only provided insights into how transferred objects enter a new environment, but also how they take hold and evolve in the new context; a topic previously relatively disregarded in the academic discourse.

These theoretical contributions have prompted further questions that should be addressed by future research. First, against the background of China's increasing importance in the global community, the insights on China urge us to understand better how the Chinese approaches to compliance and regulation as well as the idiosyncrasies of the country's regulatory regime and political economy affect global governance and international business. A topic of great importance in this context, as the case of the SCS has shown, is the layout of the national information infrastructure and the role of data in the political economy of China compared to other countries worldwide. As the importance of information increases, insights on China and other countries on this topic could not only serve actors in international business to refine their information governance and compliance management approaches, but also political decision-makers globally in reacting to trends emerging in China. Second, the similarities of the Chinese regulatory state with characteristics identified for countries in the Global South raise further questions on the applicability of findings from China for other nations in the Global South. Future research should investigate to what extent the identified transfer processes, the instrumentalization of regulatory capitalism for development purposes and the newly identified regulatory mode of managerial regulation already exist in countries of the Global South, which challenges and opportunities they entail and whether they make a positive contribution to economic development. Third, a systemic questions on political economies in the Global North versus the Global South emerges from the discussion on China: To what extent do the findings from China (e.g. technology- and data-driven compliance management, managerial regulation) as a country of the Global South also apply to nations in the Global North? And if certain features apply to both contexts, which factors drive the convergences and divergences between political economies? On the one hand, research addressing these questions could help us understand better how national trends affect political economies internationally, to what extent they spread around the world and by which factors the adoption in other countries is limited or spurred. On the other hand, insights from such inquiries could tell us whether the new trends herald the start of a new era, the era of data-driven regulatory capitalism, which transcends the mere establishment of rules-based systems by combining rules with data-driven governance to control and foster capitalism.

References

Aggarwal, N.: 2019, Machine Learning, Big Data and the Regulation of Consumer Credit Markets: The Case of Algorithmic Credit Scoring, *in* N. Aggarwal, H. Eidenmüller, L. Enriques, J. Payne and K. van Zwieten (eds), *Autonomous Systems and the Law*, Beck, München, 37–44.

Ali, M., Ahmed, K. and Henry, D.: 2004, Disclosure Compliance With National Accounting Standards by Listed Companies in South Asia, *Accounting and Business Research* 34(3), 183- 199.

Allen, F., Qian, J., Shan, C. and Zhu, J.: 2020, The Development of the Chinese Stock Market, *in* M. Amstad, G. Sun and W. Xiong (eds), *The Handbook of China's Financial System*, Princeton University Press, Princeton, 283–313.

Ameer, R. and Othman, R.: 2012, Sustainability Practices and Corporate Financial Performance: A Study Based on the Top Global Corporations, *Journal of Business Ethics* 108(1), 61–79.

Anderson, J.: 1962, *The Emergence of the Modern Regulatory State*, Public Affairs Press, Washington D.C.

Angelucci, C. and Han, M.: 2011, Monitoring Managers Through Corporate Compliance Programs, 1–48.

Asch, P. and Seneca, J.: 1976, Is Collusion Profitable?, *The Review of Economics and Statistics* 58(1), 1.

Ayres, I. and Braithwaite, J.: 1992, *Responsive Regulation: Transcending the Deregulation Debate*, Oxford University Press, Oxford.

Baer, M.: 2009, Governing Corporate Compliance, *Boston College Law Review* 50(4:4), 949–1019.

Baidu: 2021, Baidu Index [百度指数]. URL: https://index.baidu.com/v2/index.html, Accessed: 2021-07-13.

Baldwin, R., Scott, C. and Hood, C.: 1998, *A Reader on Regulation*, Oxford University Press, Oxford.

Balme, R.: 2019, Policy Transfers as Normative Interactions: The Case of Environmental Policymaking in China, *in* L. Delcour and E. Tulmets (eds), *Policy Transfer and Norm Circulation: Towards an Interdisciplinary and Comparative Approach*, Routledge, New York, 221–242.

Barnes, C.: 2007, Why Compliance Programs Fail: Economics, Ethics and the Role of Leadership, *HEC Forum* 19(2), 109–123.

Basel Committee on Banking Supervision: 2005, Compliance and the Compliance Function in Banks, *Bank for International Settlements.*

Bay, K. and Hastenrath, K.: 2016, *Compliance-Management-Systeme: Praxiserprobte Elemente, Prozesse und Tools*, 2 edn, C.H. Beck, München.

Beach, D. and Pedersen, R.: 2013, *Process-Tracing Methods: Foundations and Guidelines*, The University of Michigan Press, Ann Arbor.

Becker, G.: 1968, Crime and Punishment: An Economic Approach, *in* G. S. Becker, A. Clarke, N. G. Fielding and R. Witt (eds), *The Economic Dimensions of Crime*, Palgrave Macmillan, London, 13–68.

Beckert, J.: 2010, Institutional Isomorphism Revisited: Convergence and Divergence in Institutional Change, *Sociological Theory* 28(2), 150–166.

Behringer, S.: 2013, *Compliance Kompakt: Best Practice im Compliance-Management*, 3 edn, Erich Schmidt, Berlin.

Beijing Stock Exchange: 2021, Introduction of this Stock Exchange [本所简介]. URL: http://www.bse.cn/company/introduce.html, Accessed: 2021-12-02.

Ben-Shahar, O. and Bradford, A.: 2012, Efficient Enforcement in International Law, *Chicago Journal of International Law* 12(2), 375–431.

Benson, D. and Jordan, A.: 2011, What Have We Learned from Policy Transfer Research? Dolowitz and Marsh revisited, *Political Studies Review* 9, 366–378.

Berger, P. and Luckmann, T.: 1966, *The Social Construction of Reality. A Treatise in the Sociology of Knowledge*, Doubleday, Garden City.

Berghoff, H.: 2008, Civilizing Capitalism? The Beginnings of Credit Rating in the United States and Germany, *Bulleting of the German Historical Institute*, 9–28.

Berwick, A.: 2018, Special Report: How ZTE Helps Venezuela Create China-style Social Control. URL: https://www.reuters.com/article/us-veneuela-zte-specialreport/special-report-how-zte-helps-venezuela-create-china-style-social-control-idUSKCN1NJ1TT?feedType=RSS%5C&feedName=top News%5C%5C&, Accessed: 2018-11-20.

Beugelsdijk, S., de Groot, H. and von Schaik, A.: 2004, Trust and Economic Growth: A Robustness Analysis, *Oxford Economic Papers* 56, 118–134.

Bevir, M.: 2013, *A Theory of Governance*, University of California Press, Berkeley.

Biegelman, M.: 2008, *Building a World-Class Compliance Program: Best Practices and Strategies for Success*, John Wiley and Sons, Hoboken.

Bird, R. and Kim Park, S.: 2017, Turning Corporate Compliance Into Competitive Advantage, *University of Pennsylvania Journal of Business Law* 19(2), 285–339.

Black, J.: 2002, Regulatory Conversations, *Journal of Law and Society* 29(1), 163–196.

Bloomberg News: 2021a, China Cracks Down on Fake Divorces That Let People Buy More Properties. URL: https://www.bloomberg.com/news/articles/2021-01-22/china-cracks-down-on-fake-divorces-to-stem-real-estate-surge, Accessed: 2021-11-17.

Bloomberg News: 2021b, China Moves Forward on Credit Rating Rules as Defaults Climb. URL: https://www.bloomberg.com/news/articles/2021-03-28/china-seeks-feedback-on-rules-to-improve -credit-rating-industry, Accessed: 2021-11-09.

Borck, J. and Coglianese, C.: 2011, Beyond Compliance: Explaining Business Participation in Voluntary Environmental Programs, *in* C. Parker and V. Lehmann Nielsen (eds), *Explaining Compliance*, Edward Elgar Publishing, Cheltenham, 139–169.

Botsman, R.: 2017, China Social Credit: Big Data Meets Big Brother as China Moves to Rate Its Citizens. URL: https://www.wired.co.uk/article/chinese-government-social-credit-score-privacy-invasion, Accessed: 2020-06-12.

Braithwaite, J.: 2000, The New Regulatory State and the Transformation of Criminology, *The British Journal of Criminology* 40(2), 222–238.

Braithwaite, J.: 2002, *Restorative Justice and Responsive Regulation*, Oxford University Press, New York.

Braithwaite, J.: 2005, Neoliberalism or Regulatory Capitalism, *RegNet Occasional Paper* Regulatory (5).

Braithwaite, J.: 2006, Responsive Regulation and Developing Economies, *World Development* 34(5), 884–898.

Braithwaite, J.: 2008, *Regulatory Capitalism. How It Works, Ideas For Making It Work Better*, Edward Elgar Publishing, Cheltenham.

Braithwaite, J. and Drahos, P.: 2002, Zero Tolerance, Naming And Shaming: Is There a Case For It With Crimes of the Powerful?, *The Australian and New Zealand Journal of Criminology* 35(3), 269–288.

Braithwaite, J. and Makkai, T.: 1991, Testing An Expected Utility Model Of Corporate Deterrence, *Law and Society Review* 25(1), 7–40.

Braithwaite, J. and Makkai, T.: 1994, Trust and Compliance, *Policing and Society* 4(1), 1–12.

Bremmer, I.: 2008, The Return of State Capitalism, *Survival* 50(3), 55–64.

Brenkert, G. (ed.): 2004, *Corporate Integrity and Accountability*, SAGE Publications, Thousand Oaks.

Brokaw, C.: 2014, *The Ledgers of Merit and Demerit: Social Change and Moral Order in Late Imperial China*, Princeton University Press, Princeton.

Brown, K.: 2018, The Anti-corruption Struggle in Xi Jinping's China: An Alternative Political Narrative, *Asian Affairs* 49(1), 1–10.

Brown, M.: 2005, *Corporate Integrity: Rethinking Organizational Ethics and Leadership*, Cambridge University Press, Cambridge.

Bühr, D., Petsche, A. and Tolar, M.: 2016, *ISO 19600 – Compliance Management Systems: A Commentary for Practitioners*, LexisNexis, Vienna.

Bulmer, S., Dolowitz, D., Humphreys, P. and Padgett, S.: 2007, *Policy Transfer in European Union Governance: Regulating the Utilities*, Routledge, Abingdon.

Bunea, A.: 2018, Legitimacy Through Targeted Transparency? Regulatory Effectiveness and Sustainability of Lobbying Regulation in the European Union, *European Journal of Political Research* 57, 378–403.

Buß, E.: 1973, *Der Wettbewerb: Eine Rechtssoziologische Untersuchung*, Mohr, Tübingen.

CAAM: 2019, Introduction to the China Association of Automobile Manufacturers [中国汽车工业协会简介]. URL: http://www.caam.org.cn/chn/2/cate_7/con_5223237.html, Accessed: 2021-12-08.

CAAM: 2021, Rules of the China Association of Automobile Manufacturers [中国汽车工业协会章程]. URL: http://www.caam.org.cn/chn/2/cate_8/con_5223238.html, Accessed: 2021-12-08.

Cai, S., Jun, M. and Yang, Z.: 2010, Implementing Supply Chain Information Integration in China: The Role of Institutional Forces and Trust, *Journal of Operations Management* 28, 257–268.

Caixin: 2020, Mu Changchun: Credit is Not a Super Police [穆长春：征信不是超级警察]. URL: http://opinion.caixin.com/2020-01-08/101502177.html?mc_cid=c0c2f8d0fc&mc_eid=e77452b6ac, Accessed: 2020-04-29.

Carvalho, L. and Rodrigues, J.: 2008, Are Markets Everywhere? Understanding Contemporary Processes of Commodification, *in* J. B. Davis and W. Dolfsma (eds), *The Elgar Companion to Social Economics*, Edward Elgar Publishing, Cheltenham, 267–286.

CCP: 2017, The Chinese Communist Party's Regulation on Inspection Work [中国共产党巡视工作条例]. URL: http://news.12371.cn/2017/07/14/ARTI1500037507858103.shtml, Accessed: 2021-08-02.

Central Committee of the CCP: 2018, The Chinese Communist Party's Central Committee issued the "Plan to Deepen Party and State Institutional Reform" [中共中央印发《深化党和国家机构改革方案》]. URL: http://www.gov.cn/zhengce/2018-03/21/content_5276191.htm#1, Accessed: 2021-12-03.

Central Committee of the CCP and State Council China: 2018, The General Office of the Central Committee of the Communist Party of China and the General Office of the State Council Issue "Several Opinions on Further Strengthening the Establishment of Scientific Research Credit" [中共中央办公厅国务院办公厅印发《关于进一步加强科研诚信建设的若干意见》. URL: http://www.gov.cn/zhengce/2018-05/30/content_5294886.htm, Accessed: 2021-10-15.

Central Committee of the CCP and State Council China: 2020, Guiding Opinion of the Central Committee of the Communist Party China and the State Council on the Establishment of a More Perfect Factor Market Allocation System and Mechanism [中共中央国务院关于构建更加完善的要素市场化配置体制机制的意见]. URL: http://www.gov.cn/zhengce/2020-04/09/content_5500622.htm, Accessed: 2020-12-11.

Chan, F. and Sun, B.: 2018, The Centralisation of the Chinese Communist Party's Campaign against Corruption and Its Implications, *China Report* 54(4), 403–420.

Chen, C.: 2009, An Update on China's Capital Markets: Focus on China's Securities Industry, *in* J. Barth, J. Tatom and G. Yago (eds), *China's Emerging Financial Markets*, Springer, Boston, 547–580.

Chen, C. and Man, C.: 2020, Are Good Governance Principles Institutionalised with Policy Transfer? An Examination of Public–Private Partnerships Policy Promotion in China, *Australian Journal of Social Issues* 55(2), 162–181.

Chen, M., Engelmann, S. and Grossklags, J.: 2022, Ordinary People as Moral Heroes or Foes? Digital Role Model Narratives Propagate Social Norms in China's Social Credit System, *Proceedings of the 2022 AAAI/ACM Conference on AI, Ethics, and Society (AIES '22)*, Association for Computing Machinery, New York, 181–191.

Chen, M. and Grossklags, J.: 2020, An Analysis of the Current State of the Consumer Credit Reporting System in China, *Proceedings on Privacy Enhancing Technologies* 4, 89–110.

Chen, R.: 2020, On the Sinicization of Corporate Compliance [论企业合规的中国化问题], *Journal of Northwest University of Political Science and Law [西北政法大学学报]* 3, 34–48.

Chen, R., Qi, C. and Lin, T.: 2011, Ownership Structure and Corporate Governance Among Chinese Securities Firms, *International Journal of Management* 28(3), 789–805.

Chen, S., Chen, X., Lin, B. and Zhong, R.: 2005, The Impact of Government Regulation and Ownership on the Performance of Securities Companies: Evidences From China, *Global Finance Journal* 16(2), 113–124.

Chen, Y. and Fan, J.: 2012, Discussion on the Compliance Management Mechanism in Securities Companies' Innovative Business Fields [证券公司创新业务中的合规管理机制探讨], *China Securities Futures [中国证券期货]* 7, 21–22.

Chen, Y., He, Y. and Guang, X.: 2017, Development and Structure of the Automotive Industry in China, *in* R. Traub-Merz (ed.), *The Automotive Sector in Emerging Economies: Industrial Policies, Market Dynamics and Trade Unions*, Friedrich-Ebert-Stiftung, Berlin, 86–104.

Chen, Y., Lin, C. and Liu, H.: 2018, "Rule of Trust": The Power and Perils of China's Social Credit Megaproject, *Columbia Journal of Asian Law* 32(1), 1–36.

Chiles, T. and Mcmackin, J.: 1996, Integrating Variable Risk Preferences, Trust, and Transaction Cost Economics, *Academy of Management Review* 21(1), 73–99.

Chin, G.: 2017, The Evolution of Government-MNC Relations in China: The Case of the Automotive Sector, *in* X. Zhang and T. Zhu (eds), *Business, Government and Economic Institutions in China*, International Political Economy Series, 81–104.

China Association of Small and Medium Sized Enterprises: 2021, The Number of Corporate Credit Reporting Firms Registered in the Country is 134 [全国企业征信机构备案数量 134 家]. URL: https://ca-sme.org/content/Content/index/id/31797, Accessed: 2021-11-08.

China Insurance Regulatory Commission: 2007, Notice on Issuing the "Guidelines for Insurance Companies' Compliance Management" [关于印发《保险公司合规管理指引》的通知]. URL: http://www.law-lib.com/LAW/law_view1.asp?id=216908, Accessed: 2021-09-09.

China Organization Data Service: 2020, Public Service Platform for Standard Company Information [企业标准信息公共服务平台]. URL: https://www.cods.org.cn/c/2020-06-30/11459.html, Accessed: 2020-07-26.

China Passenger Car Association: 2021, Introduction to the China Passenger Car Association [乘用车市场信息联席会简介]. URL: http://www.cpcaauto.com/about.php, Accessed: 2021-12-08.

Chinalawtranslate: 2021, Social Credit Joint-Enforcement MOU Breakdown. URL: https://www.chinalawtranslate.com/en/social-credit-mou-breakdown-beta/, Accessed: 2021-10-20.

Chorzempa, M., Triolo, P. and Sacks, S.: 2018, China's Social Credit System: A Mark of Progress or a Threat to Privacy?, *PIIE Peterson Institute For International Economics.*

Chu, W.: 2011, How the Chinese Government Promoted a Global Automobile Industry, *Industrial and Corporate Change* 20(5), 1235–1276.

Ci, J.: 2014, *Moral China in the Age of Reform*, Cambridge University Press, New York.

CICLA, China Council for the Promotion of International Trade's Commercial Legal Service Center and Fangda Partners: 2018, China's Annual Corporate Compliance Blue Book 2017-2018 [中国年度企业合规蓝皮书 2017-2018].

CICLA, China Council for the Promotion of International Trade's Commercial Legal Service Center and Fangda Partners: 2019, China's Annual Corporate Compliance Blue Book 20182019 [中国年度企业合规蓝皮书 2018-2019].

Clarke, M.: 2000, *Regulation. The Social Control of Business between Law and Politics*, Macmillan, London.

Coase, R.: 1937, The Nature of the Firm, *Economia* 4, 386–405.

Cohen, J.: 2016, The Regulatory State in the Information Age, *Theoretical Inquiries in Law* 17(2), 369–414.

Collins, N. and Gottwald, J.: 2011, The Chinese Model of the Regulatory State, *in* D. Levi-Faur (ed.), *Handbook on the Politics of Regulation*, Edward Elgar, Cheltenham, 142–155.

Craig Smith, N., Simpson, S. and Huang, C.: 2007, Why Managers Fail to Do the Right Thing: An Empirical Study of Unethical and Illegal Conduct, *Business Ethics Quarterly* 17(4), 633– 667.

Crain, M.: 2018, The Limits of Transparency: Data Brokers and Commodification, *New Media and Society* 20(1), 88–104.

Credit China: 2018, Baihang Credit Enters the Market; Eight Shareholders Are Stripped Off Their Personal Credit Business [百行征信入场 8 家股东剥离个人征信业务]. URL: https://www.creditchina.gov.cn/gerenxinyong/gerenxinyongliebiao/201806/t20180604_117132.html, Accessed: 2021-10-18.

Credit China: 2019a, China United Property Insurance Zibo Branch Was Included in the List of Untrustworthy Entities [中华联合财产保险淄博中支被列入失信执行名单]. URL: https://www.creditchina.gov.cn/xinyongfuwu/shixinheimingdan/zhongdianguanzhuheimingdan/201910/t20191023_172857.html, Accessed: 2021-11-10.

Credit China: 2019b, CITIC Guoan Group Was Listed as Untrustworthy by the Court; Part of Its Equity Freeze was Lifted [中信国安集团被法院列入失信部分股权一度解除冻结]. URL: https://www.creditchina.gov.cn/xinyongfuwu/shixinheimingdan/zhongdianguanzhuheimingdan/201910/t20191023_172860.html, Accessed: 2021-11-10.

Credit China: 2019c, Guidelines for Credit Repair of Information about Administrative Punishments on the "Credit China" Website ["信用中国"网站行政处罚信息信用修复指南]. URL: https://www.creditchina.gov.cn/xyxf/xfzn/, Accessed: 2021-10-20.

Credit China: 2019d, Tianyancha Obtains Enterprise Credit Qualification License; The Enterprise Credit Industry Enters the Second Stage [天眼查获企业征信资质牌照企业信用领域进入下半场]. URL: https://www.creditchina.gov.cn/chengxinzhuti/xinwenjiaodian/201905/t20190513_155177.html, Accessed: 2020-04-29.

Credit China: 2021a, Announcement on the Publication of the List of Credit Service Institutions that Can Conduct Professional Credit Repair Trainings (First Batch) [关于发布可承担信用修复专题培训任务的信用服务机构名单(第一批)的公告]. URL: https://www.creditchina.gov.cn/xyxf/xfpxjgmd/, Accessed: 2021-11-08.

Credit China: 2021b, Announcement on the Publication of the List of Credit Service Institutions that Can Issue Credit Report for Credit Repair Applicants (First Batch) [关于发布可为信用修复申请人出具信用报告的信用服务机构名单（第一批）的公告]. URL: https://www.creditchina.gov.cn/xyxf/xygbfwjgmd/, Accessed: 2021-11-08.

Credit China: 2021c, China United Property Insurance Co., Ltd. Zibo Branch [中华联合财产保险股份有限公司淄博中心支公司]. URL: https://www.creditchina.gov.cn/xinyongxinxixiangqing/xyDetail.html?searchState=1&entityType=1&keyword=äÿŋåŊŐèĄŤåŘĹèťćäžğä¿İéŹľèĆąäż¡æœĽéŹŘåĔňåŔÿæůĎåŊŽäÿŋå¿ČæŤŕåĔňåŔÿ&uuid=a033e31cdd56d923d3fd638938c6a31e&tyshxydm=913703007720949595, Accessed: 2021-11-10.

Credit China: 2021d, China United Property Insurance Co., Ltd. [中华联合财产保险股份有限公司]. URL: https://www.creditchina.gov.cn/xinyongxinxixiangqing/xyDetail.html?searchState=1&entityType=1&keyword=äÿŋåŊŐèĄŤåŘĹèťćäžğä¿İéŹľèĆąäż¡æœĽéŹŘåĔňåŔÿ&uuid=dda9411753d85ac5ffaadc852387578c&tyshxydm=91110000795773161C, Accessed: 2021-11-10.

Credit China: 2021e, CITIC Guoan Group Co., Ltd. [中信国安集团有限公司]. URL: https://www.creditchina.gov.cn/xinyongxinxixiangqing/xyDetail.html?searchState=1&entityType=1&keyword=äÿŋä¿ąåŻ¡åőĽéŻĘåŻćæœĽéŹŘåĔňåŔÿ&uuid=53cb4fb2a276dbf2b371a48976968c77&tyshxydm=91100000710927046U, Accessed: 2021-11-10.

Credit China: 2021f, Guidelines for Complaints about the Public Information on the "Credit China" Website ["信用中国"网站公示信息异议申诉指南]. URL: https://www.creditchina.gov.cn/home/yyss/yysssystem/, Accessed: 2021-10-1 9.

Credit China: 2021g, Huawei Investment and Holding Co., Ltd. [华为投资控股有限公司]. URL: https://www.creditchina.gov.cn/xinyongxinxixiangqing/xyDetail.html?searchState=1&entityType=1&keyword=åŊŐäÿžæŁĂæœŕæœĽéŹŘåĔňåŔÿ&uuid=1f6edb9d832236453154fb4288660eee&tyshxydm=914403001922038216, Accessed: 2021-10-15.

Credit China: 2021h, Process Guidelines [流程指引]. URL: https://www.creditchina.gov.cn/xyxf/lczy/, Accessed: 2019-11-11.

Credit China: 2021i, Search for Companies' Credit Commitments and Their Fulfillment of Contracts [企业信用承诺及其履约践诺情况信息查询]. URL: https://www.creditchina.gov.cn/xycn/?navPage=7, Accessed: 2021-10-20.

Creemers, R.: 2015, China's Plans to Use Ratings to Keep Eye on Citizens. URL: https://www.cnn.com/2015/10/27/opinions/china-social-credit-score-creemers/index.html, Accessed: 2018-11-26.

Creemers, R.: 2018, China's Social Credit System: An Evolving Practice of Control, *SSRN Electronic Journal*.

Croall, H. and Ross, J.: 2002, Sentencing the Corporate Offender: Legal and Social Issues, *in* C. Tata and N. Hutton (eds), *Sentencing and Society: International Perspectives*, Routledge, New York, 528–547.

CSRC: 2008, China Capital Markets Development Report, 149–302.

CSRC: 2021, About the CSRC [证监会简介]. URL: http://www.csrc.gov.cn/csrc/c100002/c5c05724baf164183a5c1c7ab0da7eb34/content.shtml, Accessed: 2022-08-31.

Cyberspace Affairs Commission: 2021, The Cross-Provincial Connection of 268 Government Administrations in the Beijing-Tianjin-Suizhou Economic Development Zone [京津穗经开区 268 项政务跨省通办]. URL: http://www.cac.gov.cn/2021-08/10/c_1630186184927614.htm?mc_cid=1b71d7f6f6&mc_eid=98c5749c65, Accessed: 2021-10-14.

Dabrowski, M., Musiałkowska, I. and Polverari, L.: 2018, EU–China and EU–Brazil Policy Transfer in Regional Policy, *Regional Studies* 52(9), 1169–1180.

Dahlman, C.: 1979, The Problem of Externality, *The Journal of Law and Economics* 22(1), 141–162.

Dalley, P.: 2007, The Use and Misuse of Disclosure as a Regulatory System, *Florida State University Law Review* 34(4), 1089–1131.

Dalton, D. and Kesner, I.: 1988, On the Dynamics of Corporate Size and Illegal Activity: An Empirical Assessment, *Journal of Business Ethics* 7(11), 861–870.

Dasgupta, P.: 2000, Economic Progress and the Idea of Social Capital, *in* P. Dasgupta and I. Serageldin (eds), *Social Capital: A Multifaceted Perspectives*, The International Bank for Reconstruction and Development, Washington D.C., 325–424.

Dasgupta, S., Hettige, H. and Wheeler, D.: 2000, What Improves Environmental Compliance? Evidence From Mexican Industry, *Journal of Environmental Economics and Management* 39(1), 39–66.

de Jong, M.: 2013, China's Art of Institutional Bricolage: Selectiveness and Gradualism in the Policy Transfer Style of a Nation, *Policy and Society* 32(2), 89–101.

de Koker, L. and Symington, J.: 2014, Conservative Corporate Compliance: Reflections on a Study of Compliance Responses by South African Banks, *Law in Context: A Socio-Legal Journal* 30, 228–256.

DeLisle, J.: 2015, The Rule of Law with Xi-Era Characteristics, *Asia Policy* 20, 23–29.

Deloitte Australia: 2021, ISO 37301 Compliance Management Systems (CMS): An Opportunity for Change. URL: https://www2.deloitte.com/au/en/blog/royal-commission/2021/iso-37301-compliance-management-system-opportunity-change.html, Accessed: 2021-04-29.

den Butter, F. and Mosch, R.: 2003, Trade, Trust and Transaction Cost, 1–26.

Deng, F.: 2020, The Origin and Convergence of Corporate Compliance and Its Chinese Institutional Limitations [公司合规的源流及中国的制度局限], *Comparative Law Research [比较法研究]* 1, 34–45.

Deng, X.: 2007, *Eleven Lectures on Comparison between Chinese and Western Cultures*, Hunan Educational Press.

Denyer, S.: 2016, China Wants to Give All of Its Citizens a Score – and Their Rating Could Affect Every Area of Their Lives. URL: https://www.independent.co.uk/news/world/asia/china-surveillance-big-data-score-censorship-a7375221.html, Accessed: 2018-11-26.

DiMaggio, P. and Powell, W.: 1983, The Iron Cage Revisited: Institutional Isomorphism and Collective Rationality in Organizational Fields, *American Sociological Review* 48(April), 147– 160.

Dobbin, F., Sutton, J., Meyer, J. and Scott, W.: 1993, Equal Opportunity Law and the Construction of Internal Labor Markets, *American Journal of Sociology* 99(2), 396–427.

Dolowitz, D. and Marsh, D.: 1996, Who Learns What from Whom: A Review of the Policy Transfer Literature, *Political Studies* 44, 343–357.

Dolowitz, D. and Marsh, D.: 2000, Learning from Abroad: The Role of Policy Transfer in Contemporary Policy-Making, *Governance: An International Journal of Policy and Administration* 13(1), 5–24.

Dong, W., Han, H., Ke, Y. and Chan, K.: 2018, Social Trust and Corporate Misconduct: Evidence from China, *Journal of Business Ethics* 151, 539–562.

Drahos, P.: 2014, Regulatory Capitalism, Globalization and the End of History, *RegNet Working Paper* (33).

Drahos, P.: 2017, Regulating Capitalism's Processes of Destruction, *in* P.Drahos (ed.), *Regulatory Theory: Foundations and Applications*, ANU Press, Acton, 761–783.

Dubash, N. and Morgan, B.: 2012, Understanding the Rise of the Regulatory State of the South, *Regulation and Governance* 6, 261–281.

Dubash, N. and Morgan, B.: 2013a, The Embedded Regulatory State: Between Rules and Deals, *in* N. Dubash and B. Morgan (eds), *The Rise of the Regulatory State of the South*, Oxford University Press, Oxford, 279–297.

Dubash, N. and Morgan, B.: 2013b, *The Rise of the Regulatory State of the South*, Vol. 6, Oxford University Press, Oxford.

Dubash, N. and Morgan, B. (eds): 2013c, *The Rise of the Regulatory State of the South: Infrastructure and Development in Emerging Economies*, Oxford University Press, Oxford.

Dyer, J. and Chu, W.: 2003, The Role of Trustworthiness in Reducing Transaction Costs and Improving Performance: Empirical Evidence From the United States, Japan, and Korea, *Organization Science* 14(1), 57–68.

Economic Times: 2016, Promotion of the "Double Random, One Disclosure" Mechanism to Improve Regulatory Reform [推广"双随机、一公开"机制完善监管改革]. URL: http://www.gov.cn/xinwen/ 2016-10/30/content_5125962.htm, Accessed: 2021-09-30.

Edelman, L.: 1990, Legal Environments and Organizational Governance: The Expansion of Due Process in the American Workplace, *American Journal of Sociology* 95(6), 1401–1440.

Edelman, L.: 1992, Legal Ambiguity and Symbolic Structures: Organizational Mediation of Civil Rights Law, *American Journal of Sociology* 97(6), 1531 – 1576.

Edelman, L.: 2007, Overlapping Fields and Constructed Legalities: The Endogeneity of Law, *in* J. O'Brien (ed.), *Private Equity, Corporate Governance and the Dynamics of Capital Market Regulation*, Imperial College Press, London, 55–90.

Edelman, L., Fuller, S. and Mara-Drita, I.: 2001, Diversity Rhetoric and the Managerialization of Law, *American Journal of Sociology* 106(6), 1589–1641.

Edelman, L. and Suchman, M.: 1997, The Legal Environments of Organizations, *Annual Review of Sociology* 23, 479–515.

Edelman, L. and Talesh, S.: 2011, To Comply or Not to Comply – That Isn't the Question: How Organizations Construct the Meaning of Compliance, *in* C. Parker and V. Lehmann Nielsen (eds), *Explaining Compliance*, Edward Elgar Publishing, Cheltenham, 103–122.

El Kharbili, M. and Pulvermüller, E.: 2009, A Semantic Framework for Compliance Management in Business Process Management, *in* W. Abramowicz, L. Maciaszek, R. Kowalczyk and A. Speck (eds), *Business Process, Services – Computing and Intelligent Service Management*, Gesellschaft für Informatik e.V., Bonn, 60–80.

Engelmann, S., Chen, M., Dang, L. and Grossklags, J.: 2021, Blacklists and Redlists in the Chinese Social Credit System: Diversity, Flexibility, and Comprehensiveness, *AIES 2021 Proceedings of the 2021 AAAI/ACM Conference on AI, Ethics, and Society.*

Engelmann, S., Chen, M., Fischer, F. and Grossklags, J.: 2019, Clear Sanctions, Vague Rewards: How China's Social Credit System Currently Defines "Good" and "Bad" Behavior, *Conference on Fairness, Accountability, and Transparency*, Atlanta.

Epstein, M.: 2018, *Making Sustainability Work: Best Practices in Managing and Measuring Corporate Social, Environmental and Economic Impacts*, Routledge, London.

Ernst & Young: 2020, Is This the Moment of Truth for Corporate Integrity? Global Integrity Report 2020. URL: https://assets.ey.com/content/dam/ey-sites/ey-com/en_gl/topics/assurance/assurance-pdfs/ey-is-this-the-moment-of-truth-for-corporate-integrity.pdf, Accessed: 2021-01-12.

Etienne, J.: 2011, Compliance Theory: A Goal Framing Approach, *Law and Policy* 33(3), 305–333.

Etzioni, A.: 1975, *A Comparative Analysis of Complex Organizations: On Power, Involvement, and Their Correlates*, Collier Macmillan Publishers, London.

Eun, J. and Lee, K.: 2002, Is an Industrial Policy Possible in China? The Case of the Automobile Industry, *Journal of International and Area Studies* 9(2), 1–21.

European Union: 2014, Directive 2014/65/EU of the European Parliament and of the Council of 15 May 2014 on Markets in Financial Instruments and Amending Directive 2002/92/EC and Directive 2011/61/EU (Recast).

Evans, M.: 2004a, In Conclusion – Policy Transfer in Global Perspective, *in* M. Evans (ed.), *Policy Transfer in Global Perspective*, Ashgate, Aldershot, 211–226.

Evans, M.: 2004b, *Policy Transfer in Global Perspective*, Ashgate, Aldershot.

Evans, M. and McComb, P.: 2004, Policy Transfer Networks: An Insider Perspective, *in* M.Evans (ed.), *Policy Transfer in Global Perspective*, Ashgate, Aldershot, 45–63.

Evans, P.: 1995, *Embedded Autonomy: States and Industrial Transformation*, Princeton University Press, Princeton.

Fan, Y.: 2018, Insights from the "ZTE Incident" for Chinese Enterprises' Compliance Management ["中兴事件" 为中国企业合规管理带来的启示], *Quality and Certification [质量与认证]* 8, 33–35.

Faridi, O.: 2020, China's Reserve Bank Issues License to Pudao Credit for Collecting Personal Credit Ratings. URL: https://www.crowdfundinsider.com/2020/12/170671-chinas-reserve-bank-issues-license-to-pudao-credit-for-collecting-personal-credit-ratings/, Accessed: 2021-10-13.

Fei, X.: 1992, *From the Soil, the Foundations of Chinese Society*, University of California Press, Berkeley.

Feldman, Y. and Lobel, O.: 2010, The Incentives Matrix: The Comparative Effectiveness of Rewards, Liabilities, Duties, and Protections for Reporting Illegality, *Texas Law Review* 88(6), 1151–1212.

Feldman, Y. and Lobel, O.: 2011, Individuals as Enforcers: The Design of Employee Reporting Systems, *in* C. Parker and V. Lehmann Nielsen (eds), *Explaining Compliance*, Edward Elgar Publishing, Cheltenham, 263–284.

Feng, F. and Cheng, X.: 2009, Reflection and Construction of China's Policy Transfer under Globalization [全球化视域下中国政策转移的反思与建构], *Journal of Public Management [公共管理学报]* 6(3), 26–31.

Fewsmith, J.: 2021, *Rethinking Chinese Politics*, Cambridge University Press, Cambridge.

Fischer, D.: 2000, *Aufbau einer Wettbewerbsordnung im Transformationsprozeß: Problematisierung am Beispiel der Wettbewerbstheoretischen Diskussion und der Wettbewerbspolitik in der VR China*, Nomos Verlagsgesellschaft, Baden-Baden.

Fischer, D.: 2021, Das Chinesische Sozialkreditsystem: Durch Vertrauen zu Innovation und Wettbewerbsfähigkeit?, *Universitas* 76(903), 71–87.

Fischer, D., Habich-Sobiegalla, S. and Gohli, H.: 2021, Industrial Policies Under Xi Jinping: A Steering Theory Perspective, *Issues and Studies* 57(4), 1–27.

Fisse, B. and Braithwaite, J.: 1983, *The Impact of Publicity on Corporate Offenders*, State University of New York Press, Albany.

Flick, U.: 2009, *An Introduction To Qualitative Research*, 4 edn, SAGE Publications, London.

Florini, A.: 1998, The End of Secrecy, *Foreign Policy* 111, 50–63.

Ford, C. and Hess, D.: 2009, Can Corporate Monitorships Improve Corporate Compliance?, *Journal of Corporate Law* 34, 679–737.

Fortune: 2021, Fortune Global 500 2020: Full List of Rankings. URL: https://fortune.com/global500/, Accessed: 2021-07-29.

Foucault, M.: 1966, *The Order of Things: An Archaeology of the Human Sciences*, Routledge, London.

Fu, J. and Geng, Y.: 2019, Public Participation, Regulatory Compliance and Green Development in China Based on Provincial Panel Data, *Journal of Cleaner Production* 230, 1344–1353.

Fung, A., Graham, M. and Weil, D.: 2007, *Full Disclosure – The Perils and Promise of Transparency*, Cambridge University Press, Cambridge.

GAC: 2022, General Administration of Customs of the People's Republic of China [中华人民共和国海关总署]. URL: http://www.customs.gov.cn/customs/zsgk93/302251/index.html, Accessed: 2022-08-31.

Gallagher, M.: 2006, Mobilizing the Law in China: "Informed Disenchantment" and the Development of Legal Consciousness, *Law and Society Review* 40(4), 783–816.

Gang, C.: 2017, Reinforcing Leninist Means of Corruption Control in China: Centralization, Regulatory Changes and Party-State Integration, *Copenhagen Journal of Asian Studies* 35(2), 30–51.

Gao, A.: 2020, Research on the Application of Compliance Management in Securities Companies [证券公司合规管理应用研究], *Chinese Market [中国市场]* 5, 93–95.

Garsten, C. and Jacobsson, K.: 2007, Corporate Globalization, Civil Society and Post-political Regulation—Whither Democracy, *Development Dialogue* 49, 143–158.

Gerring, J.: 2017, *Case Study Research: Principles and Practices*, Cambridge University Press, Cambridge.

Giehler, T.: 2020, China – The Developed Developing Nation, *in* J. Kolsdorf and U. Müller (eds), *Transforming International Cooperation: Thoughts and Perspectives on Moving Beyond Aid*, Nomos Verlagsgesellschaft, Baden-Baden, 63–66.

Gilboy, J.: 1998, Compelled Third-party Participation in the Regulatory Process: Legal Duties, Culture, and Non-compliance, *Law and Policy* 20(2), 135–155.

Glawe, L. and Wagner, H.: 2016, The Middle-income Trap – Definitions, Theories and Countries Concerned: A Literature Survey.

Glawe, L. and Wagner, H.: 2017, China in the Middle-Income Trap?, *University of Hagen, Center for East Asia Macro-economic Studies* 4/2017.

Global Legal Entity Identifier Foundation: 2021a, Introducing the Legal Entity Identifier (LEI). URL: https://www.gleif.org/en/about-lei/introducing-the-legal-entity-identifier-lei, Accessed: 2021-11-05.

Global Legal Entity Identifier Foundation: 2021b, This is GLEIF. URL: https://www.gleif.org/en/ about/this-is-gleif, Accessed: 2021-11-05.

Government of the People's Republic of China: 2017, The National 12315 Internet Platform is Online, Consumer Rights Protection Can be Carried Out With Your Own Fingers [全国 12315 互联网平台上线了，动动手指即可进行消费维权]. URL: http://www.gov.cn/fuwu/2017-03/16/content_5177852.htm, Accessed: 2021-11-17.

Government of the People's Republic of China: 2018, Notice on Issuing the "Memorandum of Understanding on the Implementation of Joint Punishments against Seriously Untrustworthy Enterprises and Related Personnel in the Social Insurance Sector" [印发《关于对社会保险领域严重失信企业及其有关人员实施联合惩戒的合作备忘录》的通知]. URL: http://www.gov.cn/xinwen/2018-11/29/content_5344398.htm, Accessed: 2021-1 0-20.

Graafland, J. and Zhang, L.: 2014, Corporate Social Responsibility in China: Implementation and Challenges, *Business Ethics: A European Review* 23(1), 34–49.

Graham, D. and Woods, N.: 2005, Making Corporate Self-regulation Effective in Developing Countries, *University of Oxford, Global Economic Governance Programme (GEG)* GEG Working (2005/14), 1–26.

Gray, G.: 2002, A Socio-legal Ethnography of the Right to Refuse Dangerous Work, *Studies in Law, Politics, and Society* 24, 133–169.

Gray, G. and Silbey, S.: 2011, The Other Side of the Compliance Relationship, *in* C. Parker and V. Lehmann Nielsen (eds), *Explaining Compliance*, Edward Elgar Publishing, Cheltenham, 123–138.

Griffith, S.: 2016, Corporate Governance in an Era of Compliance, *William and Mary Law Review* 57(6), 2075–2140.

Grünberg, N.: 2021, The CCP's Nerve Center. URL: https://merics.org/en/short-analysis/ccps-nerve-center-0, Accessed: 2021-08-02.

Grünberg, N. and Drinhausen, K.: 2019, The Party Leads on Everything: China's Changing Governance in Xi Jinping's New Era, *China Monitor*.

Grüninger, S.: 2009, Werteorientiertes Compliance Management System, *in* J. Wieland, R. Steinmeyer and S. Grüninger (eds), *Handbuch Compliance-Management: Konzeptionelle Grundlagen, Praktische Erfolgsfaktoren, Globale Herausforderungen*, Erich Schmidt Verlag, Berlin, 39–70.

Grützner, T. and Bärenbrinker, V.: 2015, *Compliance From A – Z*, C.H. Beck, München.

Guangdong Province: 2021, Guangdong Province's Social Credit Regulations [广东省社会信用条例]. URL: http://www.gdqy.gov.cn/qymzj/gkmlpt/content/1/1386/post_1386630.html#8807, Accessed: 2021-10-11.

Guangming Daily: 2018, National Credit Information Sharing: Let "Laolais" Have Nowhere to Hide [全国信用信息共享：让"老赖"无处藏身]. URL: http://www.gov.cn/xinwen/2018-08/11/content_5313109.htm?_zbs_baidu_bk, Accessed: 2021-10-15.

Guinnane, T.: 2001, Cooperatives as Information Machines: German Rural Credit Cooperatives, 1883-1914, *Journal of Economic History* 61(2), 366–389.

Gunningham, N.: 2011, Strategizing Compliance and Enforcement: Responsive Regulation and Beyond, *Explaining Compliance*, Edward Elgar Publishing, Cheltenham, 199–221.

Gunningham, N., Kagan, R. and Thornton, D.: 2003, *Shades of Green: Business, Regulation, and Environment*, Stanford University Press, Stanford.

Gunningham, N., Kagan, R. and Thornton, D.: 2004, Social License and Environmental Protection: Why Businesses Go Beyond Compliance, *Law and Social Inquiry*, 307–341.

Gunningham, N. and Sinclair, D.: 2017, Smart Regulation, *in* P. Drahos (ed.), *Regulatory Theory: Foundations and Applications*, Australian National University Press, Acton, 133–148.

Gunningham, N., Thornton, D. and Kagan, R.: 2004, Motivating Management: Corporate Compliance in Environmental Protection, 1–63.

Gupta, G., Tan, K., Ee, Y. and Phang, C.: 2018, Resource-Based View of Information Systems: Sustainable and Transient Competitive Advantage Perspectives, *Australasian Journal of Information Systems* 22, 1–10.

Habisch, A.: 2012, The Broken Tables of Stone: A Decalogue Approach to Corporate Compliance Practice, *Journal of Management Development* 31(9), 912–924.

Haibao News: 2019, China United Property Insurance Zibo Branch became a "Laolai" Because of a Refusal to Comply with a Court Judgment [拒不履行判决，中华联合财产保险淄博中心支公司成"老赖"]. URL: https://baijiahao.baidu.com/s?id=1648147801707116224&wfr=spider&for=pc, Accessed: 2021-11-10.

Haider, D.: 1989, Grants as a Tool of Public Policy, *in* L.M. Salamon (ed.), *Beyond Privatization: The Tools of Government Action*, The Urban Institute, Washington D.C., 93–123.

Haines, F.: 2011, Facing the Compliance Challenge: Hercules, Houdini or the Charge of the Light Brigade?, *Explaining Compliance*, Edward Elgar Publishing, Cheltenham, 287–304.

Hall, P. and Soskice, D. (eds): 2001, *Varieties of Capitalism: The Institutional Foundations of Comparative Advantage*, Oxford University Press, Oxford.

Handy, C.: 2002, What's a Business for? URL: https://hbr.org/2002/12/whats-a-business-for, Accessed: 2021-01-11.

Hao, X.: 2019, Compliance Management: An Effective Way for High-quality Enterprise Development [合规管理：企业高质量发展的有效途径], *Enterprise Civilization [企业文明]* 1, 90–92.

Harwit, E.: 2001, The Impact of WTO Membership on the Automobile Industry in China, *The China Quarterly* 167, 655–670.

Hasan, I., Hoi, C., Wu, Q. and Zhang, H.: 2017, Does Social Capital Matter in Corporate Decisions? Evidence from Corporate Tax Avoidance, *Journal of Accounting Research* 55(3), 629–668.

Haugh, T.: 2017a, Nudging Corporate Compliance, *American Business Law Journal* 54(4), 683– 741.

Haugh, T.: 2017b, The Trouble With Corporate Compliance Programs, *MIT Sloan Management Review* . URL: https://sloanreview.mit.edu/article/the-trouble-with-corporate-compliance-programs/, Accessed: 2022-01-31.

Haugh, T.: 2018, The Power Few of Corporate Compliance, *Georgia Law Review* 53, 129–195.

Hawkins, K. and Thomas, J.: 1984, *Enforcing Regulation*, Kluwer-Nijhoff, Boston.

He, F.: 2021, Problems and Difficulties in the Construction of the Social Credit System [社会信用体系建设中存在的问题及难点], *Northern Finance Journal [北方金融]*.

He, W.: 2018, *The Regulation of Securities Markets in China*, Palgrave Macmillan, New York.

Head, P.: 1998, The Development of Compliance Programs: One Company's Experience, *Northwestern Journal of International Law and Business* 18(2), 535–548.

Healy, J. and Braithwaite, J.: 2006, Designing Safer Health Care Through Responsive Regulation, *Medical Journal of Australia* 184(10), 56–59.

Heberer, T.: 2020, Disciplining of a Society: Social Disciplining and Civilizing Processes in Contemporary China, *Ash Center for Democratic Governance and Innovation, Harvard Kennedy School.*

Heilmann, S.: 2016, *China's Political System*, Rowman and Littlefield Publishers, Lanham.

Heldt, E.: 2017, Shaping Global Trade Governance Rules: New Powers' Hard and Soft Strategies of Influence at the WTO, *European Foreign Affairs Review* 22, 19–36.

Heyes, A.: 2000, Implementing Environmental Regulation: Enforcement and Compliance, *Journal of Regulatory Economics* 17(2), 107–129.

Hodges, C.: 2015, *Law and Corporate Behavior: Integrating Theories of Regulation, Enforcement, Compliance and Ethics*, Hart Publishing, Oxford.

Holbig, H.: 2018, China after Reform: The Ideological, Constitutional, and Organisational Makings of a New Era, *Journal of Current Chinese Affairs* 47(3), 187–207.

Holstein, J. and Gubrium, J.: 2008, The Constructionist Mosaic, *in* J. Holstein and J. Gubrium (eds), *Handbook of Constructionist Research*, The Guilford Press, New York, 3–12.

Hongdao, Q., Mumtaz, A., Mukhtar, H., Saleem, H. and Azam, S.: 2018, Corruption Prevention and Economic Growth: A Mediating Effect of Rule of Law, *International Journal of Social Science Studies* 6(2), 128–143.

Honghai, B. and Bi, H.: 2021, Old Regulatory Wine in a New Bottle of Technology – a Critical Analysis of China's Social Credit System, *Asian Law Review* 16, 282–327.

Howell, J.: 2012, Civil Society, Corporatism and Capitalism in China, *Journal of Comparative Asian Development* 11(2), 271–297.

Howell, J.: 2015, Shall We Dance? Welfarist Incorporation and the Politics of State-Labour NGO Relations, *China Quarterly* 223, 702–723.

Howell, J. and Duckett, J.: 2019, Reassessing the Hu-Wen Era: A Golden Age or Lost Decade for Social Policy in China?, *China Quarterly* 237, 1–14.

Hsueh, R.: 2011, *China's Regulatory State*, Cornell University Press, Ithaca.

Hsueh, R.: 2013, Institutional Development and the Regulatory State of the South, *in* N. Dubash and B. Morgan (eds), *The Rise of the Regulatory State of the South*, Oxford University Press, Oxford, 246–255.

Hu, X., Huang, H., Pan, Z. and Shi, J.: 2019, Information Asymmetry and Credit Rating: A Quasi-Natural Experiment from China, *Journal of Banking and Finance* 106, 132–152.

Hu, Y.: 2011, The Chinese Approach to a Regulatory State: Achievements and Challenges in the Field of Drug Administration [监管型国家的中国路径：药监领域的成就与挑战], *Public Administration Review [公共行政评论]* 2, 70–96.

Huang, H.: 2010, Institutional Structure of Financial Regulation in China: Lessons from the Global Financial Crisis, *Journal of Corporate Law Studies* 10(1), 219–254.

Huang, Y.: 2008, *Capitalism with Chinese Characteristics: Entrepreneurship and the State*, Cambridge University Press, New York.

Huang, Y.: 2016, Can China Escape the Middle-income Trap?, *China Economic Journal* 9(1), 17–33.

Hutter, B. and Jones, C.: 2007, From Government to Governance: External Influences on Business Risk Management, *Regulation and Governance* 1, 27–45.

Hutter, B. M.: 2011, Negotiating Social, Economic and Political Environments: Compliance with Regulation Within and Beyond the State, *Explaining Compliance*, Edward Elgar Publishing, Cheltenham, 305–321.

International Monetary Fund and World Bank: 2017, People's Republic of China Financial Sector Assessment Program: Detailed Assessment of Observance – IOSCO Objectives and Principles of Securities Regulation.

ISO: 2014, ISO 19600: Compliance Management Systems. URL: https://www.iso.org/obp/ui/#iso:std:iso:19600:ed-1:v1:en, Accessed: 2021-04-22.

ISO: 2021a, ISO – About Us. URL: https://www.iso.org/about-us.html#5, Accessed: 2021-05-26.

ISO: 2021b, ISO 37301: 2021 – Compliance Management Systems – Requirements with Guidance for Use. URL: https://www.iso.org/obp/ui/#iso:std:iso:37301:ed-1:v1:en, Accessed: 2021-04-29.

Ite, U.: 2004, Multinationals and Corporate Social Responsibility in Developing Countries: A Case Study of Nigeria, *Corporate Social Responsibility and Environmental Management* 11, 1–11.

Jakob, S.: 2021, The Corporate Social Credit System in China and its Transnational Impact, *Transnational Legal Theory*, 1–21.

Jamali, D.: 2007, The Case for Strategic Corporate Social Responsibility in Developing Countries, *Business and Society Review* 112(1), 1–27.

Jamali, D. and Karam, C.: 2018, Corporate Social Responsibility in Developing Countries as an Emerging Field of Study, *International Journal of Management Reviews* 20, 32–61.

James, O. and Lodge, M.: 2003, The Limitations of 'Policy Transfer' and 'Lesson Drawing' for Public Policy Research, *Political Studies Review* 1, 179–193.

Jarvis, D. S. L.: 2010, Institutional Processes and Regulatory Risk: A Case Study of the Thai Energy Sector, *Regulation and Governance* 4, 175–202.

Jayasuriya, K.: 2001, Globalization and the Changing Architecture of the State: The Regulatory State and the Politics of Negative Co-ordination, *Journal of European Public Policy* 8(1), 101– 123.

Jayasuriya, K.: 2005, Beyond Institutional Fetishism: From the Developmental to the Regulatory State, *New Political Economy* 10(3), 381–387.

Jayasuriya, K.: 2013, Regulatory State with Dirigiste Characteristics: Variegated Pathways of Regulatory Governance, *in* N. Dubash and B. Morgan (eds), *The Rise of the Regulatory State of the South*, Edward Elgar Publishing, Oxford, 185–197.

Jenkins, A.: 1994, The Role of Managerial Self-efficacy in Corporate Compliance with the Law, *Law and Human Behavior* 18(1), 71–88.

Jepperson, R.: 1991, Institutions, Institutional Effects, and Institutionalism, *in* W. Powell and P. DiMaggio (eds), *The New Institutionalism in Organizational Analysis*, The University of Chicago Press, Chicago, 143–163.

Jia, C., Ding, S., Li, Y. and Wu, Z.: 2009, Fraud, Enforcement Action, and the Role of Corporate Governance: Evidence from China, *Journal of Business Ethics* 90(4), 561–576.

Jiang, M.: 2020, A Brief Prehistory of China's Social Credit System, *Communication and the Public* 5(3-4), 93–98.

Jiang, Z.: 2002, Report at the 16th National Congress of the Communist Party of China [在中国共产党第十六次全国代表大会上的报告]. URL: http://dangxiao.fudan.edu.cn/59/a0/c9736a88480/page.htm, Accessed: 2021-10-08.

Jonassen, D.: 1991, Objectivism Versus Constructivism: Do We Need a New Philosophical Paradigm?, *Educational Technology Research and Development* 39, 5–14.

Jordana, J.: 2005, Globalizing Regulatory Capitalism, *The Annals of the American Academy of Political and Social Science* 598, 184–190.

Jordana, J.: 2013, Institutional Challenges to the Regulatory State in the Developing World, *in* N. Dubash and B. Morgan (eds), *The Rise of the Regulatory State of the South*, Oxford University Press, Oxford, 198–208.

Jordana, J. and Levi-Faur, D.: 2004, The Politics of Regulation in the Age of Governance, *in* J. Jordana and D. Levi-Faur (eds), *The Politics of Regulation: Institutions and Regulatory Reforms for the Age of Governance*, Edward Elgar Publishing, Cheltenham, 1–28.

Jordana, J. and Levi-Faur, D.: 2005, The Diffusion of Regulatory Capitalism in Latin America: Sectoral and National Channels in the Making of a New Order, *Annals of the American Academy of Political and Social Science* 598, 102–124.

Kagan, R., Gunningham, N. and Thornton, D.: 2011, Fear, Duty, and Regulatory Compliance: Lessons From Three Research Projects, *in* C. Parker and V. Lehmann Nielsen (eds), *Explaining Compliance*, Edward Elgar Publishing, Cheltenham, 37–58.

Kahneman, D.: 2003, Maps of Bounded Rationality: Psychology for Behavioral Economics, *American Economic Review* 93(5), 1449–1475.

Kaspereit, T., Lopatta, K. and Zimmermann, J.: 2015, Does Compliance With the German Corporate Governance Code Pay Off?: An Investigation of the Implied Cost of Capital, *Journal of Risk Finance* 16(3), 344–376.

Kessler, B. and Jin, K.: 2020, Nutzen und Grenzen eines Multidimensionalen Sozialkreditmodells für Unternehmen, *in* O. Everling (ed.), *Social Credit Rating: Reputation und Vertrauen Beurteilen*, Springer Gabler, Wiesbaden, 493–516.

Khalifa, K.: 2010, Social Constructivism and the Aims of Science, *Social Epistemology* 24(1), 45–61.

Kipnis, A.: 2007, Neoliberalism Reified: Suzhi Discourse and Tropes of Neoliberalism in the People's Republic of China, *Journal of the Royal Anthropological Institute* 13, 383–400.

Klaes, M. and Sent, E.: 2005, A Conceptual History of the Emergence of Bounded Rationality, *History of Political Economy* 37(1), 27–59.

Klebe Trevino, L., Weaver, G., Gibson, D. and Toffler, B.: 1999, Managing Ethics and Legal Compliance: What Works and What Hurts, *California Management Review* 41(2), 131–151.

Knight, A.: 2018, In Laotianye We Trust: Credit, Morality and Governance in China's Exemplary Society, *Oxford Internet Institute.*

Knight, A. and Creemers, R.: 2021, Going Viral: The Social Credit System and COVID-19, *SSRN Electronic Journal.*

Knill, C.: 2005, Introduction: Cross-national Policy Convergence: Concepts, Approaches and Explanatory Factors, *Journal of European Public Policy*, Vol. 12, 764–774.

Kolk, A., Hong, P. and van Dolen, W.: 2010, Corporate Social Responsibility in China: An Analysis of Domestic and Foreign Retailers' Sustainability Dimensions, *Business Strategy and the Environment* 16, 289–303.

Kosti, N., Levi-Faur, D. and Mor, G.: 2019, Legislation and Regulation: Three Analytical Distinctions, *Theory and Practice of Legislation* 7(3), 169–178.

Kostka, G.: 2018, China's Social Credit Systems and Public Opinion: Explaining High Levels of Approval, *SSRN Electronic Journal.*

Kostka, G. and Antoine, L.: 2020, Fostering Model Citizenship: Behavioral Change in China's Emerging Social Credit Systems, *Policy and Internet.*

Krause, T., Chen, M., Wassermann, L., Fischer, D. and Grossklags, J.: 2022, China's Corporate Credit Reporting System: A Comparison with the United States and Germany, *Regulation and Governance*. URL: https://doi.org/10.1111/rego.12491,OnlineVersionofRecordbeforeinclusioninanissue, Accessed: 2022-08-29.

Krause, T. and Fischer, D.: 2020, An Economic Approach to China's Social Credit System, *in* O. Everling (ed.), *Social Credit Rating: Reputation und Vertrauen Beurteilen*, Springer Gabler, Wiesbaden, 437–453.

Krause, T. and Fischer, D.: 2021, Data as the New Driver for Growth? European and Chinese Perspectives on the New Factor of Production, 1–6.

Križić, I.: 2019, Regulating Public Procurement in Brazil, India, and China: Toward the Regulatory-developmental State, *Regulation and Governance*, 1–20.

Kwon, H.: 2009, Policy Learning and Transfer: The Experience of the Developmental State in East Asia, *Policy and Politics* 37(3), 409–421.

Laffont, J.: 1994, The New Economics of Regulation Ten Years After, 62(3), 507–537.

Lam, M. L.-l.: 2009, Beyond Legal Compliance: Toward Better Corporate Citizenship of Foreign Multinational Enterprises in China, *JBIB* 13, 100–109.

Lan, Z.: 2000, Understanding China's Administrative Reform, *Public Administration Quarterly* 24(4), 437–468.

Landry, P.: 2008, *Decentralized Authoritarianism in China: The Communist Party's Control of Local Elites in the Post-Mao Era'*, Columbia University Press, New York.

Lange, B.: 1999, Compliance Construction in the Context of Environmental Regulation, *Social and Legal Studies* 8(4), 549–567.

Lau, A., Wong, R. and Woo, C.: 2009, Lantian Stock: The 600-Word Spell on a Transformed State-Owned Enterprise in China, *Harvard Business Review – Case Study.*

Lau, C., Lu, Y. and Liang, Q.: 2016, Corporate Social Responsibility in China: A Corporate Governance Approach, *Journal of Business Ethics* 136, 73–87.

Lavenex, S., Serrano, O. and Büthe, T.: 2021, Power Transitions and the Rise of the Regulatory State: Global Market Governance in Flux, *Regulation and Governance* 15, 445–471.

Lee, D., Pae, J. H. and Wong, Y. H. H.: 2001, A Model of Close Business Relationships in China (Guanxi), *European Journal of Marketing* 35(1/2), 51–69.

Lee, E.: 2010, Information Disclosure and Environmental Regulation: Green Lights and Gray Areas, *Regulation and Governance* 4, 303–328.

Lee, S.: 2017, An Institutional Analysis of Xi Jinping's Centralization of Power, *Journal of Contemporary China* 26(105), 325–336.

Leeuw, F.: 1997, The Carrot: Subsidies as a Tool of Government – Theory and Practice, *in* M. Bemelmans-Videc, R. Rist and E. Vedung (eds), *Carrots, Sticks, and Sermons: Policy Instruments and their Evaluation*, Transaction Publishers, New Brundswick.

Lehmann Nielsen, V. and Parker, C.: 2008, To What Extent Do Third Parties Influence Business Compliance?, *Journal of Law and Society* 35(3), 309–340.

Lehmann Nielsen, V. and Parker, C.: 2012, Mixed Motives: Economic, Social, and Normative Motivations in Business Compliance, *Law and Policy* 34(4), 428–462.

Lemos, M. and Minzner, M.: 2014, For-profit Public Enforcement, *Harvard Law Review* 127(3), 854–913.

Levi-Faur, D.: 2005, The Global Diffusion of Regulatory Capitalism, *Annals of the American Academy of Political and Social Science* 598, 12–32.

Levi-Faur, D.: 2006, Varieties of Regulatory Capitalism: Getting the Most Out of the Comparative Method, *Governance: An International Journal of Policy, Administration, and Institutions* 19(3), 367–382.

Levi-Faur, D.: 2007, Regulatory Architectures for a Global World: On Democratic Varieties of Regulatory Capitalism, *Workshop on Multi-level Governance.*

Levi-Faur, D.: 2010, Regulation and Regulatory Governance, (1), 1–47.

Levi-Faur, D.: 2011, The Regulatory State and Regulatory Capitalism: An Institutional Perspective, *in* D. Levi-Faur (ed.), *Handbook on the Politics of Regulation*, Edward Elgar Publishing, Cheltenham, 662–672.

Levi-Faur, D.: 2013a, The Odyssey of the Regulatory State: From a "Thin" Monomorphic Concept to a "Thick" and Polymorphic Concept, *Law and Policy* 35(1-2), 29–50.

Levi-Faur, D.: 2013b, The Regulatory State and the Developmental State: Towards Polymorphic Comparative Capitalism, *in* N. Dubash and B. Morgan (eds), *The Rise of the Regulatory State of the South*, Oxford University Press, Oxford, 235–245.

Levi-Faur, D.: 2017, Regulatory Capitalism, *in* P. Drahos (ed.), *Regulatory Theory: Foundations and Applications*, ANU Press, Acton, 289–302.

Lewin, A., Kenney, M. and Murmann, J. (eds): 2016, *China's Innovation Challenge: Overcoming the Middle-Income Trap*, Cambridge University Press, Cambridge.

Li, C., Zheng, H. and Liu, Y.: 2020, The Hybrid Regulatory Regime in Turbulent Times: The Role of the State in China's Stock Market Crisis in 2015–2016, *Regulation and Governance.*

Li, J. and Lei, L.: 2014, Corporate Compliance Can Achieve Sustainable Development [企业合规方能成就可持续性发展], *Modern Business [现代商业]* 17, 152–153.

Li, L.: 2018, China's Manufacturing Locus in 2025: With a Comparison of "Made-in-China 2025" and "Industry 4.0", *Technological Forecasting and Social Change* 135, 66–74.

Li, N.: 2016, Compliance as Process: Work Safety in the Chinese Construction Industry, *Universiteit von Amsterdam.*

Li, S., Xiao, J. and Liu, Y.: 2015, The Price Evolution in China's Automobile Market, *Journal of Economics and Management Strategy* 24(4), 786–810.

Liang, F., Das, V., Kostyuk, N. and Hussain, M.: 2018, Constructing a Data-Driven Society: China's Social Credit System as a State Surveillance Infrastructure, *Policy and Internet,* 1–39.

Liao, X. and Tsai, W.: 2020, Strengthening China's Powerful Commission for Discipline Inspection under Xi Jinping, With a Case Study at the County Level, *The China Journal* 84, 29–50.

Lieberthal, K.: 1992, Introduction: the 'Fragmented Authoritarianism' Model and Its Limitations, *in* K. Lieberthal and D. Lampton (eds), *Bureaucracy, Politics, and Decision Making in Post-Mao China*, University of California Press, Berkeley, 1–30.

Liebman, B. and Milhaupt, C.: 2008, Reputational Sanctions in China's Securities Market, *Columbia Law Review* 108, 929–983.

Lin, J.: 2003, *Social Credit System Principles [社会信用体系原理]*, China Fangzheng Press [中国方正出版社], Beijing.

Lin, J.: 2011a, Social Credit System: China's Model for Efficiently Establishing a Credit Reporting System [社会信用体系：中国高校建立征信系统的模式], *Credit Reference [征信]* 2(157), 1–7.

Lin, J.: 2012, The Inheritance and Innovation of Social Credit System Theory [社会信用体系理论的传承脉络与创新], *Credit Reference [征信]* 1(162), 1–12.

Lin, K., Lu, X., Zhang, J. and Zheng, Y.: 2020, State-owned Enterprises in China: A Review of 40 Years of Research and Practice, *China Journal of Accounting Research* 13, 31–55.

Lin, L.: 2010, Corporate Social Responsibility in China: Window Dressing or Structural Change?, *Berkely Journal of International Law* 28(1), 64–100.

Lin, L. and Milhaupt, C.: 2017, Bonded to the State: A Network Perspective on China's Dorporate Debt Market, *Journal of Financial Regulation and Compliance* 3(2), 1–39.

Lin, L. and Milhaupt, C.: 2021, China's Corporate Social Credit System and the Dawn of Surveillance State Capitalism, *ECGI Working Paper Series in Law* 610.

Lin, N.: 2011b, Capitalism in China: A Centrally Managed Capitalism (CMC) and Its Future, *Management and Organization Review* 7(1), 63–96.

Ling, C.: 2016, Centralization of the Economic Policy Process under Xi Jinping, *in* S. Kennedy (ed.), *State and Market in Contemporary China: Toward the 13th Five-Year Plan*, Rowman and Littlefield Publishers, Lanham, 14–16.

Lipartito, K.: 2013, Mediating Reputation: Credit Reporting Systems in American History, *Business History Review* 87, 655–677.

Liu, N., Lo, C. W., Zhan, X. and Wang, W.: 2015, Campaign-Style Enforcement and Regulatory Compliance, *Public Administration Review* 75(1), 85–95.

Liu, P.: 2011a, Regulatory State Building in China: An Analytical Framework [中国监管型政府建设: 一个分析框架], *Public Administration Review [公共行政评论]* 2, 51–69.

Liu, P.: 2015, Campaign-style Regulation and Regulatory State Building in China: A Case Study on the Special Food Safety Campaign [运动式监管与监管型国家建设: 基于对食品安全专项整治行动的案例研究], *Chinese Public Administration [中国行政管理]* 12(366), 118–124.

Liu, X., Kirwan, B. and Martens, A.: 2018, Regulatory Compliance, Information Disclosure and Peer Effects: Evidence From the Mexican Gasoline Market, *Journal of Regulatory Economics* 54, 53–80.

Liu, X., Schwaag Serger, S., Tagscherer, U. and Chang, A.: 2017, Beyond Catch-up – Can a New Innovation Policy Help China Overcome the Middle Income Trap?, *Science and Public Policy* 44(5), 656–669.

Liu, Y.: 2011b, Issues and Reflections on the Chinese-style "Regulatory State": Taking Food Safety as an Example [中国式"监管国家"的问题与反思:以食品安全为例], *Political Studies [政治学研究]* 2, 69–79.

Liu, Y. and Cao, Y.: 2018, Looking at the Compliance Risks Faced by Chinese Companies Based on the World Bank Blacklist [从世行黑名单看中国企业面临的合规风险], *New Industrial Economy [新产经]* 9(95), 43–46.

Liu, Y. and Chen, X.: 2020, The Influence of "Golden Tax Third Period" on Enterprise Tax-related Services, *2020 International Conference on Big Data Economy and Information Management*, 74–78.

Livingston, M., Poon, W. and Zhou, L.: 2018, Are Chinese Credit Ratings Relevant? A Study of the Chinese Bond Market and Credit Rating Industry, *Journal of Banking and Finance* 87, 216–232.

Lo, C. and Fryxell, G.: 2019, Enforcement Styles Among Environmental Protection Officials in China, *Journal of Public Policy* 23(1), 81–115.

Lobel, O.: 2009, Citizenship, Organizational Citizenship, and the Laws of Overlapping Obligations, *California Law Review* 97, 433–499.

Low, P.: 2021, Special and Differential Treatment and Developing Country Status: Can the Two be Separated?, *in* B. Hoekman, X. Tu and D. Wang (eds), *Rebooting Multilateral Trade Cooperation: Perspectives from China and Europe*, CEPR Press, London, 75–102.

Lu, X. and Lorentzen, P.: 2018, Personal Ties, Meritocracy, and China's Anti-Corruption Campaign, *SSRN Electronic Journal.*

Lubman, S.: 1999, *Bird in a Cage: Legal Reform in China after Mao*, Stanford University Press, Stanford.

Lüdtke, S.: 2017, *The Secret of Lobbying in China: Who Influences Building Energy Efficiency.*

Lüthje, B. and Tian, M.: 2015, China's Automotive Industry: Structural Impediments to Socio-economic Rebalancing, *International Journal of Automotive Technology and Management* 15(3), 244–267.

Lutz, E. and Sikkink, K.: 2001, The Justice Cascade: The Evolution and Impact of Foreign Human Rights Trials in Latin America, *Chicago Journal of International Law* 2(1), 319–351.

Luwang: 2019, China United Property Insurance Zibo Branch Became a Dishonest Entity Again, and Many Other Branches Also Quickly Became Similar Professional Entities [中华联合财险淄博公司再成失信被执行人，多地公司先后进入快成"专业户"]. URL: https://news.e23.cn/shandong/2019-10-23/2019A2300272.html, Accessed: 2021-11-10.

Ma, J., Song, F. and Yang, Z.: 2010, The Dual Role of the Government: Securities Market Regulation in China 1980-2007, *Journal of Financial Regulation and Compliance* 18(2), 158- 177.

Ma, X. and Ortolando, L.: 2000, *Environmental Regulation in China*, Rowman and Littlefield Publishers, Oxford.

Maak, T.: 2008, Undivided Corporate Responsibility: Towards a Theory of Corporate Integrity, *Journal of Business Ethics* 82, 353–368.

Majone, G.: 1997, From the Positive to the Regulatory State: Causes and Consequences of Changes in the Mode of Governance, *Journal of Public Policy* 17(2), 139–167.

Makkai, T. and Braithwaite, J.: 1994, Reintegrative Shaming and Compliance With Regulatory Standards, *Criminology* 32(3), 361–385.

Malecki, E.: 2010, Global Knowledge and Creativity: New Challenges for Firms and Regions, *Regional Studies* 44(8), 1033–1052.

Malik, A.: 1992, Enforcement Costs and the Choice of Policy Instruments for Controlling Pollution, *Economic Inquiry* 30(4), 714–721.

Marquis, C., Zhang, J. and Zhou, Y.: 2011, Regulatory Uncertainty and Corporate Responses to Environmental Protection in China, *California Management Review* 54(1), 39–63.

Marsh, D. and Sharman, J.: 2009, Policy Diffusion and Policy Transfer, *Policy Studies* 30(3), 269–288.

May, P. and Winter, S.: 2000, Reconsidering Styles of Regulatory Enforcement: Patterns in Danish Agro-environmental Inspection, *Law and Policy* 22(2), 143–173.

May, P. and Winter, S.: 2011, Regulatory Enforcement Styles and Compliance, *in* C. Parker and V. Lehmann Nielsen (eds), *Explaining Compliance*, Edward Elgar Publishing, Cheltenham, 222–244.

McBarnet, D.: 2017, When Compliance is Not the Solution But the Problem: From Changes in Law to Changes in Attitude, *Taxing Democracy: Understanding Tax Avoidance and Evasion*, 229–244.

McCaleb, A.: 2015, China's Automobile Industry: Development, Policies, Internationalization, *Gdańskie Studia Azji Wschodniej* 8, 163–172.

McGowan, F. and Wallace, H.: 1996, Towards a European Regulatory State, *Journal of European Public Policy* 3(4), 560–576.

McKendall, M., Demarr, B. and Jones-Rikkers, C.: 2002, Ethical Compliance Programs and Corporate Illegality: Of the Testing the Assumptions Corporate Sentencing Guidelines, *Journal of Business Ethics* 37(4), 367–383.

McKendall, M., Sánchez, C. and Sicilian, P.: 1999, Corporate Governance and Corporate Illegality: The Effects of Board Structure on Environmental Violations, *The International Journal of Organizational Analysis* 7(3), 201–223.

McKendall, M. and Wagner, J.: 1997, Motive, Opportunity, Choice, and Corporate Illegality, *Organization Science* 8(6), 624–647.

McNally, C.: 2007, China's Capitalist Transition: The Making of a New Variety of Capitalism, *in* L. Mjøset and T. Clausen (eds), *Capitalisms Compared (Comparative Social Research, Vol. 24)*, Emerald Group Publishing Limited, Bingley, 177–203.

McNally, C.: 2012, *Sino-Capitalism: China's Reemergence and the International Political Economy*, Vol. 64.

McNally, C. and Gruin, J.: 2017, A Novel Pathway to Power? Contestation and Adaptation in China's Internationalization of the RMB, *Review of International Political Economy* 24(4), 599–628.

MEE: 2022, Responsibilities of the Ministry of Ecology and Environment [生态环境部职责]. URL: https://www.mee.gov.cn/zjhb/zyzz/201810/t20181011_660310.shtml, Accessed: 2022-08-31.

Meijer, A., Grimmelikhuijsen, S., Nell, L. and Lentz, L.: 2014, Organizational Arrangements for Targeted Transparency, *Information Polity* 19, 115–127.

Meijer, A. and Homburg, V.: 2009, Disclosure and Compliance: The 'Pillory' as an Innovative Regulatory Instrument, *Information Polity* 14, 263–278.

Meissner, M.: 2017, China's Social Credit System: A Big-data Enabled Approach to Market Regulation With Broad Implications for Doing Business in China, *MERICS China Monitor*.

Mengel, A.: 2009, *Compliance und Arbeitsrecht: Implementierung, Durchsetzung, Organisation*, C.H. Beck, München.

Mertha, A.: 2009, "Fragmented Authoritarianism 2.0": Political Pluralization in the Chinese Policy Process, *The Chinese Quarterly* 200, 995–1012.

Meseguer, C.: 2005, Policy Learning, Policy Diffusion, and the Making of a New Order, *Annals of the American Academy of Political and Social Science* 598, 67–82.

Meyer, J. and Rowan, B.: 1977, Institutionalized Organizations: Formal Structure as Myth and Ceremony, *American Journal of Sociology* 83(2), 340–363.

Mezias, S.: 1990, An Institutional Model of Organizational Practice: Financial Reporting at the Fortune 200, *Administrative Science Quarterly* 35(3), 431–457.

Miao, J.: 2018, Parallelism and Evolution in Transnational Policy Transfer Networks: The Case of Sino-Singapore Suzhou Industrial Park (SIP), *Regional Studies* 52(9), 1191–1200.

MIIT: 2015, "The Ministry of Industry and Information Technology's Main Responsibilities, Internal Organizational Set-up and Staffing Regulations" was Issued [《工业和信息化部主要职责内设机构和人员编制规定》印发]. URL: https://www.miit.gov.cn/gyhxxhb/jgzz/art/2020/art_764adf9bbab147c39c934519f8e1103b.html, Accessed: 2022-08-31.

Miller, M. J.: 2003, Credit Reporting Systems Around the Globe: The State of the Art in Public Credit Registries and Private Credit Reporting Firms, *in* M. J. Miller (ed.), *Credit Reporting Systems and the International Economy*, The MIT Press, Cambridge, Chapter 1, 25–79.

Ministry of Civil Affairs: 2021, Chinese Social Organization Government Service Platform [中国社会组织政务服务平台]. URL: https://www.chinanpo.gov.cn/, Accessed: 2021-10-15.

Minzner, C.: 2015, Legal Reform in the Xi Jinping Era, *Asia Policy* 20, 4–9.

Mirvis, P. and Googins, B.: 2006, Stages of Corporate Citizenship, *IEEE Engineering Management Review* 48(2), 104–126.

Mol, A.: 2014, Governing China's Food Quality Through Transparency: A Review, *Food Control* 43, 49–56.

Moran, M.: 2000, The Frank Stacey Memorial Lecture: From Command State to Regulatory State?, *Public Policy and Administration* 15(4), 1–13.

Morgan, B. and Yeung, K.: 2007, *An Introduction to Law and Regulation: Text and Materials*, Cambridge University Press, Cambridge.

Mukul, S., Herbohn, J., Rashid, A. and Uddin, M.: 2014, Comparing the Effectiveness of Forest Law Enforcement and Economic Incentives to Prevent Illegal Logging in Bangladesh, *International Forestry Review* 16(3), 363–375.

Murphy, E.: 1997, Constructivism: From Philosophy to Practice. URL: http://eric.ed.gov/ ERICWebPortal/contentdelivery/servlet/ERICServlet?accno=ED444966, Accessed: 2021-01-25.

Musacchio, A., Lazzarini, S. and Aguilera, R.: 2015, New Varieties of State Capitalism: Strategic and Governance Implications, *Academy of Management Perspectives* 29(1), 115–131.

Musachio, A. and Lazzarini, S.: 2014, *Reinventing State Capitalism: Leviathan in Business, Brazil and Beyond*, Harvard University Press, Cambridge.

National Congress of the CCP: 1997, Regulations of the Communist Party of China [中国共产党章程]. URL: http://cpc.people.com.cn/GB/64162/64168/64568/65445/4429244.html, Accessed: 2021-07-26.

Naughton, B.: 2007, *The Chinese Economy: Transitions and Growth*, MIT Press, Cambridge.

Naughton, J.: 2018, China is Taking Digital Control of Its People to Unprecedented and Chilling Lengths. URL: https://www.theguardian.com/commentisfree/2018/may/27/china-taking-digital-control-of-its-people-to-unprecedented-and-chilling-lengths, Accessed: 2018-11-26.

NDRC: 2018a, Guiding Opinion of the General Office of the NDRC on Further Improving the Publication of Credit Information such as Administrative Licenses and Administrative Punishments [国家发展改革委办公厅关于进一步完善行政许可和行政处罚等信用信息公示工作的指导意见]. URL: http://www.gov.cn/xinwen/2018-08/09/content_5312713.htm, Accessed: 2021-11-05.

NDRC: 2018b, List with the First Batch of Demonstration Cities for the Construction of the Social Credit System Announced [首批社会信用体系建设示范城市名单公布]. URL: http://www.ndrc.gov.cn/xwzx/xwfb/201801/t20180109_873409.html, Accessed: 2019-05-07.

NDRC: 2019, Notice of the General Office of the NDRC on Promoting the Utilization of Market Entities' Comprehensive Public Credit Evaluation Results [国家发展改革委办公厅关于推送并应用市场主体公共信用综合评价结果的通知]. URL: http://www.gov.cn/xinwen/2019-09/16/content_5430181.htm, Accessed: 2021-10-20.

NDRC: 2020, Opinion on Supporting the Healthy Development of New Business Formats and New Models and Activating the Consumer Market to Drive Employment Expansion [关于支持新业态新模式健康发展激活消费市场带动扩大就业的意见]. URL: http://www.gov.cn/zhengce/ zhengceku/2020-07/15/content_5526964.htm, Accessed: 2020-09-29.

NDRC: 2021, Announcement on Public Consultation on the "Basic Catalog of National Public Credit Information (2021 Edition) (Draft for Comments)" and the "National Basic List of Disciplinary Measures for Untrustworthiness" [关于对《全国公共信用信息基础目录（2021 年版）（征求意见稿）》和《全国失信惩戒措施基. URL: www.gov.cn/xinwen/2021-07/18/content_5625819.htm, Accessed: 2021-10-11.

NDRC and MOFCOM: 2018, Special Management Measures for Foreign Investment Access (Negative List) (2018 Edition) [外商投资准入特别管理措施（负面清单）（2018 年版）]. URL: http://www.mofcom.gov.cn/article/b/f/201806/20180602760432.shtml, Accessed: 2021-12-08.

NDRC and MOFCOM: 2020, Special Management Measures for Foreign Investment Access (Negative List) (2020 Edition) [外商投资准入特别管理措施（负面清单）（2020 年版）]. URL: https://www.ndrc.gov.cn/xxgk/zcfb/fzggwl/202006/t20200624_1231938.html?code=&state=123, Accessed: 2021-12-08.

NDRC and PBoC: 2017, Guiding Opinion on Strengthening and Regulating the Management of Targets for Joint Incentives for Trustworthiness and Joint Punishments for Untrustworthiness [关于加强和规范守信联合激励和失信联合惩戒对象名单管理工作的指导意见]. URL: https://www.creditchina.gov.cn/toutiaoxinwen/201711/t20171103_92790.html, Accessed: 2021-10-20.

NDRC and PBoC: 2018, Notice of the General Office of the NDRC and the General Office of the PBoC on Issuing the List with the First Batch of Demonstration Cities for the Construction of the Social Credit System [国家发展改革委办公厅人民银行办公厅关于印发首批社会信用体系建设示范城市名单的通知]. URL: http://www.gov.cn/xinwen/2018-01/09/content_5254715.htm, Accessed: 2021-10-12.

NDRC and PBoC: 2021, Credit China. URL: https://www.creditchina.gov.cn/qita/guanyuwomen/ 201709/t20170922_45135.html, Accessed: 2019-10-15.

NECIPS: 2021, Huawei Investment and Holding Co., Ltd. [华为投资控股有限公司]. URL: http://www.gsxt.gov.cn/%7B6BA1BEF903801F2BF0B779FA215C9D6720751EC546136E253AB9430451C1F7B07E2B561D0281EADEFB0135107BB5DE5D21E69E495568E31C2159867944778387832C832C83DD72CC5FE0E05F4415D444B4AE7508C9B779835836A536891C365D694C2772B36806953A953A953A-1634303, Accessed: 2021-12-08.

Ng, K.: 2019, Is China a "Rule-by-Law" Regime?, *Buffalo Law Review* 67(3), 793–821.

Nguyen, T., Pham, T., Le, T., Truong, T. and Tran, M.: 2020, Determinants Influencing Tax Compliance: The Case of Vietnam, *Journal of Asian Finance, Economics and Business* 7(2), 65–73.

Nielsen, J.: 2003, An Analytical Framework For Studying: Compliance and Legitimacy in Fisheries Management, *Marine Policy* 27, 425–432.

Niu, H.: 2020, Compliance Culture, Cost Stickiness and Earnings Forecast in Securities Companies [证券企业合规文化、成本粘性与分析师盈余预测], *Accounting Communications [财会通讯]* 1, 46–50.

Norman, W.: 2011, Business Ethics as Self-Regulation: Why Principles that Ground Regulations Should Be Used to Ground Beyond-Compliance Norms as Well, *Journal of Business Ethics* 102(Supplement 1: Ethics, Corporations, and Governance), 43–57.

North, D.: 1990, *Institutions, Institutional Change and Economic Performance*, Cambridge University Press, Cambridge.

Oded, S.: 2013, *Corporate Compliance: New Approaches to Regulatory Enforcement*, Edward Elgar Publishing, Cheltenham.

Odell, J.: 2001, Case Study Methods in International Political Economy, *International Studies Perspectives* 2(2), 161–176.

OECD: 2000, Reducing the Risk of Policy Failure: Challenges for Regulatory Compliance, 1–91.

OECD: 2014, OECD Best Practice Principles for Regulatory Policy: Regulatory Enforcement and Inspections, *Technical report*, OECD Publishing.

OECD: 2020, DAC List of ODA Recipients: Effective for Reporting on 2020 Flows.

Ohlberg, M., Ahmed, S. and Lang, B.: 2017, Central Planning, Local Experiments: The complex implementation of China's Social Credit System, *MERICS China Monitor*.

Oliver, C.: 1997, Sustainable Competitive Advantage: Combining Institutional and Resource-Based Views, *Strategic Management Journal* 18(9), 697–713.

O'Neill, J.: 1986, The Disciplinary Society: From Weber to Foucault, *The British Journal of Sociology* 37(1), 42–60.

O'Neill, O.: 2002, *A Question of Trust: The BBC Reith Lectures 2002*, Cambridge University Press, Cambridge.

Oxfeld, E.: 2010, *Drink Water, But Remember the Source: Moral Discourse in a Chinese Village*, University of California Press, Berkeley.

Ozel, I.: 2012, The Politics of De-delegation: Regulatory (In)dependence in Turkey, *Regulation and Governance* 6, 119–129.

Pache, T.: 2020, Betriebswirtschaftliche Betrachtungen zum Social Credit Rating, *in* O. Everling (ed.), *Social Credit Rating: Reputation und Vertrauen Beurteilen*, Springer Gabler, Wiesbaden, 539–550.

Pagel, H., Ranke, K., Hempel, F. and Köhler, J.: 2014, The Use of the Concept "Global South" in Social Science and Humanities, *Symposium "Globaler Süden / Global South: Kritische Perspektiven"*, Institut für Asien- und Afrikawissenschaften, Humboldt-Universität zu Berlin.

Paine, L. S.: 1994, Managing for Organizational Integrity, *Harvard Business Review* 72(2), 106– 117.

Parker, C.: 2003, Regulator-required Corporate Compliance Program Audits, *Law and Policy* 25(3), 221–244.

Parker, C.: 2006, The "Compliance" Trap: The Moral Message in Responsive Regulatory Enforcement, *Law and Society Review* 40(3), 591–622.

Parker, C. and Gilad, S.: 2011, Internal Corporate Compliance Management Systems: Structure, Culture and Agency, *in* C. Parker and V. Lehmann Nielsen (eds), *Explaining Compliance*, Edward Elgar Publishing, Cheltenham.

Parker, C. and Lehmann Nielsen, V.: 2006, Do Businesses Take Compliance Systems Seriously? An Empirical Study of the Implementation of Trade Practices Compliance Systems in Australia, *Melbourne University Law Review* 30, 441–494.

Parker, C. and Lehmann Nielsen, V.: 2009, Corporate Compliance Systems – Could They Make Any Difference?, *Administration and Society* 41(1), 3–37.

Parker, C. and Lehmann Nielsen, V.: 2011a, Deterrence and the Impact of Calculative Thinking on Business Compliance with Competition and Consumer Regulation, *Antitrust Bulletin* 56(2), 377–426.

Parker, C. and Lehmann Nielsen, V.: 2011b, *Explaining Compliance*, Edward Elgar Publishing, Cheltenham.

Parker, C. and Lehmann Nielsen, V.: 2011c, Introduction, *in* C. Parker and V. Lehmann Nielsen (eds), *Explaining Compliance*, Edward Elgar Publishing, Cheltenham, 1–36.

Parker, C. and Nielsen, V.: 2009, The Challenge of Empirical Research on Business Compliance in Regulatory Capitalism, *Annual Review of Law and Social Science* 5, 45–70.

Parry, R., Zhang, H. and Fu, J.: 2021, Personal Insolvency in China: Necessities, Difficulties, and Possibilities, *Brooklyn Journal of International Law* 46(2), 518–571.

Paternoster, R. and Simpson, S.: 1993, A Rational Choice Theory of Corporate Crime, *in* R. Clarke and M. Felson (eds), *Routine Activity and Rational Choice: Advances in Criminological Theory Vol. 5*, Transaction Publishers, New Jersey, 37–58.

PBoC: 2015, The PBoC issues the "Notice on the Preparation Work for Personal Credit Business" [人民银行印发《关于做好个人征信业务准备工作的通知》]. URL: http://www.pbc.gov.cn/zhengxinguanliju/128332/128352/2810010/index.html, Accessed: 2021-10-18.

PBoC: 2021, Number of Licensed National Corporate Credit Reporting Agencies [全国企业征信机构备案数量]. URL: pbc.gov.cn/zhengxinguanliju/128332/128352/2875623/index.html, Accessed: 2021-10-17.

PBoC, NDRC, Ministry of Finance, China Banking and Insurance Regulatory Commission and CSRC: 2021, Notice on Promoting the Healthy Development of the Credit Rating Industry in the Bond Market [关于促进债券市场信用评级行业健康发展的通知]. URL: http://www.pbc.gov.cn/tiaofasi/144941/3581332/4311528/index.html, Accessed: 2021-11-09.

Pearce, F. and Tombs, S.: 1990, Ideology, Hegemony, and Empiricism: Compliance Theories of Regulation, *The British Journal of Criminology* 30(4), 423–443.

Pearce, F. and Tombs, S.: 1997, Hazards, Law and Class: Contextualizing the Regulation of Corporate Crime, *Social and Legal Studies* 6(1), 79–107.

Pearson, M.: 2005, The Business of Governing Business in China: Institutions and Norms of the Emerging Regulatory State, *World Politics* 57, 296–322.

Pearson, M.: 2007, Governing the Chinese Economy: Regulatory Reform in the Service of the State, *Public Administration Review* 67(4), 718–730.

Peck, J. and Zhang, J.: 2013, A Variety of Capitalism...With Chinese Characteristics?, *Journal of Economic Geography* 13(3), 357–396.

Pei, M.: 1999, Will China Become Another Indonesia?, *Foreign Policy* (116), 94–109.

Peking University: 2021, PKU Law. URL: https://www.pkulaw.com/, Accessed: 2021-09-06.

Phillips, N.: 2006, States and Modes of Regulation in the Global Political Economy, *in* M. Minogue and L. Carino (eds), *Regulatory Governance in Developing Countries*, Edward Elgar Publishing, Cheltenham, 17–38.

Phillips, N.: 2013, States and Modes of Regulation in the Global Political Economy, *in* M. Minogue and L. Cariño (eds), *Regulatory Governance in Developing Countries*, Edward Elgar Publishing, Cheltenham, 17–38.

Pia, A.: 2016, "We Follow Reason, Not the Law:" Disavowing the Law in Rural China, *Political and Legal Anthropology Review* 39(2), 276–293.

Picciotto, S.: 2007, Constructing Compliance: Game-Playing, Tax Law and the State, *Law and Policy* 29(1), 11–30.

Pistor, K.: 2002, The Standardization of Law and Its Effect on Developing Economies.

Pistor, K. and Xu, C.: 2005, Governing Stock Markets in Transition Economies: Lessons From China, *American Law and Economics Review* 7(1), 184–210.

Pollitt, M.: 2002, The Economics of Trust, Norms and Networks, *Business Ethics: A European Review* 11(2), 119–128.

Post, D.: 2005, Standards and Regulatory Capitalism: The Diffusion of Food Safety Standards in Developing Countries, *Annals of the American Academy of Political and Social Science* 598, 168–183.

Powell, W. and Colyvas, J.: 2008, New Institutionalism, *in* S. Clegg and J. Bailey (eds), *International Encyclopedia of Organization Studies*, SAGE Publications, Thousand Oaks, 976–979.

Power, M.: 1997, *The Audit Society. Rituals of Verification*, Oxford University Press, Oxford.

Prince, R.: 2010, Policy Transfer as Policy Assemblage: Making Policy for the Creative Industries in New Zealand, *Environment and Planning A* 42, 169–186.

PwC: 2018, The Business – and Cost – of Compliance: Practical Strategies to Optimize Compliance Cost and Effectiveness, 1–12.

PwC: 2019, Compliance on the Forefront: Setting the Pace for Innovation.

Qi, B., Yang, R. and Tian, G.: 2014, Can Media Deter Management From Manipulating Earnings? Evidence From China, *Review of Quantitative Finance and Accounting* 42, 571–597.

Qichacha: 2021a, Become a VIP Immediately [立即成为 VIP]. URL: https://www.qcc.com/web/pay/vip?vf=, Accessed: 2021-11-02.

Qichacha: 2021b, Beijing Stock Exchange Co., Ltd. [北京证券交易所有限责任公司]. URL: https://www.qcc.com/firm/9b599f4c039b182587a88ecfee89226d.html, Accessed: 2021-12-02.

Qichacha: 2021c, China Securities Depository and Clearing Co., Ltd. [中国证券登记结算有限责任公司]. URL: https://www.qcc.com/firm/bd36856cd988e84d9771cf70399ca35c.html, Accessed: 2021-12-02.

Qichacha: 2021d, CITIC Guoan Group Co., Ltd. [中信国安集团有限公司]. URL: https://www.qcc.com/firm/a5c95bf80882888805b498f199137051.html, Accessed: 2021-11-10.

Qichacha: 2021e, Huawei Investment and Holding Co., Ltd. [华为投资控股有限公司]. URL: qcc.com/firm/f3c7089c90bbd4ad59cda721b4e95c0b.html, Accessed: 2021-10-17.

Qichacha: 2021f, National Equities Exchange and Quotations [全国中小企业股份转让系统有限责任公司]. URL: https://www.qcc.com/firm/ab6dd59770058c1892da6af89235ddec.html, Accessed: 2021-12-02.

Qichacha: 2021g, Qichacha. URL: https://www.qcc.com/, Accessed: 2021-10-17.

Qichacha: 2021h, Qichacha Overseas. URL: https://www.qcc.com/more_overseas, Accessed: 2021-10-17.

Qu, C.: 2018, Strengthen Compliance Management to Support the Development of Energy Companies [加强合规管理助力能源企业发展], *Shanghai Energy Conservation [上海节能]* 7, 647–650.

Radaelli, C.: 2000, Policy Transfer in the European Union: Institutional Isomorphism as a Source of Legitimacy, *Governance: An International Journal of Policy and Administration* 13(1), 25– 43.

Ramezani, E., Fahland, D., Van Der Werf, J. and Mattheis, P.: 2012, Separating Compliance Management and Business Process Management, *in* F. Daniel, K. Barkaoui and S. Dustdar (eds), *Business Process Management Workshops. BMP 2011. Lecture Notes in Business Information Processing, vol. 100*, Springer, Heidelberg, 459–464.

Renmin University of China: 2021, Wu Jingmei [吴晶妹]. URL: http://sf.ruc.edu.cn/info/1272/8128.htm, Accessed: 2021-10-28.

Reuters: 2018, Beijing to Develop 'Orwellian' Plan Of China to Rate Citizens by 2021. URL: https://www.ndtv.com/world-news/beijing-to-develop-orwellian-plan-of-china-to-rate-citizens-by-2021-1950399, Accessed: 2018-11-26.

Rohde-Liebenau, B.: 2007, Förderung der Corporate Compliance: „Mehr Zuckerbrot als Peitsche?", *ERA Forum*, 273–287.

Rudd, K.: 2022, The Chinese Economy, the 20th Party Congress, and Implications for U.S.-China Relations. URL: https://asiasociety.org/policy-institute/chinese-economy-20th-party-congress-and-implications-us-china-relations, Accessed: 2022-08-30.

SAC: 2021, Introduction of the Securities Association China [中国证券业协会简介]. URL: https://www.sac.net.cn/ljxh/xhjj/, Accessed: 2021-12-02.

Sadiq, S. and Governatori, G.: 2010, Managing Regulatory Compliance in Business Processes, *in* J. vom Brocke and M. Rosemann (eds), *Handbook on Business Process Management 2. International Handbooks on Information Systems*, Springer, Berlin, Heidelberg, 1–23.

Sahlin-Andersson, K. and Engwall, L.: 2002, *The Expansion of Management Knowledge: Carriers, Flows, and Sources*, Stanford University Press, Stanford.

SAMR: 2017, National Standard Full-Text Disclosure System [国家标准全文公开系统]. URL: http://openstd.samr.gov.cn/bzgk/gb/, Accessed: 2021-09-08.

SAMR: 2021a, Internet Platform Companies Publicly Disclose Their "Commitments of Legal and Compliant Operations" (First Batch) [互联网平台企业向社会公开《依法合规经营承诺》（第一批）]. URL: http://www.samr.gov.cn/xw/zj/202104/t20210413_327811.html, Accessed: 2021-11-15.

SAMR: 2021b, Internet Platform Companies Publicly Disclose Their "Commitments of Legal and Compliant Operations" (Second Batch) [互联网平台企业向社会公开《依法合规经营承诺》（第二批）]. URL: http://www.samr.gov.cn/xw/zj/202104/t20210414_327847.html, Accessed: 2021-11-15.

SAMR: 2021c, Internet Platform Companies Publicly Disclose Their "Commitments of Legal and Compliant Operations" (Third Batch) [互联网平台企业向社会公开《依法合规经营承诺》（第三批）]. URL: http://www.samr.gov.cn/xw/zj/202104/t20210415_327862.html, Accessed: 2021-11-15.

SAMR: 2021d, National 12315 Platform [全国 12315 平台]. URL: http://36.110.229.139/, Accessed: 2021-11-15.

SAMR: 2021e, The SAMR, the Central Cyberspace Administration of China, and the State Administration of Taxation Convene an Administrative Guidance Meeting for Internet Platform Enterprises Together [市场监管总局、中央网信办、税务总局联合召开互联网平台企业行政指导会]. URL: http://www.samr.gov.cn/xw/zj/202104/t20210413_327785.html, Accessed: 2021-11-15.

SAMR: 2022, Organization [机构]. URL: https://www.samr.gov.cn/jg/#zsdw, Accessed: 2022-08-31.

Samra-Fredericks, D.: 2008, Social Constructionism in Management and Organization Studies, *in* J. A. Holstein and J. F. Gubrium (eds), *Handbook of Constructionist Research*, The Guilford Press, New York, 129–152.

Schaefer, K.: 2020, China's Corporate Social Credit System: Context, Competition, Technology and Geopolitics, *Trivium*.

Schaefer, K. and Yin, E.: 2019, Understanding China's Social Credit System, *Trivium*, 1–58.

Schneider, U.: 2003, Compliance als Aufgabe der Unternehmensleitung, *Zeitschrift für Wirtschaftsrecht* 24(15), 645–650.

Schubert, G. and Alpermann, B.: 2019, Studying The Chinese Policy Process in the Era of ‚Top-Level Design': The Contribution of 'Political Steering' Theory, *Journal of Chinese Political Science* 24(2), 1–26.

Schwartz, M. S.: 2004, Effective Corporate Codes of Ethics: Perceptions of Code Users, *Journal of Business Ethics* 55(4), 323–343.

Scott, C.: 2004, Regulation in the Age of Governance: The Rise of the Post-regulatory State, *in* J. Jordana and D. Levi-Faur (eds), *The Politics of Regulation*, Edward Elgar Publishing, Cheltenham, 145–174.

Scott, C.: 2017, The Regulatory State and Beyond, *in* P. Drahos (ed.), *Regulatory Theory: Foundations and Applications*, ANU Press, Acton, 265–287.

Securities Industry Association: 2005, White Paper on the Role of Compliance, *SIFMA*.

Securities Industry and Financial Markets Association: 2013, The Evolving Role of Compliance.

Seidl, D., Sanderson, P. and Roberts, J.: 2013, Applying the 'Comply-or-explain' Principle: Discursive Legitimacy Tactics With Regard to Codes of Corporate Governance, *Journal of Management and Governance* 17, 791–826.

Seidman, H. and Gilmour, R.: 1986, *Politics, Position, and Power: from the Positive to the Regulatory State*, Oxford University Press, New York.

Selznick, P.: 1949, *TVA and the Grass Roots*, University of California Press, Berkeley.

Selznick, P.: 1985, Focusing Organizational Research on Regulation, *in* R. Noll (ed.), *Regulatory Policy and the Social Sciences 1*, University of California Press, Berkeley, 363–367.

Serrano, O., Selmanovic, S., Lee, B. and Arndt, L.: 2022, Techno-Regulation in China: How are Bavarian Firms Faring Under the Social Credit System?, *bidt Analyses and Studies* 8.

Serrano Oswald, O.: 2019, The New Architects: Brazil, China, and Innovation in Multilateral Development Lending, *Public Administration and Development* 39, 203–214.

Shamir, R.: 2008, Corporate Social Responsibility: Towards a New Market-Embedded Morality?, *Theoretical Inquiries in Law* 9(2), 371–394.

Shandong Province: 2020, Shandong Province Social Credit Regulations [山东省社会信用条例]. URL: https://www.creditchina.gov.cn/zhengcefagui/xinyonglifa/202008/t20200807_205997.html, Accessed: 2021-10-11.

Shi, N. and Wang, X.: 2018, An Analysis of the Role of the Government in the Construction of the Social Credit System [政府在社会信用体系建设中的作用法分析], *Business and Economics [商业经济]* 8(504), 1–3.

Shi, X.: 2020, Zur Historischen Entwicklung des Kreditbegriffs, *in* O. Everling (ed.), *Social Credit Rating: Reputation und Vertrauen Beurteilen*, Springer Gabler, Wiesbaden.

Sichuan Province Bureau of Statistics: 2021, Notice on Issuing the "Work Plan for the Recognition of Statistical Integrity Demonstration Enterprises in Sichuan Province" [关于印发《四川省统计诚信示范企业认定工作方案》的通知]. URL: http://tjj.sc.gov.cn/scstjj/c105843/2021/1/27/2f6460ebb9ee4702ac054e5e8b3385be.shtml, Accessed: 2021-11-08.

Siedenbiedel, G.: 2014, *Corporate Compliance: Grundelemente der Strukturellen Integration von Compliance-Konzepten*, NWB Verlag, Herne.

Simon, H.: 1972, Theories of Bounded Rationality, *in* C. McGuire and R. Radner (eds), *Decision and Organization: A Volume in Honor of Jacob Marschak*, North-Holland Publishing Company, Amsterdam, 161–176.

Simpson, S.: 2002, *Corporate Crime, Law, and Social Control*, Cambridge University Press, New York.

Simpson, S., Garner, J. and Gibbs, C.: 2007, Why Do Corporations Obey Environmental Law? Assessing Punitive and Cooperative Strategies of Corporate Crime Control, 216.

Simpson, S. and Rorie, M.: 2011, Motivating Compliance: Economic and Material Motives For Compliance, *in* C. Parker and V.Lehmann Nielsen (eds), *Explaining Compliance*, Edward Elgar Publishing, Cheltenham, 59–77.

Sina Finance: 2020, Tianyancha and Qichacha Provoke Public Anger and Collective Complaints; Domestic Commercial Search Business Urgently Needs to be Regulated [天眼查、企查查惹众怒遭集体投诉国内商查领域亟待规范]. URL: https://finance.sina.com.cn/roll/2020-04-23/doc-iircuyvh9314317.shtml, Accessed: 2021-11-04.

Sinolytics and European Union Chamber of Commerce in China: 2019, The Digital Hand: How China's Corporate Social Credit System Conditions Market Actors, 1–37.

Sohu: 2019, CITIC Guoan's Hundred Billion Crisis: Will CITIC Group help this company which is listed as dishonest? [中信国安千亿危局：被列失信人，中信集团会否援手？]. URL: https://www.sohu.com/a/349025398_324659, Accessed: 2021-11-10.

Sohu: 2021, The Preparation Meeting for the Adoption of ISO 37301 as a National Standard and the Revision of GB/T 35770 "Guidelines for Compliance Management Systems" was Held in Beijing [ISO 37301 采用为我国国家标准暨 GB/T 35770《合规管理体系指南》修订预备会在京召开]. URL: https://www.sohu.com/a/462951138_120056211, Accessed: 2021-09-08.

Sokol, D.: 2012, Cartels, Corporate Compliance, and What Practitioners Really Think About Enforcement, *Antitrust Law Journal* 78, 201–240.

Soltes, E.: 2018, Evaluating the Effectiveness of Corporate Compliance Programs: Establishing a Model for Prosecutors, Courts, and Firms, *New York University Journal of Law and Business* 14(3), 965–1011.

Song, B.: 2015, State-owned Enterprises' Compliance Management Strategy [国有企业合规管理策略], *SME Management and Technology [中小企业管理与科技]* 30, 1.

Song Lei and Li Jing: 2019, Economic Ideas，Government Structure and Unfinished Policy Transfer: The Process of Industrial Policy Sinicization [经济理念、政府结构与未完成的政策转移:对产业政策的中国化过程的分析], *Public Administration Review [公共行政评论]* 12(1), 5–23.

S&P Global: 2020, S&P Global (China) Ratings Registered to Rate in China's Exchange Bond Market. URL: https://press.spglobal.com/2020-10-26-S-P-Global-China-Ratings-Registered-to-Rate-in-Chinas-Exchange-Bond-Market, Accessed: 2021-11-08.

State Council China: 1990, Notice of the State Council on Launching the Work of Clearing "Triangular Debts" across the Country [国务院关于在全国范围内开展清理"三角债"工作的通知]. URL: http://www.gov.cn/zhengce/content/2010-12/17/content_2477.htm, Accessed: 2021-10-08.

State Council China: 1997, The State Council's Institutional Reform Program [国务院机构改革方案]. URL: http://cpc.people.com.cn/GB/64162/64168/64568/65445/4429253.html, Accessed: 2021-07-26.

State Council China: 2014, State Council's Outline for Issuing the Plan for Building a Social Credit System (2014-2020) [国务院关于印发社会信用体系建设规划纲要（2014—2020 年）的通知]. URL: http://www.gov.cn/zhengce/content/2014-06/27/content_8913.htm#, Accessed: 2019-05-02.

State Council China: 2015, Guiding Opinion of the State Council on Actively Promoting the 'Internet Plus' Action [国务院关于积极推进"互联网+"行动的指导意见]. URL: http://www.gov.cn/zhengce/content/2015-07/04/content_10002.htm, Accessed: 2020-09-29.

State Council China: 2018a, Explanations of the State Council's Organizational Reform Program [关于国务院机构改革方案的说明]. URL: https://baike.baidu.com/reference/22428897/0ee3rYbBwuTVCN3rw1gdn45yfiRQk02zMRY2PXslTkGxKOFqa52Nu6RoS3QPTV5dqXevlW4c0knLAMsTIZoQERPOMJS469KXZxqN6V3MTjTiiilE88yzNVZnWmyCvR4F9A, Accessed: 2021-05-27.

State Council China: 2018b, Provisions on the Jurisdictions, Departments and Staffing of the State Administration for Market Regulation [国家市场监督管理总局职能配置、内设机构和人员编制规定]. URL: http://www.gov.cn/zhengce/2018-09/10/content_5320813.htm, Accessed: 2022-01-25.

State Council China: 2020, Guiding Opinion of the General Office of the State Council on Further Improving the System for Restraining Untrustworthiness and Building a Long-term Effective Mechanism for Building Honesty [国务院办公厅关于进一步完善失信约束制度构建诚信建设长效机制的指导意见]. URL: www.gov.cn/zhengce/content/2020-12/18/content_5570954.htm, Accessed: 2021-10-11.

Steinmüller, H.: 2013, *Communities of Complicity: Everyday Ethics in Rural China*, Berghahn Books, Oxford.

Stone, D.: 2004, Transfer Agents and Global Networks in the 'Transnationalization' of Policy, *Journal of European Public Policy* 11(3), 545–566.

Stone, D.: 2010, Private Philanthropy or Policy Transfer? The Transnational Norms of the Open Society Institute, *Policy and Politics* 38(2), 269–287.

Street, D. and Gray, S.: 2002, Factors Influencing the Extent of Corporate Compliance With International Accounting Standards: Summary of a Research Monograph, *Journal of International Accounting, Auditing and Taxation* 11, 51–76.

Stretesky, P. and Lynch, M.: 2011, Does Self-Policing Improve Environmental Compliance?, *in* L. Paddock, D. Qun, L. Kotzé, D. Markell, K. Markowitz and D. Zaelke (eds), *Compliance and Enforcement in Environmental Law: Toward More Effective Implementation*, Edward Elgar Publishing, Cheltenham, Chapter 9, 223–244.

Stucken, B.: 2015, *Compliance Management in China: Praxishandbuch für Manager*, Haufe, Freiburg.

Suchman, M. and Edelman, L.: 1996, Legal Rational Myths: The New Institutionalism and the Law and Society Tradition, *Law and Social Inquiry* 21(4), 903–941.

Sunstein, C.: 2014, Nudging: A Very Short Guide, *Journal of Consumer Policy* 37, 583–588.

Sunstein, C. and Ullmann-Margalit, E.: 1998, Second-Order Decisions, 1–38.

Supreme People Procuratorate: 2021, Guiding Opinion on Establishing a Third-Party Supervision and Evaluation Mechanism for the Compliance of Enterprises Involved in Litigations (Pilot) [关于建立涉案企业合规第三方监督评估机制的指导意见（试行）]. URL: https://www.spp.gov.cn/spp/xwfbh/wsfbh/202106/t20210603_520224.shtml, Accessed: 2021-09-09.

Supreme People's Court: 2017, Decision of the Supreme People's Court on Amending "Several Regulations of the Supreme People's Court on the Disclosure of Lists of Untrustworthy Persons that Have Been Subject to Enforcement" [最高人民法院关于修改《最高人民法院关于公布失信被执行人名单信息的若干规定》的决定]. URL: http://www.court.gov.cn/fabu-xiangqing-37172.html, Accessed: 2021-10-18.

Supreme People's Court: 2020, Guiding Opinion of the Supreme People's Court on Several Issues Concerning the Proper Handling of the Enforcement Cases Related to the COVID-19 Pandemic [最高人民法院关于依法妥善办理涉新冠肺炎疫情执行案件若干问题的指导意见]. URL: http://www.court.gov.cn/zixun-xiangqing-229541.html, Accessed: 2021-05-04.

Supreme People's Court: 2021, China Administrative Information Disclosure Website [中国执行信息公开网]. URL: http://zxgk.court.gov.cn/xgl/, Accessed: 2021-10-18.

Suzhou Government: 2021, Notice on Jiangsu Province's Cities' Recommendation Work to Support the Identification of Redlisted Enterprises for Statistical Creditworthiness in 2021 [关于做好 2021 年江苏省统计信用红名单企业认定我市推荐工作的通知]. URL: http://www.suzhou.gov.cn/szsrmzf/bmwj/202109/360c575100244d25a6bb3cabba90d518.shtml, Accessed: 2021-11-08.

Taghiabadi, E. R.: 2016, Understanding Non-compliance, *Technische Universiteit Eindhoven.*

Talesh, S.: 2009, The Privatization of Public Legal Rights: How Manufacturers Construct the Meaning of Consumer Law, *Law and Society Review* 43(3), 527–562.

Tan, Y.: 2014, Transparency Without Democracy: The Unexpected Effects of China's Environmental Disclosure Policy, *Governance: An International Journal of Policy, Administration, and Institutions* 27(1), 37–62.

Tang, R.: 2012, China's Auto Sector Development and Policies: Issues and Implications, 1–36.

Tang, S., Lo, C. and Fryxell, G.: 2003, Enforcement Styles, Organizational Commitment, and Enforcement Effectiveness: An Empirical Study of Local Environmental Protection Officials in Urban China, *Environment and Planning* 35, 75–94.

Ten Brink, T.: 2019, *China's Capitalism: A Paradoxical Route to Economic Prosperity*, University of Pennsylvania Press, Philadelphia.

Tencent: 2021a, China United Property Insurance Co., Ltd. Fined for Compiling False Financial Information [编制虚假财务资料中华联合财产保险股份有限公司被罚款]. URL: https://new.qq.com/rain/a/20210112A0CVXB00, Accessed: 2021-11-10.

Tencent: 2021b, Many Branches of China United Property Insurance Were Fined With a Total Fine of 1.79 Million [中华联合财险多家分支公司被处罚合计罚款 179 万]. URL: https://new.qq.com/omn/20211110/20211110A05D4Y00.html, Accessed: 2021-11-10.

Tencent Anti-Fraud Investigation Department: 2021, Tencent Group Anti-Fraud Announcement [腾讯集团反舞弊通报]. URL: https://mp.weixin.qq.com/s/j5Q66SW1Vza5AEK_mHoi3A, Accessed: 2021-11-05.

Teubner, G.: 2001, Legal Irritants: How Unifying Law Ends Up in New Divergencies, *in* P. Hall and D. Soskice (eds), *Varieties of Capitalism: The Institutional Foundations of Comparative Advantage*, Oxford University Press, Oxford, 417–441.

The Economist: 2016, Big Data, Meet Big Brother: China Invents the Digital Totalitarian State. URL: https://www.economist.com/briefing/2016/12/17/china-invents-the-digital-totalitarian-state, Accessed: 2018-11-26.

The Guardian: 2011, China's Good Samaritans Count the Cost of Their Altruism. URL: https://www.theguardian.com/world/2011/sep/08/chinas-good-samaritans-count-cost, Accessed: 2021-10-12.

The New York Times: 2018, Beijing Pioneering Citizens' 'Points' System Critics Brand 'Orwellian'. URL: https://www.nytimes.com/reuters/2018/11/21/world/asia/21reuters-china-society-points.html, Accessed: 2018-11-26.

The World Bank: 1997, *Clear Water, Blue Skies: China's Environment in the New Century*, The World Bank, Washington D.C.

The World Bank: 2010, Summary of World Bank Group Integrity Compliance Guidelines.

The World Bank: 2018, China – Systematic Country Diagnostic: Towards a More Inclusive and Sustainable Development, 1–112.

The World Bank: 2021a, GDP Growth (annual percentage): China. URL: https://data.worldbank.org/indicator/NY.GDP.MKTP.KD.ZG?end=2020&locations=CN&start=1978, Accessed: 2021-08-03.

The World Bank: 2021b, Gross Domestic Product 2020. URL: https://databank.worldbank.org/data/download/GDP.pdf, Accessed: 2021-08-03.

The World Bank: 2021c, Procurement – World Bank Listing of Ineligible Firms and Individuals. URL: https://www.worldbank.org/en/projects-operations/procurement/debarred-firms, Accessed: 2021-08-13.

Thornton, D., Gunningham, N. and Kagan, R.: 2005, General Deterrence and Corporate Environmental Behavior, *Law and Policy* 27(2), 262–288.

Thornton, P.: 2007, *Disciplining the State: Virtue, Violence, and State-Making in Modern China*, Harvard East Asian Monographs 283, Cambridge.

Thornton, P.: 2012, The New Life of the Party: Party-Building and Social Engineering in Greater Shanghai, *The China Journal* 68, 58–78.

Thun, E.: 2004, Industrial Policy, Chinese-Style: FDI, Regulation, and Dreams of National Champions in the Auto Sector, *Journal of East Asian Studies* 4, 453–489.

Thun, E.: 2006, *Changing Lanes in China: Foreign Direct Investment, Local Governments, and Auto Sector Development*, Cambridge University Press, Cambridge.

Transparency International: 2017, Corruption Perceptions Index 2017. URL: https://www.transparency.org/news/feature/corruption_perceptions_index_2017, Accessed: 2020-12-06.

Transparency International: 2020, Corruption Perceptions Index 2020. URL: https://www.transparency.org/en/cpi/2020/index/deu, Accessed: 2021-10-12.

Trevaskes, S.: 2018, A Law Unto Itself: Chinese Communist Party Leadership and Yifa Zhiguo in the Xi Era, *Modern China* 44(4), 347–373.

Trivium: 2019, China to Speed Up Release of National Legal Framework for Social Credit. URL: http://socialcredit.triviumchina.com/2019/09/china-to-speed-up-release-of-national-legal-framework-for-social-credit/, Accessed: 2020-08-03.

Tsai, W., Wang, H. and Lin, R.: 2021, Hobbling Big Brother: Top-level Design and Local Discretion in China's Social Credit System, *The China Journal* 86, 1–20.

Tversky, A. and Kahneman, D.: 1987, Rational Choice and the Framing of Decisions, *in* R. Hogarth and M. Reder (eds), *Rational Choice: The Contrast Between Economics and Psychology*, University of Chicago Press, Chicago, 67–94.

Tyler, T.: 2011, The Psychology of Self-regulation: Normative Motivations for Compliance, *in* C. Parker and V. Lehmann Nielsen (eds), *Explaining Compliance*, Edward Elgar Publishing, Cheltenham, 78–99.

Tyler, T. and Degoey, P.: 1996, Trust in Organizational Authorities, *in* R. Kramer and T. Tyler (eds), *Trust in Organizations: Frontiers of Theory and Research*, SAGE Publications, Thousand Oaks, 331–356.

U.S. Department of Justice Criminal Division: 2020, Evaluation of Corporate Compliance Programs.

Van Erp, J.: 2010, Regulatory Disclosure of Offending Companies in the Dutch Financial Market: Consumer Protection or Enforcement Publicity?, *Law and Policy* 32(4), 407–433.

Van Erp, J.: 2011, Naming and Shaming in Regulatory Enforcement, *in* C. Parker and V. Lehmann Nielsen (eds), *Explaining Compliance*, Edward Elgar Publishing, Cheltenham, 322–342.

Van Rooij, B.: 2006, *Regulating Land and Pollution in China: Lawmaking, Compliance, and Enforcement; Theory and Cases*, Leiden University Press, Leiden.

Van Rooij, B., Fryxell, G., Lo, C. and Wang, W.: 2013, From Support to Pressure: The Dynamics of Social and Governmental Influences on Environmental Law Enforcement in Guangzhou City, China, *Regulation and Governance* 7, 321–347.

Vogel, D. and Funck, B.: 2018, Immer Nur die Zweitbeste Lösung? Protokolle als Dokumentationsmethode für Qualitative Interviews, *Forum Qualitative Sozialforschung* 19(1), 1–29.

Von Blomberg, M.: 2020, The Social Credit System and China's Rule of Law, *in* O. Everling (ed.), *Social Credit Rating: Reputation und Vertrauen Beurteilen*, Springer Gabler, Wiesbaden.

Von Busekist, K.: 2016, *International Compliance: Legal Requirements of Business Organisation in Over 30 Countries*, C.H. Beck, München.

Von Glaserfeld, E.: 1995, A Constructivist Approach to Teaching, *in* L. Steffe and J. Gale (eds), *Constructivism in Education*, Routledge, New York, 3–16.

Wang, D., Wu, Q. and Xiao, Y.: 2017, Research on the Selection of Risk Control and Compliance Management Models of Securities Companies under the New Normal [新常态下证券公司风控合规管理模式选择研究], *Securities Market Herald [证券市场导报]* 1, 57–62.

Wang, J.: 2011, The Political Logic of Securities Regulation in China, *in* G. Yu (ed.), *The Development of the Chinese Legal System: Change and Challenges*, Routledge, London and New York, 227–250.

Wang, T.: 2014, *The Cultural Revolution and Overacting: Dynamics between Politics and Performance*, Lexington Books, London.

Wang, W.: 2021, On the Choice of a Legislative Mode for the Social Credit Law [论社会信用法的立法模式选择], *China Legal Science [中国法学]* 1, 228–247.

Wang, Z.: 2012, Chinese Multinationals Should Strengthen Compliance Management [中国跨国公司需要强化合规经营], *Asia Pacific Economy [亚太经济]* 4, 103–109.

Weaver, G. and Klebe Trevino, L.: 2001, The Role of Human Resources in Ethics/Compliance Management: A Fairness Perspective, *Human Resource Management Review* 11, 113–134.

Weber, J. and Wasieleski, D.: 2013, Corporate Ethics and Compliance Programs: A Report, Analysis and Critique, *Journal of Business Ethics* 112(4), 609–626.

Weber, M.: 1952, *The Protestant Ethic and the Spirit of Capitalism*, Scribner, New York.

Webnews of the CCP: 2005, Socialism and the Harmonious Society Should be Understood as a Society in Which People and the Environment Live Together Harmoniously [怎样理解社会主义和谐社会是人与自然和谐相处的社会]. URL: http://cpc.people.com.cn/GB/34727/48916/ 48918/3435287.html, Accessed: 2021-01-14.

Webnews of the CCP: 2006, What are the Eight Honors and Eight Shames? [什么是八荣八耻？]. URL: http://cpc.people.com.cn/GB/64156/64157/4544006.html, Accessed: 2021-01-14.

Webnews of the CCP: 2008, The Four Cardinal Principles [四项基本原则]. URL: http://cpc.people.com.cn/GB/134999/135000/8103346.html, Accessed: 2021-0 1-14.

WeChat: 2020, This Score Will Affect Your Street Stall [这个分数，会影响你摆地摊]. URL: https://mp.weixin.qq.com/s/d0qoEbQPlcrDgrMCnvEZyQ, Accessed: 2021-11-09.

Wei, Y.: 2005, The Development of the Securities Market and Regulation in China, *Loyola of Los Angeles International and Comparative Law Review* 479, 479–514.

Weil, D., Fung, A., Graham, M. and Fagotto, E.: 2006, The Effectiveness of Regulatory Disclosure Policies, *Journal of Policy Analysis and Management* 25(1), 155–181.

Weithmann, S.: 2018, *The Evolvement of Standards in China: Insights from the Electric Vehicle Sector*, Nomos Verlagsgesellschaft, Baden-Baden.

Wenzel, M.: 2002, Principles of Procedural Fairness in Reminder Letters: A Field-Experiment, *Centre for Tax System Integrity* 42(43).

Werbach, K.: 2021, Panopticon Reborn: Social Credit as Regulation for the Age of AI, *University of Illinois Law Review.*

What's on Weibo: 2018, Baihang and the Eight Personal Credit Programmes: A Credit Leap Forward. URL: https://www.whatsonweibo.com/baihang-and-the-eight-personal-credit-programmes-a-credit-leap-forward/, Accessed: 2019-05-07.

What's on Weibo: 2019, "Be as Good as Your Word": The Chinese Social Credit Song is Here. URL: https://www.whatsonweibo.com/be-as-good-as-your-word-the-chinese-social-credit-song-is-here/, Accessed: 2019-11-05.

Whiting, S. H.: 2017, Authoritarian "Rule of Law" and Regime Legitimacy, *Comparative Political Studies* 50(14), 1907–1940.

Whitley, R.: 1999, *Divergent Capitalisms: The Social Structuring and Change of Business Systems*, Oxford University Press, Oxford.

Whitley, R. (ed.): 1992, *European Business Systems: Firms and Markets in Their National Contexts*, SAGE Publications, London.

Wieland, J.: 2009, Compliance Management als Corporate Governance – Konzeptionelle Grundlagen und Erfolgsfaktoren, *in* J. Wieland, R. Steinmeyer and S. Grüninger (eds), *Handbuch Compliance-Management. Konzeptionelle Grundlagen, Praktische Erfolgsfaktoren, Globale Herausforderungen*, Erich Schmidt Verlag, Berlin, 15–38.

William, E., Turley, M. and Kishnani, P.: 2018, The Regulator's New Toolkit: Technologies and Tactics for Tomorrow's Regulator, *Deloitte Insights.*

Williams, C.: 2005, *A Commodified World? Mapping the Limits of Capitalism*, ZED Book, London.

Williamson, O.: 1981, The Economics of Organization: The Transaction Cost Approach, *The American Journal of Sociology* 87(3), 548–577.

Williamson, O.: 1993, Calculativeness, Trust, and Economic Organization, *The Journal of Law and Economics* 36(1, Part 2), 453–486.

Williamson, P., Hoenderop, S. and Hoenderop, J.: 2018, An Alternative Benchmark for the Validity of China's GDP Growth Statistics, *Journal of Chinese Economic and Business Studies* 16(2), 171–191.

Winter, S. and May, P.: 2001, Motivation for Compliance with Environmental Regulations, *Association for Public Policy Analysis and Management* 20(4), 675–698.

Wiseman, J.: 1977, The Economics of Subsidies: Some Taxonomic and Analytical Problems, *SPOUDAI-Journal of Economics and Business* 27(2), 455–461.

Witt, M. A.: 2010, China: What Variety of Capitalism?, *Faculty and Research Working Paper*.

Wolfson, D.: 1990, Towards a Theory of Subsidization, *in* R. Gerritse (ed.), *Producer Subsidies*, Pinter Publishers, New York, 1–20.

World Value Survey Association: 2014, World Value Survey Database – Wave 7 2010-2014. URL: http://www.worldvaluessurvey.org/WVSOnline.jsp, Accessed: 2018-12-06.

Wu, J.: 2012, Analysis on the Compliance Management of Securities Companies [浅析证券公司合规管理问题], *Eastern Corporate Culture [东方企业文化]* 9, 64–65.

Wu, J.: 2013, *The Three-Dimensional Credit Theory [三维信用论]*, Contemporary China Publishing House [当代中国出版社], Beijing.

Wu, J.: 2019a, Reflections on the Future of China's Credit Service System: Conception and Prospects of "Five Types of Services" [我国信用服务体系未来："五大类"构想与展望], *Credit Reference [征信]* 8(247), 7–10.

Wu, J.: 2019b, The Status Quo, Problems and Approaches of Our Country's Credit Industry [我国征信业的现状、问题和进路], *Unity [团结]* 3, 25–28.

Wu, J.: 2020a, On Elevating China's Social Credit System Construction to a Higher Level [社会信用体系建设要更上一层楼], *Credit Reference [征信]* 4(255), 1–5.

Wu, J.: 2020b, Reflections on China's Credit Reporting Practice, *in* O. Everling (ed.), *Social Credit Rating: Reputation und Vertrauen Beurteilen*, Springer Gabler, Wiesbaden, 3–22.

Wu, J. and Liu, H.: 2017, Give Play to Credit Service Institutions in the Construction of Local Credit Systems [发挥信用服务机构在地方信用体系建设中的作用], *Credit Reference [征信]* 7(222), 8–10.

Wu, Q.: 2007, The Making of a Market Economy in China: Transformation of Government Regulation of Market Development, *European Law Journal* 13(6), 750–771.

Wu, W.: 2015, Development and Insights from Foreign Securities Firms' Compliance Management System [境发外展变证券迁公及启司合示规管理制度的发展变迁及启示], *Securities Law Center [证券法苑]* 16, 291–306.

Wu, W.: 2018, Theory, Policy, Problems and Countermeasures of Social Credit System Construction [社会信用体系建设的理论、政策、问题与对策], *Globalization [全球化]* 6, 55–73.

Wu, W. and Zhang, X.: 2017, *Credit of Great Powers: Global vision of China's Social Credit System [大国信用-全球视野的中国社会信用体系]*, China Planning Press [中国计划出版社], Beijing.

Wu, X. and Liang, H.: 2015, Issues and Countermeasures of Enterprise Compliance Management in China, *WHICEB 2015 Proceedings* 46, 643–646.

Wu, X. and Liang, H.: 2016, Discussion the Urgency of Implementing Compliance Management Systems Guidelines Standard in China, *International Conference on Advanced Education and Management Engineering*, 110–115.

Wu, Y.: 2017, Exploration on the Compliance Management in Central Construction Enterprises [建筑施工中央企业合规管理探索], *Journal of Railway Engineering Society [铁道工程学报]* 4(223), 96–100.

Xi, C. and Pan, X.: 2017, Public Enforcement of Securities Laws: A Case of Convergence?, *in* Y. Zhao and M.Ng (eds), *Chinese Legal Reform and the Global Legal Order*, Cambridge University Press, Cambridge, 81–103.

Xia, M.: 2011, Social Capital and Rural Grassroots Governance in China, *Journal of Current Chinese Affairs* 40(2), 135–163.

Xinhua: 2005, Banned Dye Sudan I Found in KFC Sauce. URL: https://www.chinadaily.com.cn/english/doc/2005-03/17/content_425856.htm, Accessed: 2021-07-26.

Xu, G. and Yano, G.: 2017, How Does Anti-corruption Affect Corporate Innovation? Evidence From Recent Anti-corruption Efforts in China, *Journal of Comparative Economics* 45(3), 498– 519.

Xu, M.: 2016, Analysis on the Problems and Causes of the Chinese Government's Market Regulation System [我国政府市场监管体制存在的问题及成因分析], *Journal of Chongqing University of Technology [重庆理工大学学报]* 30(9), 62–68.

Xue, L. and Liou, K.: 2012, Government Reform in China: Concepts and Reform Cases, *Review of Public Personnel Administration* 32(2), 115–133.

Yan, X. and Huang, J.: 2017, Navigating Unknown Waters: The Chinese Communist Party's New Presence in the Private Sector, *China Review* 17(2), 37–63.

Yang, D.: 2004, *Remaking the Chinese Leviathan: Market Transition and the Politics of Governance in China*, Stanford University Press, Redwood City.

Yang, D.: 2017a, China's Illiberal Regulatory State in Comparative Perspective, *Chinese Political Science Review* 2, 114–133.

Yang, F.: 2017b, Is Xinlian the answer to the Individual Credit Checking System in China? URL: https://www.kapronasia.com/china-banking-research-category/is-xinlian-the-answer-to-the-individual-credit-checking-system-in-china.html, Accessed: 2019-05-07.

Yang, J., Chi, J. and Young, M.: 2011, A Review of Corporate Governance in China, *Asian-Pacific Economic Literature* 25(1), 15–28.

Yang, J. and Yu, X.: 2021, Jack Ma's Ant in Talks to Share Data Trove With State Firms. URL: https://www.wsj.com/articles/jack-mas-ant-in-talks-to-share-data-trove-with-state-firms-11624442902?mc_cid=06248546c1&mc_eid=e77452b6ac, Accessed: 2021-10-13.

Yang, L.: 2017c, Ris Points, Index Curves and Challenges of Corporate Compliance in China [中国企业合规的风险点、变化曲线与挑战应对], *Political and Legal Essays [政法论丛]* 4(2), 3–16.

Yang, Y. and Liu, N.: 2019, Alibaba and Tencent refuse to hand loans data to Beijing. URL: https://www.ft.com/content/93451b98-da12-11e9-8f9b-77216ebe1f17, Accessed: 2021-10-18.

Yang, Z. and Jiang, L.: 2015, Managing Corporate Crisis in China: Sentiment, Reason, and Law, *Business Horizons* 58, 193–201.

Yao, Y.: 2017, Construction of State-owned Enterprises' Compliance Management Mechanisms [国有企业合规管理机制的构建], *Legal Economy [青年法苑]* 11, 175–176.

Yao, Z.: 2015, How Can China Avoid the Middle Income Trap?, *China and World Economy* 23(5), 26–42.

Ye, X.: 2015, Social Credit System Construction: Innovations and Challenges of the Chinese Model [中国模式社会信用体系建设的创新与挑战], *Innovation [创新]* 9(58), 25–32.

Yee, W., Tang, S. and Lo, C.: 2016, Regulatory Compliance When the Rule of Law Is Weak: Evidence From China's Environmental Reform, *Journal of Public Administration Research and Theory* 26, 95–112.

Yeo, Y. and Pearson, M.: 2008, Regulating Decentralized State Industries: China's Auto Industry, *China Review* 8(2), 231–259.

Yeung, K.: 2004, *Securing Compliance: A Principled Approach*, Hart Publishing, Oxford.

Yin, R.: 2009, *Case Study Research: Design and Methods*, 5 edn, SAGE Publications, Thousand Oaks.

Yu, L.: 2016, Research on Foreign Social Credit System Construction Models and Insights for China [国外社会信用体系建设模式研究及对我国的启示], *Journal of Jincheng Vocational and Technical College [晋城职业技术学院学报]* 9(1), 50–60.

Yu, S.: 2018, Rethinking the Construction of Our Country's Social Credit System [对我国社会信用体系建设的再思考], *Hubei Social Sciences [湖北社会科学]* 1, 26–44.

Zaheer, A., McEvily, B. and Perrone, V.: 1998, Does Trust Matter? Exploring the Effects of Interorganizational and Interpersonal Trust on Performance, *Organization Science* 9(2), 141– 159.

Zak, P. and Knack, S.: 2001, Trust and Growth, *The Economic Journal* 111(470), 295–321.

Zhang, C.: 2019, How Much Do State-Owned Enterprises Contribute to China's GDP and Employment?, *World Bank*.

Zhang, J., Zhang, Y. and Farazmand, A.: 2021, Policy Transfer: The Case of Founding the Growth Enterprise Board in China's Security Market, *International Journal of Public Administration* 44(13), 1165–1174.

Zhang, L., Zhang, Y. and Dong, Z.: 2019, Financial Sector Opening and Financial Constraints: An Empirical Study Based on China's Experiences, *China Economic Journal* 12(3), 272–296.

Zhang, Y.: 2016, *Theory and Practice of Policy Transfer in a Changing China*, Paths International Ltd, Reading.

Zhang, Y. and Marsh, D.: 2016, Learning by Doing: The Case of Administrative Policy Transfer in China, *Policy Studies* 37(1), 35–52.

Zhang, Y. and Yu, X.: 2021, Policy Transfer: The Case of European Union–China Cooperation in Public Administration Reform, *International Review of Administrative Sciences* 87(1), 3–20.

Zhao, B. and Feng, Y.: 2021, Mapping the Development of China's Data Protection Law: Major Actors, Core Values, and Shifting Power Relations, *Computer Law and Security Review* 40, 1–16.

Zhejiang Daily: 2018, The Promotion of the "Run at Most Once" Reform Continuously Progresses [推动"最多跑一次"改革不断前行]. URL: http://www.gov.cn/zhengce/2018-04/20/content_5284540.htm, Accessed: 2021-09-15.

Zheng, M. and Wei, S.: 2019, Research on the Failure of Policy Transfer in the Chinese Government's Governance: An Analysis of Policy Transfer Based on "Circuit Breakers" [我国政府治理中的政策转移失灵研究:基于股市"熔断机制"政策转移分析], *Journal of Northeastern University [东北大学学报]* 21(3), 283–290.

Zhima Credit: 2021, Overview [概述]. URL: https://www.zmxy.com.cn/%7B%5C#%7D/detail/4-2, Accessed: 2021-11-09.

Zhou, F. and Cheng, J.: 2011, Discussion on the Effectiveness Evaluation of Securities Companies' Compliance Management -Reference to and Enlightenment from the Experience of Canadian Securities Companies [证券公司合规管理有效性评估探讨—加拿大证券公司评估经验的借鉴及启示], *Internal Audit China [中国内部审计]* 10, 27–29.

Zhou, R. and Zhang, M.: 2020, Research on the Legalization Approach of the Institutional Arrangement for the Social Credit System Construction [社会信用体系建设制度安排的合法化进路研究], *Journal of Suzhou University [苏州大学学报]* 3(7), 73–81.

Zhu, J.: 2021, Chinese State Firms to Take Big Stake in Ant's Credit-Scoring JV. URL: https://www.reuters.com/technology/exclusive-chinese-state-firms-take-big-stake-ants-credit-scoring-jv-sources-2021-09-01/?mc_cid=47fce754c2&mc_eid=e77452b6ac&mc_cid=bb0f9e5f4e&mc_eid=e77452b6ac, Accessed: 2021-10-13.

Zhu, X. and Wang, H.: 2012, Roles of International Organizations in Policy Transfer: The Participation of the UNDP in the Micro-Credit Policy in China [国际组织在政策转移中的作用研究:以 UNDP 参与中国小额信贷政策为例], *Chinese Public Administration [中国行政管理]* 2(320), 45–49.